# The Gender Knot

# The Gender Knot

Unraveling Our Patriarchal Legacy

## Revised and Updated Edition

## ALLAN G. JOHNSON

TEMPLE UNIVERSITY PRESS
PHILADELPHIA

Allan G. Johnson is a writer and sociologist with more than thirty years of college teaching experience. The author of numerous books, including *The Forest and the Trees: Sociology as Life, Practice, and Promise* (Temple), he speaks on issues of inequality and privilege on campuses all over the United States. For more information about his work, see www.agjohnson.us.

Temple University Press
1601 North Broad Street
Philadelphia PA 19122
*www.temple.edu/tempress*

Printed in the United States of America

⊗ The paper used in this publication meets the requirements of the American National Standard for Information Sciences—Permanence of Paper for Printed Library Materials, ANSI Z39.48-1992

Library of Congress Cataloging-in-Publication Data
Johnson, Allan G.
The gender knot : unraveling our patriarchal legacy / Allan G. Johnson.—
Revised and updated ed.
p.  cm.
Includes bibliographical references and index.
ISBN 1-59213-382-7 (cloth : alk. paper)
ISBN 1-59213-383-5 (pbk. : alk. paper)
1. Sex role.  2. Patriarchy.  3. Feminism.  I. Title.

HQ1075.J64 2005
305.3—dc22          2004062081

6  8  9  7  5

ISBN-13: 978-1-59213-383-3

# FOR NORA L. JAMIESON

*Life partner, dearest friend, comrade and soul companion
in the journey toward understanding
how to live a life that
makes a difference*

# Contents

# Part III
## Unraveling the Patriarchal Legacy

# Preface and Acknowledgments

The *Gender Knot* flows from many parts of my life. It is based on more than thirty years of work around issues of gender inequality, from reading and teaching and research to giving speeches at rallies to testifying before legislative committees to writing op-ed pieces to working in corporations and schools with men and women trying to understand what living in a patriarchal world is about.

It has been shaped by my experience growing up and living as a male in the United States. As a boy who liked literature more than football, for example, I often felt on the outside of the young-boy macho in-crowd, a vantage point that ultimately enabled me, I think, to see many things about gender more clearly and notice many other things that I would otherwise have missed. I've also had to come to terms with my mother and father and how their lives and our relationships were shaped by the choices they made within patriarchy as it shaped their generation. I've had to navigate the aggressive ritual of status competition among boys and men. I've had to move from avoiding men as dangerous and untrustworthy to, during five years in a weekly men's group, rediscovering what men can be beneath the distortions of patriarchal masculinity. I've had to resolve the massive contradictions between my need and love for women and the horrendous damage patriarchal culture does to gender relations and sexuality. I've had to learn to accept the social fact of male privilege and the damage it does to women, without taking it personally as saying something bad about me simply because I'm a man.

This work has been touched in powerful ways by the people I've known who share in the struggle to understand what patriarchy means for the world and their lives. From knowing them has come an unshakable belief that oppression is not an inevitable feature of human life, that the choices each of us makes matter more than we can ever know, and that we must find ways for both men and women to become part of the solution rather than just part of the problem.

This book comes from a place in me once described by a writer friend as "an edificial turn of soul." It bends me toward the underlying structure of things and the work of making sense and finding ways to share that with others. It draws me to build bridges that connect a diversity of life experiences, ideas, and ways of seeing, to create a common ground for people who might otherwise feel driven apart.

This book also arises from a lifelong preoccupation with the moral nature of human life and its connection to fundamental questions about the world and us in it. What *is* this that we are about here? What binds us together in a common lot and what drives us to inflict such suffering on one another? Such questions make it impossible to ignore issues of social inequality, injustice, and disregard for human dignity. They also go to the heart of a moral imperative to do something, however small, for change. But to act, I've needed to find a way to think about what it means to take responsibility for things that seem so huge and beyond my ability to affect anything. This has led me to what is perhaps the most important bridge of all, the one that enables me to find ways to make a difference.

## Notes on the Revised Edition

The revised edition benefits from several years of speaking on college and university campuses, an experience that has prompted three significant changes. The first is to describe in greater detail the characteristics of patriarchy, especially male identification. The second is to reposition Chapter 4 to become Chapter 2, moving the discussion of patriarchy to where it's needed most. The third expands the discussion of individuals and systems, with the addition of a graphic that I've found very useful with a wide variety of audiences.

I've also made a point of telling more about Robert Bly and Sam Keen, whose work I often use to exemplify typical "men's movement" takes on patriarchy and gender inequality. Because many readers may be unfamiliar with them, I hope this will make the discussion more useful.

Definitions of key—and controversial—terms such as *sexism, privilege,* and *political correctness* are found in footnotes attached to their first use (denoted by an asterisk with the footnote appearing at the bottom of the page).

Finally, I've tried to respond to suggestions from a variety of helpful sources (see *Acknowledgments*) as well as bring the book generally up to date in its references to current figures, events, and resources. A lot has happened in the world since the first edition was published, most notably the violent events of September 11, 2001 and the virtual state of war embodied in the violent U.S. response to them. Some argue that the terrorist attack on the United States forever altered the basic outlines of social life, but as I believe the chapters to follow make clear, violence is a manifestation of patriarchal dynamics that have been around for a long, long time.

Such changes are in keeping with my most important consideration in preparing the revised edition, which has been to keep a steady focus on the book's original purpose—to illuminate the basic character of patriarchy, the relationship of individuals to it, and the kinds of thinking that get in the way of seeing both in a clear and critical way.

## Acknowledgments

When I think about where this book comes from and the parts other people have played in it, the line between "me" and "them" quickly becomes a mysterious and elusive thing. It never would have occurred to me to write this book were it not for the many writers whose work on gender issues has been part of the air I've breathed for most of my adult life. I am especially grateful to Marilyn French, whose monumental book, *Beyond Power,* profoundly shaped my understanding of patriarchy.

The work and the result would have been enormously different without the people who cared enough to read what I wrote and tell me the truth of what they thought of it. As I prepared the first edition, Jeanne Bonaca read the entire manuscript and gave freely of her enthusiasm and support, her fine ear for clarity and the simple elegance of good prose, and her uncanny grasp of things structural. Nicholas Ayo, Michael Kimmel, Jeffrey McChristian, Michael Schwalbe, Sharon Toffey Shepela, and an anonymous reviewer for Temple University Press all shared thoughtful and useful comments. Many of my students at Hartford College for Women read portions of the book, especially the chapter on feminism. In addition to their feedback, they gave the gift of pushing for things to make sense and to go beyond describing the problem to identifying what we can do about it once we know it's there.

In preparing the revised edition, I benefited from the suggestions of Susan Barger (Idaho State University), Joanne Callahan, Donna Garske (Marin Abused Women's Services), Dr. Lori Handrahan (Oxford University), Heather Howard-Bobiwash (Michigan State University), Judy Jordon (Wellesley Center for Research on Women), Margaret Lazarus (Cambridge Documentary Films), Tamah Nakamura (Kyushu University), The Path of Greater Resistance Group at North Seattle Community College, V. Spike Petersen (University of Arizona), Michael Schwalbe (North Carolina State University), and John Stoltenberg. I thank you all. I am also grateful for the resources available through the WMST-L listserv archives, its extraordinary moderator, Joan Korenman (University of Maryland–Baltimore campus), and the thousands of subscribers who have contributed to them.

I also want to express my profound debt to the generations of activists, scholars, and writers whose courage and vision and hard work have given me the basis for most of what I know about these issues. And to those authors whose work I encountered so long ago that their insights have inadvertently slipped into my store of "common knowledge," I can only offer both my appreciation and my apologies for being unable to give them proper attribution.

Writing about problems is always easier than doing something about them. I've been fortunate to know people like Bettina Borders, Kim Cromwell, Donna Garske, Annalee Johnson, Charles Levenstein, Anne Menard, and Jane Tuohy, who provide models of how to think about the world and act on what they think. They have profoundly affected my writing of this book, especially the last two chapters.

I have also benefited from the kindness of strangers whose generous response to my call for help in finding the right agent to represent this book spoke volumes about the possibilities of a feminist future. Although I'd never met any of them, when I wrote out of the blue to Barbara Ehrenreich, Susan Faludi, and Marilyn French, they surprised me by writing back with suggestions and support. Arnold Kahn's help came via the women's studies Internet discussion list, whose subscribers have reminded me daily for years with their ongoing conversation that this work is alive and well and goes on all over the world. My publishing journey led to literary agents Gail Ross and Howard Yoon, who from the start believed in this book and the importance of getting it published, and published well. Their faith and good work led in turn to Temple University Press, its director David Bartlett, and its editor-in-chief Michael Ames. Their enthusiasm and commitment to *The Gender Knot*'s potential are gratifying reminders of the wisdom of patience.

For this revised edition, I thank my editor, Janet M. Francendese, for all her support; Charles Ault and David M. Wilson for expertly guiding the manuscript into print; and Ann-Marie Anderson and Gary Kramer for all they do to ensure that *The Gender Knot* reaches the broadest possible audience.

Closer to home are people who believe not simply in the writing but, more important, in the writer. Writing is solitary work, but sorrounding it have been people whose loving presence and support make the solitude possible. I am especially mindful of my sister Annalee, of my father, Valdemar, my late mother, Alice, and my second mother, Geraldine; and of Annie Barrett, Jeanne Bonaca, Kristin Flyntz, and Cat Proper.

Last and most important is Nora L. Jamieson, to whom the book is dedicated. It is hard for me to grasp the significance of having lived together as life partners these past twenty-five years. As a feminist healer and wise woman, Nora lives and works in the thick of patriarchy and its consequences. In that sense we have breathed the same air of attention, swum in a common sea of ideas, and struggled with the same issues. And yet we are in such different places as woman and man under patriarchy, a fact that both divides us and, in our facing it together, joins us in common purpose. The paths of our work and lives run parallel and cross, diverge and draw near in a continuing flow that enriches beyond measure not only the work, but the experience of being alive. It has been twenty-five years of "Can I run something by you?" and "getting it" and "not getting it," of bedside tables piled high with books, of play and passion and silent meditation, of struggling with the patriarchal legacy as it lives in each of us and, unavoidably, between us. And it has been twenty-five years of learning how a woman and man can share life and love each other in spite of patriarchy, of learning what is possible across the great gender divide we were born into, of the many meanings that "we're in this together" can have.

And, of course, she read every word of every draft, and brought to it her uncannily accurate "crap detector" that invariably goes off whenever something doesn't make sense or reads badly. And she's brought to it her belief in the work and in me—I can only wonder at the depth of difference that has made to both.

Allan G. Johnson
*Collinsville, Connecticut*
*www.agjohnson.us*

# Part I

## What Is This Thing Called Patriarchy?

# 1

# Where Are We?

Twenty-five men and women gather for a workshop on gender issues in the workplace. In a simple opening exercise, they divide into small single-gender groups and brainstorm four lists: the advantages and disadvantages their own gender has in the workplace, and their perception of the advantages and disadvantages the other gender has. The women dive into the task with energy to spare that gets more intense as their lists of women's disadvantages and men's advantages spill over onto second and third flipchart pages. Sometimes the energy comes in waves of laughter that roll out into the room and wash up on the still quiet shore of the men's groups. At other times it's felt simply in women's furious scribbling of one item after another: paid less, held to higher or double standards, worked harder, granted little power or respect, judged on physical attractiveness more than performance or ability, confined by glass ceilings, not taken seriously, harassed, given little support or mentoring, allowed little space or privacy, excluded from informal networks, patronized, expected to do "housekeeping" chores from taking notes to getting coffee, treated as weaker and less intelligent, often denied credit for ideas appropriated by men, and treated without recognition of the family roles that also claim their time and energy in a society that makes few such demands on men.

On it goes. The men work in tight-knit little groups on the fringes of the women's energy. Surprisingly for many, their lists are quite similar to the women's lists, if a bit shorter. Men miss many of the forms that advantage and disadvantage take, but in a basic sense, they know very well what's going on. They know what they've got and what women don't.

When the men are done, they stand in awkward silence and watch the women, still at work. After a while each group shares what it's come up with. There is some good-natured if somewhat nervous laughter over the inevitable throw-away items: men don't have to wait in line to use the bathroom; men can get away with simpler wardrobes. But there soon follows a steady stream of undisputed facts about how gender shapes the lives of women and men in the workplace and beyond.

The accumulated sum hangs heavy in the air. There are flashes of anger from some of the women, but many don't seem to know what to do with how they feel. The men just stand and listen, muted, as if they'd like to find a safe place to hide or same way to defend themselves, as if all of this is about them personally. In response to questions about how the lists make them feel, one man says that he wants to hang on to the advantages without being part of their negative consequences for women. "Depressed" is a frequent response from the women.

In the silence that falls over the room, two things become clear: The lists say something powerful about people's lives. And we don't know how to talk about the lists. If we don't know how to talk about them, we certainly don't know what to do about them.

The result is a kind of paralysis that reflects not only where this particular group—and countless others like it—finds itself as it confronts the reality of gender inequality, but where entire societies are in relation to these issues. Where we are is stuck. Where we are is lost. Where we are is deep inside an oppressive gender legacy, faced with the knowledge that what gender is about is tied to a great deal of suffering and injustice. But we don't know what to do with the knowledge, and this binds us in a knot of fear, anger, and pain, of blame, defensiveness, guilt, and denial. We're unsure of just about everything except that something is wrong and we're in it up to our necks. The more we pull at the knot, the tighter it gets.

## Patriarchy

We are trapped inside a legacy and its core is patriarchal. To understand it and take part in the journey out, we have to find ways to unravel the knot, and this begins with getting clear about what it means to be inside a patriarchal legacy. To get clear, we first have to get past the defensive reaction of many people–men in particular–to the word "patriarchy" itself, which they routinely interpret as a code word for "men." It will take an entire chapter (Chapter 2) to do justice to this issue, but, for now, the gist of the answer is this: Patriarchy is *not* simply another way of saying "men." Patriarchy is a kind of society, and a society is more than a collection of people. As such, "patriarchy" doesn't refer to me or any other man or collection of men, but to a kind of society in which men *and* women participate. By itself this poses enough problems without the added burden of equating an entire society with a group of people.

What is patriarchy? A society is patriarchal to the degree that it promotes male privilege* by being *male dominated, male identified,* and *male centered.* It is also organized around an obsession with control and involves as one of its key aspects the oppression of women.

## Male Dominance

Patriarchy is male dominated in that positions of authority—political, economic, legal, religious, educational, military, domestic—are generally reserved for men. Heads of state, corporate CEOs and board members, religious leaders, school principals, members of legislatures at all levels of government, senior law partners, tenured professors, generals and admirals, and even those identified as "head of household" all tend to be male under patriarchy. When a woman finds her way into such positions, people tend to be struck by the exception to the rule and wonder how she'll measure up against a man in the same position. It's a test rarely applied to men ("I wonder if he'll be as good a president as a woman would be") except, perhaps, on those rare occasions when men venture into the devalued domestic and other "caring" work typically done by women. Even then, men's failure to measure up can be interpreted as a sign of superiority, a trained incapacity that actually protects their privileged status ("You change the diaper. I'm no good at that sort of thing").

---

* I use the term *privilege* according to the definition developed by Peggy McIntosh in her classic article, "White Privilege and Male Privilege," in *Gender Basics: Feminist Perspectives on Women and Men,* 2nd ed., edited by Anne Minas (Belmont, CA: Wadsworth, 2000). Privilege refers to any unearned advantage that is available to members of a social category while being systematically denied to others. In patriarchy, for example, what men say tends to have greater credibility than what women say, even when they're saying the same thing. Access to privilege depends on the prevailing definition of categories such as "male" and "female" and the advantages and disadvantages socially attached to them. It also depends on related characteristics—a man's access to male privilege, for example, will vary according to other status characteristics such as race, sexual orientation, disability status, and social class. McIntosh's approach is important to any understanding of privilege because it refers not to individuals, but to the organization of social systems in which people live.

In the simplest sense, male dominance creates power differences between men and women. It means, for example, that men can claim larger shares of income and wealth. It means they can shape culture in ways that reflect and serve men's collective interests by, for example, controlling the content of films and television shows, or handling rape and sexual harassment cases in ways that put the victim rather than the defendant on trial.

Male dominance also promotes the idea that men are superior to women. In part this occurs because we don't distinguish between the superiority of *positions* in a hierarchy and the kinds of people who usually occupy them.[1] This means that if men occupy superior positions, it's a short leap to the idea that *men must be superior*. If presidents, generals, legislators, priests, popes, and corporate CEOs are all men (with a few token women as exceptions to prove the rule), then men as a group become identified with superiority even though most men aren't powerful in their individual lives. In this sense, *every* man's standing in relation to women is enhanced by the male monopoly over authority in patriarchal societies.

Note that male dominance does not mean that all men are powerful. Most men in patriarchies are not powerful individuals, and spend their days doing what other men tell them to do whether they want to or not. Male dominance does mean that where there is a concentration of power, men are the ones most likely to have it—they are the default.

Nor does male dominance mean that all women are powerless. Supreme Court Justices Sandra Day O'Connor and Ruth Bader Ginsberg, for example, or National Security Advisor Condoleezza Rice or Hewlett-Packard Chair and CEO Carelton "Carly" Fiorina, are all far more powerful than most men will ever be. But, they stand out as exceptions because male dominance is the rule. Like all subordinate groups, women also manage to have some power by making the most of what is left to them by men. Just as patriarchy turns women into sex objects who are supposed to organize their lives around men's needs, for example, so, too, does this arrangement grant women the power to refuse to grant men sexual access.[2]

## Male Identification

Patriarchal societies are *male identified* in that core cultural ideas about what is considered good, desirable, preferable, or normal are associated with how we think about men and masculinity. The simplest example of this is the still widespread use of male pronouns and nouns to represent people in general. When we routinely refer to human beings as "man" or to doctors as "he," we construct a symbolic world in which men are in the foreground and women are in the background, marginalized as outsiders and exceptions to the rule.[3] (This practice can back people into some embarrassingly ridiculous corners, as in describing man as a "species that breast-feeds his young.")

But male identification amounts to much more than this, for it also takes men and men's lives as the standard for defining what is normal. The idea of a career, for example, with its sixty-hour weeks, is defined in ways that assume the career holder has something like a wife at home to perform the vital support work of taking care of children, doing laundry, and making sure there's a safe, clean, comfortable haven for rest and recuperation from the stress of the competitive male-dominated world. Since women generally don't have wives, they find it harder to identify with and prosper within this male-identified model.

Another aspect of male identification is the cultural description of masculinity and the ideal man in terms that closely resemble the core values of society as a whole. These include qualities such as control, strength, competitiveness, toughness, coolness under pressure, logic, forcefulness, decisiveness, rationality, autonomy, self-sufficiency, and control over any emotion that interferes with other core values (such as invulnerability). These male-identified qualities are associated with the work valued most in patriarchal societies—business, politics, war, athletics, law, and medicine—because this work has been organized in ways that require such qualities for success. In contrast, qualities such as cooperation, mutuality, equality, sharing, compassion, caring, vulnerability, a readiness to negotiate and compromise, emotional expressiveness, and intuitive and other nonlinear ways of thinking are all devalued *and* culturally associated with femininity and femaleness.

Of course, femaleness isn't devalued entirely. Women are often prized for their beauty as objects of male sexual desire, for example, but as such they are often possessed and controlled in ways that ultimately devalue them. There is also a powerful cultural romanticizing of women in general and mothers in particular, but it is a tightly focused sentimentality (as on Mothers Day or Secretaries Day) that has little effect on how women are regarded and treated on a day-to-day basis. And, like all sentimentality, it doesn't have much weight when it comes to actually doing something to support women's lives by, for example, providing effective and affordable child day-care facilities for working mothers, or family-leave policies that allow working women to attend to the caring functions for which we supposedly value them so highly, without compromising their careers.

Because patriarchy is male identified, when most women look out on the world they see themselves reflected as women in a few narrow areas of life such as "caring" occupations (e.g., teaching, nursing, child care) and personal relationships. To see herself as a leader, for example, a woman must first get around the fact that leadership itself has been gendered through its identification with maleness and masculinity as part of patriarchal culture. While a man might have to learn to see himself as a manager, a woman has to be able to see herself as a *woman* manager who can succeed in spite of the fact that she isn't a man.

As a result, any woman who dares strive for standing in the world beyond the sphere of caring relationships must choose between two very different cultural images of who she is and who she ought to be. For her to assume real public power—as in politics, corporations, or her church—she must resolve a contradiction between her culturally based identity as a woman, on the one hand, and the male-identified *position* that she occupies on the other. For this reason, the more powerful a woman is under patriarchy, the more "unsexed" she becomes in the eyes of others as her female cultural identity recedes beneath the mantle of male-identified power and the masculine images associated with it. With men the effect is just the opposite: the more powerful they are, the more aware we are of their maleness. In other words, power looks sexy on men but not on women.

But for all the pitfalls and limitations, some women do make it to positions of power. What about Margaret Thatcher, for example, or Queen Elizabeth I, Catherine the Great, Indira Gandhi, and Golda Meir? Doesn't their power contradict the idea that patriarchy is male dominated? The answer is that patriarchy can accommodate a limited number of powerful women so long as the society retains its essential patriarchal character, especially its male identification. Although a few individual women have wielded great power in patriarchal societies, each has been surrounded by powerful men—generals, cabinet ministers, bishops, and wealthy aristocrats or businessmen—whose collective interests she must support by embracing core patriarchal values. Indeed, part of what makes these women stand out as so exceptional is their ability to embody values culturally defined as masculine: they've been tougher, more decisive, more aggressive, more calculating, and more emotionally controlled than most men around them.[4]

These women's power, however, has nothing to do with whether women in general are subordinated under patriarchy. It also doesn't mean that putting more women in positions of authority will by itself do much for women unless we also change the patriarchal character of the systems in which they operate. Indeed, without such change, the Margaret Thatchers and Condoleezza Rices of the world tend to affirm the very systems that subordinate women by fostering the illusion of gender equality and by embracing the patriarchal values on which male power and privilege rest. This does *not* mean we shouldn't try to get women into positions of power, only that making some women powerful will not be enough to bring about fundamental change.

Since patriarchy identifies power with men, the vast majority of men who aren't powerful but are instead dominated by other men can still feel some connection with the *idea* of male dominance and with men who *are* powerful. It is far easier, for example, for an unemployed working-class man to identify with male leaders and their displays of patriarchal masculine toughness than it is for women of any class. When upper-class U.S. President George Bush "got tough" with Saddam Hussein, for example, men of all classes could identify with his acting out of basic patriarchal values. In this way, male identification gives even the most lowly placed man a cultural basis for feeling some sense of superiority over the otherwise most highly placed woman (which is why a construction worker can feel within his rights as a man when he sexually harasses a well-dressed professional woman who happens to walk by).[5]

Lina Wertmuller beautifully portrays this dynamic in her film, *Swept Away*, in which a working-class man is marooned on an island with an upper-class woman. Although disadvantaged by class, he's very aware of his right to sexually dominate any woman he chooses, which he uses to accomplish a temporary overthrow of her class privilege. Under patriarchy, this scenario would have little credibility or mainstream audience appeal if we reversed the situation and had a lower-class woman subdue and dominate an upper-class man. The objection is based not on social class but on the threat to the gender order that subordinates women. She wouldn't be seen as bold or heroic; rather, *he* would be judged for his lack of masculine power and control.

When a society identifies a particular group such as men as the standard for human beings in general, it follows that men will be seen as superior, preferable, and of greater value than women. Not only will maleness be culturally defined as superior, but whatever men do will tend to be seen as having greater value. Occupations performed primarily by men, for example, will tend to be more highly regarded and better paid than occupations done primarily by women even when women's jobs require the same or even higher levels of skill, training, and responsibility. In the nineteenth century, most secretaries, telephone operators, librarians, and nurses were men and those occupations consequently commanded higher pay and status than they do now when most are performed by women.[6]

And just as what men do tends to be valued more highly than what women do, those things that are valued in a social system's culture will tend to be associated with men more than with women. God, for example, is of enormous importance in human life, and so it should come as no surprise that every monotheistic patriarchal religion worships a male-identified God gendered as masculine. As Mary Daly argues in her book, *Beyond God the*

*Father*, this, in turn, puts men in the highly favorable position of having God identified with *them*, which further reinforces the position of women as "other" and the legitimacy of men's claim to privilege and dominance.[7]

## Male Centeredness

In addition to being male dominated and male identified, patriarchy is *male centered*, which means that the focus of attention is primarily on men and what they do. Pick up any newspaper or go to any movie theater and you'll find stories primarily about men and what they've done or haven't done or what they have to say about either. With rare exceptions, women are portrayed as along for the ride, fussing over their support work of domestic labor and maintaining love relationships, providing something for men to fight over, or being foils that reflect or amplify men's heroic struggle with the human condition. If there's a crisis, what we see is what men did to create it and how men dealt with it.

If you want a story about heroism, moral courage, spiritual transformation, endurance, or any of the struggles that give human life its deepest meaning, men and masculinity are usually the terms in which you must see it. Male experience is what patriarchal culture uses to represent *human* experience, even when it is women who most often live it. Films about single men taking care of children, for example, such as *Sleepless in Seattle,* have far more audience appeal than those focusing on women, even though women are much more likely to be single parents. And stories that focus on deep bonds of friendship—which men have a much tougher time forming than women do—are far more likely to focus on men than women.[8]

In another example, the closing scenes of *Dances with Wolves* show, the white male hero and his Native American-raised wife leaving his recently adopted tribe, which is also the only family she has known since early childhood. The focus, however, is clearly on the drama of *his* moment as she looks on supportively. *She* is leaving her adoptive parents, but we see only the emotionally charged parting (with a touching exchange of gifts) between son- and father-in-law. And the last words we hear are the deeply moving cries of a newfound warrior friend testifying to the depth of feeling between these two men (of which, oddly, this is the only expression we ever see).

By contrast, films that focus on women, such as *Elizabeth, Girlfriends, Leaving Normal, Passion Fish, Strangers in Good Company, Beaches,* and *Thelma and Louise,* are such startling exceptions that they invariably sink quickly into obscurity, are dismissed as clones of male themes ("female buddy movies"), or are subjected to intense scrutiny as aberrations needing to be explained.

**TABLE 1**   Films Winning the Oscar for
Best Picture, 1965–2003

| | |
|---|---|
| 2003 | Lord of the Rings |
| 2002 | Chicago |
| 2001 | A Beautiful Mind |
| 2000 | Gladiator |
| 1999 | American Beauty |
| 1998 | Shakespeare in Love |
| 1997 | Titanic |
| 1996 | The English Patient |
| 1995 | Braveheart |
| 1994 | Forrest Gump |
| 1993 | Schindler's List |
| 1992 | The Unforgiven |
| 1991 | The Silence of the Lambs |
| 1990 | Dances with Wolves |
| 1989 | Driving Miss Daisy |
| 1988 | Rain Man |
| 1987 | The Last Emperor |
| 1986 | Platoon |
| 1985 | Out of Africa |
| 1984 | Amadeus |
| 1983 | Terms of Endearment |
| 1982 | Gandhi |
| 1981 | Chariots of Fire |
| 1980 | Ordinary People |
| 1979 | Kramer vs. Kramer |
| 1978 | The Deer Hunter |
| 1977 | Annie Hall |
| 1976 | Rocky |
| 1975 | One Flew Over the Cuckoo's Nest |
| 1974 | The Godfather, Part II |
| 1973 | The Sting |
| 1972 | The Godfather, Part I |
| 1971 | The French Connection |
| 1970 | Patton |
| 1969 | Midnight Cowboy |
| 1968 | Oliver! |
| 1967 | In the Heat of the Night |
| 1966 | A Man for All Seasons |
| 1965 | The Sound of Music |

To get a full sense of what I mean, look at Table 1, which lists films awarded the Oscar for Best Picture since 1965. Of the almost forty films, only four tell a story through the life of someone who is female—*Chicago, Out of Africa, Terms of Endearment,* and *The Sound of Music*—and only the middle two focus on a serious subject, the other two being musicals.

A male center of focus is everywhere. Research makes clear, for example, what most women probably already know: that men dominate conversations by talking more, interrupting more, and controlling content.[9] When women suggest ideas in business meetings, they often go unnoticed until a man makes the same suggestion and receives credit for it (or, as a cartoon caption put it, "Excellent idea Ms. Jones. Perhaps one of the men would like to suggest it"). In classrooms at all levels of schooling, boys and men typically command center stage and receive most of the attention.[10] Even when women gather, they must often resist the ongoing assumption that no situation can be complete or even entirely real unless a man is there to take the center position. How else do we understand the experience of groups of women who go out for drinks and conversation and are approached by men who ask, "Are you alone?"

Many men, however, will protest that they don't *feel* at the center, and this is one of the many ironic consequences of male privilege. In *A Room of One's Own*, Virginia Woolf writes that women often serve as "looking-glasses possessing the magic and delicious power of reflecting the figure of man at twice its natural size."[11] Woolf's insight suggests several things about what happens to men in patriarchal societies. As part of men's training, they are affirmed through what they accomplish.[12] This contrasts with women, whose training mirrors them in different ways, affirming them less for what they accomplish than for their ability to empathize and mirror others as they form and maintain personal relationships. If men want to satisfy the human need to be seen and acknowledged by others, it will be through what they do and how well they live up to the standards of patriarchal manhood (which is one reason why male friendships tend to focus so heavily on competition and doing things together). This affects both individual men and patriarchy as a system, for men's focus on themselves ("See me!") and women's focus on others reinforce patriarchy's male-identified, male-centered aspects. These, in turn, support male dominance by making it easier for men to concentrate on enhancing and protecting their own status.

Another consequence of patriarchal mirroring is that heterosexual men in particular are encouraged to relate to women with the expectation of seeing only themselves. When men's reflection is obscured by the reality and demands of women's own lives, men are vulnerable to feeling left out and neglected. Like cold-blooded animals that generate little heat of their own, this dynamic makes it hard for men to feel warm unless the light is shining on them at the moment, something well-known to women who spend inordinate amounts of time worrying about whether they're paying enough attention to their male partners, about whether they should be sitting quietly and reading a book or spending time with women friends when they could be with the men in their lives. It is a worry few men wrestle with unless women complain.

All of this is compounded by the expectation that in order to feel normally alive, patriarchal men must be reflected as larger than life. This makes it difficult to develop an acceptable sense of self as an ordinary human being with a relatively stable center from which to relate to other people. As a result, feeling themselves the focus of a one-way flow of attention is the closest that patriarchal training allows many men to come to authentic personal relationships.

This shouldn't be confused with most of what passes for "male bonding." When men get together with other men, they typically are male centered in the general sense of focusing attention on men and what men do. On an interpersonal level, however, men generally don't put other men at the center of their attention because they are in competition with one another and because they are too busy looking for someone to put *them* at the center. As I've wrestled with the difficulty of forming friendships with other men, for example, it's been both puzzling and painful to realize how rarely it occurs to me to telephone a male friend simply to ask how he is, to place his life at the center of my attention at my own initiative. For many years I simply couldn't see the point. I was in the middle of one of many patriarchal paradoxes: that men live in a male-centered society and yet act as though the reality of other men's inner lives matters very little.

Although men generally don't provide one another with the kind of mirroring they expect from women, they do play a part in fostering the illusion of being larger than life, especially through competition. When men compete, they enter the pumped-up world of winners and losers, in which the number of times a ball goes through a hoop or is carried over a line elevates some men over other men (and, by default, over all women) in ways judged to be important in patriarchal culture. If ever there were an assertion of larger-than-life status, the triumphant shout of "We're number one! We're number one!" is it. (Not asked is, For how long? Compared to whom? So what?) Even the losers and the male spectators share in the reflected glow of the noble masculine striving after the coveted opportunity to stand before the mirror that makes us look bigger than we are, if only for a little while— until the next season begins or someone faster, stronger, younger, or smarter comes along.

All of this, of course, is impossible for men to sustain. Women have distracting lives of their own in spite of their training to keep men at the center of attention. And the fleeting moments of actually living up to the expectation of being larger than life are just that. As a result, patriarchal expectations that place men at the center paradoxically perch men just a short drop away from feeling that they are not at the center—and, therefore, on some level, that they don't exist at all.

## The Obsession with Control

The fourth characteristic of patriarchy is an obsession with control as a core value around which social life is organized. As with any system of privilege that elevates one group by oppressing another, control is an essential element of patriarchy: men maintain their privilege by controlling women and anyone else who might threaten it. Given the primacy of control, it becomes the cultural standard for a truly superior human being, which is then used to justify men's privileged position. Men are assumed (and expected) to be in control at all times, to be unemotional (except for anger and rage), to present themselves as invulnerable, autonomous, independent, strong, rational, logical, dispassionate, knowledgeable, always right, and in command of every situation, especially those involving women. These qualities, it is assumed, mark them as superior and justify their privilege. Women, in contrast, are assumed (and expected) to be just the opposite, especially in relation to men.

It would be misleading to suggest that control is inherently bad or inevitably leads to oppression. Control is, after all, one of the hallmarks of our species. It is our only hope to bring some order out of chaos or to protect ourselves from what threatens our survival. We imagine, focus, and act—from baking bread to composing music to designing a national health plan—and all of this involves control. Even small children delight in a sense of human agency, in being able to make things happen. Under patriarchy, however, control is more than an expression of human essence or a way to get things done. It's valued and pursued to a degree that gives social life an oppressive form by taking a natural human capacity to obsessive extremes.

Under patriarchy, control shapes not only the broad outlines of social life but also men's inner lives. The more men see control as central to their sense of self, well-being, worth, and safety, the more driven they feel to go after it and to organize their inner and outer lives around it. This takes men away from connection to others and themselves and toward disconnection. This is because control involves a relationship between controller and controlled, and disconnection is an integral part of that relationship. In order to control something, we have to see it as a separate "other." Even if we're controlling ourselves, we have to mentally split ourselves into a "me" that's being controlled and an "I" that's doing the controlling. And if we're controlling other people, we have to justify the control and protect ourselves from an awareness of how our control affects them.

As a result, controllers come to see themselves as subjects who intend and decide what will happen, and to see others as objects to act upon. The controlled are seen without the fullness and complexity that define them as human beings. They have no history, no dimensions to give them depth or command the controllers' *attention* or *understanding* except by interfering with control. When parents control small children, for example, they often act as though children aren't full human beings, and justify punishment by saying that children can't reason and don't understand anything else. As children grow older, it becomes more difficult to see them as "other" and control becomes more difficult, especially in that memorable moment when a parent looks at a maturing child and sees a person looking back. Suddenly, control that once seemed justified may feel awkward, inappropriate, or even foolish.

Because patriarchy isn't organized around simply an obsession with control, but around an obsession with *male* control, the more men participate in the system, the more likely they are to see themselves as separate, autonomous, and disconnected from others. They may become versions of the western hero who rides into town from nowhere, with no past, and leaves going nowhere, with no apparent future. Women's lives, of course, also involve control, especially in relation to children. But the idea and practice of control as a core principle of social life is part of what defines patriarchal *man*hood, not womanhood, and so women are discouraged from pursuing it and criticized if they do. A woman perceived as controlling a man is typically labeled a "castrating bitch" or a "ball buster," and the man she supposedly controls is looked down upon as "henpecked," "pussy whipped," and barely a man at all. But there are no insulting terms for a man who controls a woman—by having the last word, not letting her work outside the home, deciding when she'll have sex, or limiting her time with other women—or for the woman he controls. There is no need for such words because men controlling women is a core aspect of patriarchal manhood.

## Women and Patriarchy

An inevitable consequence of patriarchy is the oppression of women, which takes several forms. Historically, for example, women have been excluded from major institutions such as church, state, universities, and the professions. Even when they've been allowed to participate, it's generally been at subordinate, second-class levels. Marilyn French goes so far as to argue that historically women's oppression has amounted to a form of slavery:

What other term can one use to describe a state in which people do not have rights over their own bodies, their own sexuality, marriage, reproduction or divorce, in which they may not receive education or practice a trade or profession, or move about freely in the world? Many women (both past and present) work laboriously all their lives without receiving any payment for their work.[13]

Because patriarchy is male identified and male centered, women and the work they do tends to be devalued, if not made invisible, and women are routinely repressed in their development as human beings through neglect and discrimination in schools[14] and in occupational hiring, development, promotion, and rewards. Anyone who doubts that patriarchy is an oppressive system need only consult the growing literature documenting not only economic, political, and other institutionalized sexism, but pervasive violence, from pornography to the everyday realities of wife battering, sexual harassment, and sexual assault.[15] And there are also the daily headlines—such as recent revelations of a long history of sexual assault at the U.S. Air Force Academy that was allowed to continue for years before a public scandal forced corrective action.

This is not to deny that much has changed in women's position over the last hundred years—from the appointment of women to the U.S. Supreme Court to assigning women to combat zones during the Iraq War. There is less tolerance for overt sexist behavior toward women in many settings. An elite of women has managed to enter the professions and, to a degree, upper levels of corporate management. And most laws that blatantly discriminate against women have been repealed.

To a great degree, however, such highly publicized progress supports an illusion of fundamental change. In spite of new laws, for example, violence and sexual harassment against women are as pervasive as ever, if not more so. Inequality of income and wealth has not changed much from the 1950s, and women are still heavily concentrated in a small number of low-level service and pink-collar occupations. In spite of the huge influx of married women, many of them mothers, into the paid labor force, and in spite of a great deal of talk about the joys of fatherhood, there's been no substantial increase in men's sense of responsibility for domestic labor or their willingness to actually participate.[16] And women's share of authority in major institutions—from the state to organized religion to corporations to science, higher education, and the mass media—remains low.[17] In short, the basic features that define patriarchy as a type of society have barely budged, and the women's movement has stalled in much the same way that the civil rights movement stalled after the hard-won gains of the 1960s.

Thus far, mainstream women's movements have concentrated on the liberal agenda, whose primary goal has been to allow women to do what men do in the ways that men do it, whether in science, the professions, business, or government. More serious challenges to patriarchy have been silenced, maligned, and misunderstood for reasons that aren't hard to fathom. As difficult as it is to change overtly sexist* sensibilities and behavior, it is much harder to raise critical questions about how sexism is embedded in major institutions such as the economy, politics, religion, and the family. It is easier to allow women to assimilate into patriarchal society than to question society itself. It is easier to allow a few women to occupy positions of authority and dominance than to question whether social life should be organized around principles of hierarchy, control, and dominance at all, to allow a few women to reach the heights of the corporate hierarchy rather than question whether people's needs should depend on an economic system based on dominance, control, and competition. It is easier to allow women to practice law than to question adversarial conflict as a model for resolving disputes and achieving justice. It has even been easier to admit women to military combat roles than to question the acceptability of warfare and its attendant images of patriarchal masculine power and heroism as instruments of national policy. And it has been easier to elevate and applaud a few women than to confront the cultural misogyny that is never far off, waiting in the wings and available for anyone who wants to use it to bring women down and put them in their place.

"Easier," yes, but not easy or anything close to it. Like all movements that work for basic change, women's movements have come up against the depth to which the status quo is embedded in virtually every aspect of social life. The power of patriarchy is especially evident in the ongoing backlash against even the liberal agenda of women's movements—including the Supreme Court's retreat on abortion rights, the widespread effort to discredit feminism resulting in women's growing reluctance to embrace or identify with it, and the emergence of a vocal movement of men who portray themselves as victims not only of the sex/gender system but of women's struggle to free themselves from their own oppression under it.

---

* The words *sexism* and *sexist* are commonly used to describe a personal prejudice or the person who holds it. As sociologist David Wellman argues in *Portraits of White Racism*, however, that approach is far too narrow to be of use because male privilege requires far more than this to continue. Following his lead, I use the term to indicate anything that has the effect of promoting male privilege, regardless of the intentions of the people involved. By judging actions, policies, and institutional arrangements solely in terms of their consequences, Wellman's conceptualization allows us to focus on the full range of forces that perpetuate male privilege, and saves us from the trap of personalizing what is essentially a social and systemic phenomenon.

The power of patriarchy is also reflected in its ability to absorb the pressures of superficial change as a defense against deeper challenges. Every social system has a certain amount of "give" in it that allows some change to occur, and in the process leaves deep structures untouched and even invisible. Indeed, the "give" plays a critical part in maintaining the status quo by fostering illusions of fundamental change and acting as a systemic shock absorber. It keeps us focused on symptoms while root causes go unnoticed and unremarked, and it deflects the power we need to take the risky deeper journey that leads to the heart of patriarchy and our involvement in it.

Like all social systems, patriarchy is difficult to change because it is complex and its roots run deep. It is like a tree rooted in core principles of control, male dominance, male identification and male centeredness.[18] Its trunk is the major institutional patterns of social life as shaped by the roots—family, economy, politics, religion, education, music and the arts. The branches— first the larger, then the progressively smaller—are the actual communities,

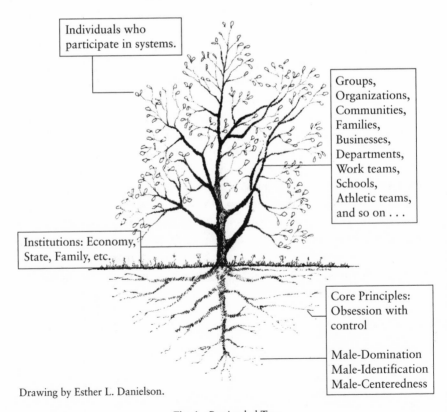

Individuals who participate in systems.

Groups, Organizations, Communities, Families, Businesses, Departments, Work teams, Schools, Athletic teams, and so on . . .

Institutions: Economy, State, Family, etc.

Core Principles: Obsession with control

Male-Domination
Male-Identification
Male-Centeredness

Drawing by Esther L. Danielson.

**Fig. 1**   Patriarchal Tree

organizations, groups, and other systems in which we live our lives, from cities and towns to corporations, parishes, marriages, and families. And in all of this, individuals are the leaves who both make possible the life of the tree and draw their form and life from it.

Obviously, we're in something that's much larger than ourselves, that isn't us. But equally obvious is our profound connection to it through the social conditions that shape our sense of who we are and what kinds of alternatives we can choose from. As a system, patriarchy encourages men to accept male privilege and perpetuate women's oppression, if only through silence. And it encourages women to accept and adapt to their oppressed position even to the extent of undermining movements to bring about change. We can't avoid participating in patriarchy. It was handed to us the moment we came into the world. But we can choose *how* to participate in it.

In this sense, we are far more than passive leaves on a tree, for human beings think and feel and, most important, make choices through which we either perpetuate or challenge the status quo. But as later chapters show, our relationship to the system of patriarchy is complex and full of paradox, challenging us to do the necessary work to understand what's going on and what it has to do with us.

## Deep Structures and the Way Out

Over the last century or so, a lot has happened around the subject of male privilege and patriarchy. There's been an enormous amount of feminist writing and social action in Western industrial societies. And for the first time, the potential exists to challenge patriarchy in a serious and sustained way. Most people's attention is on the surface storms raging around particular issues such as abortion, pornography, sexual harassment and violence, and political and economic discrimination. But these struggles rarely if ever raise critical questions about the nature of patriarchy itself. In spite of the important feminist work being done on the patriarchal roots of pornography and men's violence against women, for example, public discussion rarely gets beyond issues of free speech, constitutional rights, and individual psychopathology.[19] In part this is because we don't know how to get beyond such questions to explore the trunk and roots of patriarchal society, but it is also a way to avoid going deeper into our own lives and the world that shapes them.

To go deeper, we need both inner and outer awareness, which flow from different yet related kinds of insight. I've come to know the first as a client in psychotherapy, which more than anything else introduced me to the existence of deep structures inside each of us—webs of belief, experience, and feeling that help shape the patterns in our lives. They affect us so deeply in part because we aren't aware of them in a critical way. Most people, for example, have a strong personal sense of what it means to be a woman or a man, a sense that profoundly affects how they think, feel, and act. But rarely do we think about such ideas critically. Rarely do we look closely at how they affect us or explore alternatives to them.

We're unaware because awareness is hard work (try to monitor your thoughts for just five minutes), and also because we're easily threatened by anything that questions our basic assumptions. As a result, we live as if these deep structures did not exist at all, as if life's surface that presents itself most immediately to us is all there is. This makes us least aware of aspects of our selves that most affect us, except, perhaps, when a crisis forces us to look deeper, to overcome our resistance simply because we feel we have no other choice. We're like spouses who confront the reality of how they actually experience each other only when their marriage is falling apart.

A second kind of insight is grounded in my work as a sociologist, through which I've been able to see a similar phenomenon at a larger level. As a matter of course, we go about our daily lives without any ongoing awareness of the deep underlying structures and shared understandings that define the social terms on which we live. It's as if the other leaves and small branches to which they cling are all there is to the patriarchal tree. To some degree, we're unaware of deeper social realities because we don't know *how* to be aware. We lack a clear working sense of what a society actually is, for example, or how to think about large systems like industrial capitalism, much less about how we're involved in them. In part, this is just a matter of training. Two hundred years ago, for example, psychology didn't exist, and barely a century ago Freud still hadn't come along to suggest the existence of the subconscious and offer his ideas on personality and the meaning of dreams. And yet today a basic psychological language for making sense of inner experience has become the stuff of everyday conversation. In a similar way, we need to incorporate into common usage ways of making sense of societies and our relation to them.

What is perhaps most important about the deep structures of individuals and societies is how closely they're connected to one another. It's easy to think, for example, that reality is just what we think it is, that a phenomenon like sexuality is a fixed concrete "thing" that simply exists, waiting for us to discover and experience it. But as Michel Foucault has argued, our intensely personal experience of ourselves as sexual beings is profoundly shaped by the society we live in and ways of thinking about sex that are part of its culture.[20]

In a heterosexist culture, for example, when people say "sexual" they typically mean "heterosexual" and exclude all other forms of sexual expression as possible meanings. In ancient Greece, however, "sexual" included a much broader range of human potential and experience which, in turn, shaped people's perceptions and experience as sexual beings. And only a century or so ago in Europe and the United States, "homosexual" was a term that described behavior but not people: People could behave in homosexual ways, but this didn't make them "homosexuals." The word "homosexuality" first appeared in print in Germany in 1869 and was first used in the *New York Times* in 1926.[21] Today, by contrast, being gay, lesbian, bisexual, or transgendered is treated as an aberration at the core of people's social identities and an oppressive system of heterosexual privilege that excludes and persecutes them.[22]

Just what we think sexuality *is*, then, depends on which society we're participating in and shapes our sense of who we are. "Female" and "male," for example, are in the simplest sense words used to categorize people. We tend to experience them as more than words, however, treating them as representing some fixed, objective reality. We act as though "sex" is a word that refers to just one thing, regardless of culture, and that it includes two and only two possible categories, male and female. But in fact, things don't divide up so neatly. An estimated 2 to 3 percent of babies are born with physical characteristics that don't fall clearly into one sex category or another. A baby might be born genetically female, for example, with a "normal" vagina and a clitoris that has developed as a penis. In cultures that admit only two sexes, there's little tolerance for such ambiguity, and parents usually feel compelled to do something about it, from infanticide to surgically assigning one sex or the other to the newborn.[23]

From this perspective, words like "female" and "male" are cultural categories that have as much (if not more) to do with creating reality as they do with objectively naming it. Since the categories are cultural creations, they inevitably differ across cultures and shift over time. In general, for example, the idea that everyone must have a clear and fixed identity as male or female is relatively new in human societies, and contrasts with societies that provide other alternatives.[24] The Native American Navahos allow those born with sexual "ambiguities" to occupy a third sex category (called *nadle*) with its own legitimate social standing. In some other cultures, people have been allowed to choose their gender regardless of what it appears to be "objectively," as was the case historically in several Native American Plains tribes, where men sometimes responded to a spiritual vision by taking on the dress and social standing of women.[25]

In our everyday lives we pay scant attention to the deep patriarchal roots that shape both the world we live in and our seemingly private selves. There are many reasons for this and much that gets in the way that thread together to make a tangled knot. Finding a way to unravel that knot is the major purpose of this book.

## We'd Rather Not Know

We're as stuck as we are primarily because we can't or won't acknowledge the roots of patriarchy and our involvement in it. We show no enthusiasm for going deeper than a surface obsession with sex and gender. We resist even saying things like "patriarchy" or "male privilege" in polite conversation. We act as if patriarchy isn't there, because the realization that it does exist is a door that swings only one way and we can't go back again to not knowing. We're like a family colluding in silence over dark secrets of damage and abuse, or like "good and decent Germans" during the Holocaust who "never knew" anything terrible was being done. We cling to the illusion that everything is basically all right, that bad things don't happen to good people, that good people can't participate in the production of injustice and cruelty, and that if we only leave things alone they'll stay pretty much as they are and, we often like to think, always have been.

Many women, of course, and a few men do dare to see and speak the truth, but they are always in danger of being attacked and discredited in order to maintain the silence. Even those who would never call themselves feminists often know there is something terribly wrong with the structures of privilege that are so central to life in modern societies and without which we think we cannot survive. The public response to feminism has been ferociously defensive precisely because feminism touches such a deep nerve of truth and the denial that keeps us from it. If feminism were truly ridiculous, it would be ignored. But it isn't ridiculous, and so provokes a vigorous backlash.

We shouldn't be too hard on ourselves for hanging on to denial and illusions about patriarchy. Letting go is risky business, and patriarchy is full of smoke and mirrors that make it difficult to see what has to be let go of. It's relatively easy to accept the idea of patriarchy as male dominated and male identified, for example, and even as male centered. Many people, however, have a much harder time seeing women as oppressed.[26] This is a huge issue that sparks a lot of argument, and for that reason it will take several chapters to do it justice. Still, it's worthwhile outlining a basic response here.

The reluctance to see women as oppressed has several sources. The first is that many women have access to privilege based on race, class, disability status or sexual orientation and it's difficult for many to see women as oppressed without insulting "truly oppressed" groups such as the lower classes or racial minorities.[27] How, for example, can we count upper-class women among the oppressed and lower-class men among their oppressors?

Although this objection has a certain logic to it, it rests on a confusion between the position of women and men as groups and their experience as individuals. Identifying "female" as an oppressed status under patriarchy doesn't mean that every woman suffers its consequences to an equal degree, just as living in a racist society doesn't mean that every person of color suffers equally or that every white person shares equally in the benefits of white privilege. Living in patriarchy does mean, however, that every woman must come to grips with an inferior gender *position* and that whatever she achieves will be *in spite of* that position. With the exception of child care and other domestic work and a few paid occupations related to it, women in almost every field of adult endeavor must labor under the presumption that they are inferior to men, that they are interlopers from the margins of society who must justify their participation. Men may have such experiences because of their race or other subordinate standing, but rarely if ever because they're men.

It is in this sense that patriarchies are male dominated even though most individual men may not *feel* dominant, especially in relation to other men. This is a crucial insight that rests on the fact that when we talk about societies, words like *privilege* and *oppression* describe relations between categories of people such as whites and people of color, lower and upper classes, or women and men. How privilege and oppression actually play out among individuals is another issue. Depending on other social factors such as race or class, individual men will vary in their access to male privilege. We can make a similar argument about women and the price they pay for belonging to a subordinate group. Upper-class women, for example, may be insulated to some degree from the oppressive effects of being women under patriarchy, such as discrimination in the workplace. Their class privilege, however, exists *in spite of* their subordinate standing as women, which they can never completely overcome, especially in relation to husbands.[28] No woman is immune, for example, to the cultural devaluing of women's bodies as sexual objects to be exploited in public and private life, or the ongoing threat of sexual and domestic violence. To a rapist, the most powerful woman in the land is first and foremost a woman—and this more than anything else culturally marks her as a potential victim.

Along with not seeing women as oppressed, we resist seeing men as a privileged oppressor group. This is especially true of men who are aware of their own suffering, who often argue that both men and women are oppressed because of their gender and that neither oppresses the other. Undoubtedly men do suffer because of their participation in patriarchy, but it isn't because men are oppressed *as men*. For women, gender oppression is linked to a cultural devaluing of femaleness itself. Women are subordinated and treated as inferior because they are culturally defined as inferior *as women*. Men, however, do not suffer because maleness is a devalued, oppressed status in relation to some higher, more powerful one. Instead, to the extent that men suffer as men—and not because they're also gay or of color—it's because they belong to the dominant gender group in a system of gender oppression, which both privileges them and exacts a price in return.

A key to understanding this is that a group cannot oppress itself. A group can inflict injury on itself, and its members can suffer from their position in society. But if we say that a group can oppress or persecute *itself* we turn the concept of social oppression into a mere synonym for socially caused suffering, which it isn't.[29] Oppression is a social phenomenon that happens between different groups in a society. It is a system of social inequality through which one group is positioned to dominate and benefit from the exploitation and subordination of another. This means not only that a group cannot oppress itself, but also that it cannot be oppressed *by society*. Oppression is a relation that exists *between groups*, not between groups and society as a whole.

To understand oppression, then, we must distinguish it from suffering that has other social roots. Even the massive suffering inflicted on men through the horrors of war is not an oppression of men *as men*, because there is no system in which a group of non-men subordinates men and enforces and benefits from their suffering. The systems that control the machinery of war are themselves patriarchal, which makes it impossible for them to oppress men as men. Warfare *does* oppress people of color and the lower classes, who are often served up as cannon fodder by privileged classes whose interests war most often serves. Some 80 percent of all U.S. troops who served in Vietnam, for example, were from working- and lower-class backgrounds.[30] But this oppression is based on race and class, not gender. When Warren Farrell, a leading figure in the men's rights movement, argues that men are "disposable," he confuses male gender, which is privileged, with classes and races that are indeed regarded as disposable.[31] If war made men truly disposable *as men*, we wouldn't find monuments and cemeteries in virtually every city and town in the United States dedicated to fallen soldiers (with no mention of their race or class), or endless retrospectives on the anniversary of every milestone in World War II.

Rather than devalue or degrade patriarchal manhood, warfare celebrates and affirms it. As I write this on the anniversary of D-Day and the Normandy invasion, I can't help but feel the power of the honor and solemn mourning accorded the casualties of war, the deep respect opponents often feel for one another, and the countless monuments dedicated to men killed while trying to kill other men whose names, in turn, are inscribed on still more monuments.[32] But these ritual remembrances do more than sanctify sacrifice and tragic loss, for they also sanctify war itself and the patriarchal institutions that promote it. Leaders whose misguided orders, blunders, and egomaniacal schemes bring death to tens of thousands, for example, earn not ridicule, disgust, and scorn but a curious historical immunity framed in images of noble tragedy and heroic masculine endeavor. In stark contrast to massive graveyards of honored dead, the memorials, the annual speeches and parades, there are no monuments to the millions of women and children caught in the slaughter and bombed, burned, starved, raped, and left homeless. An estimated nine out of ten wartime casualties are civilians, not soldiers, and these include a huge proportion of children and women.[33] During the U.S. invasion and occupation of Iraq, it has been official military policy to *not* keep count of civilian deaths and injuries. And so, there are no great national cemeteries devoted to *them*. War, after all, is a man's thing.

Perhaps one of the deepest reasons for denying the reality of women's oppression is that we don't want to admit that a real basis for conflict exists between women and men. We don't want to admit it because, unlike other groups involved in oppressive systems of privilege, such as whites and people of color, females and males really need each other, if only as parents and children. This can make us reluctant to see how patriarchy puts us at odds regardless of what we want or how we feel about it. Who wants to consider the role of gender oppression in everyday married and family life? Who wants to know how dependent we are on patriarchy as a system, how deeply our thoughts, feelings, and behavior are embedded in it? Men resist seeing the oppression of their mothers, wives, sisters, and daughters because we've participated in it, benefited from it, and developed a vested interest in it. We resist seeing our fathers as members of a privileged oppressor group and may prefer to see them as hapless victims of women and unseen social forces in which male interests magically play no part. We resist, perhaps because in our fathers we see ourselves and because we're still trying to figure out why they didn't love us very well, or were never around, or were around but in the wrong ways. And we struggle to figure all that out in the hope that if we do, we might be able to have them after all and become something different ourselves.

Harder still is seeing our fathers linked to the oppression of our mothers, or our mothers' unavoidable participation in their own oppression, playing at being less than they are or giving themselves away in the name of perfect motherhood or tolerating neglect and abuse. All of this we resist, because we couldn't help taking our mothers and fathers into ourselves and making them part of our deepest longings and most enduring expectations. And in the process we also drew into our deepest selves core elements from the patriarchal roots of gender privilege and oppression.

But, once again, we must remember that as deeply as the patriarchal tree shapes our lives, we are the leaves and not the roots, trunk, or branches. We're too easily blinded by the good/bad fallacy that says that only bad people can participate in and benefit from societies that produce bad consequences. We act as though patriarchy can be reduced to personality types, as if our participation shows we've failed as people. But like any social system, patriarchy can't be reduced to personal feelings, intentions, and motivations.

It's impossible, for example, to live in this world and not participate in industrial capitalism. We read about the sweatshops in Southeast Asia and the United States in which workers (mostly women and children) labor for little pay under appalling conditions, and we may feel anger at such cruelty and comfort ourselves that our good intentions somehow lift us above such things. But a quick look through our closets and the labels on our clothing will probably show otherwise, that yesterday's bargain was made in Thailand or Mexico and subsidized by the exploitation of those very same workers. This doesn't make us bad people, as if we had set out to do harm; but it does *involve* us in the social production of injustice and unnecessary suffering. In the same way, men don't have to feel cruel or malevolent toward women in order to participate in and benefit from patriarchy as a system. This is a crucial distinction that makes the difference between being stuck in a defensive moral paralysis and seeing how to participate in change.

There are many ways to avoid facing the world in ourselves and ourselves in the world. But it has to get done sooner or later, because any society that doesn't take seriously enough the critical process of creating alternatives to itself probably doesn't have much of a future. Change work is both frightening and exciting. It loosens the boundaries of our taken-for-granted reality, and when we feel lost we need to learn how to be "lost comfortably," like the mountain man who never got lost in spite of long periods when he didn't know how to get where he was going.[34]

We can move toward a clearer and more critical awareness of what patriarchy is about, of what gets in the way of working to end it, and new ways for all of us—men in particular—to participate in its long evolutionary process of turning into something else. Patriarchy is our collective legacy, and there's nothing we can do about that or the condition in which we received it. But we can do a lot about what we pass on to those who follow us.

# 2

# Patriarchy, the System:
# An It, Not a He,
# a Them, or an Us

"When you say patriarchy," a man complained from the rear of the audience, "I know what you *really* mean—me!" A lot of people hear "men" whenever someone says "patriarchy," so that criticism of male privilege and the oppression of women is taken to mean that all men—each and every one of them—are oppressive people. It's enough to prompt many men to take it personally, bristling at what they often see as a way to make them feel guilty. And some women feel free to blame individual men for patriarchy simply because they're men. Some of the time, men feel defensive because they identify with patriarchy and its values and don't want to face the consequences these produce or the prospect of giving up male privilege. But defensiveness can also reflect a common confusion about the difference between patriarchy as a kind of society and the people who participate in it. If we're ever going to work toward real change, it's a confusion we'll have to clear up.

To do this, we have to realize that we're stuck in a model of social life that views everything as beginning and ending with individuals. Looking at things in this way, the tendency is to think that if bad things happen in the world, it's only because there are bad people who have entered into some kind of conspiracy. Racism exists, then, because white people are racist bigots who hate members of racial and ethnic minorities and want to do them harm. The oppression of women happens because men want and like to dominate women and act out hostility toward them. There is poverty and class oppression because people in the upper classes are greedy, heartless, and cruel. The flip side of this individualistic model of guilt and blame is that race, gender, and class oppression are actually not oppression at all, but merely the sum of individual failings on the part of blacks, women, and the poor, who lack the right stuff to compete successfully with whites, men, and others who know how to make something of themselves.

What this kind of thinking ignores is that we are all participating in something larger than ourselves or any collection of us. On some level, most people are familiar with the idea that social life involves us in something larger than ourselves, but few seem to know what to do with that idea. Blaming everything on "the system" strikes a deep chord in many people.[1] But it also touches on a basic misunderstanding of social life, because blaming "the system" (presumably society) for our problems, doesn't take the next step to understanding what that might mean. What exactly *is* a system, for example, and how could it run our lives? Do *we* have anything to do with shaping *it*, and if so, how? How, for example, do we participate in patriarchy, and how does that link us to the consequences? How is what we think of as "normal" life related to male privilege, women's oppression, and the hierarchical, control-obsessed world in which everyone's lives are embedded?

Without asking such questions, we can't understand gender fully and we avoid taking responsibility either for ourselves or for patriarchy. Instead, "the system" serves as a vague, unarticulated catch-all, a dumping ground for social problems, a scapegoat that can never be held to account and that, for all the power we think it has, can't talk back or actually *do* anything.

A powerful example of this is found in the work of Sam Keen and Robert Bly, whose influential books on gender were part of the mythopoetic men's movement, which attracted a wide following, especially during the 1990s. Although younger readers probably won't have heard of it, the movement is still important to understand because it expresses views of gender inequality that are still widely used to reject feminism and defend male privilege.

Both Keen and Bly blame much of men's misery on industrialization and urbanization.[2] The solutions they offer, however, amount to little more than personal transformation and adaptation, not changing society itself. So, the system is invoked in contradictory ways. On the one hand, it's portrayed as a formidable source of all our woes, a great monster that "runs us all." On the other hand, it's ignored as a nebulous blob that we think we don't have to include in any solutions.

But we can't have it both ways. If society is a powerful force in social life, as it surely is, then we have to understand it and how we are connected to it. To do this, we have to change how we think about it, because how we think affects the kinds of questions we ask. The questions we ask in turn shape the kinds of answers and solutions we'll come up with.

If we see patriarchy as nothing more than men's and women's individual personalities, motivations, and behavior, for example, then it probably won't even occur to us to ask about larger contexts—such as institutions like the family, religion, and the economy—and how people's lives are shaped in relation to them. From this kind of individualistic perspective, we might ask why a particular man raped, harassed, or beat a woman. We wouldn't ask, however, what kind of society would promote persistent *patterns* of such behavior in everyday life, from wife-beating jokes to the routine inclusion of sexual coercion and violence in mainstream movies. We'd be quick to explain rape and battery as the acts of sick or angry men, but we'd rarely take seriously the question of what kind of society would produce so much male anger and pathology or direct it toward sexual violence rather than something else. We'd rarely ask how gender violence might serve other more "normalized" ends such as male control and domination. We might ask why a man would like pornography that objectifies, exploits, and promotes violence against women, or debate whether the Constitution protects an individual's right to produce and distribute it. But it'd be hard to stir up interest in asking what kind of society would give violent and degrading visions of women's bodies and human sexuality such a prominent and pervasive place in its culture to begin with.

In short, the tendency in this society is to ignore and take for granted what we can least afford to overlook in trying to understand and change the world. Rather than ask how social systems produce social problems such as men's violence against women, we obsess over legal debate and titillating but irrelevant case histories soon to become made-for-television movies. If the goal is to change the world, this won't help us. We need to see and deal with the social roots that generate and nurture the social problems that are reflected in and manifested through the behavior of individuals. We can't do this without realizing that we all participate in something larger than ourselves, something we didn't create but that we have the power to affect through the choices we make about *how* to participate.

Some readers have objected to "participate" as a way to describe women's relation to patriarchy. This is based on the idea that participation is something voluntary, freely chosen, entered into as equals, and it therefore makes little sense to suggest that women can participate in their own oppression. But that is not my meaning here, nor is it a necessary interpretation of the word. To *participate* is simply to have a *part* in what goes on, to do something (or *not*) and to have the choice affect the consequences, regardless of whether it is conscious or unconscious, coerced or not. Of course, the *terms* of women's participation differ dramatically from those that shape men's, but it is participation, nonetheless.

This concept is similar to the participation of workers in the system of capitalism. They do not participate as equals to the capitalists who employ them or on terms they would choose if they could. Nevertheless, without them, capitalism cannot function as a system that oppresses them.

The importance of participation can be seen in the great variety of ways that women and working-class people respond to oppression—all the forms that fighting back or giving in can take. To argue that women or workers do not participate is to render them powerless and irrelevant to patriarchy's and capitalism's past and future, for it is only as participants that people can affect anything. Otherwise, women and workers would be like pieces of wood floating down a river which, as history makes clear, has never been the case.

The something larger we all participate in is patriarchy, which is more than a collection of individuals (such as "men"). It is a system, which means it can't be reduced to the people who participate in it. If you go to work in a corporation, for example, you know the minute you walk in the door that you've entered "something" that shapes your experience and behavior, something that isn't just you and the other people you work with. You can feel yourself stepping into a set of relationships and shared understandings about who's who and what's supposed to happen and why, and all of this limits you in many ways. And when you leave at the end of the day you can feel yourself released from the constraints imposed by your participation in that system. You can feel the expectations drop away and your focus shift to other systems such as family or a neighborhood bar that shape your experience in different ways.

To understand a system like a corporation, we have to look at more than people like you, because all of you aren't the corporation, even though you make it run. If the corporation were just a collection of people, then whatever happened to the corporation would by definition also happen to them, and vice versa. But clearly this isn't so. A corporation can go bankrupt or cease to exist altogether without any of the people who work there going bankrupt or disappearing. Or everyone who works for a corporation could quit, but that wouldn't necessarily mean the end of the corporation, only the arrival of a new set of participants. We can't understand a system, then, just by looking at the people who participate in it, for it is something larger and has to be understood as such.

Even more so, we cannot understand the world and our lives in it without looking at the dynamic relationship between individual people and social systems. Nor can we understand the countless details—from sexual violence to patterns of conversation to unequal distributions of power—that make up the reality of male privilege and the oppression of women.

As the accompanying figure shows, this relationship has two parts. The arrow on the right side represents the idea that as we participate in social systems, we are shaped as individuals. Through the process of *socialization*, we learn how to participate in social life—from families, schools, religion, and the mass media, through the examples set by parents, peers, coaches, teachers, and public figures—a continuing stream of ideas and images of people and the world and who we are in relation to them.

Through all of this, we develop a sense of personal identity—including gender—and how this positions us in relation to other people, especially in terms of inequalities of power. As I grew up watching movies and television, for example, the message was clear that men are the most important people on the planet because they're the ones who supposedly do the most important things as defined by patriarchal culture. They're the strong ones who build, the heroes who fight the good fight, the geniuses, writers and artists, the bold leaders, and even the evil—but always interesting—villains. Even God is gendered male.

Among the many consequences of such messages is to encourage in men a sense of entitlement in relation to women—to be tended to and taken care of, deferred to and supported no matter how badly they behave. In the typical episode of the television sitcom, *Everybody Loves Raymond*, for example, Ray Barone routinely behaves toward his wife, Debra, in ways that are insensitive, sexist, adolescent, and downright stupid, but by the end of each half hour we always find out why she puts up with it year after year—for some reason that's never made clear, she just loves the guy.

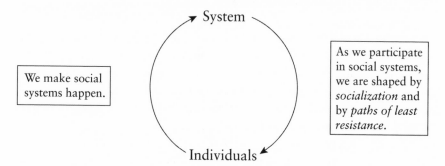

**Fig. 2**  Individuals and Systems

This sends the message that it's reasonable for a heterosexual man to expect to "have" an intelligent and beautiful woman who will love him and stay with him in spite of his behaving badly toward her a great deal of the time.

Invariably, some of what we learn through socialization turns out not to be true and then we may have to deal with that. I say "may" because powerful forces encourage us to keep ourselves in a state of denial, to rationalize what we've learned in order to keep it safe from scrutiny, if only to protect our sense of who we are and ensure our being accepted by other people, including family and friends. In the end, the default is to adopt the dominant version of reality and act as though it's the only one there is.

In addition to socialization, participation in social systems shapes our behavior through *paths of least resistance,* a concept that refers to the conscious and unconscious choices we make from one moment to the next. When a man hears other men tell sexist jokes, for example, there are many things he *could* do, but they vary in how much social resistance they're likely to provoke. He could laugh along with them, for example, or remain silent or ignore them or object. And, of course, there are millions of other things he could do—sing, dance, go to sleep, scratch his nose, and so on. Most of these possibilities won't even occur to him, which is one of the ways that social systems limit our options. But of those that do occur to him, usually one will risk less resistance than all the rest. The path of least resistance is to go along, and unless he's willing to deal with greater resistance, that's the choice he's most likely to make.

Our daily lives consist of an endless stream of such choices as we navigate among various possibilities in relation to the path of least resistance in each social situation. Most of the time, we make choices unconsciously without realizing what we're doing. It's just what seems most comfortable to us, most familiar, and safest. The more aware we are of what's going on, however, the more likely it is that we can make conscious, informed choices, and therein lies our potential to make a difference.

This brings us to the arrow on the left side of the figure, which represents the fact that human beings are the ones who make social systems happen. A classroom, for example, doesn't happen as a social system unless and until students and teachers come together and, through their choices from moment to moment, *make* it happen in one way or another. Because people make systems happen, then people can also make systems happen differently. And when systems happen differently, the consequences are different as well. In other words, when people step off the path of least resistance, they have the potential not simply to change other people, but to alter the way the system itself happens. Given that systems shape people's behavior, this kind of change has enormous potential. When a man objects to a sexist joke, for example, it can shake other men's perception of what's socially acceptable and what's not so that the next time they're in this kind of situation, their perception of the social environment itself—not just of other people as individuals, whom they may or may not know personally—may shift in a new direction that makes old paths (such as telling sexist jokes) more difficult to choose because of the increased risk of social resistance.

The model in the figure represents a basic sociological view of the world at every level of human experience, from the global capitalist economy to sexual relationships. Patriarchy fits this model as a social system in which women and men participate. As such, it is more than a collection of women and men and can't be understood simply by understanding *them*. *We* are not patriarchy, no more than people who believe in Allah *are* Islam or Canadians *are* Canada. Patriarchy is a kind of society organized around certain kinds of social relationships and ideas that shape paths of least resistance. As individuals, we participate in it. Paradoxically, our participation both shapes our lives and gives us the opportunity to be part of changing or perpetuating it. But *we are not it*, which means patriarchy can exist without men having "oppressive personalities" or actively conspiring with one another to defend male privilege.

To demonstrate that gender privilege and oppression exist, we don't have to show that men are villains, that women are good-hearted victims, that women don't participate in their own oppression, or that men never oppose it. If a society is oppressive, then people who grow up and live in it will tend to accept, identify with, and participate in it as "normal" and unremarkable life. That's the path of least resistance in any system. It's hard not to follow it, given how we depend on society and its rewards and punishments that hinge on going along with the status quo. When privilege and oppression are woven into the fabric of everyday life, we don't need to go out of our way to be overtly oppressive for a system of privilege to produce oppressive consequences, for, as Edmund Burke tells us, evil requires only that good people do nothing.

## "The System"

In general, a system is any collection of interrelated parts or elements that we can think of as a whole. A car engine, for example, is a collection of parts that fit together in certain ways to produce a "whole" that is identified by a culture as serving a particular purpose. A language is also a collection of parts—letters of the alphabet, words, punctuation marks, and rules of grammar and syntax—that fit together in certain ways to form something we can identify as a whole. And societies include a variety of interrelated aspects that we can think of as a whole. All of these are systems that differ in what they include and how those elements are organized.

The crucial thing to understand about patriarchy or any other social system is that it's something people participate in. It's an arrangement of shared understandings and relationships that connect people to one another and something larger than themselves. In some ways, we're like players who participate in a game. Monopoly, for example, consists of a set of ideas about things such as the meaning of property and rent, the value of competition and accumulating wealth, and various rules about rolling dice, moving around a board, buying, selling, and developing property, collecting rents, winning, and losing. It has positions—player, banker, and so on—that people occupy. It has material elements such as the board, houses and hotels, dice, property deeds, money, and "pieces" that represent each player's movements on the board. As such, the game is something we can think of as a social system whose elements cohere with a unity and wholeness that distinguish it from other games and from non-games.[3] Most important, we can describe it as a system without ever talking about the personal characteristics or motivations of the individual people who actually play it at any given moment.

If we watch people play Monopoly, we notice certain routine patterns of feeling and behavior that reflect paths of least resistance inherent in the game itself. If someone lands on a property I own, for example, I collect the rent (if I happen to notice); and if they can't pay, I take their assets and force them from the game. The game encourages me to feel good about this, not necessarily because I'm greedy and merciless, but because the game is about winning, and this is what winning consists of in Monopoly. Since everyone else is also trying to win by driving me out of the game, each step I take toward winning protects me and alleviates some anxiety about landing on a property whose rent I can't pay.

Because these patterns are shaped by the game far more than by the individual players, we can find ourselves behaving in ways that might seem disturbing in other situations. When I'm not playing Monopoly, I behave quite differently, even though I'm still the same person. This is why I don't play Monopoly anymore—I don't like the way it encourages me to feel and behave in the name of "fun," especially toward people I care about. The reason we behave differently outside the game doesn't lie in our personalities but in the *game's* paths of least resistance, which define certain behavior and values as appropriate and expected. When we see ourselves as Monopoly players, we feel limited by the rules and goals the game defines, and experience it as something external to us and beyond our control.

It's important to note how rarely it occurs to people to simply change the rules. The relationships, terms, and goals that organize the game aren't presented to us as ours to judge or alter. The more attached we feel to the game and the more closely we identify ourselves as players, the more likely we are to feel helpless in relation to it. If you're about to drive someone into bankruptcy, you can excuse yourself by saying, "I've got to take your money, those are the rules," but only if you ignore the fact that you could choose not to play or could suggest a change in the rules. Then again, if you can't imagine life without the game, you won't see many alternatives to doing what's expected.

If we try to explain patterns of social behavior only in terms of individual people's personalities and motives—people do greedy things, for example, because they *are* greedy—then we ignore how behavior is shaped by paths of least resistance found in the systems people participate in. The "profit motive" associated with capitalism, for example, is typically seen as a psychological motive that explains capitalism as a system: Capitalism exists because there are people who want to make a profit. But this puts the cart before the horse by avoiding the question of where wanting to make a profit comes from in the first place. We need to ask what kind of world makes such wants possible and encourages people to organize their lives around them, for although we may pursue profit as we play Monopoly or participate in real-world capitalism, the psychological profit motive doesn't originate with us. We aren't born with it. It doesn't exist in many cultures and was unknown for most of human history. The profit motive is a historically developed aspect of market systems in general and capitalism in particular that shapes the values, behavior, and personal motives of those who participate in it.

To argue that managers lay off workers, for example, simply because managers are heartless or cruel ignores the fact that success under capitalism often depends on this kind of competitive, profit-maximizing, "heartless" behavior. Most managers probably know in their hearts that the practice of routinely discarding people in the name of profit and expedience is hurtful and unfair. This is why they feel so bad about having to be the ones to carry it out, and protect their feelings by inventing euphemisms such as "downsizing" and "outplacement." And yet they participate in a system that produces these cruel results anyway, not because of cruel personalities or malice toward workers, but because a capitalist system makes this a path of least resistance and exacts real costs from those who stray from it.

To use the game analogy, it's a mistake to assume that we can understand players' behavior without paying attention to the game they're playing. We create even more trouble by thinking we can understand the *game* without ever looking at it as something more than what goes on inside the people who play it. One way to see this is to realize that systems often work in ways that don't reflect people's experience and motivations. If we try to explain warfare, for example, by looking at what soldiers actually do and the consequences that result, we might attribute war to some human tendency to be aggressive and slaughter one another, to some "natural" brutality. But if we look for such tendencies in the participants themselves, the soldiers, we won't find much, for account after account shows that the typical soldier is motivated by anything but aggressive, bloodthirsty impulses to kill, maim, and destroy.

Most soldiers are simply following paths of least resistance. They want nothing more than to do what they think is expected of them—especially to live up to cultural images of what it means to be patriotic and a man—and to get themselves and their friends safely home. Many are there because they couldn't find any other way to make a living or wanted job training or a subsidized college education and never imagined they'd wind up in combat. Or they get caught up in a wave of nationalism that sends them off to fight for things they dimly perceive and barely understand. Once in battle, their aggressive behavior is more often than not a defensive reaction to fear created by confronting other men who feel compelled to kill them so *they* can do what's expected of them and get home safely.[4]

If we look to the personal motivations of national leaders to explain war, we won't do much better. Leaders often seem to feel caught in webs of obligations, contingencies, and alternatives they didn't create and cannot control, and feel compelled to commit armies to war in spite of personal misgivings over the probable result. During the 1962 Cuban missile crisis, for example, U.S. President John F. Kennedy and Soviet Premier Nikita Khrushchev brought the world to the brink of nuclear war. The evidence suggests that both felt trapped between what they saw as the imperatives of national interest and the terror that things might get beyond their control and result in nuclear holocaust. Surely their personal motivations pale beside the incalculable horror of what their actions might have caused.[5]

In spite of all the good reasons to not use individual models to explain social life, doing so constitutes a path of least resistance because personal experience and motivation are what we know best. As a result, we tend to see something like patriarchy as the result of poor socialization through which men learn to act dominant and masculine and women learn to act subordinate and feminine. While there is certainly some truth to this, it doesn't work as an explanation of patterns like privilege and oppression. It's no better than trying to explain war as simply the result of training men to be warlike, without looking at economic systems that equip armies at huge profits and political systems that organize and hurl armies at one another.

It's like trying to understand what happens during Monopoly games without ever talking about the game itself and the kind of society in which it would exist. Of course, soldiers and Monopoly players do what they do because they've learned the rules, but this doesn't tell us much about the rules themselves and why they exist to be learned in the first place. Socialization is merely a process, a mechanism for training people to participate in social systems. Although it tells us how people learn to participate, it doesn't illuminate the systems themselves. As such, it can tell us something about the *how* of a system like patriarchy, but very little about the *what* and the *why*.

Without some sense of how systems work and how people participate in them, we can't do much about either. Robert Bly and others in the mythopoetic men's movement, for example, want to change cultural definitions of masculinity and femininity. They want men to become "spiritual warriors" in touch with the "deep masculine," who feel good about themselves as men and who don't need to rely on coercion and violence. And they want the "old men"—the fathers—to initiate the young men into this new way of being. However, because the concept of a patriarchal system has no place in Bly's analysis, changing cultural definitions will have no affect on that system. In other words, masculinity will be transformed without confronting the control-driven system of patriarchal power relations and male competition and all the ways they are embedded in social institutions.

Where, then, will we find these old men who are prepared to give up their male privilege and adopt, promote, and welcome young men into ways of seeing men (and women) that contradict the prevailing patriarchal order that gives those same old men the most to lose? And where will we find young men willing to follow their lead? Quite simply, we won't, except among a relative few who adopt "new masculinities" as personal styles. These new masculinities, however, are generally reserved for ritual observances among the like-minded and otherwise kept from public view, or, as seems to be the case in the "new men's movement," they turn out to be not so new after all.[6]

Either way, the individualistic model offers little hope of changing patriarchy because patriarchy is more than how people think, feel, and behave. As such, patriarchy isn't simply about the psychic wounding of sons by their fathers, or the dangers and failures of heterosexual intimacy, or boys' feelings about their mothers, or how men treat women and one another. It *includes* all of these by producing them as symptoms that help perpetuate the system, but these aren't what patriarchy *is*. It is a way of organizing social life through which such wounding, failure, and mistreatment can occur. If fathers neglect their sons, it is because fathers move in a world that makes pursuit of goals other than deeply committed fatherhood a path of least resistance.[7] If heterosexual intimacy is prone to fail, it is because patriarchy is organized in ways that set women and men fundamentally at odds with one another in spite of all the good reasons they otherwise have to get along and thrive together. And men's use of coercion and violence against women is a pervasive pattern only because force and violence are supported in patriarchal society, because women are designated as desirable and legitimate objects of male control, and because in a society organized around control, force and violence *work*.

We can't find a way out of patriarchy or imagine something different without a clear sense of what patriarchy is and what it's got to do with us. Thus far, the alternative has been to reduce our understanding of gender to an intellectual gumbo of personal problems, tendencies, and motivations. Presumably, these will be solved through education, better communication skills, consciousness raising, "heroic journeys," and other forms of individual transformation. Since this isn't how social systems actually change, the result is widespread frustration and cycles of blame and denial, which is precisely where most people in this society seem to have been for many years.

We need to see more clearly what patriarchy is about as a system. This includes cultural ideas about men and women, the web of relationships that structure social life, and the unequal distribution of power, rewards and resources that underlies privilege and oppression. We need to see new ways to participate by forging alternative paths of least resistance; for the system doesn't simply "run us" like hapless puppets. It may be larger than us, it may not *be* us, but it doesn't happen except *through* us. And that's where we have power to do something about it and about ourselves in relation to it.

# Patriarchy

The key to understanding any system is to identify its various aspects and how they're arranged to form a whole. To understand a language, for example, we have to learn its alphabet, vocabulary, and rules for combining words into meaningful phrases and sentences. With a social system such as patriarchy, it's more complicated because there are many different aspects, and it is often difficult to see just how they're connected.

Patriarchy's defining elements are its male-dominated, male-identified, male-centered, and control-obsessed character, but this is just the beginning. At its core, patriarchy is based in part on a set of symbols and ideas that make up a culture embodied by everything from the content of everyday conversation to literature and film. Patriarchal culture includes ideas about the nature of things, including women, men, and humanity, with manhood and masculinity most closely associated with being human and womanhood and femininity relegated to the marginal position of "other." It's about how social life is and how it's supposed to be, about what's expected of people and about how they feel. It's about standards of feminine beauty and masculine toughness, images of feminine vulnerability and masculine protectiveness, of older men coupled with younger women, of elderly women alone. It's about defining women and men as opposites, about the "naturalness" of male aggression, competition, and dominance and of female caring, cooperation, and subordination. It's about the valuing of masculinity and maleness and the devaluing of femininity and femaleness. It's about the primary importance of a husband's career and the secondary status of a wife's, about child care as a priority in women's lives and its secondary importance in men's. It's about the social acceptability of anger, rage, and toughness in men but not in women, and of caring, tenderness, and vulnerability in women but not in men.

Above all, patriarchal culture is about the core value of control and domination in almost every area of human existence. From the expression of emotion to economics to the natural environment, gaining and exercising control is a continuing goal. Because of this, the concept of power takes on a narrow definition in terms of "power over"—the ability to control others, events, resources, or one's self in spite of resistance—rather than alternatives such as the ability to cooperate, to give freely of oneself, or to feel and act in harmony with nature.[8] To have power over and to be prepared to use it are culturally defined as good and desirable (and characteristically "masculine"), and to lack such power or to be reluctant to use it is seen as weak if not contemptible (and characteristically "feminine"). This is a major reason that patriarchies with the means to do so are often so quick to go to war. Studies of the (mostly) men who formulate U.S. military strategy, for example, show that it is almost impossible to lose standing by advocating an excessive use of force in international relations (such as the U.S. response to terrorism and the 2003 invasion of Iraq). But anyone—especially a man—who advocates restraint in the use of force, runs the serious risk of being perceived as less than manly and, therefore, lacking credibility.[9]

The main use of any culture is to provide symbols and ideas out of which to construct a sense of what is real. As such, language mirrors social reality in sometimes startling ways. In contemporary usage, for example, the words *crone, witch, bitch,* and *virgin* describe women as threatening, evil, or heterosexually inexperienced and thus incomplete. In prepatriarchal times, however, these words evoked far different images.[10] The crone was the old woman whose life experience gave her insight, wisdom, respect, and the power to enrich people's lives. The witch was the wise-woman healer, the knower of herbs, the midwife, the link joining body, spirit, and Earth.

The bitch was Artemis-Diana, goddess of the hunt, most often associated with the dogs who accompanied her. And the virgin was merely a woman who was unattached, unclaimed, and unowned by any man and therefore independent and autonomous. Notice how each word has been transformed from a positive cultural image of female power, independence, and dignity to an insult or a shadow of its former self so that few words remain to identify women in ways both positive and powerful.

Going deeper into patriarchal culture, we find a complex web of ideas that define reality and what's considered good and desirable. To see the world through patriarchal eyes is to believe that women and men are profoundly different in their basic natures, that hierarchy is the only alternative to chaos, and that men were made in the image of a masculine God with whom they enjoy a special relationship. It is to take as obvious the idea that there are two and only two distinct genders; that patriarchal heterosexuality is "natural" and same-sex attraction is not; that because men neither bear nor breast-feed children, they cannot feel a compelling bodily connection to them; that on some level every woman, whether heterosexual or lesbian, wants a "real man" who knows how to "take charge of things," including her; that females can't be trusted, especially when they're menstruating or accusing men of sexual abuse. In spite of all the media hype to the contrary, to embrace patriarchy still is to believe that mothers should stay home and that fathers should work outside the home, regardless of men's and women's actual abilities or needs.[11] It is to buy into the notion that women are weak and men are strong, that women and children need men to support and protect them, all in spite of the fact that in many ways men are not the physically stronger sex, that women perform a huge share of hard physical labor in many societies (often larger than men's), that women's physical endurance tends to be greater than men's over the long haul, that women tend to be more capable of enduring pain and emotional stress.[12] And yet, as Elizabeth Janeway notes, such evidence means little in the face of a patriarchal culture that dictates how things *ought* to be and, like all cultural mythology, "will not be argued down by facts. It may seem to be making straightforward statements, but actually these conceal another mood, the imperative. Myth exists in a state of tension. It is not really describing a situation, but trying by means of this description *to bring about* what it declares to exist."[13]

To live in a patriarchal culture is to learn what's expected of men and women—to learn the rules that regulate punishment and reward based on how individuals behave and appear. These rules range from laws that require men to fight in wars not of their own choosing to customary expectations that mothers will provide child care. Or that when a woman shows sexual interest in a man or merely smiles or acts friendly, she gives up her right to say no and to control her own body. And to live under patriarchy is to take into ourselves ways of feeling—the hostile contempt for femaleness that forms the core of misogyny and presumptions of male superiority, the ridicule men direct at other men who show signs of vulnerability or weakness, or the fear and insecurity that every woman must deal with when she exercises the right to move freely in the world, especially at night and by herself in public places.

Such ideas make up the symbolic sea we swim in and the air we breathe. They are the primary well from which springs how we think about ourselves, other people, and the world. As such, they provide a taken-for-granted everyday reality, the setting for our interactions with other people that continually fashion and refashion a sense of what the world is about and who we are in relation to it. This doesn't mean that the ideas underlying patriarchy determine what we think, feel, and do, but it does mean they define what we'll have to deal with as we participate in it.

The prominent place of misogyny in patriarchal culture, for example, doesn't mean that every man and woman consciously hates all things female. But it does mean that to the extent that we don't feel such hatred, it's *in spite of* paths of least resistance contained in our culture. Complete freedom from such feelings and judgments is all but impossible. It is certainly possible for heterosexual men to love women without mentally fragmenting them into breasts, buttocks, genitals, and other variously desirable parts. It is possible for women to feel good about their bodies, to not judge themselves as being too fat, to not abuse themselves to one degree or another in pursuit of impossible male-identified standards of beauty and sexual attractiveness. All of this is possible, but to live in patriarchy is to breathe in misogynist images of women as objectified sexual property valued primarily for their usefulness to men. This finds its way into everyone who grows up breathing and swimming in it, and once inside of us it remains, however unaware of it we may be. So, when we hear or express sexist jokes and other forms of misogyny, we may not recognize it, and even if we do, we may say nothing rather than risk other people thinking we're "too sensitive" or, especially in the case of men, "not one of the guys." In either case, we are involved, if only by our silence.

The symbols and ideas that make up patriarchal culture are important to understand because they have such powerful effects on the structure of social life. By *structure,* I mean the ways privilege and oppression are organized through social relationships and unequal distributions of power, rewards, opportunities, and resources. This appears in countless patterns of everyday life in family and work, religion and politics, community and education. It is found in family divisions of labor that exempt fathers from most domestic

work even when both parents work outside the home and in the concentration of women in lower-level pink-collar jobs and male predominance almost
everywhere else. It is in the unequal distribution of income and all that goes
with it, from access to health care to the availability of leisure time. It is
in patterns of male violence and harassment that can turn a simple walk in
the park or a typical day at work or a lovers' quarrel into a life-threatening
nightmare. More than anything, the structure of patriarchy is found in the unequal distribution of power that makes male privilege possible, in patterns of
male dominance in every facet of human life, from everyday conversation to
global politics. By its nature, patriarchy puts issues of power, dominance, and
control at the center of human existence, not only in relationships between
men and women, but among men as they compete and struggle to gain status, maintain control, and protect themselves from what other men might
do to them.

To understand patriarchy, we have to identify its cultural elements and
see how they are related to the structure of social life. We must see, for
example, how cultural ideas that identify women primarily as mothers and
men primarily as breadwinners support patterns in which women do most
domestic work at home and are discriminated against in hiring, pay, and
promotions at work. But to do anything with such an understanding, we
also must see what patriarchy has to do with us as individuals—how it
shapes us and how we shape *it*.

## The System in Us in the System

One way to see how people connect with systems is to think of us as occu-
pying social positions that locate us in relation to people in other positions.
We connect to families, for example, through positions such as "mother,"
"daughter," and "cousin"; to economic systems through positions such as
"vice president," "secretary," or "unemployed"; to political systems through
positions such as "citizen," "registered voter," and "mayor"; to religious systems through positions such as "believer" and "clergy." How we perceive
the people who occupy such positions and what we expect of them depend
on cultural ideas—such as the belief that mothers are naturally better than
fathers at child care. Such ideas are powerful because we use them to construct a sense of who we and other people are. When a woman marries, for
example, how people (including her) perceive and think about her changes
as cultural ideas about what it means to be a wife come into play—ideas
about how wives feel about their husbands, what's most important to wives,
what's expected of them, and what they may expect of others.

From this perspective, *who* we and other people think we are has a lot to do with *where* we are in relation to social systems and all the positions we occupy in them. We wouldn't exist as social beings if it weren't for our participation in one social system or another. It's hard to imagine just who we'd be and what our existence would consist of if we took away all our connections to the symbols, ideas, and relationships that make up social systems. Take away language and all that it allows us to imagine and think, starting with our names. Take away all the positions that we occupy and the roles that go with them—from daughter and son to occupation and nationality—and with these all the complex ways our lives are connected to other people. Not much would be left over that we'd recognize as ourselves.[14]

We can think of a society as a network of interconnected systems within systems, each made up of social positions and their relations to one another. To say, then, that I'm white, male, college educated, nondisabled, and a writer, sociologist, U.S. citizen, heterosexual, middle-aged, husband, father, grandfather, brother, and son identifies me in relation to positions which are themselves related to positions in various social systems, from the entire world to the family of my birth. In another sense, the day-to-day reality of a society only exists through what people actually do as they participate in it. Patriarchal culture, for example, places a high value on control and maleness. By themselves, these are just abstractions. But when men and women actually talk and men interrupt women more than women interrupt men, or men ignore topics introduced by women in favor of their own or in other ways control conversation,[15] or when men use their authority to harass women in the workplace, then the reality of patriarchy as a kind of society and people's sense of themselves as female and male within it actually happen in a concrete way.

In this sense, like all social systems, patriarchy exists only through people's lives. Through this dynamic relationship, patriarchy's various aspects are there for us to see over and over again. This has two important implications for how we understand patriarchy. First, to some extent people experience patriarchy as external to them. But this doesn't mean that it's a distinct and separate thing, like a house in which we live. Instead, by participating in patriarchy we are *of* patriarchy and it is *of* us. Both exist *through* the other and neither can exist without the other. Second, patriarchy isn't static. It's an ongoing *process* that's continuously shaped and reshaped. Since the thing we're participating in is patriarchal, we tend to behave in ways that create a patriarchal world from one moment to the next. But we have some freedom to break the rules and construct everyday life in different ways, which means that the paths we choose to follow can do as much to change patriarchy as they can to perpetuate it.

We're involved in patriarchy and its consequences because we occupy social positions in it, which is all it takes. Because patriarchy is, by definition, a system of inequality organized around gender categories, we can no more avoid being involved in it than we can avoid being female or male. *All* men and *all* women are therefore involved in this oppressive system, and none us can control *whether* we participate, only *how*. As Harry Brod argues, this is especially important in relation to men and male privilege:

> We need to be clear that there is no such thing as giving up one's privilege to be "outside" the system. One is always *in* the system. The only question is whether one is part of the system in a way which challenges or strengthens the status quo. Privilege is not something I *take* and which I therefore have the option of *not* taking. It is something that society *gives* me, and unless I change the institutions which give it to me, they will continue to give it, and I will continue to *have* it, however noble and egalitarian my intentions.[16]

Because privilege is conferred by social systems, people don't have to *feel* privileged in order to *be* privileged. When I do presentations, for example, I usually come away feeling pretty good about what happened and, therefore, about myself. If anyone were to ask me to explain why things went so well, I'd probably mention my ability, my years of experience in public speaking, the quality of my ideas, and so on, as well as the interest and contributions of the audience. The last thing that would occur to me, however, would be that my success was aided by my gender, that if I'd performed in exactly the same way but was perceived to be a woman, research shows quite clearly that I'd have been taken less seriously, evaluated less positively, and have less of my success attributed to my own efforts and ability. The difference between the two outcomes is a measure of male privilege, and there is little I can do to get rid of it, because its authority doesn't rest in me but in society itself, especially in cultural images of gender. The audience doesn't know it is conferring male privilege on me, and I may not be aware that I'm receiving it. But the privilege is there, nonetheless. That all this may feel "natural" and nonprivileged only deepens the system's hold on all who participate in it.

## A Case in Point: Rethinking Gender Violence

It's a sociological truism that problems produced by social systems can't be solved without changing systems, but one would never know it to judge from most discussions of how to cure what ails us. No matter how liberals and conservatives approach a problem like poverty, for example, the focus always comes around to changing individuals but not systems, which amounts to an agreement to perpetuate the status quo. Conservatives blame the poor, leaving it to them to pull themselves together, adopt the right values, and work harder. Liberals turn to government for the answer, but this shouldn't be mistaken for systemic change. Liberals use government programs to change individuals—poor people—by giving them money, job training, food stamps, or health care rather than trying to change how society generates poverty in the first place.

The industrial capitalist economic system allows a small portion of the population to appropriate most of the income and wealth created each year through people's labor—as anyone can see from readily available sources. In the United States, the richest 10 percent controls roughly 80 percent of all the wealth, including 87 percent of the cash and more than 90 percent of business assets, stocks, and bonds. The wealthiest 20 percent controls half of annual income, leaving the "bottom" 80 percent to compete over the rest.[17] When most of the population is left to fight over half the income and a fifth of the wealth, it's inevitable that large numbers of people will wind up with too little or just barely enough to live a decent life no matter how hard they work, including huge numbers of "working poor" who have full-time jobs. In the end, both liberal and conservative solutions call on individuals to work harder and compete more effectively, but the predictable result is that tomorrow's losers will simply be better educated and harder working than today's. What neither side dares to hint is that a system organized to produce such gross inequality might need to be changed.

As with poverty, so too with patriarchy. Instead of focusing on patriarchy as a system and understanding people's relation to it, most discussions psychologize and individualize gender issues and concentrate on education, self-help workshops, psychotherapy, and other programs for individual change. This may make some people happier, better adjusted, or more successful, but without a critical awareness of patriarchy as a system, there's little reason to push beyond personal change. Men, for example, are often motivated to avoid accusations of sexism, and once they've achieved a socially acceptable level of interpersonal sensitivity, they may enjoy some sense of relief and relative safety from criticism, if not a certain smugness in relation to men who still don't "get it" (even here, the patriarchal game continues). And, having found a safe haven, they are unlikely to risk making anyone, including themselves, uncomfortable by digging deeper into questions about what patriarchy is, how it works, and why and how it needs to be changed. The same can be said of women who manage to rise to the top of their occupations; for, having achieved acceptance by the patriarchal system, they risk losing power, rewards, and recognition if they then challenge that same system. As a result, they often serve patriarchal interests by accusing feminists who focus on patriarchy of "playing victim" instead of working to succeed as individuals.

We must focus on patriarchy as a system, but this doesn't mean we should ignore individuals, only that we include them as participants in a larger system rather than treat them as the beginning and end of everything. Consider, for example, the problem of male violence and harassment against women. Between one quarter and one half of American women can expect to suffer some form of sexual violence during their lives, and women are equally likely to be physically abused in other ways, especially by men close to them. Battering by intimates has become the most frequent cause of injury to women, occurring in some states more often than mugging, car accidents, and sexual assault combined. Sexual harassment is pervasive in the workplace, with the proportion of women who say they've been harassed ranging from just under one half to more than three quarters, depending on the occupation. Men's violence against women is so widespread that the United Nations declared it to be "the most pervasive form of human rights abuse."[18]

With the exception of some feminist analyses[19] (which rarely receive mass media coverage), most discussions of gender violence and harassment focus on questions about individuals rather than patriarchy. What kind of men rape and harass? What kind of personality problems do they have? What were their childhoods like? And what bad experiences did they have with women, especially their mothers? This last reason is especially popular, but it makes sense only if we ignore questions about how individuals and their experience are connected to social systems.

Why, for example, should bad experiences with members of a particular group lead to a lifetime of prejudice, hatred, and violence against them? Having a bad experience with someone who wears glasses is unlikely to cause antipathy toward people who wear glasses, but people often say their prejudice against groups such as blacks, women, or Jews is based on a few bad experiences during their younger years. The difference between people who wear glasses, on the one hand, and Jews, blacks, and women on the other is that the latter are all regarded and treated as a devalued subordinate group in a racist, anti-Semitic, sexist society, while the former are not. What turns a bad individual experience into a pattern of prejudicial, discriminatory, and violent behavior is a social environment that encourages and supports just that sort of generalization. It does this by presenting such groups in a way that makes it easy to attribute bad experiences with individuals to their stereotypical group characteristics. So if an individual Jew treats a non-Jew badly, the latter is culturally supported in attributing the bad treatment to

Jewishness itself rather than, say, to that individual's personality or mood. The same dynamic occurs with all subordinate groups, including people of color and women. Without such cultural linkages, people would interpret unpleasant incidents with individuals as no more than that, and the particular social characteristics of the other person would take on no special *social* significance. But when such linkages are provided as paths of least resistance, it's all too easy to seize upon devalued characteristics and generalize to them from what is otherwise an isolated individual experience.

Individual psychology and experience are of course important keys to understanding social life. By themselves, however, they can't possibly explain social *patterns* such as prejudice, discrimination, and violence inflicted by members of one group against another. It's like trying to explain the pervasive lynching of blacks in the post–Civil War South by analyzing the personalities of individuals who took part while ignoring how the long history of white privilege and racial oppression shaped white people's perceptions, expectations, and judgments of what they thought they could do to people of color. It's as if we don't need to consider the racist social environment in which lynchers acted, that gave whites something to gain by oppressing blacks and keeping them in a state of intimidation and fear, that defined blacks as suitable targets for hostility and violence and made it clear that whites who tortured and murdered blacks would go unpunished. It would seem almost silly to suggest that this pattern of lynching occurred simply because one community after another just happened to have some number of people whose troubled personalities led to racial hatred and violence. And it would seem equally silly to suggest that we could stop lynching by identifying troubled individuals and trying to change them—through re-education and psychotherapy, perhaps—rather than focusing on a social system that promoted and protected their behavior.

And yet that's precisely what we've done in relation to men's violence against women. There is a phenomenal amount of public resistance to the idea that such patterns could involve anything more than individual misbehavior and psychopathology. Several years ago, for example, I testified before a state commission charged with finding ways to stop violence against women. I asked the commission to consider that (1) the vast majority of violence against women is perpetrated by men; (2) this takes place in a society that is clearly male dominated, male identified, and male centered; and (3) we need to understand how these two are connected, how the patriarchal character of the society contributes to patterns of violence by members of the gender-dominant group against members of the gender-subordinate group. This generated considerable interest and I was invited to meet with a subcommittee responsible for public education and awareness.

My argument was fine, they said, but what could be done with it? I suggested a first step that was both simple and radical: Become perhaps the first governmental body in the United States to acknowledge openly that men's violence against women is widespread, that we live in a patriarchal society, and that we need to devote serious resources to studying how those two are connected. This was greeted with a nervous murmur that circled the room, for apparently even to acknowledge that patriarchy both exists and is problematic is a risky thing to do. Needless to say, patriarchy remained safely invisible in the commission's final report. In other such groups, the response has been similar—clear recognition of the scope of the problem but an unwillingness to come out and speak the plain truth. "It'll make a lot of men angry," goes a typical response, which, of course, is probably true. But the alternative is to go along as we have, shielding the system by pretending problems like violence aren't about systems, only about individuals who have somehow gone astray.

Like lynching, men's violence against women is something that individual men do and for which they can and should be held accountable. But it's *more* than that, and this means we have to pursue its causes in a broader and deeper way. In addition to being something that individual men do, violence against women is also a pattern of behavior that reflects the oppressive patriarchal relationships that exist between men and women as dominant and subordinate groups in society as a whole. Individuals don't behave in a vacuum—everything about us takes shape in relation to social contexts larger than ourselves. As such, our perceptions, thoughts, feelings, and behavior are neither self-contained nor simply "out there" in society. Rather, they emerge through and reflect our *participation* in patriarchal society. If we ignore this, then we perpetuate the status quo by focusing on the individual *manifestations* of social forces while ignoring the social forces themselves. And that is one reason why an individualistic approach serves patriarchal and other status quo interests so well.

To understand violence against women as both a social and a psychological problem, we have to ask what kind of society would provide fertile ground for it to take root and flourish as a recurring pattern of behavior. Decades of research have established a clear link between pervasive sexual violence against women and a patriarchal environment in which control and dominance are highly valued in men.[20] Under patriarchy, for example, "normal" heterosexuality is male identified and male centered, emphasizing men's access to women and equating "real" sex with intercourse, a practice that's far more conducive to men's pleasure than women's.[21] Such a system encourages men to value women primarily in terms of their ability to meet men's needs and desires and to support men's self-images as potent and in control.[22] The huge pornography industry, for example, exists primarily to provide men with female images available for them to appropriate and incorporate into masturbatory fantasies. As a result, men's use of coercion and violence to control women sexually and their use of women as objects on which to act out feelings of rage, shame, frustration, or fear are commonplace, not only in behavior, but as popular themes in literature, films, and other mass media. In other words, given the values promoted by patriarchal culture, men resort to violence against women because it *works*.[23]

None of this can be divorced from a society organized around male privilege and oppressive relations between men and women as groups. To the degree that violence, control, domination, objectification, and sexuality are bound up with one another under patriarchy, we need to look at how patriarchal culture defines normal sexuality. What we take for granted as "natural" sexuality is not. It is and always has been socially constructed, and the context in which this occurs as well as what goes into it are profoundly bound up with the culture and structure of patriarchal systems.[24] This means that although sexual violence certainly involves how some men feel and behave, it goes beyond this to include patterns that are rooted in patriarchy as a whole. Specific acts of violence directed at women *because* they are women are related to the social oppression of women as a group, just as specific acts of violence directed against blacks *because* they are black are related to the existence of racial oppression in society as a whole. This means that men's violence against women involves *everyone* who participates in the life of patriarchal society, *even though only a minority of individuals may actually do it or be directly victimized by it.*

The challenge for individuals—men in particular—is to figure out what it means to be involved in patriarchy and, therefore, to also be involved in consequences such as sexual violence. When Susan Brownmiller writes, in *Against Our Will*, that rape "is nothing more or less than a conscious process of intimidation by which *all* men keep *all* women in a state of fear,"[25] many men feel offended by what they think is an accusation that all men are rapists. Regardless of what Brownmiller actually means, men wouldn't react so defensively if they realized that "involvement" in a system like patriarchy doesn't necessarily reflect their personal motives and behavior. Regardless of whether I, as an individual man, rape anyone, I am connected to the pattern of violence through which other men do. I am connected if only because I participate in a society that encourages the sexual domination, objectification, and exploitation of women, all of which normalize and support sexual violence as a pattern of behavior.

Whether I personally encourage or support this behavior is beside the point. That women, for example, will tend to fear and therefore defer to me simply because they identify me as a man, or that they'll seek me out for protection against other men, or that they'll curtail their freedom of movement in ways that are unnecessary for me, all affect me, regardless of how I think, feel, or behave. In such a world, being able to walk freely about at night or look people in the eye and smile when you pass them on the street or dress as you please becomes a privilege precisely because it is denied to some and allowed to others, and the privilege exists regardless of whether men experience it as such.[26] That I don't rape women doesn't mean I'm not involved in a patriarchal society that promotes both male privilege and men's violence as a means to control women.

If we think about problems like violence in a way that appreciates both the power of systems and the importance of our role in them, the choice we face becomes clearer. The choice isn't about whether to be involved in privilege and oppression. It isn't about accepting blame for a system we didn't create. Nor is it about whether to make ourselves better people so that we can consider ourselves above and beyond sexism as a social problem. The choice is how to participate in this system differently so that we can help to change not only ourselves, but the world that shapes our lives and is, in turn, shaped by them. Ultimately, the choice is about empowering ourselves to take our share of responsibility for the patriarchal legacy that we've all inherited.

If you're already starting to wonder what people can do in order to take responsibility, or if you start feeling that way as you read on, feel free to turn to Chapter 10 which is devoted entirely to that question.

# 3

# Why Patriarchy?

Patriarchy is full of paradox, not least of which is the mere fact that it exists at all. Consider this: In union, female and male bring new life into the world. They live and work together to make families and communities. They trace their deepest time–space sense of who they are and where they came from through ties of blood and marriage that join them as children, parents, siblings, or life partners who bring with them some of the profoundest needs for intimacy, belonging, and caring that humans beings can have. And yet here we are, stuck in patriarchy, surrounded by privilege and oppression, fundamentally at odds. Obviously, something powerful is going on and has been for a long time. What kind of social engine could create and sustain such an oppressive system in the face of all the good reasons against it? In short, why patriarchy?

The answer that first occurs to many people is that patriarchy is rooted in some natural order of things, reflecting "essential" differences between women and men based on biology or genetics (which is why such arguments are called "essentialist").[1] Men tend to be physically stronger than women, for example, which might explain their dominance. Or men must protect pregnant or lactating women from wild beasts and other men, and female dependency requires men to be in charge. Or men are naturally predisposed to dominance, and patriarchy simply *is* men and what they do to one another and to women. In other words, patriarchy comes down to guys just being guys.

If we take such arguments seriously, it's hard not to conclude that male privilege and oppression are simply part of what we are as a species. This will appeal to anyone who wants to perpetuate patriarchy or who wants to blame men for it. For people like me, who sometimes feel overwhelmed by men's violence, it is also hard to resist the idea that there's something fundamentally wrong with maleness itself. Unfortunately, though, essentialism offers little hope short of changing human nature, getting rid of men, or finding a way for women and men to live completely apart (which won't do anything about the awful things many men do to one another).[2] Given this, it makes little sense to embrace essentialism unless there's solid evidence to support it. But there isn't. Essentialism requires us to ignore much of what we know about psychology, biology, genetics, history, and how social life actually works. We have to be willing to reduce incredibly complex patterns of social life not just to biology and genetics, but to the even thinner slice of human life that defines sex, a position that gets little support even from biologists, including sociobiologists like E. O. Wilson.[3] And if we believe in evolution, essentialism backs us into the corner of arguing that privilege and oppression are actually a *positive* adaptation, that societies organized in this way will thrive more than those that aren't.

Essentialism also implies that patriarchy is the only system that's ever been, since what makes something "essential" is its universal and inescapable nature. Some things, of course, are essentially human, such as small children's period of dependence on adults to feed, protect, and care for them. When it comes to patriarchy, however, all kinds of evidence from anthropology, archaeology, and history point to anything but a universal natural order. There is, for example, a lot of archaeological evidence from prepatriarchal times that dates back to about seven thousand years ago, when goddess imagery held a central place throughout modern-day Europe, Africa, and the Middle East.[4] We also know that the status of women varies a great deal among pre-industrial tribal societies. In many cases, for example, kinship is traced through women, women are neither subordinated nor oppressed, misogyny and sexual violence are unheard of, and women control property and have political authority.[5] Since essentialism assumes that all humans share the same human "essence," it falls apart in the face of such striking and widespread variations.

The best reason to pass up essentialism may be that it doesn't fit with what we know about gender. Essentialism, for example, can't account for the enormous variability we find *among* women and *among* men, or for the similarities between men and women in similar situations.[6] On various measures of mental ability, men differ as much from other men as they do from women; and men and women placed in the same situation, such as having sole responsibility for child care, tend to respond in ways that are far more similar than different.[7] Essentialism also can't explain why so much coercion is needed to keep patriarchy going. If male privilege is rooted in some male essence, for example, then why do so many men experience such pain, confusion, ambivalence, and resistance during their training for patriarchal manhood and their lives as adult men?[8] And if women's essence is to be subordinate, how do we explain their long history of resisting oppression and learning to undermine and counteract male dominance?[9]

In spite of its appeal, essentialism doesn't hold up as a way to understand patriarchy. The alternative takes us into the deep root structures of social forces powerful enough to drive patriarchy in spite of all the good reasons against it. And it takes us deep into ourselves, where the terms of life under patriarchy often seem to permeate to the core of who we are.

## Missing Links: Control, Fear, and Men

Perhaps more than anything else, what drives patriarchy as a system—what fuels competition, aggression, and oppression—is a dynamic relationship between control and fear.[10] Patriarchy encourages men to seek security, status, and other rewards through control, to fear other men's ability to control and harm them, and to identify being in control as both their best defense against loss and humiliation and the surest route to what they need and desire. In this sense, although we usually think of patriarchy in terms of women and men, it is more about what goes on *among men*. The oppression of women is certainly an important part of patriarchy, but, paradoxically, it may not be the *point* of patriarchy.

Why does control have such cosmic importance under patriarchy? One possibility is that control may be inherently so terrific that men just can't resist organizing their lives around it. In other words, men control because they *can*. But this puts us back in the arms of dead-end essentialism and up against the fact that the more people try to control other people and themselves, the more miserable they seem to be. And the idea that what men might get through control, such as wealth or prestige, is inherently so appealing that they would participate routinely in the oppression of their mothers, sisters, daughters, and wives isn't much better. For that to be true, we would first have to explain how control and its rewards could possibly outweigh the horrendous consequences of oppression, especially involving groups as intimately involved as women and men are. A common explanation is, "That's the way people (men) are. They'll always compete for wealth, power, and prestige." But that's the kind of circular reasoning that essentialism so often gets us into: Men are that way because that's the way men are.

An essentialist approach also ignores the prominent role that fear plays in most men's lives. Unlike control, fear may be one of the most powerful and primal of all human motivations, more deeply rooted than greed, desire, lust, or even love. Nothing matches fear's potential to twist us out of shape, to drive us to abandon everything we otherwise hold dear, to oppress and do violence to one another—fear of death, of loss, of pain, of shame or rejection. And the most powerfully oppressive systems are organized in ways that promote fear. What patriarchy accomplishes is to make men fear what other men might do to us—how control might be turned on us to do us harm and deprive us of what matters most to us. This encourages men to feel afraid of being ridiculed and deprived of recognition as real men.[11] We're afraid men will use economic power to take away jobs or hold us back or make our work lives miserable. We're afraid they'll beat us up or kill us if we're unlucky enough to provoke the wrong one. We're afraid they'll wage war against us, destroy our communities and homes, beat, torture, rape, and kill those we love. In short, patriarchy encourages men to fear all the things that other men might do to exert control and thereby protect and enhance their standing as real men in relation to other men.

Women, of course, have many reasons to fear men, but this isn't what shapes and defines patriarchy as a way of life. Men's fear of other men is crucial because *patriarchy is driven by how men both cause and respond to it*. Because patriarchy is organized around male-identified control, men's path of least resistance is to protect themselves by increasing their own sense of control, and patriarchy provides many ways to do that. For some, it's holding their own in aggressive male banter, whatever their particular group's version of "doing the dozens"[12] happens to be. Or keeping their feelings to themselves rather than being vulnerable at the wrong moment to someone looking for an advantage. Or learning to win an argument, always having an answer, and never admitting they're wrong. They learn early on not to play with girls unless it's in the back seats of cars, and may go out of their way to avoid the appearance that women can control them. They may pump iron, talk and follow sports, study boxing and martial arts, learn to use guns, play football or hockey or rugby. In all these ways they may try to cope with their own fear and at the same time inspire it in others, all the while maintaining an underlying commitment to men, what men do, and the system of privilege that binds them together.

Men's participation in patriarchy tends to lock them in an endless pursuit of and defense against control, for *under patriarchy, control is both the source of and the only solution offered for their fear.* The more invested a man is in the control–fear spiral, the worse he feels when he doesn't feel in control. And so on some level he's always on the lookout for opportunities to renew his sense of control while protecting himself from providing that same kind of opportunity for others, especially men. As each man pursues control as a way to defend and advance himself, he fuels the very same response in *other* men. This dynamic has provided patriarchy with an escalating driving force for thousands of years.

Men pay an enormous price for participating in patriarchy. The more in control men try to be, for example, the less secure they feel. They may not know it because they're so busy trying to be in control, but the more they organize their lives around being in control, the more tied they are to the fear of *not* being in control. As Marilyn French put it, "A religion of power is a religion of fear, and . . . those who worship power are the most terrified creatures on the earth."[13] Dig beneath the surface appearance of "great men," and you'll often find deep insecurity, fear, and a chronic need to prove themselves to other men. As president of the United States, for example, one of the most powerful positions on Earth, George H. W. Bush was obsessed that people might think he was a "wimp." Before him, President Lyndon Johnson continued the Vietnam War in part because he was afraid of being considered "less than manly" if he didn't.[14] Rather than making men feel safe, great power makes them need still greater control to protect themselves from still more powerful men locked into the same cycle. To make matters worse, control itself is a fleeting, momentary experience, not a natural, stable state. And so, as Marilyn French and Simone Weil argue, control is always on the edge of slipping away or falling apart:

> Power is not what we think it is. Power is not substantial; not even when it takes substantive form. The money you hold in your hand can be devalued overnight. . . . A title can be removed at the next board meeting. . . . A huge military establishment can disintegrate in a few days . . . a huge economic structure can collapse in a few weeks.[15]
>
> All power is unstable. . . . There is never power, but only a race for power. . . . Power is, by definition, only a means . . . but power seeking, owing to its essential incapacity to seize ahold of its object, rules out all consideration of an end, and finally comes . . . to take the place of all ends.[16]

The religion of fear and control also blocks men's need for human connection by redefining intimacy. Men are encouraged to see everything and everyone as other, and to look on every situation in terms of how it might enhance or threaten their sense of control. Every opportunity for control, however, can also be an occasion for a failure of control, a fact that can inject issues of control and power into the most unlikely situations. Intimacy is lost as a chance to be open and vulnerable on the way to a deeper connection. Sexual intimacy in particular can go from pleasure in a safe place to a male performance laced with worry about whether the penis—that notorious and willful "other" that so often balks at men's efforts at control—will "perform" as it's supposed to. Dictionaries typically define impotence as a man's *inability to achieve or sustain an erection*, as if an erection were something a man *did* and not something he experienced, like sweating or having his heart beat rapidly or feeling happy. The more preoccupied with control men are, the more lovers recede as full people with feelings, thoughts, will, and soul, and become vehicles for bolstering manhood and relieving anxiety. And even though a woman's opinion of a man's sexual "performance" may seem to be what matters, her words of reassurance are rarely enough, for it's always a patriarchal male gaze that's looking at him over her shoulder and judging him.

Patriarchy is grounded in a Great Lie that the answer to life's needs is disconnection, competition, and control rather than connection, sharing, and cooperation. The Great Lie separates men from what they need most by encouraging them to be autonomous and disconnected when in fact human existence is fundamentally relational. What is a "me" without a "you," a "mother" without a "child," a "teacher" without a "student"? Who are we if not our ties to other people—"I *am* . . . a father, a husband, a worker, a friend, a son, a brother"?[17] But patriarchal culture turns the truth inside out, and "self-made man" goes from oxymoron to cultural ideal. And somewhere between the need for human connection and the imperative to control, the two merge, and a sense of control becomes the closest many men ever come to feeling connected with anything, including themselves.

## Patriarchy as a Men's Problem

Patriarchy is usually portrayed as something that's primarily between women and men. At first blush this makes a lot of sense given that "male" and "female" define each other and that women occupy an oppressed position in relation to male privilege. Paradoxically, however, the cycle of control and fear that drives patriarchy has more to do with relations among men than with women, for it is men who control men's standing *as men*. With few exceptions, men look to other men—not women—to affirm their manhood, whether as coaches, friends, teammates, co-workers, sports figures, fathers, or mentors.

This contradicts the conventional wisdom that women hold the key to heterosexual men's sense of manhood. It's true that men often use women to show they measure up—especially by controlling women sexually—but the standards that are used are men's, not women's. Men also may try to impress women as "real men" in order to start and keep relationships with them, to control them, or to get sexual access and personal care. This isn't enough to prove they're real men, however. For affirmation of that, they have to go to a larger male-identified world—from the local bar to sports to work—which is also where they're most vulnerable to other men. Whether in locker rooms or the heat of political campaigns, when a man is accused of being a "wimp" or of otherwise failing to measure up, it almost always comes from another man. And when a man suspects *himself* of being less than a real man, he judges himself through a patriarchal male gaze, not from a woman's perspective.

Although men often use women as scapegoats for their bad feelings about themselves, women's role in this is indirect at most. If other men reject a man's claim to "real man" standing, how his wife or mother sees him usually makes little difference, and if women's opinions *do* matter to him, his manhood becomes all the more suspect to other men.[18] Women's marginal importance in the manhood question is plain to see in the risks men take to prove themselves in spite of objections from wives, mothers, and other women who find them just fine the way they are. The record books are full of men who seize upon *anything*—from throwing Frisbees to extreme sports to being the first to get somewhere or discover something—as a way to create competitive arenas in which they can jockey for position and prove themselves among men.[19] If a man must choose between men's and women's views of what makes a real man, he'll choose men's views most of the time. "A man's gotta do what a man's gotta do," is typically spoken by a man to a woman (often as he goes off to do something with other men). And just what it is he's got to do is determined by men and patriarchy, not by women. It isn't up to women to decide what a real man is. Her role is to reassure men that they meet the standards of a male-identified patriarchal culture.

When a woman does question or attack a man's masculinity, the terms of the attack and the power behind it are based on men's standards of patriarchal manhood. She's not going to attack his manhood, for example, by telling him he isn't caring enough. When she uses what are culturally defined as *women's* terms—"You're not sensitive, nurturing, open, or vulnerable and you're *too* controlling"—the attack has much less weight and produces far less effect. But when women don't play along—when they criticize or

question or merely lose enthusiasm for affirming patriarchal manhood—
they risk the wrath of men, who may feel undermined, abandoned, and
even betrayed. Men may not like being criticized for failing to measure up
to "women's" ideas of what men should be, but it's nothing compared to
how angry and violent men can be toward women who dare to use "men's"
weapons against them by questioning their manhood.

In the patriarchal cycle of control and fear, no man is safe from challenges
to his real-man standing, which is why even the rich and powerful can be
so quick to defend themselves. In his analysis of John F. Kennedy's presi-
dency, for example, David Halberstam argues that Kennedy initiated U.S.
involvement in the Vietnamese civil war in part because he failed to appear
sufficiently tough and manly at his 1961 Vienna summit meeting with Soviet Premier Nikita Khrushchev. Khrushchev challenged Kennedy from the
start, and Kennedy, surprised, responded in kind only toward the end. Upon
returning home, he felt the need for an opportunity to right the impression
he'd made and remove any doubts about his manhood. "If he [Khrushchev]
thinks I'm inexperienced and have no guts," Kennedy told New York Times
reporter James Reston, " . . . we won't get anywhere with him. So we have
to act . . . and Vietnam looks like the place."[20] And so the horror of U.S. involvement in Vietnam turned on a political system organized in part around
men's ability to impress one another with their standing as real men. And
this no doubt played a prominent role in the tortured progress of that war
and the stubborn refusal of all sides to compromise or admit defeat.

In addition to what Kennedy's dilemma says about patriarchal politics,
it also challenges the stereotype that macho displays of manhood are largely
confined to lower- and working-class subcultures. The roots of men proving
their manhood run deep in the upper classes, from President George W. Bush
taunting and daring Iraqi guerrillas to "bring it on" and attack U.S. troops
to the enthusiastic stampede of Britain's elite to the killing fields of World
War I to the sexually compulsive behavior of Bill Clinton and John Kennedy
to the San Francisco Bohemian Grove retreats where captains of business
and government gather to make deals, mock women in cross-dressing skits,
and otherwise relax in the comfort of male privilege.[21] Men, of course, aren't
born to this. They must be trained and given ongoing incentives.

In the early 1960s, for example, I was a middle-class first-year student
at an all-male Ivy League college, a training ground for the sons of the elite.
Among my classmates' fathers were prominent figures in business, government, and the professions, who fully expected their sons to follow in their
footsteps. In late fall, dorm residents who'd been accepted to fraternities prepared for "sink night," a time to celebrate their newfound "brotherhood"
by getting very drunk. Before they went off, they warned freshmen not to

lock our doors when we went to bed because they intended to pay us a visit later on and didn't expect to be stopped by a locked door. We didn't know what was coming, but there was no mistaking the dense familiar weight of men's potential for violence.

When they returned that night, screaming drunk, they went from door to door, rousting us from our beds and herding us into the hall. They lined us up and ordered us to drop our pants. Then one held a metal ruler and another a *Playboy* magazine opened to the centerfold picture, and the two went down the line, thrusting the picture in our faces, screaming "Get it up!" and resting our penises on the ruler. The others paced up and down the hall behind them, yelling, screaming, and laughing, thickening the air with a mixture of alcohol and held violence. None of us protested, and of course none of us "measured up." We weren't supposed to (any man who'd managed an erection would have become a legend on the spot). That, after all, was the point: to submit to the humiliation, to mirror (like women) men's power to control and terrorize in what we later learned was a rite of passage known as "the peter meter."

For them, perhaps, it was a passage to a fraternal bond forged in their shared power over the "others." For us, it was a grant of immunity from having to submit again, at least in this place, to these men, in this way. But our lack of outrage and the general absence of talk about it afterward suggest we got something else as well. As outrageous as the peter meter was, it touched a core of patriarchal truth about men, power, and violence that, as men, we found repellant and yet ultimately acceptable. The truth is, we, too, got a piece of real-man standing that night, for by deadening and controlling ourselves in the face of an assault, we showed that we had the right stuff. Had anyone protested, he wouldn't have been seen as the more manly for his courage. More likely, he'd have been called a sissy, a pussy, a little mama's boy who couldn't take it. And so we both lost and gained during our late-night dip in the patriarchal paradox of men competing and bonding at the same time.[22]

## What about Women?

In one sense, women, like all else under patriarchy, are something for men to control. The consequences of this are enormous because of the damage it does to women's lives, but controlling women is neither the point of patriarchy nor the engine that drives it. This means that women's place is more complicated than it might seem, especially in relation to competition among men.[23]

This works in several ways. First, heterosexual men are encouraged to use women as badges of success to protect and enhance their standing in the eyes of other men. People routinely compliment a man married to a beautiful woman, for example, not because he had a hand in making her beautiful but because he has proprietary rights of access to her. In contrast, people are much less likely to compliment a man whose wife is financially successful—especially if she earns more than he does—because this threatens rather than enhances his status as a real man.

Men's use of women as badges of success is a prime example of how men can compete and ally with one another at the same time.[24] On the one hand, they may compete over who has the highest standing and is therefore least vulnerable to other men's control, as when they vie for a specific woman or use women in general as a way to keep score on their manhood. A man who lacks enthusiasm for pursuing women may have his masculinity questioned, if not attacked, especially by being "accused" of being gay. In this sense, "getting laid" is more than a badge of success. It's also a safe-conduct pass through perpetually hostile territory.

At the same time that men may compete with one another, they're also encouraged to bond around a common view of women as objects to be competed for, possessed, and used. When men tell sexist jokes, for example, or banter about women's bodies, they usually can count on other men to go along (if only in silence), for a man who objects risks becoming an outcast. Even if the joke is directed at his wife or lover, he's likely to choose his tie to men over loyalty to her by letting it pass with a shrug and perhaps a good-natured smile that leaves intact his standing as one of the guys.

In this sense, the competitive dynamic of patriarchal heterosexuality brings men together and promotes feelings of solidarity by acting out the values of control and male domination. This is partly why there is so much male violence against gay men: Since gays don't use women in this way, their sexual orientation challenges not so much heterosexuality per se but *male solidarity* around the key role of control and domination in *patriarchal* heterosexuality.[25] John Stoltenberg argues that violence against gays also protects male solidarity by protecting men from sexual aggression at the hands of other men:

> Imagine this country without homophobia: There would be a woman raped every three minutes and a man raped every three minutes. Homophobia keeps that statistic at a manageable level. The system is not fool-proof. It breaks down, for instance, in prison and in childhood—when men and boys are often subject to the same sexual terrorism that women live with almost all the time. But for the most part homophobia serves male supremacy by keeping males who act like real men safe from sexual assault.[26]

A second part that women play in men's struggle for control is to support the idea that men and women are fundamentally different, because this gives men a clear and unambiguous turf—masculinity—on which to pursue control in competition with one another.[27] Women do this primarily by supporting (or at least not challenging) femininity as a valid view of who women are and how they're supposed to be. The idea that male sexuality is inherently aggressive, predatory, and heterosexual, for example, defines a common ground for men in relation to both women and other men. To protect this, it's important that women *not* be sexually aggressive or predatory because this would challenge the idea of a unique male sexuality as a basis for male solidarity, competition, and dominance.

When women challenge stereotypically feminine ways of acting, it makes it harder for men to see themselves clearly as men. This muddles men's relationships with women and their standing as real men under patriarchy. In the film *Fatal Attraction*, for example, the villain embodied a predatory, violent female sexuality that sent shock waves through audiences across the country. The history of film includes legions of obsessive, murderous men, but with the appearance of the first such woman there was a rush to analyze and explain how such a thing could happen. Perhaps her greatest transgression was to trespass on male turf by violating the strictures of cultural femininity. How fitting, then, that everything should be "set right" when her lover's wife—who embodied all the feminine virtues of good mother, faithful wife, and constrained sexuality—killed the madwoman who'd invaded the sanctity of this "normal" patriarchal household.

In a third sense, a woman's place is to support the key patriarchal illusion that men are independent and autonomous. An unemployed wife who sees herself as dependent, for example, props up images of male independence that mask men's considerable dependence on women for emotional support, physical comfort, and a broad range of practical services. On the average, for example, men tend to have a much harder time adjusting to the loss of a spouse than women do, especially at older ages. And the standard model for a career still assumes a wife at home to perform support work, putting any man (or woman) who doesn't have one at a disadvantage.[28]

The illusion of male independence and female dependence is amplified whenever men complain about the burdens of the provider role. In fact, however, most husbands would have it no other way, because for all its demands, the provider role brings with it power and status and exempts men from domestic work such as cleaning and child care. As a result, many men feel threatened when their wives earn as much or more than they do. They cling to the idea that earning a living is a man's responsibility that anchors male gender identity, and that women are little more than helpers in that role[29] if not "little women" waiting for a man to bring home the bacon. This arrangement, however, was created largely by working- and middle-class white men who fought for the "family wage" in the early 1900s. This enabled them to support their families by themselves and justified keeping wives at home, where they would be financially dependent and available to provide personal services.[30]

You might think that such arrangements are a thing of the past, that with so many married women working outside the home, the provider role is no longer male-identified. But the superficial appearance of gender equity and balance masks a continuing imbalance that's revealed when we consider how men and women would be affected by leaving paid employment. If the woman in a two-earner household were to give up her job, it might create hardships and negative feelings, but these probably wouldn't include making her feel less than a real woman. But for a man to give up his job, he'd have to contend with far more serious threats to his sense of himself as a real man, and both women and men know it. This is why, when someone in a marriage has to leave paid employment—to take care of children or ailing relatives, for example—it is generally understood that it will be the woman, regardless of who earns more.[31]

A fourth aspect of women's place is to help contain men's resentment over being controlled *by other men* so that it doesn't overpower the male solidarity that is essential to patriarchy. Most men are dominated by other men, especially at work, and yet judge their manhood by how much control they have in their own lives. It's a standard against which they're bound to fall short. If they rebel against other men—as when workers go on strike—the risks can be huge and the gains short-lived. A safer alternative is compensation in the form of social support to control and feel superior to women. This provides both individual men and patriarchy with a safety valve for the frustration and rage that might otherwise be directed toward other men and at far greater risk to both individuals and the system as a whole. No matter what other men do to a man or how deeply they control his life, he can always feel culturally superior to women and entitled to take out his anger and frustration on them.[32]

In this way, men are allowed to dominate women as compensation for their being subordinated to other men because of social class, race, or other forms of inequality. Ironically, however, their dominance of women supports the same principles of control that enable other men to subordinate them, a contradiction that is typical of systems of privilege. Men may buy into this so long as they can, in turn, enjoy the dominance that comes with applying those principles to women. The use of such compensation to stabilize systems also works with race and class inequality where one oppression is used to compensate for another. Working-class people, for example, can always look down on people receiving welfare, just as lower-class whites can feel superior to people of color. The playing off of one oppression against another helps explain why overt prejudice is most common among the most disadvantaged groups—because these are the people most in need of some kind of compensation.[33]

Related to men's use of women as compensation is the expectation that women will take care of men who have been damaged by other men. When he comes home from work, her role is to greet and take care of him, whether or not she's been at work all day herself. On a deeper level, she is supposed to make him feel whole again, to restore what he loses through his disconnected pursuit of control, to calm his fears—all, of course, without requiring him to face the very things about himself and patriarchy that produce the damage in the first place. When women fail to "make it better"—and they are bound to fail eventually—they are also supposed to be there to accept the blame and receive men's disappointment, pain, and rage. Men who feel unloved, incomplete, disconnected, battered, humiliated, frightened, and anxious routinely blame women for not supporting or loving them enough. It's a responsibility women are encouraged to accept, which is one reason so many victims of domestic violence stay with the men who abuse them.[34]

## Misogyny

These days, even the slightest criticism of men or male dominance can prompt accusations of "man hating" or "male bashing." But only feminists seem to care about the woman hating that's been around for thousands of years as part of everyday life under patriarchy.[35]

The cultural expression of *misogyny*—the hatred (*mis-*) of femaleness (*gyny*)—takes many forms.[36] It's found in ancient and modern beliefs that women are inherently evil and a primary cause of human misery—products of what the Greek philosopher and mathematician Pythagoras called the "evil principle which created chaos, darkness, and woman."[37] There is misogyny in pornography that portrays women as willing victims of exploitation and abuse, in jokes about everything from mothers-in-law to the slapping around or "good fuck" that some women supposedly "need." Misogyny shaped the historical transformation of ancient wise-women healers into modern-day images of witches who roast and eat children. It has been the basis for the torture and murder of millions of women from the witch hunts of the Middle Ages to Serb terrorism in Bosnia. It is reflected in the everyday reality of sexual coercion, abuse, violence, and harassment, in the mass media display of women's bodies as objects existing primarily to please men and satisfy the male gaze, in cultural ideals of slenderness that turn women against their own bodies and inspire self-hatred and denial, and in the steady stream of sensationalized and sexualized mass media "entertainment" in which men terrorize, torture, rape, and murder women.[38]

Not to be overlooked is the insulting of males with names that link them to females—sissy (sister), girl, son of a bitch, mama's boy. Notice, however, that the worst way to insult a woman isn't to call her a man or a "daddy's girl." It's to *still* call her a woman but by names that highlight or maligns femaleness itself—bitch, whore, pussy, cunt.[39] The use of such words as insults is made even worse by the fact that prior to patriarchy, many had neutral or positive meanings for women. A "whore" was a lover of either sex, "bitch" was associated with the pre-Christian goddess of the hunt, Artemis-Diana, and "cunt" derives from several sources, including the goddesses Cunti and Kunda, the universal sources of life.[40]

It's difficult to accept the idea that in the midst of wanting, needing, and loving women, men are involved—if only as sons in relation to mothers—in a system that makes misogynist feelings, thoughts, and behavior paths of least resistance. Most men would probably deny this affects them in any way. Often the most sexist men are among the first to say how much they love women. But there's no escaping misogyny, because it isn't a personality flaw. It's part of patriarchal culture. We're like fish swimming in a sea laced with it, and we can't breathe without passing it through our gills.[41] Misogyny infuses into our cells and becomes part of who we are because by the time we know enough to reject it, it's too late. As with everything else in a culture, some people are exposed to more of it than others, but to suppose that anyone escapes untouched is both wishful and disempowering. It's wishful because it goes against what we know about socialization and the power of culture to shape reality. It's disempowering because if we believe that misogyny doesn't involve us, we won't feel compelled to do anything about it.

Misogyny plays a complex role in patriarchy. It fuels men's sense of superiority, justifies male aggression against women, and works to keep women on the defensive and in their place. Misogyny is especially powerful in encouraging women to hate their own femaleness, an example of internalized oppression. The more women internalize misogynist images and attitudes, the harder it is to challenge male privilege or patriarchy as a system. In fact, women won't tend to see patriarchy as even problematic since the essence of self-hatred is to focus on the self as the sole cause of misery, including the self-hatred.

In another sense, patriarchy promotes the hatred of women as a reaction to men's fear of women. Why should men fear women? Because every system of privilege depends to some degree on subordinate groups going along with their own subordination. The other side of this, however, is the potential to undermine and rebel by not going along. This makes privilege inherently unstable, which makes dominant groups vulnerable. Throughout the slaveholding South, for example, white people's fear of slave revolts was woven into the fabric of everyday life and caused many a restless night. And I suspect that much of the discomfort that whites typically feel around blacks today, especially black men, also reflects a fear that the potential for challenge and rebellion is never far from the surface.[42] In a patriarchal system the fear for men is that women will stop playing the complex role that allows patriarchy to continue, or may even go so far as to challenge male privilege directly. Women's potential to disrupt patriarchy and make men vulnerable is why it's so easy for women to make men feel foolish or emasculated through the mildest humor that focuses on maleness and hints at women's power to stop going along with the status quo. Making fun of men, however, is just the tip of the iceberg of what women can do to disturb the patriarchal order, and on some level most men know this and have reason to feel threatened by it.

In more subtle ways, misogyny arises out of a system that offers women to men as a form of compensation. Because patriarchy limits men's emotional and spiritual lives, and because men rarely risk being vulnerable with other men, they often look to women as a way to ease the resulting sense of emptiness, meaninglessness, and disconnection. However, the patriarchal expectation that "real men" are autonomous and independent sets men up to both want and resent women at the same time. This is made all the worse by the fact that women can't possibly give men what they want, since autonomy and indepence are illusions. Caught in this bind, men could face the truth of the system that put them there in the first place. They could look at patriarchy and how their position in it creates this dilemma. The path of least resistance, however, is to resent and blame women for what men lack, by accusing women of not being loving or sexual enough, of being manipulative, withholding, selfish bitches who deserve to be punished.[43]

In a related sense, misogyny can reflect male envy of the human qualities patriarchy encourages men to devalue and deny in themselves as they avoid association with anything remotely female. Under patriarchy, women are viewed as trustees of all that makes a rich emotional life possible—of empathy and sympathy, vulnerability and openness to connection, caring and nurturing, sensitivity and compassion, emotional attention and expressiveness—all of which tend to be driven out of men's lives by the cycle of control and fear. On some level, men know the value of what they don't have and see women as privileged for being able to hold on to it. As a result, women live a double bind: The patriarchal ideology that supports male privilege and women's oppression devalues the human qualities associated with being female, yet it also sets men up to envy and resent women for being able to weave those same qualities into their lives.[44]

Finally, misogyny can be seen as a cultural result of men's potential to feel guilty about women's oppression. Rather than encourage men to feel guilty, patriarchal culture projects negative judgments about men onto women. When men do feel guilty, they can blame women for making them feel this way: "If you weren't there reminding me of how oppressed women are, then I wouldn't have to feel bad about myself as a member of the group that benefits from it." Anger and resentment play this kind of role in many systems of privilege. When middle-class people encounter the homeless on the street, for example, it's not uncommon for them to feel angry simply for being reminded of their privilege and their potential to feel guilty about it. It's easier to hate the messenger than it is to take some responsibility for doing something about the reality behind the message.

As a mainstay of patriarchal culture, misogyny embodies some of the most contradictory and disturbing aspects of male privilege. When love and need are bound up with fear, envy, resentment, and the obsession with control, the result is an explosive mixture that can twist our sense of ourselves and one another beyond recognition. If misogyny were merely a problem of bad personal attitudes, it would be relatively easy to deal with. But its close connection to the cycle of control and fear that makes patriarchy work will make it part of human life as long as patriarchy continues.

## The Look of Modern Patriarchy

Over its long history, patriarchy has changed dramatically in some ways and very little in others. As societies have developed new forms of control and domination, systems of privilege have changed in order to make use of them. Under European feudalism, for example, class privilege depended on military force, control over land, and traditional obligations between nobles and peasants. With industrial capitalism, however, class is based primarily on control over complex organizations such as corporations, government, universities and the mass media. In similar ways, patriarchy has shifted from one base of power to another in response to social change. This hasn't happened in a uniform way since no single patriarchal model applies to all societies, but it has always involved some mix of the core qualities that define patriarchy as male dominated, male identified, and male centered.

In pre-industrial patriarchies, the main objects of control are land and women's reproductive potential. Since families produce most of the wealth, male privilege is based primarily on men's authority as husbands and fathers and their title to land and other property. To the extent that pre-industrial societies have institutions outside the family—such as separate religious, medical, military, or state institutions—men dominate these as well.

This is how it was in most patriarchies until industrial capitalism began to revolutionize social life several centuries ago. The most dramatic change was to shift production away from agriculture and the land and into urban factories. This made land less valuable as a source of wealth and power, lowered the economic value of children and their labor, and drew increasing numbers of men and women into wage labor in a money-driven economy. As a result, men could no longer use the family as a basis of privilege because the family no longer had a central place in economic production. A great deal of work was still done in families, but it wasn't done for money. Since power revolved increasingly around money and wealth was valued in terms of money, family work couldn't be used as a basis for privilege.

Male privilege now depended on controlling capital or earning the money that families needed to purchase goods and services in an exploding market economy. Men moved quickly to appropriate this for themselves. Since children's contribution to industrial labor quickly lost its economic value as production became more complex, their worth became something figured primarily in emotional terms. This encouraged fathers to lose interest in children and limited women's lives ever more narrowly to child care.[45] As a result, child custody no longer went automatically to fathers, but more typically to mothers.[46] In some ways, the position of the father lost so much of its traditional authority under industrial capitalism that, technically speaking, the gender system was no longer patriarchal but androcratic, based on male (andro-) rather than father (patri-) dominance.

As industrial capitalism transformed patriarchy, it also profoundly affected women. Before industrialization, there wasn't much that women couldn't and didn't do, and husbands and wives depended on one another for survival.[47] Industrial capitalism changed all of that, however. Individuals now could survive on their own by earning wages, which broke the age-old bond of mutual dependence between women and men. The work women did at home was marginalized and devalued because it didn't involve an exchange of money,[48] and without earnings of their own, middle-class women who stayed home became what may have been the first major group of productive yet economically dependent women in human history.[49] As a result, women confronted the novel choice of whether to depend on men or make their way as second-class, unwelcome workers in the new patriarchal world of work where wealth, power, dignity, and prestige were distributed.

Industrial capitalism was shrinking the family's sphere of influence and shifting the focus of power outward to rapidly growing institutions such as the state, science, industry, and schools. These institutions grew out of a new way of thinking that emphasized the power of the human intellect to understand and ultimately control all it could imagine. Both natural scientists and early sociologists believed the world was governed by social and natural laws that, once understood, would enable *men* to exercise revolutionary degrees of control over themselves and their environments. "Man's place in the physical universe," a Nobel laureate declared not so long ago, "is to be its master . . . to be its king through the power he alone possesses—the Principle of Intelligence."[50] This kind of thinking carried the evolution of patriarchy through a quantum leap that expanded dramatically the cultural importance attached to the idea of control as an organizing principle of social life on every level, from self to society to the entire natural world. For most people, patriarchy went from being a relatively simple family system to something much larger and more complex as the tools and settings for practicing the religion of power multiplied.

The rapid rise of science, technology, politics, and other forms of control also changed how people thought about and justified male dominance. As Arthur Brittan put it,

> Instead of the religious justification of gender differences, in the six-teenth and seventeenth centuries these differences were beginning to be explained in a new way. Previously, they had been codified in philosophical and political doctrines. They had a rationale legiti-mated by God, by reason and by the nascent political authority. But, from this time onward, differences were not decreed by the church, but by "science" and its *spokesmen*, the "discoverers" of the essential nature of men and women. Since all human beings are subject to the laws of nature, they could be "worked on" and manipulated like other "natural" objects. Where the church had demanded that women obey men because God willed it, the new science argued that women were inferior because they were made this way.[51]

It's important to realize that much of this change reshaped how men competed with one another for power and control. Under the European feudalism that preceded industrial capitalism, for example, power struggles revolved around the military, the landed aristocracy, the church, and the fledgling state—all of which were patriarchal. Capitalism developed as a revolt against feudalism by a new patriarchal middle class of entrepreneurs who wanted the freedom to compete in markets. The landed aristocracy stood in their way, which made for conflict and sometimes violent revolution. None of this, however, ended the religion of power. It merely changed the terms of the struggle to control over markets rather than control over land and peasants, and later to control over production, labor, and the environment. The social landscape was transformed, but the major players were still men, and the new social systems were still thoroughly patriarchal.

We can lose sight of patriarchy in all of this social upheaval and transformation if we overlook the fact that industrial capitalism was male dominated, male centered, and male identified and sprang from and embodied the core patriarchal valuing of control. Writers such as Robert Bly and Sam Keen, for example, have a lot to say about the evils of industrialization but don't mention its connection to patriarchy.[52] What changed the world wasn't mere capitalist industrialization, but *patriarchal* capitalist industrialization. The same can be said of the socialist alternatives that developed in response to capitalism, such as in the Soviet Union and China, that for all their progressive reforms, in many ways represented little more than a new form of competition between patriarchal systems. As Hazel Henderson put it, capitalism and socialism have merely been two contenders in the struggle over what form industrialization would take.[53]

## The Mystery of How We Got Here

Whenever I speak about patriarchy, someone always asks where it came from in the first place. The question usually comes from a man, and I suspect he's saying, "If I'm going to give up the essentialist idea that patriarchy is universal and inevitable, I want something to put in its place." If patriarchy isn't hard-wired into the species, then it had to *start* for some reason. The problem is that what we know as history doesn't reach back very far and can't tell us what we want to know without a lot of speculation mixed in. That won't stop us from wondering about where patriarchy came from, however, because this huge hole in our understanding nags for something to fill it up. And we need some reason to hope that something better is possible, which we can't have if we settle for essentialist explanations. What, after all, is the point of trying to change something that's inevitable?

Another reason to look at the question of where patriarchy came from is that whatever model we use to explain what drives patriarchy now is more credible if it fits with a plausible argument about where it came from in the first place. If we're right about patriarchy as it *is*, we should be able to extend our understanding back in time and see a connection between how it is now and how it most likely *was*. This won't *prove* anything, for the forces that bring a social system into being aren't necessarily the same as those that keep it going. But if one framework can make sense of patriarchy's past *and* its present, we can quiet some nagging questions that distract us from doing something about it.

What, then, do we know about nonpatriarchal societies, and how do we know it?[54] Some evidence comes from anthropological and historical studies of tribal societies, from the !Kung in Africa to Native American tribes to the New Guinea Arapesh.[55] From these we know of numerous societies in which women have not been devalued or subordinated but have, in fact, played prominent roles in social life. Matrilineal and matrilocal societies[56] have been quite common and have often included substantial female control over land and other property. Although every known society divides some tasks by gender, there is often a great deal of overlap, and in either case men's and women's work are valued equally. Sexual violence and the treatment of women as property are almost unknown in these societies, and historically have increased only with advances in male dominance.[57]

When we consider the rich store of archaeological evidence from prehistoric civilizations such as ancient Crete, it's difficult to deny that something other than patriarchy existed as recently as seven thousand years ago.[58] Artifacts dating to before that time, for example, suggest the existence of Middle Eastern societies in which women and men were equally well regarded. Women's graves were as centrally located and richly appointed with statues and other artifacts as those of men. In addition, the accumulation of statuary from ancient sites shows far more female than male figures. These consist mostly of women with prominent breasts, belly, and vagina, suggesting a clear focus on women's role in renewing life. Only in later periods of emerging male dominance do artistic themes shift away from women and begin to portray phallic images. Evidence also suggests that organized warfare was rare if not unknown. Excavations in ancient Crete, for example, find no evidence of fortifications in the prepatriarchal period.

It's reasonable to argue from such evidence that for most of humanity's 250,000 years on Earth, social life has not been organized around control and domination. It is also reasonable to argue that male dominance and the oppression of women are relatively recent. Not only has women's work been regarded as central to social life, but on a deeper level, the belief that women could create life seems to have placed female imagery at the core of religious traditions.[59] The abundant goddess imagery found in archaeological digs, for example, suggests that prepatriarchal societies were organized around a world view centered on the idea of the female as a symbolic link between humanity and the flow of nature from which all life comes. As Miriam Johnson notes, this doesn't mean that men were marginalized or subordinated, only that there was reverence for cultural *principles* associated with femaleness:

> Matrifocality [a cultural focus on mothers] . . . does not refer to domestic maternal dominance so much as it does to the relative cultural prestige of the *image* of mother, a role that is culturally elaborated and valued. . . . It is not the absence of males (males may be quite present) but the centrality of women as mothers and sisters that makes a society matrifocal, and this matrifocal emphasis is accompanied by a minimum of differentiation between women and men.[60]

Nonetheless, we're so used to the patriarchal obsession with control that it's hard to imagine that a society might exist without a dominant group. From a narrow patriarchal perspective, the logical assumption is that if the world was ever nonpatriarchal, it must have been matriarchal, especially if femaleness was valued and even revered.

Once we accept the idea that something came before patriarchy and that valuing women and gender equality was one of its core aspects, then we have to deal with the question of what happened to turn all of this into a system based on control, privilege, and gender oppression. What social engine could be powerful enough to break down bonds of equality between women and men? What could create new forms of family life in which women and children became men's property? How could kinship systems organized around mothers and their blood relatives become male identified?[61] Why would systems of cooperation and peaceful coexistence give way to systems of competition and warfare?

Although we can never answer such questions once and for all, Riane Eisler, Elizabeth Fisher, Marilyn French, Gerda Lerner, and others have made a good case that certain social conditions played an important part.[62] The first was the discovery of how to grow crops, which took place some nine thousand years ago. As using plows to cultivate fields replaced small-garden horticulture, societies could produce a surplus of goods. This, in turn, made it possible for some people to accumulate wealth at the expense of others. This didn't *cause* inequality, since sharing is as much a possibility as hoarding. Surpluses were, however, a precondition that made inequality *possible*.[63] Perhaps even more important, agriculture introduced the *idea* of control into many human cultures as people settled into more permanent communities and discovered they could affect their environment through such practices as clearing forests and cultivating the soil. Some degree of control has probably always been part of human life, but never before had the concept of control emerged so forcefully as part of culture, or been so conducive to seeing the rest of the natural world as a nonhuman "other" to be controlled.[64]

This changing relationship of humans to nature was related to the discovery, some nine thousand to eleven thousand years ago, of how reproduction worked in both plant and animal species, and the resulting domestication of goats, cattle, and other animals. Elizabeth Fisher believes this helped lay the groundwork for patriarchy in several ways. First, it transformed a relatively equal and balanced relation between humans and other animals into one of control and dominance. When hunters killed wild animals for food, they had reason to see them as creatures of equal standing in the nature of things whose deaths warranted appreciation, often in the form of ritual honoring. The lives of domesticated animals, however, are from the start dominated and controlled by people, their entire existence subordinated to human needs and ends.

Second, when animals were bred for slaughter or work, reproduction took on an economic value it didn't have before.[65] From this it was a short leap to the idea that human reproduction also has economic value, especially given how much labor was needed to cultivate large fields. This, in turn, created an incentive to control women's reproductive potential, for the more children a man had, the more workers there were to produce surplus goods, which men invariably controlled.

Third, domesticating animals created an emotional dilemma around nurturing and caring for animals with the intention of slaughtering them later.[66] Short of letting the animals live, the only way people could resolve the tension was to distance themselves from both the nurturing and the killing, to see nature as a separate and alien exploitable resource, an object of control and domination, even an adversary—all of which more advanced patriarchies have done to greater and greater degrees.

Fisher believes the split between humanity and the rest of nature sowed the seeds for a more general and profound disconnection in social life. It did this by providing a model for control and domination based on the distinction between self and other, an "us" and a "them." Instead of seeing all life as an undifferentiated whole, the stage was now set for dividing the world into the controllers and the controlled. This was crucial to the development of patriarchy, especially given how an understanding of reproduction must have undermined the cultural reverence for women's reproductive powers. If reproduction wasn't a matter of female magic and could be controlled like anything else, then women's special connection to the universal life force was lost and men could put themselves at the center of things. Knowledge that men played a role in reproduction, for example, opened the door to the belief that men, not women, are the source of life—men who plant their seed in the passive, fertile fields of women's wombs.

Fisher's arguments fit quite well with observations that the first known patriarchies were nomadic herding societies (the first to depend on raising livestock) and that male privilege annd women's oppression reach their height in advanced agrarian societies that dependend heavily on both human labor and animal breeding.[67] As Riane Eisler reads the evidence, aggressive herding tribes from the northern reaches of Eurasia swept down on goddess civilizations such as that at Crete and converted them by force to the patriarchal model.[68] In this we can see various factors coming together to set the stage for the emergence of patriarchy: surplus production and the possibility of inequality, development of control as a human potential and cultural ideal, an economic value placed on reproduction and the ability to control it, and the potential for competition among tribes for grazing land, water, and other resources. But the puzzle still has missing pieces, for although these conditions made patriarchy *possible*, they aren't the social engine we're looking for.

The problem is that just because control and oppression became possible, it doesn't follow that they had to take over social life, just as people don't necessarily do something just because they can, whether it be hoarding wealth, killing disobedient children, or conquering neighbors. It might seem that conflict and aggression among nomadic tribes or expanding settlements were inevitable,[69] since these are ways to deal with conditions of scarcity. But cooperation, compromise, and sharing are even more effective solutions to the problem of scarcity, especially in the long run. Being able to produce a surplus makes it possible for some to hoard at the expense of others, but surpluses also can be used to create leisure and plenty for all.

But isn't it human nature to hoard, compete, and aggress? Of course it is, but compromise, cooperation, and compassion are also part of human nature, although under patriarchy they are culturally associated with women and devalued as not fitting the male-identified standard of "human nature." If a society is organized around one set of human capabilities rather than another, human nature won't tell us why. The answer lies in the social forces that shaped it in this way.[70]

All of which brings us back to the nagging question of what could be powerful enough to move humanity toward male privilege and the oppression of women. This is where we need to connect what we know about the present with what is reasonable to suppose about the past. What both have in common is the patriarchal cycle of fear and control. Modern patriarchy is driven by the dynamic between control and fear, of men seeking status and security through control, fearing other men's control over them, and seeing still more control as the only solution. And if we look at our reasonable speculations about the past, it is more than credible to suppose that this same dynamic provided the key to the origins and evolution of patriarchy. Just as men are at the center of this powerful cycle now, so too were they at the center when that cycle emerged thousands of years ago.

But why would men be the ones at the center of the fear–control whirlwind? For men to be at the center, they had to be more likely than women to embrace the emerging cultural idea of control and to run with it. For this to happen, they had to be more likely to experience themselves and others in a disconnected way. There is no reason to believe that men did not feel a strong connection to the nature-centered goddess cultures of their societies. But there are good reasons to believe that men's connection was weaker than women's and that this left them more open to the cycle of control and fear and the religion of power that patriarchy embodied.

Men's connection to the creation of new life is invisible—they must imagine how intercourse produces a child rather than feel it in their own bodies—and prepatriarchal cultures lacked even the abstract knowledge of how reproduction works. Nor do men bleed in monthly cycles in tune with the moon. As a result, men have fewer reminders of the body and its relation to natural rhythms of birth, renewal, and death. This makes it easier to live as though it were possible to stand apart from such rhythms, and this is the first step to rising above, transcending, and ultimately trying to control the self and everything else as "other." None of this means that men can't feel deeply connected to nature and the body, or that women can't feel disconnected and separate. But it does mean that men are more open to feeling this way and more vulnerable to being drawn into the cycle of control and fear that became the driving force behind patriarchy.

Because pursuing control goes hand in hand with disconnection from the object of control, it is reasonable to suppose that as the *idea* of control emerged as a natural part of cultural evolution, men were more likely than women to see it as something to develop and exploit. Women's lives, of course, also involved the idea of control—over children, for example, or gardens, or materials involved in producing goods and services that have always met a huge portion of human needs. But women have more to overcome in order to develop a sense of disconnection, and for this reason they would be less likely to pursue control to its extremes. This would fall to men, and the result would be patriarchy.

At first, the idea of control was most likely applied to the simple mechanics of altering the environment by making things and growing food. It was only a matter of time, however, before the potential to control other people became apparent. Women and children may have been the first human objects of this new potential as husbands and fathers looked for ways to enhance their resources and standing in relation to other men. But why would men do this, given all the good reasons not to? How could the idea of control be powerful enough to reorder a world rooted in connection, unity, and equality? Why couldn't the powerful and complex bonds that joined people together in prepatriarchal societies withstand the allure of control?

I believe the answer lies in the same dynamic that drives patriarchy today. It seems reasonable to suppose that as populations grew and nomadic societies moved about in search of food, they must have gotten in one another's way. If men were most open to the idea of control as a solution to such problems, then they must have learned to fear what other men might do to them as well as women and children in their societies. It wouldn't take much to realize how control could be used to do harm, to take away liberty and the means of survival. It's here that men find themselves caught in a cycle, for the same reliance on control that created the fear in the first place can also be seen as an effective response to it. And so the path of least resistance was for men to respond to their fear of other men by increasing their own ability to control and dominate, gradually making this a central focus of social life. As Marilyn French observes, once this dynamic is set in motion, it forms the basis for an escalating spiral of control and fear. The result is an extended patriarchal history marked not only by the accomplishments that control makes possible, but also by domination, warfare, and oppression, all of which are male-dominated, male-identified, male-centered pursuits that revolve around affirming, protecting, and enhancing men's standing and security in relation to other men.

This dynamic also encourages men to incorporate into their core sense of self the ability to always be in control and to invest themselves in the appearance of being in control as a way to present themselves to others. This becomes a valued and sought-after zone of safety and comfort, even though its ultimate effect is to undermine both. It does so by provoking fear in others (who then seek to defend themselves through a still more-convincing demonstration of control) and because, like every illusion, it carries with it the potential to come crashing down with devastating effect. So, the patriarchal obsession with control is no testament to the inherent appeal of control, but rather springs from being trapped in the dynamic relationship between fear and control that seems to offer no way out.

Maybe it all happened this way and maybe it didn't. But the inability to prove where patriarchy came from won't stop people from reaching their own conclusions about it. The argument that patriarchy is rooted in a cycle of fear, control, and domination is no less plausible than alternative explanations, and far more plausible than many. It also has the advantage of providing continuity between what we can reasonably know and speculate about the past and how patriarchy works today. This gives us a more solid and hopeful base to push off from as we work toward change. After all, if control and domination are inherently so appealing to men that they'd oppress half the human race in pursuit of them, then working for change may be a hopeless war against men's "nature." But what if patriarchy is rooted in men's paradoxical fixation on control, fear, competition, and solidarity with other men? Then the way is open to changing not men per se, but the patriarchal system and its paths of least resistance, which we can see as only one of many possible forms that the natural human potential for control can take.

# The Journey Out

There are many reasons to deny patriarchy its future. There is the obvious one of ending the injustice and unnecessary suffering that constitute women's oppression—their exclusion from equal power and participation in social life, the pervasive misogyny and violence directed against them, and the denial of the fullness of their independence, autonomy, sexuality, spirituality, and dignity as human beings. Obvious reasons also include the damage men suffer for their participation in patriarchy—damage to their emotional, spiritual, and physical well-being, to their relationships with children, women, and other men, and to their sense of themselves as people. Although such goals get the most attention, they are just a beginning, because patriarchy isn't simply about relationships between women and men. It encompasses an entire world organized around principles of control, male domination, male identification, and male centeredness.

Patriarchy's roots are also the roots of most human misery and injustice, including race, class, and ethnic oppression and the destruction of the natural environment.[72] The spiral of control and fear underlies a worldwide reliance on militarism and toughness to solve problems and resolve disputes, from Vietnam to Bosnia to terrorism to the U.S. invasion of Iraq. Patriarchal nation states and militant movements arm themselves to the teeth and develop rigid hierarchies to control their own people and "defend" themselves as the potential victims of other patriarchal entities. The "others" are locked in the same cycle, presenting themselves as victims of unfair claims, unjustified aggression, outrageous insult, and so on and on. In this sense, the war/terror system is a self-perpetuating and self-justifying cycle of control and fear supported by the illusion that there are bad guys and good guys, with everyone laying claim to the latter. When each side defines the other as its opposite, they mask what each has in common, which is the underlying basis for their use of violence as a means of control. Beneath the good guy/bad guy mask is a system controlled by a deadly patriarchal cycle in which control as a response to fear simply causes more fear.

The religion of power drives patriarchy onward in politics, in religion, in economics, in the smallest details of personal life. Even as the world seems to move toward political democracy, for example, economic power is increasingly concentrated under global capitalism to a degree that may soon dwarf the resources of all but the most powerful nation-states.[73] Capitalists are driven by the fear of failing at competition, on the one hand, and on the other, by their ongoing struggle to control and dominate labor and markets in order to maximize profit and survive. Greed isn't the problem, and a "kinder, gentler capitalism"—a kinder, gentler cycle of control and fear—isn't the solution.[74] Even in quasi-socialist societies like Sweden, patriarchy is alive and well, although in a somewhat muted form.[75] We're running scared most of the time. While politicians and corporate managers struggle in vain for some semblance of control over events, bookstore shelves bulge with self-help guides telling us that the answer to our problems lies in learning to have more control—over the body, mind, spirit, love, sex, death, taxes, stress, memory, bosses, spouses, children. None of this obsession with control works—for individuals or societies—for still more control won't free us from the patriarchal obsession with control.

The depth of brutishness we see today in the world isn't what human life needs to be about. Even in the jungle, the human idea of the "law of the jungle" doesn't apply. We're living in a jungle of our own making, and the journey out begins with seeing how it operates and what it does to us, how we participate in it and how we might choose differently. For this, we need new ways to think about ourselves and the world, and the path to these revisits some old familiar territory—which is where we go next.

# 4

# Ideology, Myth, and Magic:
# Femininity, Masculinity,
# and "Gender Roles"

"**Y**ou just don't get it!" is a common complaint these days, often directed at men who are slow to grasp some aspect of male privilege. It's for men who don't understand why their repeated sexual advances at work are offensive and intolerable, for example, or men who don't see why wives get so upset over who cleans the bathroom. In some ways, "not getting it" is part of privilege—the "luxury of obliviousness."[1] It is also an effective way to defend privilege, a kind of dead-weight passive oppression that leaves to women the hard work of consciousness and understanding. No matter how much energy women expend to get men to "get it," it won't amount to much unless men *want* it to, which, most of the time, judging from their behavior, they don't.

But the problem of seeing—of getting it—is more complicated than privilege. It is also a general social phenomenon that affects everyone because, like water to a fish, the social environment is about the last thing we're likely to notice as something to be studied and understood. Everyone, for example, speaks a language without much trouble, but it takes real effort to be aware from moment to moment of how language is used to shape the world and us in it. When people insult women by calling them witches, they rarely are aware that "witch" originally referred to highly respected wise-women healers and midwives who for centuries were the main providers of health care (and much of whose knowledge of medicinal plants is being "discovered" by a now male-dominated medical profession).[2] To use "witch" as a way to insult a woman, then, contributes to an ongoing cultural degradation of women and their historical role as healers.

In many ways, people don't "get it" in the same way that audiences don't get the sleight of hand in a magician's magic. The secret of magic lies in directing attention away from one thing that's happening to other things that distract us from what becomes the magical event. Performance magic is what happens while our attention is elsewhere, and what makes us experience it as magic is our inability to tell the difference. We think we're paying attention to what counts and yet somehow we miss it. That's because the magic lies not in what the magician actually does but in our relation to it and our perceptions of it, and therein lie both the magician's artful power *and* our participation in it. Such magic, in other words, is inherently relational and happens only when everyone does their part.

Societies aren't magicians out to fool us. Since they aren't living beings, after all, they can't actually do anything. But our relation to societies and how we participate in them can have some magical effects on how we see things. Culture, for example, consists largely of words and ideas that we use to define and interpret almost everything we experience and do. Since every culture is finite and therefore limited in what it can include, it tends toward some versions of reality more than others. If a language doesn't include pronouns that distinguish by sex, such as *she* and *he*, people who speak that language will be less likely to see female and male as important distinctions. Whether or not to note the sex of the person who occupied a social position— as in chairman, policewoman, male nurse, or actress—wouldn't come up as an issue or call for a specialized vocabulary. This doesn't mean that people would experience women and men as being the same, only that the distinction between male and female would be less salient, less critical to how they make sense of social life and themselves. Many cultures, however, make heavy use of gender pronouns and suffixes (such as heir and heiress) which encourage us to see sex distinctions as relevant to every aspect of life and not merely reproduction or sexuality.

Although culture powerfully shapes what we experience as reality, we're rarely aware of this, especially while it's happening. When we use gender pronouns, we don't set out to shape reality in a gender-conscious way. We just obey rules of grammar and usage and fit into a culture that makes a great deal of gender. The words are just words to us, second nature and taken for granted, as is the gendered reality we assume they represent.

In this way, living in any culture is somewhat like participating in the magician's magic because all the while we think we're paying attention to what's "really" happening, alternative realities unfold without even occurring to us. These alternative realities include an awareness of culture itself *as culture*, as one set of symbols and ideas among many that people might use to construct and interpret reality. Since we don't see our own culture as something to understand, we don't ask critical questions about it, but assume instead that what we experience as reality *is* reality. We defend it, and in defending it we also defend ourselves, because our involvement in it runs as deep as our need to think we know the difference between what's real and what's not. As reality goes, it's all we've got—or so we think.

To see patriarchy clearly, we have to start by seeing how the reality of gender is put together in patriarchal societies. To "get" the magic, we need new ways to pay attention and a willingness to acknowledge that what we've always accepted as self-evident probably *is* which is just the problem, for it winds up obscuring more than it reveals.

## Why Do We Make So Much of Gender?

Until the 1970s or so, the word "sex" was used to refer to anything related to being female or male—as in "sex differences" or "sex change operation." "Gender" was about grammatical constructions, which often had nothing to do with sex—such as classifying French and Spanish nouns as masculine or feminine. In French, for example, the gender of the noun "table" is feminine and the gender of the noun "virus" is masculine. In practical terms, all this means is that adjectives used to modify the two kinds of nouns have different endings and the nouns take different articles—*le* and *la* (the masculine and feminine forms of "the")—none of which has much of anything to do with being male or female.

This worked well enough until feminists pointed out the difference between biological and social factors that shape people's lives. From this they argued that male privilege and women's oppression are rooted in society, not biology, and therefore aren't inevitable or immutable. Having a clitoris, for example, is a matter of biology. The nineteenth-century expectation that women weren't supposed to enjoy sex, however, and the continuing practice in some areas of the world of removing women's clitorises in order to control their sexuality have nothing to do with biology and everything to do with women's position in patriarchal societies.[3] To make such distinctions clear, feminists appropriated "gender" from the realm of grammar and gave it a new meaning focused on social aspects of being female or male. In the new version of things, *having* a clitoris is about sex, while ideas and practices *about* the clitoris are matters of gender.

Although the distinction between biological and social forces is important, it also creates problems by making it seem as though sex isn't in any way social, but rather exists as a concrete biological reality that we're simply naming in an objective way. It is of course true that the human body isn't a cultural creation, but as Michel Foucault argues, how we think about the body certainly is.[4] When girls reach puberty, for example, the biology of being female dictates that they will rapidly acquire most of their adult body weight. This includes a naturally higher percentage of fat than is usually found in males. By itself, this isn't a problem, but in some patriarchal societies, male-identified standards of female beauty encourage pubescent girls to view their natural growth with a sense of alarm that can stay with them for their entire lives.[5] This contrasts sharply with other cultures, such as most of Europe, whose classical art is rich with full-bodied women (and where women today tend to gain far more weight during pregnancy than do women in the United States) or Western Samoa, where large women are admired for their erotic dancing during some public events. Even in the United States, it wasn't so long ago that "sex goddesses" such as Marilyn Monroe were idolized for bodies that would be considered not thin enough by current Hollywood standards. The obsession with female thinness—the denial of a natural body fullness rooted in biology—is nothing less than a cultural transformation of what it *means* to be female. In this sense, what a female actually *is* as a living being takes a back seat to the ideas a culture makes available for thinking about what she is.

Why cultures would include two categories—male and female—isn't hard to see, since no society can continue without reproducing its population and it takes males and females to do it. In other words, sex makes a distinction that is certainly relevant to human existence. But it's one thing to make a clear distinction and quite another to give it cosmic importance, as if who people are as female or male were at the core of their lives, the linchpin of personal identity, and the rock foundation of society and social life. As Sam Keen tells it, for example, we are men and women before we are people, for "God did not make persons . . . only men and women."[6] Robert Bly goes even further, into every cell where men's and women's bodies supposedly "vibrate" at different frequencies, "sing" different songs, and "dance" a different dance.[7] Jungians (who are especially popular with the mythopoetic men's movement) see human existence as organized around a universal core of male and female archetypes—animus and anima—that presumably exist regardless of time or place.[8] And John Gray would have us believe that women and men are so completely and fundamentally different that they might as well come from different planets.[9]

From a strictly biological perspective, it's hard to see what all the fuss is about since what actually makes us male or female depends on a tiny bit of genetic information out of all other factors, genetic and otherwise, that shape who we are. Some would argue, though, that however "simple" sex differences may be, they are crucial and central to human life because of their role in reproduction. This has a lot of intuitive appeal, especially since reproduction brought each of us into the world. It can't, however, carry the weight of explaining why humans have organized so much of social life around an obsession with gender. It can't carry that weight because if we look closely, we find that humans and human societies don't assign as much importance to reproduction as we might think.

For thousands of years, societies worshipped fertility and used images of pregnant women as religious symbols. Studies of these traditions suggest, however, that the object of reverence and awe wasn't simply human regeneration or women's part in it, but the seemingly miraculous process through which *all* forms of life are renewed and sustained. It's not at all clear that ancient people were obsessed with human reproduction per se rather than with the regeneration of life in general on which human survival depends. Goddess figures were associated with human mothers, for example, but, more important, they were also associated with the Earth itself and all the manifestations of its fertile abundance, much of which is plant based and essentially asexual. In short, before humans worry about reproducing themselves, they have to worry about the ability of all the species that provide food to reproduce *themselves* so that people who are already born can eat.

Of course, there has to be a certain amount of human reproduction in order for social life to continue. This doesn't mean, however, that reproduction and gender are any more important than other necessary ingredients of human existence. This is especially so given that in its fullest sense, reproduction is a long and complicated process that doesn't end with birth. Human societies don't need babies in order to survive. They need fully functioning adults, and compared with what it takes to produce an adult, sexual reproduction is a walk in the park.

Some might argue that the socialization of children into adults lacks the grand mystery—and hence the fascination and importance—of sexual reproduction and, by extension, sex and gender. But why limit our capacity for wonder to that? I was awed when I saw my children being born, but my sense of wonder didn't end there. I will never be able to account for the mysteries of children learning to speak and think and struggle with love, death, and loss. I will never be able to explain my feeling that my children are connected to my body and my soul even though I never carried them inside myself, neither birthed nor nursed them—indeed, like every father, had no body experience that unequivocally said they were "mine." Is any of this less amazing, less mysterious, or less vital to the human condition and experience than the male–female coupling in sexual reproduction? And yet we attribute no cosmic importance to the amazing and difficult process through which people come into being or to the caring work that makes it possible—work that both men and women are capable of doing.[10]

Even reproduction in its fullest sense, however, is not much more important than numerous other human necessities. In fact, it may be less so if we judge from how children are actually treated. Throughout most of human history, the death of babies and infants has been a common and relatively uneventful occurrence, as have abortion and infanticide, and where infant mortality is high, babies are often left unnamed until they show they're likely to survive beyond infancy. For children who do survive, the historical record of child care is unremarkable in much of the world. Children have a long history of being forced to work under appalling conditions or being killed, sold, bartered, and otherwise neglected and abused. This is especially true for females (who, one would think, would be cherished for their reproductive potential) in societies most obsessed with gender distinctions.

None of this means that reproduction doesn't matter. It does suggest, however, that the obsession with sex and gender isn't based on some vital interest in human reproduction. What this obsession *does* serve are the interests of patriarchy, by anchoring the whole idea of a male-dominated, male-identified, and male-centered society. After all, if we were human beings first and women or men second, the patriarchal order wouldn't make much sense. Patriarchy, not some inherent human condition, requires that gender assume mythic proportions and take its place as the most defining and confining human characteristic, dwarfing all others by comparison. This is true of most systems of privilege: Race distinctions, for example, would barely exist, much less matter, without their link to white privilege.

Using gender to define the core of what makes us human creates huge contradictions by requiring us to define men and women as fundamentally different from each other and yet also as full human beings. On the one hand, this can't be done, because as soon as human traits are made gender specific, each gender is encouraged to alienate itself from a substantial portion of what makes us human. On the other hand, patriarchy depends on such divisions, because there's no basis for men to dominate women if we see the genders as fundamentally the same in their common humanity. And this is what sets up a contradiction that can be sustained only through some peculiar thinking.

This includes, for example, the strange notion that men's place in society is defined more by their manhood than their adulthood. What it takes to be an adult is fairly constant across societies—the ability and willingness to take responsibility, to care for others, to be productive and contribute to family, community, and society; to be courageous, to live creatively and with awareness. Under patriarchy, however, manhood has to amount to more than this. It has to differ from adult *womanhood* enough to justify organizing social life in a male-identified, male-centered way. This calls for a vision of male adulthood based on a social, psychological, spiritual, and physical territory that men can identify with and defend as exclusively male.

The only way to accomplish this cultural sleight of hand is to gender what are essentially human qualities by pretending they define manhood rather than adulthood. The idea of heroism, for example, has been appropriated almost entirely by patriarchal manhood. From movies and television to literature to the nightly news, our ideas of who and what is heroic focus almost entirely on men and what they do. Where the cultural magic comes in is in the pretense that women are not heroic, which we can see when we look at what heroism actually consists of. Sam Keen, for example, describes the "heroic male identity" as a capacity to feel outrage in the face of cruelty, to protect the powerless, and to heal those who are broken.[11] This kind of real man knows how "to take care of the place to which he has been entrusted . . . to practice the art of stewardship, to oversee, to make judicious use of things, and to conserve for the future . . . to make a decision to be in a place, to make commitments, to forge bonds, to put down roots, to translate the feeling of empathy and compassion into an action of caring."[12]

These are all wonderful human qualities, but why should we associate them primarily with manhood, and not adulthood? The answer is that gendering such qualities distinguishes and elevates men in relation to women. The falseness of this practice is even more striking when we consider that in many ways what is described as heroic above is more common among women than men. If anyone puts down roots, commits to relationships, and organizes a life around empathy, compassion, caring, healing, and even protecting the powerless, it's women. This is especially true in relation to children, whom many fathers seem all too willing to abandon and all too unwilling to provide for when the going gets rough. In contrast, women rarely feel they have a choice about whether to stay with and care for their children, and usually will do what's necessary to hold families together. Why, then, is heroism gendered as an essential element of manhood even though men are no more heroic than women? The answer is that under patriarchy it perpetuates the ruse that women and men are fundamentally different and in the process elevates men by appropriating for them a valuable chunk of symbolic territory.

Robert Bly provides another example of such contradictions when he argues that for "soft" men to get in touch with the true spirit of the "wild man", they must overcome their fear of "wildness, irrationality, hairiness, intuition, emotion, the body, and nature."[13] Ironically, almost all of these traits are culturally associated with women, not men. In other words, Bly is telling men to become more like women as a key to being true wild men. He gets into the same kind of trouble when he complains about the suppression of the wild man, because even more striking is the suppression of wildness in women. It is women, not men, who shave the hair from their bodies, who feel compelled to deny their inherent juiciness lest they be accused of being bitches or sluts, who learn to look upon their own flesh as an enemy, who are taught that anger and rage are unbecoming in them. Women's potential wildness so threatens patriarchy that it's been suppressed and twisted to the point of being unrecognizable and shows itself on rare and predictably controversial occasions (such as in the film *Thelma and Louise*). Instead of female wildness, patriarchy churns out images of evil witches, castrating bitches, vengeful feminists, mass media caricatures such as Madonna, and the proverbial "slut," whose wildness, for all the myths about nymphomania, serves men's imaginations more than women's lives.

When we gender what are inherently human qualities, we lock ourselves in a web of lies whose main consequence is to keep patriarchy going, for if society is to remain male dominated, male identified, and male centered, women and men must be seen as fundamentally different so that men can control women as "other." But the lie cannot abide the underlying truth that all people share a common biological, spiritual, and psychological core, and that qualities such as heroism, caring, and wildness are no more about maleness than they are about femaleness. Rather than confront the contradiction, we obsess about gender and define it as the core of social order and ourselves. And in struggling to hold the lie together, we keep ourselves from knowing what's really going on and what it's got to do with us.

## Patriarchy as a Personality Problem: Feminine and Masculine

The obsession with sex and gender revolves around two concepts—femininity and masculinity—that encourage us to think about men and women as different kinds of people. As the patriarchal story goes, women are essentially feminine and men are essentially masculine, and so long as each stays in their own designated territory, life goes on as it's supposed to. To some feminists, this splitting of the human species is the heart of the gender system and what needs to be changed to improve women's lot. From this perspective, patriarchy *is* men acting masculine and women acting feminine; and the freedom to break the bonds of narrowly defined ways of being is the key to women's liberation (and, some say, men's liberation as well). In fact, however, femininity and masculinity aren't what they seem. As cultural ideas that shape how we think about gender, they play a key role in keeping patriarchy going. This occurs primarily because we spend so much time fo-cusing on what are essentially personality issues that we pay no attention to patriarchy as a system and the privilege and oppression it produces.

In the simplest sense, masculinity and femininity are cultural ideas about who men and women are and who they're supposed to be. Typically, they are expressed in terms of personality traits that portray women and men as "opposite sexes." According to patriarchal culture, for example, men are aggressive, daring, rational, emotionally inexpressive, strong, cool headed, in control of themselves, independent, active, objective, dominant, decisive, self-confident, and unnurturing. Women are portrayed in opposite terms, such as unaggressive, shy, intuitive, emotionally expressive, nurturing, weak, hysterical, erratic and lacking in self-control (especially when menstruating), dependent, passive, subjective, submissive, indecisive, and lacking in self-confidence. As this shapes how we think about gender, it creates a great divide, with men on one side and women on the other. So long as everyone buys into the split, whether or not it actually describes them, all can have a relatively clear and stable sense of who they are and what's what. The problem, though, is that femininity and masculinity *don't* describe most people as they actually are.

Part of the problem with masculinity and femininity is that the "trait" approach to describing people is a shaky business with questionable validity even among psychologists.[14] How people feel and behave depends more on the social situation they're in than it does on some rigid set of underlying traits that define them in every circumstance. A woman might be passive and submissive as a wife in relation to her husband, for example, but very active and totally in charge as a mother in relation to her children. Or a man may be dominating as husband and father in relation to his wife and children but submissive as an employee in relation to his boss or as a son in relation to his parents. Which is he, then—dominant or submissive? Is she active or passive? The answer depends to a large extent on the social situation and the facets of the human repertoire that paths of least resistance call for. Masculinity and femininity tell us relatively little about who we are, then, in part because we are complicated beings who reveal ourselves differently from one situation to another. We are not self-contained and autonomous "personalities" but relational beings whose feelings and behavior are shaped in an ongoing way through our interactions with other people in particular social environments.

A related problem with femininity and masculinity is that when we split humanity in half we tend to see women and men in polar opposite terms that don't allow for alternatives. Dualities such as dominant–submissive, for example, or rational–irrational imply that if you aren't dominant, then you must be submissive, or if you aren't rational you must be irrational. But there is more than one alternative to being dominant (such as being independent, autonomous, or cooperative), or to being rational (such as being intuitive and nonlinear, which aren't *irrational*).

Things get even murkier when supposed pairs of opposites aren't in fact opposite, which happens often with feminine and masculine imagery. "Passive" and "aggressive," for example, are routinely paired, even though the opposite of passive is *active*, not aggressive. When we pair aggression with passivity, we mute negative associations with aggression because now it's seen as an alternative to passivity, which is generally devalued and regarded with contempt for what Plutarch called "the lowest of the low."[15] And so we transform aggression into a masculine virtue and a lack of aggression into feminine weakness or "passivity."[16] This bit of cultural magic serves patriarchal interests by elevating the social standing of aggression and making it look better than it otherwise would and by making a lack of aggression suspect.

When we disentangle aggression and passivity, we can see how patriarchal culture promotes the fiction that women are essentially inactive.[17] This borders on the ludicrous, for it obscures the truth of women's work, which historically has accounted for the bulk of productive labor, especially in nonindustrialized societies.[18] The common portrayal of women as passive is simply wrong, and yet it persists because it helps sustain male privilege. As such, it is both mythological and ideological—it both embodies and promotes core patriarchal ideas about the nature of women and men.

How is this cultural sleight of hand accomplished? One answer is that in practice, femininity applies only to women's place in heterosexual relationships, and we conveniently ignore everything else. In characteristic patriarchal style, the entirety of women's being is reduced to their ties with men, particularly lovers and husbands. In heterosexual relations, for example, feminine "passivity" takes the form of being "receptive" to men who are "penetrating," "sexually aggressive," and otherwise "active" during intercourse. Even in this narrow context, however, the notion that women are passive paints a false picture of what really goes on. It takes only a little imagination to think of intercourse as a joining together of two active parties in which the vagina embraces the penis as much as it is penetrated by it.[19] In fact, the muscles in the vaginal wall are quite active during intercourse and can hold or expel the penis. In addition, successful conception depends on the wavelike action of thousands of cilia that direct the sperm along their path to the egg, which then changes chemically to "select" which sperm will actually join with the egg. So even "passive" women really aren't, except perhaps in the patriarchal imagination.[20]

Part of the confusion about women's essentially active role in heterosexual intercourse is based on a confusion between receptivity and passivity. Receptivity is more than a state of being. To "receive" someone requires energy and will, not passivity (imagine, for example, what it takes merely to make someone feel truly "well-received" into your home).[21] If receptivity were nothing more than passivity—a state of do-nothing limp inactivity—then the ultimate receptive person would be either unconscious or dead, which clearly is *not* what receptivity is about.

Unless she's being coerced, when a woman *takes* a man into her vagina she most certainly is *doing* something to make it happen, and not merely being done to. But patriarchal feminine/masculine imagery obscures women's active ways of being and creates the illusion that activity is the exclusive province of men.[22]

There are similar problems with how we view nurturing, caring, and intuition. We tend to think that women nurture, care, and draw on "female intuition" simply because that's the way women *are*. But in truth these activities require considerable practice, effort, initiative, and commitment. Intuition is not inborn, but rather flows from "careful attention to the nuances of personal relationships, from an intelligence trained on the minutely perceptible exterior signs in people around them of loneliness, pride, disappointment, and changes of heart."[23]

The only thing that keeps the masculine/feminine framework going in spite of its contradictions and distortions is some cultural magic. This is aided by the practice of noticing when women and men behave according to masculine and feminine expectations, but ignoring or discounting much that contradicts them. The path of least resistance is to see male leaders as logical, decisive, and capable, for example, but not women who juggle the financial, emotional, and practical work that it takes to run a household, especially when they also work outside the home. In the same way, we tend to see women who cry as emotionally expressive, but not men who get angry or approach problems with detached, dispassionate "objectivity," even though emotion has a lot to do with their behavior. There is cultural magic at work here, too, in what we choose to call emotion, which we can see if we think for a moment about how emotionally loaded a phrase like "cold blooded" really is. What we call "unemotional" is actually a controlled emotional flatness that is no less an emotional state than hysteria, rage, or grief. In not seeing this, we buy into the illusion that masculine men are emotionally inexpressive, rational, objective, in control, and "above it all," and that being emotionally expressive precludes being rational, objective, or anything other than out of control. In truth, being masculine is not about being unemotional. It's about acknowledging or expressing only those emotions that enhance men's control and status—anger and rage—and it's about renaming or explaining away all the rest.

There is a double standard here that shapes perceptions of men and women in ways that support patriarchy as a system. What is culturally valued is associated with masculinity and maleness, and what is devalued is associated with femininity and femaleness, regardless of the reality of men's and women's lives. Courage and heroism, for example, are culturally associated with masculinity. This makes us quick to identify as courageous those people who expose themselves to physical danger rather than risk losing power or social dominance. Since courage is valued in patriarchal culture, it is identified with men in expressions such as "having balls," while cowardice is routinely associated with being female, as reflected in the practice of insulting a man by calling him a "girl," a "sissy," or a "pussy." There are no equivalent female images for courage—"having ovaries" has yet to catch on, but it's not that unusual to hear brave women described as "having balls."

Related to this is the use of "castration" to refer to disempowerment by removing the testes, which implies that women don't have such power to lose in the first place. Technically, removal of the ovaries is also a form of castration, but since ovaries have no cultural association with courage, castration—and the loss of power as a traumatic and significant experience— is never linked to women.[24] This is consistent with the fact that the courage shown by women and men who reject patriarchal masculinity is rarely acknowledged unless it takes stereotypically masculine forms. Daring to separate from an abusive husband and taking on the daunting challenge of single parenthood are not identified as courageous, nor is daring to be emotionally vulnerable, which is often dismissed as a "natural" part of being a woman, like intuition. Far from being identified as courageous, emotional risk taking is more often defined as a sign of weakness, as if making ourselves emotionally vulnerable entails no risk.

And so, men who avoid vulnerability are seen to lack not courage but the requisite "skills" or predispositions. Indeed, more often than not they're actually seen as strong. All of this serves patriarchy well, for if emotional risk taking were socially identified as courageous, then men would feel compelled to pursue and measure themselves against it. This, in turn, would undermine male dominance, since men need emotional detachment and the appearance of *in*vulnerability in order to enhance and protect their position in a system based on control. Through this bit of cultural magic, men can think of themselves as courageous and manly without ever having to see their *lack* of courage for what it is.

When all is said and done, masculinity and femininity do a terrible job of describing women and men as they actually are, and have done so across history and across cultures. In eighteenth- and nineteenth-century Europe, for example, women were seen as "naturally frail" or "naturally tough," depending on whether the focus was on the upper class or the peasantry. There are similar problems with comparing women of different social classes and races today, or men and women who differ on sexual orientation. Such considerations lead Robert Connell and others to argue that it's a mistake to assume that a society has only one version of masculinity or femininity. The gay male subculture, for example, includes several versions of masculinity that differ in many respects from the heterosexual, female-dominating masculinity prevalent in patriarchal society as a whole.[25]

Although femininity and masculinity badly describe people as they actually are, many argue that they do describe us as we're *supposed* to be. As the reasoning goes, masculinity and femininity make up "gender roles" that define how men and women are expected to appear and behave, and this is the core of what makes patriarchy work. But a closer look reveals far more—and less—going on than we might think.

## Patriarchy as Role: The Myth of Gender Roles

Talk about gender rarely goes on for long without involving the idea that femininity and masculinity are organized into gender (or sex) roles that almost magically account for most of what goes on around gender. As we'll see in Chapter 5, this is a classic liberal perspective that reduces patriarchy to men and women enacting male and female roles that they learned in childhood, and that pins hopes for change on education and individual enlightenment. The problem with this approach is that although it may help explain how people participate in patriarchy, it doesn't tell us much about the system itself. And what the gender roles tell us about men and women as individuals doesn't amount to much, because as strange as it may seem, it's far from clear that such roles even exist. Many who study gender have all but abandoned the concept as a distraction from the core dynamics that make patriarchy work.[26]

The easiest way to see the problem is to consider what social roles are. Roles are sets of ideas about what is expected of people based on the positions they occupy in social relationships. Lawyer and client, for example, are positions in a relationship, and their associated roles shape how people participate in it. Clients are supposed to tell their lawyers the truth and lawyers aren't supposed to betray the confidence. Similarly, mother and child are positions with roles attached—mothers are expected to love, nurture, and protect their children, and children are expected to love and obey their mothers.

Such expectations help define the terms of relationships between people who occupy various positions in social systems. In this, roles both identify people and locate them socially. Ask a woman who's spoon-feeding her child, "What role are you playing now?" and she'll reply that she's being a mother. But that same woman who's spoon-feeding her invalid mother will answer differently because although her behavior is the same, the relationship and her position in it are different. Notice, then, how roles are tied to identifiable positions in relationships. That's what counts more than anything else in understanding roles and social behavior.

If we now try to think of what a "gender role" might be, the first problem we run into is that "male" and "female" don't name positions in relationships in the way that lawyer and client or mother and child do. Rarely, if ever, would someone answer the question, "What role are you playing right now?" simply with "I'm being a male" or "I'm being a female," because the mere fact of gender is never enough to tell us who someone *is* in a social situation. When a mother disciplines her child, is she playing the role of mother or the role of female? And if we reply that they are one and the same, since you can't be a mother without being female, what do we say about that same woman when she defers respectfully to her grandmother (as granddaughter) or heroically runs into a burning building to rescue her brother (as sister)? Is she playing the same role in each case, the "gender role" of "female"? Since only females can be sisters, do we explain her risking her life to save her brother as conforming to the "female role"? No, because "sister" tells us who she is socially in that situation while "female" does not.

It's true that we play many roles that are culturally *associated* with gender, but never are we simply being male or female. Men behave very differently as sons, brothers, uncles, husbands, grandsons, or fathers even though they are men in every case. They behave differently because although they are always men, none of those relationships is primarily about that. If they neglect or abuse an ill parent, for example, they fail in their role as sons, not as men, just as abandoning their children violates their role as fathers. It's true that failing at being fathers, mothers, employees, and such may seem to damage our standing as women and men, but this has more to do with adulthood than gender.

Having said all this, there's no denying that whether we're identified as female or male has real and powerful effects on perceptions, feelings, and expectations. As I'll argue shortly, however, this takes the form of a general ideology that can be invoked as needed to help maintain male privilege and the patriarchal order. Ideas about gender, for example, play an important part in how people are sorted into various social positions: The relative absence of women among scientists, motion picture directors, presidents, prime ministers, and corporate CEOs has much to do with how gender is used as a basis for hiring, firing, and distributing power and rewards. The same is true of the relative absence of men among secretaries, elementary schoolteachers, nurses, and day-care workers.[27]

Ideas about gender also affect how people perform occupational and other roles and how others perceive and treat them. Sexual harassment on the job, for example, isn't part of any job description. There's nothing about working for a government official, studying with a college professor, or working on a construction project that remotely calls for sexual harassment. What *does* promote sexual harassment are the gendered inequalities of power inherent in such situations and how power, sexuality, and a sense of male entitlement are linked together under patriarchy. When a male manager interprets his authority as a legitimate basis for sexually coercing a woman he supervises, he draws on a patriarchal ideology that goes far beyond job descriptions.

In an important sense, then, gender is linked with ideas about people that color our perceptions and expectations as we participate in role relationships. This means that while gender may have no direct connection to a given role, it nonetheless can have powerful indirect effects. This is true of many social characteristics such as race, age, ethnicity, and social class. There are no "race roles" or "class roles," for example, but race and class relations are shaped by ideologies that profoundly affect how we perceive and treat ourselves and one another. As concepts, then, femininity and masculinity play an important part in social life, but not as gender roles or ways of describing men and women as they actually are. Instead, they are a key element in perpetuating male privilege. In particular, they help control potential threats to patriarchy, manage men's competition with other men, and make oppression appear to be a normal part of everyday life.

## Maintaining the Patriarchal Gender Order

In perpetuating patriarchy, femininity and masculinity are important tools for social control. This works primarily through people's investment in maintaining a socially acceptable gender identity. Everyone needs to have a relatively stable sense of who they are and a secure place in the world. Given the importance of gender identity in patriarchal societies, attacking people as being insufficiently masculine or feminine can do a lot to control them because it both challenges their sense of who they are and makes them feel like outsiders. This can be a serious enough threat to keep people from doing anything that might undermine or even question the status quo. Attacks on people's gender identities are also effective because masculinity and femininity are such sloppy, contradictory categories, much like "insanity" and "sanity."

Sanity and insanity are vaguely defined concepts full of inconsistency when applied to people in everyday life, so much so that mental health professionals shun them in their work.[28] Whether someone is sane or insane is hardly a matter of scientific certainty (how, for example, would you *prove* you were sane?) and whether a particular behavior is regarded as evidence of insanity depends pretty much on who does it and the social situation. What's "eccentric" in a wealthy recluse may qualify as "nuts" in a homeless person walking through a shopping mall, and what's considered pathological in one society or historical period may be seen as normal, inspired, brilliant, or even holy in another.

And yet, for all their arbitrary sloppiness, the categories of "sane" and "insane" can be used to devastate people's lives and grant enormous power to anyone authorized to decide who belongs in which. During the slavery era in the United States, for example, the legitimacy of recapturing escaped slaves was reinforced by the medical diagnosis of "drapetomania," defined as "an insane desire to run away."[29] In the former Soviet Union, diagnoses of mental illness were often used to justify the imprisonment of political dissidents in "mental hospitals."[30] And throughout the last century, mental illness diagnoses have been used to pathologize and control women's unhappiness and tendency to rebel against patriarchal constraints.[31]

Femininity, masculinity, sanity, and insanity are all concepts plagued by ambiguity, inconsistency, imprecision, and lack of clarity. This wouldn't be a problem if it weren't for what happens when they're used to attack someone. Since no one's masculinity or femininity can ever be proved conclusively, anyone's can be challenged, and the more importance we give to gender in building a sense of who we are, the more anxious we are likely to feel about it. This is especially true for men, who, as members of the dominant gender group, have the most to lose, which helps explain why men typically get much more worked up over proving their manhood than women do over proving their womanhood.

In this sense, femininity and masculinity are powerful weapons of social control that help maintain the patriarchal order. The truth of this is reflected in how inconsistently and unevenly they are applied, for it is primarily when someone threatens patriarchy and its core values that they're invoked. Men and women often appear and behave in ways that don't fit masculine and feminine expectations but without anyone making an issue of it. With children, for example, women may be assertive and powerful and men may be emotionally expressive and tender without inviting criticism that they're being insufficiently feminine or masculine. But when appearance or behavior raises questions about the male-identified, male-dominated, and male-centered nature of patriarchy, the heavy cultural artillery comes rolling out and gender identities get attacked left and right.

Nowhere is this more apparent than in the treatment of gays and lesbians, much of whose persecution and oppression has relatively little to do with sexual behavior or orientation per se. Instead, they are attacked because they undermine the patriarchal model that defines maleness in sexual terms.[32] A key aspect of male privilege and women's oppression is rooted in heterosexual relations that subordinate women to men's right to sexual access and control. Gay men undermine this by not relating to women in this way,[33] as do lesbians who choose women rather than men as sexual partners. By the examples set by their own lives, lesbians and gays challenge basic patriarchal assumptions and arrangements. In the process, they often provoke feelings of fear, betrayal, and rage in men who depend on male solidarity and female acquiescence in order to feel secure in themselves and their privilege.

The role of gay and lesbian oppression in maintaining patriarchy is clear when we look at how it works in practice. When public attention was first focused on lesbians and gays, it was common to stereotype couples as conforming to the model of patriarchal heterosexuality with one partner in a dominant "male" role ("butch") and the other in a subordinated "female" role ("femme"). In other words, in order to deflect a potential challenge to patriarchy, gays and lesbians were portrayed as *sexually* deviant but *socially* conforming to the most important element of patriarchal heterosexuality— the domination of one partner by the other and the identification of dominance with men and masculinity (hence the tendency to describe the "dominant" partner in a lesbian relationship as masculine). This has a long social history, as anthropologist David Gilmore notes in his study of masculinity. The ancient Greeks, for example, allowed a man to have male lovers without forfeiting his standing as a truly masculine man *unless* he "accepted the passive or receptive role in the sex act, because then he surrendered the male prerogative of control or domination." Similarly, the Romans equated maleness with being sexually active, regardless of the lover's sex.[34] This dynamic is also reflected today in gay behavior among men in prisons, where heterosexual men don't see themselves as gay so long as they're dominant.

A related practice is the use of terms for lesbians and gays as insults against heterosexuals in order to control behavior or gain competitive advantage. Among young men, for example, I suspect that those called "faggots," "fairies," or "queers" are often heterosexuals. Rarely is sexual behavior or orientation the issue, since many younger males know little about either. Instead, what occasions such attacks is often a reluctance to support male

solidarity by playing the control and domination game, especially in relation to athletics and females. The target may be a boy who enjoys playing
with girls, for example, or a young man who shuns aggressive behavior, who
shows little interest in contact sports, who's reluctant to take a dare, who
seems emotionally sensitive or vulnerable, or who holds back from joining in
banter about women as objects of male sexual conquest. Whether he's gay is
irrelevant, because it is only his solidarity with patriarchal values and other
males that matters. Often the target of the attack is simply someone chosen
more or less at random to be a foil against which other males can measure
their patriarchal masculinity. It also creates "outsiders," who then serve to
heighten the feeling of being an "insider." So a quiet boy in gym class may
be taunted as "queer" simply as a way to embody the "other" and clarify
and affirm the masculine standing of male classmates.

In this way, a man can elevate himself or make himself feel more secure
simply by challenging other men's credentials as "real men," like the stereotypical Old West tough guy picking a fight.[35] There seems to be no area of
social life where this doesn't happen—from adolescent boys trading dares
to national leaders going out of their way to foster images of "toughness"
("Bring it on.") and dispel suspicion that they might be "wimps" or otherwise lacking in manly virtues. As most men learn early in life, this is almost
every man's Achilles' heel in patriarchal systems, and the only sure protection is to find a way not to care whether other men think he's masculine. But
this brings on a whole new set of risks that come with being identified as
an outsider, if not a traitor to one's gender. As a result, for men who don't
identify with patriarchal values, the path of least resistance is not to make a
public show of it. When they're with other men and someone tells a sexist
joke, for example, they may remain silent and thereby join in the collusion
of male solidarity. Though they may be able to sustain inner lives and intimate relationships relatively free of patriarchal values, their public lives are
a different story, especially in the company of men.

It's worth pointing out that when women deviate from feminine
expectations, the social response tends to be quite different in both quality
and intensity. A woman who dons a tuxedo gets far less negative attention,
for example, than a man who wears a dress. At the least he will provoke
laughter—intentionally in the case of comedians—and at most he may be
suspected of mental instability or risk being assaulted. A major reason
for this is that a woman in man's clothing is seen as "dressing-up" in the
uniform of her social superiors, a socially acceptable act of identifying with
the dominant group. A man who dresses as a woman, however, will be seen
either as making fun of women (which is acceptable) or as identifying with
women (which is not). Since solidarity with male dominance is at issue in

either case, ambiguity is intolerable, and there is always a reaction of one sort or another. There is less ambiguity when women dress "as men" because it's assumed they are identifying with men rather than making fun of them. This pattern repeats itself among all kinds of dominant groups, who tend to be blind to the idea that someone might actually ridicule them. This is why there are so few jokes about WASPs in Anglo-identified societies and why men are so hypersensitive when women make even the slightest fun of them *as men*.

## Normalizing Privilege and Oppression

As elements of patriarchal culture, femininity and masculinity are part of a way of thinking that makes privilege and oppression seem acceptable and unremarkable—as simply the way things are in everyday life. They are used to portray women and men in ways that justify the oppression of one by the other, that make it seem normal that men should control women, and that give the various aspects of privilege and oppression a taken-for-granted, "of course" quality that hardly bears notice, much less analysis or challenge. This is common in all systems of privilege. In the heyday of colonialism, for example, white Europeans typically saw themselves as advanced and civilized compared to the "primitive," "backward," even "subhuman" peoples of color whom they colonized. This made it seem only natural that "superior" Europeans would control and exploit non-Europeans, much as they controlled and exploited domestic animals (also defined as "other").[36] As Albert Memmi writes, much of colonial ideology is grounded not in real differences, but in a racism rooted as deeply as the body itself: "Racism . . . penetrates the flesh, the blood and the genes of the victim. It is transformed into fate, destiny, heredity. From then on, the victim's very *being* is contaminated, and likewise *every manifestation of that being*: behavior, body, and soul."[37]

Under patriarchy, gender is defined in similar ways with masculine and feminine imagery portraying male and female as two opposite sorts of human beings. In patriarchal ideology, each gender is assigned an immutable nature fixed in the body and permanently set apart from the other. This is to maintain an almost cosmic polarity upon which the universe supposedly depends for balance and order. The fact that human variation doesn't take the form of opposites—that we're all fundamentally alike with far more in common than whatever distinguishes us—makes no difference at all when it comes to ideology.[38] As a result, women are objectified and relegated to the position of other. And men, like any dominant group, become the standard against which others are evaluated, just as colonized peoples were measured against European cultures. As under colonialism, a critical part of this process has been the practice of identifying subordinate groups with nature and the Earth and of identifying dominant groups with civilization, science, and other institutional means of control.[39] In patriarchy, this is used to justify male dominance and to portray women as marginal to what really counts in the patriarchal view of civilization and how it works.

The concepts of femininity and masculinity also normalize privilege and oppression by creating images of men and women as harmonious, complementary, and equal, and therefore not involved in a system of privilege at all. We're encouraged to embrace images of women and men as yin and yang, as inherently incomplete beings whose only hope for wholeness lies in joining with the other. Each has a role to play in the life of the other if only we align ourselves in the proper way and accept our predestined positions in the gendered order of things. What this has to do with patriarchal control and male privilege is lost in a haze of longing and romantic imagery.

A critical approach to femininity, masculinity, and gender roles doesn't mean women and men are somehow the same and that any idea to the contrary is just an ideological prop. It does mean, however, that we need to pay attention to how we think about gender differences and what happens when we attach such great importance to them. The patriarchal vision of men and women as separate types of human beings whose differences assume cosmic importance in social life has little to do with the differences themselves. It has a lot to do with perpetuating patriarchy, its core values, and the consequences they produce.

## Looking for a Way Out

The path of least resistance is to see femininity, masculinity, and gender roles as the core of gender issues, but this is the stuff of cultural magic that in the end does little more than confuse and set us against one another. And keep us stuck in patriarchy. Using femininity and masculinity to describe people puts us in a straightjacket that denies the inherent complexity of what we and our experience are all about. It backs us into a tight little corner where we are always just a step or two away from having to defend against challenges to our legitimacy as men and women. And it sets us up to struggle endlessly with contradiction, ambiguity, and denial as we search for an authentic sense of who we are.

At work here is a core patriarchal illusion that we are split between our "natural" masculine and feminine characters as women or men. Instead of asking questions about patriarchy, we're encouraged to busy ourselves "healing" the imagined "split" with inventions like "androgyny" and workshops on how to appreciate our masculine and feminine "sides."[40] But this just fixes our attention on the cultural fiction that feminine and masculine sides even exist, while the perpetuation of patriarchy continues undisturbed by questions about how it works and the privilege and oppression it produces.

# 5

# Feminists and Feminism

Every struggle to change the world needs a way to make sense of where we are, how we got here, and where to go—and the women's movement is no exception. It has developed feminism as a diverse and evolving framework for understanding gender inequality and interpreting women's experience in relation to men, other women, and patriarchy. After more than two centuries, feminism is a rich body of thought that is both analytical and ideological: It makes sense of reality and supports work for something better.

Every struggle for change is also resisted in ways ranging from subtle to overt, from peaceful to violent; again, the women's movement is no exception. Trashing feminism is now so routine that most women won't openly identify with feminism even when they support feminist goals and ideas. The backlash has been so successful that "feminism" carries a vague and highly distorted meaning for the average person, and "feminist" is increasingly used as an accusation or insult needing neither explanation nor justification: "What are you, some kind of feminist?" or, "Don't get me wrong, I'm no feminist, but . . . "

Before rushing to explain this as something peculiar to feminism, it's important to realize how typical this is for any way of thinking that challenges basic cultural ideas and the social arrangements those ideas support. Galileo nearly lost his life for pointing out that Earth revolves around the sun. Critics of capitalism are dismissed as communists and reds in the West, just as critics of communism were castigated as reactionaries and counter-revolutionaries in Soviet and Chinese orthodoxy. Apparently, the fact that progressive change is impossible without new ways of thinking doesn't protect innovators from accusations of heresy and being punished, dismissed, discredited, and excluded as a result. Whether the heresy is religious or political or familial, it is attacked because it scares people and undermines powerful interests. It challenges root structures and ideas that prop up social systems and give everyday life its seamless, acceptable appearance.

Like many heresies, feminism is often attacked by those who understand it least. The less that people actually know, the easier it is to assume they know all they need to know and to fall back on stereotypes that leave the status quo undisturbed. Most people in the United States are staunchly "anti-Marxist," for example, but know next to nothing of what Marx wrote about capitalism and how it works and affects people's lives. At most, they might recognize a famous phrase or two from *The Communist Manifesto* (a pamphlet written for a popular audience and reflecting only a small portion of Marx's work) or, more likely, something said by Lenin, Mao, or some other communist leader. In the same way, critics of feminism rarely know much of what feminism consists of in spite of the rich body of writings available to anyone with a library card. Most people don't even know how much published feminist thought there is, largely because hardly anyone talks about it outside of university women's studies programs. Increasingly, feminist writers work as academics who, true to the values and rules of that patriarchal system, write primarily for one another and not for the public at large. When their work does get wider attention, mass media coverage is at best superficial, typically limited to the blandest forms of feminism or feminism's most sensational ideas taken out of context and distorted beyond recognition. While feminism continues to broaden and deepen its analysis of patriarchy, all that most people see is the mass media recycling the same shallow analyses—about why men won't express their feelings or how women and men have such a hard time communicating—trotting them out periodically like seasonal recipes and household hints.

Most of the time, feminism isn't censored openly. It isn't shouted down or burned in public. Instead, it's simply contained and ignored in a kind of passive oppression by writers, editors, publishers, teachers, film and television producers, and public officials.[1] When radical feminists write about patriarchy and its legacy of men's violence against women, they don't make the front cover of the *New York Times* magazine or Book Review, but when Katie Roiphe wrote an astonishingly uninformed book about campus sexual violence, she was embraced by the media and made the front page of *both*.[2]

When, in 1991, law professor Anita Hill accused Supreme Court nominee Clarence Thomas of sexual harassment, the U.S. Senate held closely watched hearings that not once sought out feminist thinking and research—the only source with much to say about what they supposedly were trying to understand. Without comment, feminism and the social reality of sexual harassment were kept invisible. Instead, we were treated to a media event and a national debate about who was telling the truth, complete with "Honk if you believe Anita" bumper sticker politics.

If feminism is invisible, patriarchy is invisible. And if feminism is distorted and discredited, patriarchy is safe from scrutiny, for feminism is the only critical perspective on patriarchy we've got. Without feminism, we're left to understand gender inequality in patriarchal terms that invariably ignore it or justify it by turning reality upside down and calling it something else. Without feminism, it's easy not to see male dominance at all, or if we do, to explain it away as human nature or "what every woman wants deep down." Without feminism, it's easy to see feminists who talk about men's violence against women as just troublemakers with private axes to grind. And it's easy to hop on the bandwagon in the mythical "postfeminist" Oz in which inequality is no longer a problem for *real* women. But once we accept the reality that patriarchy exists, we open a door that swings just one way, and once we pass through it to the other side, feminism is our best hope for figuring out where we are and what to do next.

Since anyone can walk through the door of feminist awareness, feminism is not for women only. As members of the dominant group, men are limited in how deeply they can understand and engage with feminism, and there is always a danger that men will try to co-opt it for their own purposes. If we think of feminism as a way for women to understand their own experience, then there is little that men can bring to it, and it would be presumptuous for any man, including me, to try to explain what it's about. But a large chunk of feminism is about how patriarchy works and shapes social life. This involves men just as deeply as it does women, although in dramatically different ways. While women are in the best position to speak about their own experience of oppression, men have a lot to contribute to understanding patriarchy as a whole, and particularly male privilege and men's participation in it.[3]

Any full understanding of patriarchy must of course include women's experience, but this isn't going to be enough, unless we believe that women's experience encompasses the entire reality of patriarchy. To the extent that feminism is about patriarchy as a whole and how we all participate in it, then change requires that both men and women understand it, since each brings distinct points of view to the work. Undoubtedly, feminism speaks to women in unique and powerful ways that men can understand only indirectly, but we all can use feminism to understand what patriarchy is about.[4]

## Feminists and Feminism

The word *feminism* is an umbrella that covers many approaches to gender and patriarchy.[5] In the most general sense, feminism is a way of thinking critically about gender and its place in social life, but from here it ranges in many directions. All forms of feminism take gender to be problematic in some way, but just what this means—how prominent the concept of patriarchy is, for example—varies from one branch of feminism to another. As such, feminism lends itself to many different purposes. We can use it as an intellectual framework for analyzing how social life works, from love and sex to family violence to work to the meaning of art, literature, and spirituality to the conduct of science to the dynamics of ecology and global capitalism. Feminism also provides an ideological basis for change on every level of human existence, from intimate behavior to transforming patriarchy and its core values of dominance and control. By focusing on how we participate in the patriarchal gender order, feminism challenges us to live in new ways, to question assumptions about gender and human nature, and to confront the everyday realities of male privilege and the oppression of women.

Because feminism challenges the status quo, it gets attacked from many sides. Instead of criticizing feminism as it really is, however, most critics focus on two substitutes—"issues feminism" and feminists. It is easier to deal with these because this avoids confronting men and leaves patriarchy largely intact. "Issues feminism" defines feminism as little more than positions on issues such as abortion or pornography.[6] The result is a fractured and divisive view of feminism as a collection of contending positions—anti-pornography feminism, pro-choice feminism, pro-life feminism, middle-class white feminism, black feminism, lesbian feminism, Latina feminism, second-wave feminism, third-wave feminism, and so on. This way of looking at things often does more to divide women from common struggle than unite them. Many women, for example, refuse to call themselves feminists because they think it automatically implies a particular position on abortion or censorship or sexual orientation. Many women of color are put off by feminism because they associate it with the interests of white middle-class women to the neglect of other classes or races.

How such divisive dynamics play out can be seen in a *Village Voice* interview with the award-winning actor, Isabella Rossellini, on the occasion of a 2001 performance of the *Vagina Monologues* in New York to raise money to combat men's violence against women.

"I don't know about feminist," said Isabella Rossellini. "Is this about feminism really? Violence against women is a feminist issue? I don't think it is." OK, but does she consider herself a feminist? Rossellini looked as if she were smelling something unpleasant. "Well, I don't know what you mean. I would not label tonight a feminist night; it's a women's night. I mean, there are Republican women, there are Democratic women, there are feminist women, and women who don't define themselves, they're just women against violence."[7]

In this exchange, Rossellini does more than reject the feminist label. She also overlooks basic questions about what patriarchy is, how it works, and how we participate in it. Such questions don't necessarily hinge on taking particular positions on any given issue. You don't have to be a pro-choice on the abortion issue, for example, to see patriarchy as problematic and try to understand it as such. Nor do you have to be a white middle-class professional woman bumping up against the glass ceiling. But if the focus is solely on issues such as abortion or workplace discrimination to the neglect of the system that creates and shapes them, the result is the kind of endless, divisive debate that we've been stuck in for a long time.

When feminism isn't being fragmented into a jumble of topical issues, it is being attacked through women associated with it. Femin*ists* are regularly trashed through stereotypes portraying them as humorless, man-hating, angry, whining, antifamily, and lesbian. Sam Keen, for example, applauds femin*ism* for drawing attention to patriarchy's oppressive consequences, including the obsession with control and dominance. And yet, rather than take the next step of figuring out how to take responsibility for and *do* something about patriarchy, he switches almost immediately from talking about feminism to talking about the behavior and motives of "some" feminists. He energetically attacks what he calls "ideological feminism" which is "animated by a spirit of resentment, the tactic of blame, and the desire for vindictive triumph over men that comes out of the dogmatic assumption that women are the innocent victims of a male conspiracy."[8] And having established himself as an innocent victim of such irrational, vindictive hatred of men, he never looks back or bothers to ask just what this phenomenon tells us about feminism or the women's movement as a whole. Nowhere, for example, does he ask what men might *do* with all those "enlightening perspectives and prophetic insights of the women's movement" for which he says he has such high regard.[9] That gets no more than an approving nod as he wades into what he seems to see as the *real* problem—women's anger at men.

Keen has a lot of company, for it's easier and safer to dwell on caricatures, extreme factions of complex movements, personal smears, and slogans than it is to understand a new way of thinking and what it might tell us about the world and ourselves in it. From Rush Limbaugh's sneering references to "femi-Nazis" to Camille Paglia's smug characterization of Gloria Steinem as Stalin,[10] stereotypes are vivid and powerful in the human imagination and potent weapons against change. Even Naomi Wolf, author of *The Beauty Myth*, a powerful feminist analysis of the role of beauty in women's oppression,[11] goes on in a later book to confuse feminists and feminism, to the detriment of both. In *Fire with Fire*, she criticizes what she calls "victim feminism," which she presents as a mixture of theory, selected issues, and, most important, personal attitudes and behavior of individual feminists who, for the most part, are referred to only as "them" or "some feminists." She seems to see no significant difference, for example, between arguing that patriarchy is problematic and being personally humorless or rigid or grim in one's dealings with other people. Seeing both as feminism makes it impossible to distinguish feminism as a framework for thought and action—which is what threatens patriarchy most—from feminism as an attitude or personal style. Such fusing of feminism and feminists has taken over the public imagination, which means that to see femin*ism* clearly we have to cut through the many stereotypes about femin*ists*.

## Feminists Are Antifamily

Feminists are often described as antifamily, but most feminists I've encountered in print or in person have nothing against the family per se as a group in which children are reared and people's emotional and material needs get met by loving adults. Many feminists do object, however, to the subordination of women inside the *patriarchal* family and the way this can damage the potential for nurturing, caring, and growth. They do oppose the organization of family life in ways that suffocate women's emotional and productive lives and foster a climate for the ongoing epidemic of physical abuse of women and children. They don't deny the vital importance of women's connection to children, but many do oppose how patriarchy enables and encourages men to use that connection to control women's bodies, to restrict where they go and with whom they spend their time, and to deny them the independence and autonomy that paid employment provides.

If the patriarchal family is the only kind of family we can imagine, then many feminists will appear to be antifamily when in fact they are simply antipatriarchy.[12] This was especially true during the feminist heyday of the 1970s, when many women were reeling from the realization of how oppressive family life can be when it's organized on a patriarchal model. The patriarchal model was so pervasive that the only alternative often appeared to be no family life at all, which easily lent itself to the impression that feminists devalued marriage and the vital work that mothers do. This may have been true of some feminists, but the underlying theme was alarm over what has *become* of marriage, motherhood, and the family under patriarchy.

## Feminists Are No Fun

Feminists are also accused of being angry and humorless and not knowing how to have a good time. Aside from not being true, it's a peculiar criticism to make of a group whose primary work is to deal with the reality of privilege and oppression.

For women, however, getting angry is socially unacceptable, even when the anger is over violence, discrimination, misogyny, and other forms of oppression.[13] Anger is unacceptable because angry women are women in touch with their passion and power, especially in relation to men, which threatens the entire patriarchal order. It's unacceptable because it forces men to confront the reality of male privilege and women's oppression and their involvement in it, even if only as passive beneficiaries. Women's anger challenges men to acknowledge attempts to trivialize oppression with "I was only kidding." And women's anger is unacceptable to men who look to women to take care of them, to prop up their need to feel in control, and to support them in their competition with other men. When women are less than gracious and good-humored about their own oppression, men often feel uncomfortable, embarrassed, at a loss, and therefore vulnerable. And it places women and their concerns at center stage in a male-centered world.

But what James Baldwin said about blacks, that "to be a relatively conscious African-American is to be in a rage almost all the time,"[14] is also true for women. For this reason, women often protect themselves from feeling (and appearing) perpetually angry by keeping themselves only partially aware of what's going on. But it's unreasonable to expect women to feel no anger about day-to-day oppression often lived in intimate relation to men who not only benefit from patriarchy, but typically show little interest in knowing what it's about or doing anything about it.

And yet that's precisely what's expected of women who are called on to please, nurture, and soothe men and never cause them discomfort, embarrassment, or alarm. As wives and employees, women are supposed to be perpetually good natured, smiling, accepting, accessible, and yielding, lest they be thought of as cold, frigid bitches. This means that all a man has to do to challenge or discredit a woman is point out that she's angry or, even worse, accuse her of being angry at men. Women are a unique minority in this respect. Malcolm X, for example, was often criticized for his expressions of rage at white racism, as was Louis Farrakhan. But while their rage may make them unpopular political figures among whites, if anything it enhances their standing as *men*.

## Man-Hating Male Bashers

There is probably no more effective weapon against feminists than to accuse them of hating men and to characterize feminist criticism of patriarchy and male privilege as "male bashing." The tactic works in part because attacking men challenges the male-identified character of society itself. In other words, since men are assumed to be the standard, to criticize men in general is to take on society as a whole, which both men and women have a stake in resisting. Just the opposite is true, however, of the demeaning prejudice routinely directed at women and other subordinate groups.

Mainstream sexist and racist culture, for example, is full of negative images of women and blacks that devalue the *idea* of being female or black, but we rarely hear about "female bashing" or "black bashing" as a result. This is especially true of misogyny, which simply has no place in most people's active vocabularies in spite of, or perhaps because of, its pervasiveness as an integral part of everyday life. It is unremarkable and taken for granted. When feminists and people of color *do* call attention to sexist and racist speech, however, and demand that it stop, a hue and cry goes up about the tyranny of "political correctness"* and infringements on free speech.

Calling feminists man haters and male bashers protects patriarchy and male privilege by turning what otherwise would be criticism of patriarchy into questions about feminists' personalities and motives. They're accused of creating feminism and the women's movement as a way to act out personal hostility, bitterness, and discontent, all presumably fueled by being

---

* The term *political correctness* was first used by social activists as a way to monitor and ensure their behavior and speech were consistent with their political principles. Talking about male privilege and the oppression of women, for example, in ways that focus entirely on the experience of white women would be considered politically incorrect because while opposing one form of privilege, it tacitly supports another. Since then, the term has been appropriated copied, and distorted by gender equity opponents who use it to refer to any infringement on any dominant groups' freedom to speak and behave without considering the consequences for members of subordinate groups and without regarding the maintenance of privilege. As such, the term has strayed from its original meaning in ways that trivialize the reality of privilege and oppression.

unattractive to men or wanting to be men themselves. Such feelings supposedly result from personal experience, maladjustment, and pathologies having
nothing to do with patriarchy or the oppression of women it produces. In
short, feminism is reduced to the ravings of a bunch of bitter malcontents
and all of its critical insights into patriarchy are conveniently tossed aside.

The accusation of man hating and male bashing also shifts attention
away from women and onto men in a sympathetic way that reinforces patriarchal male centeredness while putting women on the defensive for criticizing
it. In the process, it portrays men as victims of a gender prejudice that on
the surface seems comparable to the sexism directed at women. Like many
such false parallels, this ignores the fact that antifemale and antimale prej-
udices have different social bases and produce very different consequences.
Resentment and hatred of women are grounded in a misogynist *culture* that
devalues femaleness itself as part of male privilege and female oppression.
For women, however, mainstream patriarchal culture offers no comparable
antimale ideology, and so their resentment is based more on experience as a
subordinate group and men's part in it.

It is true, of course, that men sometimes are made fun of, as in television
sitcoms, and this can hurt their feelings. As Marilyn French argues, however,
in almost every case, it is women who appear to make men laughable by
turning them into fools trapped in the home as husbands, the one setting
where women have some real power.[15] It is more as *husbands* than as men
that men are made to look foolish, and even in this the status of manhood
is never at much risk. Even though male characters may sometimes look
foolish in the narrow confines of television or the Sunday comics, they're
surrounded by an overwhelmingly male-identified, male-centered world in
which misandry—the hatred of maleness—simply has no place. A few henpecked (by women) husbands may bumble their way through life for our
entertainment, but it's funny precisely because it is such a departure from
the exalted value placed on maleness, from which every man benefits. There
wouldn't be much of an audience for a show based on a husband's ability to
belittle and control his wife.

Accusations of male bashing and man hating also work to discredit feminism because, as Chapter 2 shows, people often confuse men as individuals
with men as a dominant and privileged category of people. Given the reality
of women's oppression, male privilege, and men's enforcement of both, it's
hardly surprising that *every* woman should have moments when she resents
or even hates "men."[16] Even Phyllis Schlafly, a leader in the antifeminist
backlash, led the fight against the Equal Rights Amendment by arguing in
part that without protective laws, mothers wouldn't be able to count on
fathers to support their children, a judgment that reflects little regard for

men. In spite of such mainstream criticism of men—and its thinly veiled dissatisfaction and hostility—it's politically expedient for opponents of feminism to attribute such negative judgments and feelings to feminists. It makes feminists seem marginal and extreme. It obscures the fact that many feminists have deep ties to men and thereby alienates them from other women who also depend on men. And it gives many women someone to take the heat for feelings they themselves dare not express.

There's a big difference, however, between hating a dominant group in an oppressive system like patriarchy and hating the individuals who belong to it. Angela Davis once said that as an African American she often feels hatred for *white* people, but her feelings for particular white *people* depend on the individual.[17] She hates white people's collective position of dominance in a racially oppressive society, she hates the privilege they enjoy at her expense, and she hates the racist culture that whites take for granted as unremarkable while she must struggle with the oppression it creates in everyday life. But Davis also knows that while individual whites can never be free of racism, they can participate in racist systems in many different ways, which include joining people of color in the fight for racial justice. The same can be said of men and women.[18]

The distinction between groups and individuals, however, is subtle and easy to lose sight of when you're up to your ears in an oppressive system. Of course women are going to feel and express anger, resentment, and even hatred toward individual men who may not have it coming in just that way or to that degree or at that moment. Of course men are sometimes going to get their feelings hurt or be called on to take responsibility for themselves in ways they may not be used to. When I heard Davis talk about hating white people, and when I've heard women talk about hating men, I've had to get clear in my own mind about how these words refer to me and how they don't, and it often takes some effort to get there. And as a white male who benefits from both male and white privilege, I've also had to see that it's up to me—and not to women or people of color—to distinguish one from the other. Too often men react to women's anger by calling on women to take care of them, and in this way recreate the male-centered principle of the very gender order that women, feminist and otherwise, are angry about.

Feminists do exist who passionately and unapologetically hate all males simply for being male, although in all my years of work on gender I've encountered very few of them. The author of the infamous 1960s *SCUM Manifesto* comes to mind as one candidate.[19] Although it's unclear whether the "Society for Cutting Up Men" ever had more than one member, I've heard men cite it as a general characterization of how feminists feel about men. Given the existence of many nonfeminists who are angry at men, and given how much work lies ahead of us to understand patriarchy and what we can do about it, putting the subject of women who hate men at the center of attention is nothing more than a defensive distraction.

## Here Come the Lesbians

A favorite way to dismiss feminists and feminism in a single stroke is to associate both with lesbianism. It's true that many lesbians are feminists and that many feminists are lesbians. But it's also true that many lesbians aren't feminists, many feminists are heterosexual, and the women's movement is full of disagreement among feminists of varying sexual orientations.[20] More to the point, however, is that when the label "lesbian" is used to smear and dismiss feminists and feminism, it silences women who fear being labeled if they identify themselves as feminist or even talk openly about patriarchy.[21] Such "lesbian-baiting" leaves no room to ask about the meaning of lesbianism and its significance under patriarchy.

Adrienne Rich, for example, argues that lesbianism isn't simply about women who want to have sex with other women, but is a continuum of women's sense of identification and desire to be with other women.[22] There are reasons for this to exist in any society, beginning with every girl's intimacy with her mother. In a male-identified, male-centered system, however, women must contend with paths of least resistance that encourage them to see and evaluate themselves as men would. As Ellyn Kaschak puts it, "The most notable aspect of current gender arrangements is that the masculine always defines the feminine by naming, containing, engulfing, invading, and evaluating it. The feminine is never allowed to stand alone or to subsume the masculine."[23]

This means that when women look for role models, they usually find men and women who measure themselves by male-identified cultural standards— what has been called the "male gaze."[24] Most Western art, for example, is created as if its intended audience were primarily male, especially when the subject is women. Similarly, when heterosexual women look in a mirror, they often see themselves as they think men would see them, and judge themselves when they fail to conform to feminine ideals promoted by patriarchal culture.[25] When women leave the patriarchal frame of reference, however, by *also* turning to one another for mirroring and standards, they challenge the assumption that the world revolves around men and men's point of view, and that women exist primarily to please and take care of them.

Becoming more woman identified is a critical part of feminist practice, regardless of women's sexual orientation. It is a process that *every* oppressed group goes through as part of its struggle to redefine itself. It is a way to throw off negative self-images constructed through lifetimes of gazing into cultural mirrors that devalue them in order to maintain the privilege of dominant groups. In this sense it's not surprising that many lesbians are attracted to a movement to free women from patriarchal oppression. But it also makes sense for women of *all* sexual orientations to shift toward woman-identified living even while participating in marriages and raising families with men.

As heterosexual women reclaim a positive, autonomous sense of themselves in nonpatriarchal terms, this will most likely happen as it has thus far—through other women acting as mirrors that help define what it means to be women. This means, of course, that women's movement toward being woman identified threatens men's place at the center of women's attention and what security women have been able to attain for themselves in relation to that center. At the same time, it challenges the male-identified, male-centered core of patriarchy as a system, calling on men to develop their own sense of themselves apart from the exploitative dependency on women that patriarchy promotes. From this perspective, the persecution of lesbians and the use of "lesbian" as accusation or insult is really a defensive attack on the larger movement of women away from patriarchal existence and toward fuller and more self-defined lives. As lesbian baiting intimidates all women into silence and blunts feminism's potential to change how they think about gender, it defends patriarchy as a whole and the privilege and oppression that go with it.

### Feminists as Victims

A more recent attack on feminists has been the peculiar accusation that focusing on patriarchy and its oppressive consequences for women actually demeans and disempowers women by portraying them as "mere" victims. Feminists have been characterized as whining "victim feminists" and "rape-crisis feminists" who portray women as too weak to defend themselves from men who would harass, beat, sexually assault, or discriminate against them.[26] What's most bizarre about this accusation is that the women who work against male violence and exploitation are some of the strongest, toughest, most articulate, and courageous people around, and to describe them as whining victims who passively sit around feeling sorry for themselves is about as far from reality as one could imagine. What makes whining so unappealing is that it is both a call for help and a form of focused self-pity that is so intense that nothing in the way of help has much chance of getting through. In other words, whining is a manipulative setup in which actually making things better isn't the point. But this is a far cry from feminist demands for an end to discrimination, violence, and sexual exploitation.

In spite of its loose hold on reality, the "victim feminism" criticism works because it draws attention away from men as victimizers and focuses instead on women who are victimized. In one sense, critics are correct that focusing on women as victims is counterproductive, but not because we should instead ignore victimization altogether. The real reason to avoid an exclusive focus on women as victims is to free us to concentrate also on the compelling fact that men are the ones who victimize, and such behavior and the patriarchal system that encourages it are the problem. Otherwise we might find ourselves concentrating on male victimization of women as something that *happens to* women without being *done by* men.

The shift in focus can be as simple as the difference between saying "Each year 100,000 women are sexually assaulted" and "Each year men sexually assault 100,000 women." Many people feel less comfortable with the second version because it draws attention to *male* violence against women and thereby to the male gender as problematic. Placing men at the center of the issue also makes it more difficult to explain away sexual violence as a matter of chance (like catching a cold or being in a traffic accident) or of women's failures to be careful enough or of women somehow "asking for it." Sexual violence doesn't fall on women out of thin air, and referring to a woman as a victim doesn't tell us anything about her except that she suffered the consequences of what some man *did*. To call attention to that simple fact, as many feminists do, in no way demeans or diminishes women. What it does do is challenge men and women to look more carefully at what is really going on.

The "victim feminist" label also works because it taps a core feature of patriarchal masculinity: the importance of "taking it like a man" in order to be "one of the guys." Men's abuse of other men is a staple ingredient of patriarchal culture, from high school locker rooms to fraternity hazing to military training. The man who takes abuse without complaint improves his chance of being accepted as a real man who deserves to share in male privilege. A man who objects, however, who dares identify abuse for what it is, risks being ostracized as a sissy, a mama's boy who can't take it and who belongs with "the girls" ("Aww, what's the matter? Gonna cry and run home to mama?"). In the same way, when feminists point out that sexual harassment is abusive or that coerced sex is rape, they may be chided for being the equivalent of whining sissies who don't give women enough credit for being tough and able to take it—like a man. The "like a man" part usually isn't spoken, but in a patriarchal culture it's implicit and doesn't have to be voiced. And some of the loudest voices in the chorus are women who have achieved acceptance and success in a man's world.

As the attacks continue, many feminists are distracted and harried by having to explain and defend themselves from the latest provocation. More to the point, perhaps, is that the ongoing waves of criticism—whether warranted or not—are combined with a general absence of thoughtful public discussion of what feminism is about. Over time, this creates the illusion that patriarchy either doesn't exist or, if it does, it doesn't deserve serious attention. While the reality of feminism's world-changing potential remains invisible in the public eye, gender privilege and oppression continue largely unabated. To do something about that, we need a clear sense of what feminism is and how it can help us understand what's going on.

## What Is Feminism?

As a matter of principle, some feminists prefer not to define feminism at all because it's so diverse that no single version of it could possibly do justice to the many forms it takes. In addition, a commitment to being inclusive and nonhierarchical makes many feminists leery of definitions, since definitions can be used to establish an exclusive "one true feminism" that separates "insiders" from "outsiders."

Nonetheless, people do use the word to describe how they think and work. Like any word, *feminism* can't be used unless it has meaning, and any meaning necessarily sets it apart from other possibilities. Without taking anything away from feminism's diversity, I think it's possible to identify some core ideas that most forms of feminism have in common. I've never encountered anything called feminism, for example, that didn't in some way begin with the assumption that gender inequality exists and that it's problematic. How and why inequality exists, what forms it takes, and what to do about it are questions with different and sometimes conflicting answers. But the questions all reflect a common focus of attention, and this is how feminism can encompass a diversity of answers.

Having said this, it's important to emphasize the distinction between feminism as a framework for analysis and two other possibilities. Feminism can refer to a set of opinions about social issues such as abortion or equal pay. It can also simply be about being "pro-woman,"[27] as when people identify themselves as feminists because they favor gender equality or the right to choose abortion. But neither of these necessarily points to a particular way of analyzing gender inequality that one might call feminism. For my purpose here, feminism is a way of thinking—of observing the world, asking questions, and looking for answers—that may lead to particular opinions *but doesn't consist of the opinions themselves.* One could be pro-choice or in favor of equal pay, for example, on purely moral or liberal political grounds without any basis in a feminist analysis of gender. In this sense, feminism refers to ways of *understanding* such issues from various points of view, all of which share a common focus of concern.

Although all feminist thought begins with gender inequality as problematic, from there it follows various paths, especially in relation to patriarchy. In general, I think it's useful to distinguish among branches of feminism according to the degree to which:

- They understand various aspects of social life—such as sexual domination and violence, religion, warfare, politics, economics, and how we treat the natural environment—in relation to gender;
- They explicitly recognize patriarchy as a system, as problematic, as historically rooted, and in need of change; and
- They see men as a dominant group with a vested interest in women's subordination, the perpetuation of patriarchal values, and control over the political, economic, and other institutions through which those values operate.

Some brands of feminism, for example, have little use for the term "patriarchy," not seeing men as particularly problematic and avoiding anything that might challenge men or make them feel uncomfortable or raise the possibility of conflict between men and women. Others define patriarchy, male privilege, gender oppression, and conflict as basic points of departure for any understanding of gender. In some cases the focus of change is quite narrow, as it was in the turn-of-the-century struggle for women's suffrage, while in others, such as ecofeminism or feminist spirituality, the focus is global change spanning multiple dimensions of human experience.

Most feminist work draws to varying degrees on a handful of major approaches best known as liberal, radical, Marxist, and socialist feminism. These aren't the only kinds of feminist thought—psychoanalytic and postmodern feminism are two notable additions to the list—but they certainly have played a part in most attempts to understand and do something about patriarchy and its consequences. They also aren't mutually exclusive. Although liberal and radical feminism, for example, differ dramatically in some ways, they also have a lot in common and trace back to similar roots. As such, "liberal," "socialist," "Marxist," and "radical" aren't little boxes into which feminists can neatly and unambiguously fit themselves. If I tried to identify the feminist approaches that have shaped the writing of this book, for example, I'd find them all in one way or another even though I lean more toward some than others. It helps, then, to think of various feminist approaches as threads woven together to form a whole. While the threads are distinctive in many ways, they are strongest in relation to one another.

## Liberal Feminism

The basic idea behind liberal feminism—and liberal thinking in general—is that humans are rational beings who, with enough knowledge and opportunity, will realize their potential as individuals to the benefit of themselves and society as a whole. Things go wrong primarily through ignorance, bad socialization, and limited access to opportunities. Equality of opportunity and freedom of choice are seen as the bedrock of individual well-being, which in turn makes possible an enlightened society and progressive social change. Liberalism assumes that the individual person is the highest good and the key to social life. From this perspective, societies are little more than collections of people making choices, and social change is largely a matter of changing how individuals think and behave, especially through education and other means of enlightenment.[28]

From a liberal feminist perspective, the main gender problem is that prejudice, values, and norms deny women equal access to the opportunities, resources, and rewards that society offers. Forcing women to choose between child care and employment; excluding women from positions of authority in economic, political, religious, and other organizations; segregating women in the job market; devaluing, objectifying, and portraying women as inferior in a wide variety of cultural stereotypes; and socializing women and men in ways that enhance all of the above are identified as central to gender equality.

The liberal feminist solution is to remove the barriers to women's freedom of choice and equal participation, from restrictions on reproductive control to providing day care to breaking the glass ceiling at work. The liberal method is to persuade people to change by challenging stereotypes and demanding equal access and treatment. This includes rewriting school textbooks and curricula; reforming legal codes; breaking the glass ceiling and promoting women's advancement through networking; providing victimized women with resources such as battered women's shelters and rape crisis services; and lobbying for child-care facilities and equal access to professions, corporate management, and elected office. Liberal feminism calls on men to change how they think about and behave toward women, to be less violent, harassing, and exploitative and more supportive, emotionally sensitive and expressive, and committed to their roles as fathers and partners. And it calls on women to assert and believe in themselves, to strive to achieve and not be deterred by the barriers they must overcome.

In short, liberal feminism ultimately relies on men to be decent and fair, to become enlightened and progressive as they learn the truth about gender inequality and women's true potential, to give women their due by allowing them to participate as equals in social life, and to support this by doing their fair share of domestic work. And it relies on women to believe in themselves, to strive and achieve, to push against barriers until they give way. All of this strikes a deep chord, especially in the "American Dream" consciousness, whose root ideology extols the virtues of individual freedom as the answer to most social problems. This is one reason why the liberal perspective has shaped so much of the women's movement and general public perceptions of what gender issues are all about.

Liberalism has certainly improved the lives of many women, but after several decades of hard-won gains, the women's movement seems nearly swamped by the backlash and stalled by stiff resistance to further change. A recent study conducted by the U.S. Department of Labor's Women's Bureau, for example, found that a majority of working women, and especially women of color, continue to be devalued, underpaid, and not taken seriously, and still struggle with the demands of domestic responsibilities with little help from employers, government, or, most important, husbands. None of this is the fault of liberal feminism, but it does reflect its underlying limitations as a way to make sense of patriarchy and find alternatives to it.

A basic problem with liberal feminism (and liberalism in general) is that its intense focus on the individual obscures the power of social systems. This is one reason why liberal feminism doesn't recognize patriarchy as something to be reckoned with. It rarely looks at the underlying structures that produce male privilege and women's oppression and that shape the individual men and women liberal feminism aims to change. A liberal feminist approach to getting fathers more involved in child care, for example, emphasizes changing men one at a time (or perhaps in small groups). This might be done by appealing to a sense of fairness or the importance of having closer relations with children.

By ignoring patriarchy, however, liberal feminism turns male privilege into an individual problem only remotely connected to larger systems that promote and protect it. In the case of child care, this misses the fact that when men don't do their "fair share" of domestic labor, they gain in terms of nondomestic rewards such as power, income, and status as "real men." In the dominant patriarchal culture, these rewards are valued far more highly than the emotional satisfactions of family life. In opinion polls, many men *say* that family life is more important than work, but when it comes to actual choices about where to invest themselves, the results reflect a different set of cultural values embedded in powerful paths of least resistance. Liberal feminism, then, often puts women in the position of negotiating from a position of weakness, depending on men to give up male privilege and endanger their standing in relation to other men because it's the right thing to do and might enrich their or their children's emotional lives.[29]

Liberal feminism's individualism also backs us into a no-win position between denying that patriarchy even exists, on the one hand, and claiming that all men are engaged in a conspiracy to oppress women on the other. If nothing significant exists beyond the rational individual, then by definition the only thing larger than ourselves in which we might participate is a conspiracy or other form of deliberate planning among individuals. Since it's easy to refute the existence of a massive conspiracy in which men gather to plot a patriarchal future, any kind of systemic understanding of privilege and oppression becomes virtually impossible, as does the hope of doing much about it.

Liberal feminism is also limited by its ahistorical character. It offers no way to explain the origins of the social arrangements it's trying to change, nor does it identify a social engine powerful enough to keep them going. Liberal feminism's main assumption is that privilege and oppression result from ignorance whose removal through enlightened education will clear the road to equality and a better life for all. But when ignorance and misunderstanding perpetuate an oppressive system of privilege, they become more than a passive barrier that dissipates in the light of truth. Instead, they become part of a willful defense that puts up a fight, and a good one at that. Liberal feminism is ill equipped to deal with this, for the closest liberalism comes to acknowledging the forces that perpetuate patriarchy is its frequent reference to "tradition" (as in "traditional roles"). There is no theory of history or systemic privilege here. Instead, we have a vague sense that things have been this way for a long time and for reasons that are apparently not worth exploring beyond "it's hard for people to change."

Liberal feminism's "tradition" catch-all obscures the underlying dynamics that make patriarchy work, and it trivializes privilege and oppression by making them seem a matter of habit. Imagine, by comparison, how unacceptable it would be to attribute racism or anti-Semitism to nothing more than tradition, as in "Racism is a matter of tradition in the United States," or "Persecuting Jews is just the way we've done things here—for as long as I can remember." "Tradition" doesn't *explain* anything, it merely characterizes one aspect of how it's practiced and woven into the fabric of everyday life so that it's taken for granted and perceived as normal.

Liberal feminism's lack of historical perspective has serious consequences because it leads away from questions about patriarchy which has little place in liberal thinking. Patriarchy is treated as a shadow concept with no serious analytical role to play in making sense of gender. Avoiding patriarchy also fits nicely with the liberal focus on individuals as the be-all and end-all of human life, with little appreciation for how feelings, motivations, thoughts, and behavior are shaped by participation in larger social contexts. From a liberal perspective, for example, men who rape are merely sick individuals, and there's no reason to ask why such "sickness" is more common in some societies than others or how the violent coercion practiced by rapists might be related to the less violent coercion that figures so prominently in "normal" patriarchal heterosexuality, especially in some of its more romanticized versions. Unless we want to argue that men are conspiring to produce violence against women on a massive scale, we're stuck with no larger understanding of what's going on.

A deeper problem is liberal feminism's single-minded focus on the right of women to be men's equals—to do what men do in the way that men do it. In asserting this, it doesn't ask what might be wrong with a way of organizing the world that encourages men to do what they do in the way they do it. As a result, when women demand access to positions of power in corporations, the military, government, religion, universities, and the professions, they also affirm the basic patriarchal character of social life. Rather than question warfare as a way to conduct international relations, for example, liberal feminism champions the right of women to serve in combat. Rather than question capitalism as a way to produce and distribute what people need in order to live, liberal feminism targets glass ceilings that keep women from moving up in corporate hierarchies. Rather than challenge the values that shape how professions are practiced—from medicine and law to science—liberalism focuses on equal access to graduate schools, legal partnerships, and the tenured ranks of university faculties.

This is essentially what Naomi Wolf promotes as "power feminism": Women should beat men at their own game and run the world—hence the title of her book, *Fire with Fire*. Initially, she seems to favor the more radical goal of changing the game itself rather than merely winning at it. She disagrees with Audre Lorde's proposition that "The Master's tools will never dismantle the Master's house,"[30] arguing instead that patriarchy can be undone through the use of patriarchal forms of power and domination, whether political, economic, or interpersonal. But it soon becomes clear that Wolf isn't concerned with dismantling the Master's house, but with breaking down the door and getting into it. "Women," Wolf writes, "should be free to exploit or save, give or take, destroy or build, to exactly the same extent that men are."[31]

On the face of it, Wolf is simply calling for the right of women to run their own lives, a core tenet of liberal thinking. As important as this is, unless it is informed by an explicit critical analysis of patriarchy as the prevailing social system, it runs the risk of failing to ask whether *men* should be free to do such things to the extent that they are, or whether that is a good standard for organizing the world. This is a problem with liberalism in general and liberal feminism in particular—the tendency to assume that the main thing wrong with the status quo is unequal opportunity for women to participate in it as men do. It is not surprising, then, that Wolf never tells us what the Master's house is by describing patriarchy and how it works.

Of course equal opportunity, equal access, and equality under the law are important goals. But there are some serious unanticipated consequences to working for equal access to a system without *also* asking what kind of system it is and how it produces privilege and oppression, especially when based on characteristics other than gender, such as race, sexual orientation, disability status, and social class. One consequence of following a liberal feminist agenda is that successful women often join men at the top of systems that oppress working-class white men and women and people of color, obscuring the fact that equality for "women" comes to mean in effect equality for white women of a certain class. This does *not* mean that women shouldn't pursue power now held predominantly by men. It does mean, however, that the liberal feminist perspective that shapes and informs such striving omits huge chunks of reality. As such, it can't be the only feminist approach to understanding gender oppression or doing something about it.

Because liberal feminism has little to say about how patriarchy organizes male competitive bonding and women's oppression, it focuses on the consequences of oppression without looking at the system that produces them. Sexist behavior and attitudes, for example, are discussed out of their social context, as if they were simply the result of "bad training," to be replaced with "good training" at home and in school. But socialization and education are social mechanisms that serve much larger patriarchal interests, including the perpetuation of male privilege and social institutions organized around core patriarchal values. As such, socialization isn't the problem, any more than programs that train workers in weapons factories are the key to understanding war.

Perhaps the most ironic problem with liberal feminism is that by focusing on equality only in terms of individual choice and opportunity *within* patriarchy, it actually undermines the liberal ideal of free choice. By ignoring how patriarchy shapes and limits the alternatives from which people might "freely" choose, it ignores the power to determine just what those alternatives will be. This means that the freedom to participate in the world on patriarchal terms is freedom only in a context that ignores the *non*patriarchal alternatives that patriarchal culture doesn't tell us about. This also means that the limited liberal agenda for change assumes that society as it currently exists defines the limits of what is possible. But as Marilyn French points out, the freedom to choose among existing alternatives is only part of a larger feminist agenda:

> For although feminists do indeed want women to become part of the structure, participants in public institutions; although they want access for women to decision-making posts, and a voice in how society is managed, *they do not want women to assimilate to society as it presently exists but to change it*. Feminism is not yet one more of a series of political movements demanding for their adherents access to existing structures and their rewards. . . . [I]t is a revolutionary moral movement, intending to use political power to transform society. . . . The assimilation of women to society as it presently exists would lead simply to the inclusion of certain women . . . along with certain men in its higher echelons. It would mean continued stratification and continued contempt for "feminine" values. Assimilation would be the cooption of feminism.[32]

In the above sense, critics of liberal feminism would take feminism well beyond issues of gender equality. A broader and deeper feminism is about the very terms on which equality is figured. It is about women's right to participate as men's equals in society, but also about the power to shape the alternatives from which both women and men may choose. It's about the power to affect the forces that shape experience, thought, feeling, and behavior. It's about the power to change society itself. It's about fundamentally changing the Master's house, if not dismantling it altogether, which is a far cry from just getting in the door. This goes well past the limits of liberal feminism to the roots—the radicals—of the patriarchal tree, which leads us into the kinds of questions that so often provoke a backlash of resistance and denial. This is a major reason why liberal feminism is so widely viewed as the only legitimate and socially acceptable form that feminism can take, because it's also the most palatable, the least threatening, and the most compatible with the status quo. This is also why one of its major alternatives, radical feminism, is so routinely maligned, misunderstood, and ignored.

## Radical Feminism

As we move toward more radical areas of feminist thought, the landscape is taken up with far more than issues like unequal pay. Radical feminism of course pays attention to patriarchy's consequences and how people experience them. But unlike liberal feminism, radical feminism carries that attention to the underlying male-dominated, male-identified, male-centered, control-obsessed patriarchal system that produces male privilege and the oppression of women. Radical feminism aims to make sense of patriarchy in relation to history and social contexts that help explain not only where it came from, but how and why it persists and affects us so deeply.

As we saw in Chapter 2, for example, male violence against women is more than an individual pathology. It is also a path of least resistance that patriarchy lays down for men to follow and for women to accept. From a radical perspective, that path doesn't exist in isolation from the rest of social life but is rooted in and helps to maintain male privilege in patriarchy as a system. In similar ways, a radical perspective on family divisions of labor that still saddle women with most domestic work is quite different from a liberal view. Radical feminism sees this as more than "tradition" or an expression of female and male personality tendencies or a lack of appropriate training or encouragement for men. The family is an institution with a complex history as a vehicle for keeping women in their place, and men's resistance to domestic labor has been an important part of that dynamic.[33] Whatever reasons individual men may offer for not doing child care and housework, it is rooted in male privilege, and its cumulative effect is to reinforce that privilege.

The connection with male privilege also appears in radical analyses of things as mundane as the difficulties women and men have communicating with each other. From Deborah Tannen's liberal feminist perspective, for example, power and control are secondary issues in gender communication. The real problem is that men and women use different conversational "styles" that reflect men's concern with status and women's concern with intimacy and relationships. Tannen believes these styles are "different *but equally valid*" and result from being socialized into different cultures, each with its own traditions.[34]

If men interrupt and otherwise dominate conversation, for example, it's because that's "their way," just as the Spanish enjoy siesta and Japanese traditionally remove their shoes before entering a house. Since there's a lot of pressure these days to respect cultural differences, Tannen's somewhat anthropological approach to gender dynamics tends to make it off limits to criticism. Her perspective offers some comfort to those feeling stressed from gender conflict: There's no problem here that can't be cured with a good dose of education and tolerance for differences—the classic liberal remedy for just about everything. But the comfort masks the messier reality that men and women don't grow up in separate cultures in any sense of the term but share common family, school, and work environments and swim in the same cultural sea of media imagery. However soothing it might be to think of gender issues as a matter of "East meets West," or "Mars meets Venus," it simply isn't so.

A radical critique of Tannen's feminism might begin with her liberal pre-occupation with individual motives and how she confuses these with social consequences. Tannen bends over backward to discourage women's anger at men who behave in dominating, aggressive ways, arguing that men don't *mean* to be this way. What she misses is that a hallmark of privilege is not having to mean it in order to exercise or benefit from socially bestowed privilege, whether it be taking up conversational space or being taken more seriously and given credit for ideas. Awareness and intention require commitment and work, in comparison to which arrogance or innocence is relatively easy. And when men's conversational style promotes privilege, whether it's intended or not is irrelevant to the social consequences that result.

A radical perspective assumes from the start that patriarchy is real, that it doesn't spring from some vague wellspring of cultural "tradition," and that it sets men and women fundamentally at odds with one another, regardless of how they might feel about it as individuals.[35] Radical feminism's historical perspective identifies patriarchy as the first oppressive system, the originator of the religion of control, power, and fear that provided a model for all other forms of privilege and oppression.[36] As such, patriarchy is also the most deeply rooted and pervasive system of privilege and the most resistant to change. It manifests itself in every aspect of social life, making privilege and oppression part of something much larger and deeper than what they may appear to be within the rhythms of everyday life.

Because radical feminism takes patriarchy to be real, it looks hard at men as the prime beneficiaries and enforcers of the patriarchal order. Regardless of how individual men may behave or see themselves, they participate in a system that grants them privilege at the expense of women and encourages them to protect and take advantage of it. The truth of this can be seen not only in obviously sexist men but in men who consider themselves sensitive to gender issues and supportive of the women's movement, for all too often they do little about it. Sometimes known as "sensitive New Age guys," these men rarely take the initiative to learn more about patriarchy or their participation in it. They don't speak out publicly against male privilege and women's oppression or confront other men about sexist behavior. They may protest that they don't want women to be oppressed and hate the idea of benefiting from it, but they also show little interest in making themselves uncomfortable to the extent of confronting the reality of what's going on beyond their good intentions. Unless prodded into action by women, most men choose to leave things as they are, which, by default, includes their unearned privilege. This is especially striking when it appears in men whose politics are otherwise progressively left. In fact, radical feminism emerged from women's experience in new left civil rights and antiwar movements of the 1960s in which male colleagues often treated them as subordinate, objectified "others" whose primary purpose was to meet men's needs.[37]

The distinction between liberal and radical feminism is important not because one is right and the other is wrong, but because they focus on different kinds of questions and problems. As a result, they also lead to different kinds of answers and solutions. Liberal feminism, for example, tends to interpret sexist stereotypes as false beliefs and bad attitudes that can be corrected through exposure to the truth. The belief that women are weak and dependent, for example, can be undone by showing people how strong and independent women can be or male attitudes of contemptuous superiority can be changed by making men aware of how injurious, unfair, and groundless such views are.

Radical feminism, however, reminds us that negative stereotypes about women don't exist in a vacuum. Especially when something is so persuasive in a society, we have to ask what *social* purpose it serves beyond the motives and intentions of individuals. Whose interests does sexism support, and what kind of social order does it perpetuate? From this perspective, misogyny and other forms of sexist thinking are more than mistaken ideas and bad attitudes. They are also part of a cultural ideology that serves male privilege and supports women's subordination. As such, a sexist attitude is more than mere prejudice: *it is prejudice plus the power to act on it.*

The belief that women are weak and dependent, for example, and the cultural identification of strength and independence with maleness combine to make women's strength and independence invisible. It also masks most men's essential vulnerability and dependence on women and promotes the illusion that men are in control—all of which are keys to maintaining patriarchy. As a form of sexism, misogyny also helps stabilize patriarchy by encouraging men to use women as targets for the feelings of contempt, frustration, and anger that arise from their competitive relations with other men.[38] Patriarchy sets men against other men, but it also rests on male solidarity in relation to women. Using women as scapegoats for negative feelings maintains this delicate balance while minimizing the personal risk to men.

Because radical and liberal perspectives interpret sexism differently, they also suggest different solutions to it. From a radical perspective, the liberal reliance on socialization is short-sighted and futile, for anything that truly undermines the definition of women as inferior and men as superior challenges the entire patriarchal system and therefore will provoke resistance. By itself, socialization won't bring about fundamental change because families, schools, and other agents of socialization are dedicated to raising children who will be accepted and succeed in society as it is, not risk living their lives in the shunned status of troublemaker or radical. This is what makes liberal feminism so appealing and also what limits its ability to create fundamental change. After decades of liberal feminist activism, for example, a small minority of elite women has been allowed to embrace patriarchal masculine values and achieve some success in male-identified occupations, but for women as a group, oppression is still the rule. The problem isn't how we train children to fit into the world. The problem is the world into which we fit them and into which they'll feel compelled to fit if they're going to "get along" and "succeed."

If sexism reflected no more than a need for the light of truth to shine on the reality of men and women as they are, then it wouldn't have much of a future, given how much knowledge is readily available. But sexism isn't simply about individual enlightenment. It isn't a personality problem or a bad habit. Sexism is rooted in a social reality that underpins male privilege. As such, sexism isn't going to disappear from patriarchal culture through appeals to people's sense of fairness and decency or their ability to distinguish stereotypes from the facts of who people are.[39]

For all its limitations—or perhaps because of them—liberal feminism is all that most people actually know of feminist thought, and it therefore defines gender issues in public discussion. Radical feminism is virtually invisible in the mainstream except for the occasional distorted sound bite references to its most provocative expressions or its ideas taken out of context. As a result, radical feminism is known primarily as an attitude (such as man hating), or as rigid orthodoxy ("only lesbians are real feminists"), or as a form of essentialism ("women are superior and ought to rule the world"). To be sure, all of these can be found somewhere in feminist thought, but they pale beside the overwhelming bulk of radical analysis of patriarchy, whose insights can help both men and women work for something better.

Liberal feminism has more popular appeal than radical feminism because it focuses on gender without confronting the reality of patriarchal oppression and without seriously threatening male privilege. It avoids the uncomfortable work of challenging men to take some responsibility for patriarchy rather than merely being sensitive to "women's issues" or helping women out with domestic responsibilities when it suits them. And liberal feminism allows us to stay within the relatively comfortable familiarity of an individualistic, psychological framework in which individual pathology and change are the answers to every problem.

Under the liberal umbrella, women can comfort themselves with the idea that the men in *their* lives are personally okay and uninvolved in patriarchy.

Successful women can enjoy their status without having to question the patriarchal terms on which they achieved it, except when criticizing "victim
feminists" who "spoil" things by calling attention to patriarchy and what
it does to women. Men can reassure themselves that so long as they don't
behave with conscious malevolence toward women, they aren't part of the
problem. Men who don't rape, harass, or discriminate against women can
wash their hands of gender issues and get on with their lives, with an occasional acknowledgment of the ever-fascinating "battle of the sexes" and
men's and women's "cultures" and all the ins and outs of getting along with
one another and appreciating gender "differences."

Radical feminism is avoided, dismissed, and attacked precisely because
it raises critical questions that most people would rather ignore in the hope
that they will go away. Radical feminism forces us to confront relationships
that most men and women depend on to meet their needs. It challenges
us to see how patriarchy divides women and men into subordinate and
dominant groups with different interests that put them at odds with one
another. And it violates one of patriarchy's core principles by daring to place
women rather than men at the center of the discussion, focusing women's
energy on themselves and other women and encouraging even heterosexual
women to identify with women rather than with a male-identified system
that marginalizes and oppresses them.

It shouldn't surprise us, then, that the mass media and so many people
are content to settle for negative caricatures of radical feminism, to make
it invisible, discredited, and ghettoized in the underground press and the
shelves of alternative bookstores. But the liberal alternative isn't enough
to work our way out of patriarchy because it can't provide a clear view
of patriarchy and how it works. We wind up in Naomi Wolf's confusion
between dismantling the Master's house and getting into it, a confusion
based on having no clear idea of just what the Master's house *is* or what it
would mean to dismantle it. To change the system, we can't just focus on
individuals. We also have to find ways to focus on the *system*, and for that
we have to go to its roots, which is what radical feminism is all about. A
purely liberal approach to gender—or to race or class or any other form of
privilege and oppression—can take us just so far, as is painfully clear from
the current anti-feminist backlash, a stalled civil rights movement, and a
resurgence of xenophobia and racism in the United States, especially since
the events of September 11, 2001. Liberalism is a crucial first step in the
journey away from oppressive systems. But that's all it is, because it can take
us only as far as the system will allow, and in systems of privilege, that isn't far
enough.

# Patriarchy and Capitalism: Marxist and Socialist Feminism

From a Marxist perspective, it's economics, not love, that makes the world go around. Since nothing is possible without material necessities such as food, clothing, and shelter, Marxism argues that every aspect of social life is shaped by how those material needs are met in a society. Everything from religion to the family to literature will look different in a feudal society, for example, than it will in an industrial capitalist one or in a band of hunter-gatherers. If the family is small, mobile, and nuclear in capitalist societies, and large, fixed, and extended in agrarian ones, it's because families accommodate themselves to different economic conditions and, as a result, survive within different systems of inequality.

How production is organized in a society can give rise to various kinds of social classes. In feudal societies, for example, production centered on the land, and class inequality was defined in relation to it. The land-owning class was thereby the dominant class, while the class that worked but didn't own the land was subordinate. By comparison, in industrial capitalist societies the central importance of land has been replaced by machinery and other technology. Under capitalism, the class that owns or controls the means of producing wealth is the dominant class, and instead of agrarian peasants, we now have various kinds of workers who must sell their labor in exchange for wages.

In the simplest sense, Marx argued that social life is always organized around such basic aspects of economic life. The state, for example, will generally act to preserve a given economic system and the class that dominates it, such as capitalist control over capital, working conditions, and profit. Schools will socialize children to accept their position in the class structure and perform appropriately, whether as obedient workers or take-charge managers or members of the upper class. Art, literature, and popular culture all become commodities valued primarily by how much someone is willing to pay for them. Because it's hard to think of anything that can't be bought or sold in a capitalist system, capitalism shapes almost every aspect of human existence.

Ask a strict Marxist about gender inequality and the response will invariably center on economics. Through a Marxist lens, male privilege is just a variation on class privilege, with men being the ruling class who control the most important resources and women the subordinate class whose childrearing and other domestic labor are exploited for men's benefit. Or women's oppression is a by-product of capitalist exploitation that feeds on women's free or cheap labor and ready availability as part-time workers who can be hired when needed and discarded when not.

In short, the Marxist version of feminism argues that women's oppression has more to do with the class dynamics of capitalism than with male privilege and dominance as forces in their own right. It is true that the working class includes both women and men, and women are often exploited in different ways than men—such as by performing unpaid child care and other domestic labor that produces new workers and cares for existing ones. But Marxist feminism argues that women's oppression is nonetheless primarily a matter of economics. If women are kept out of the paid labor force, for example, it's because capitalism took production out of the home and into the factory, making it difficult for women to do both paid and domestic labor.[40] In keeping with the Marxist perspective, then, women's subordinate status is defined in terms of capitalist class relations, not gender relations per se.

Economics also lies at the heart of a Marxist feminist solution to gender oppression. This would be accomplished by closing the split between family and work and replacing capitalism with socialism or some other alternative. Such changes would integrate women into the paid labor force— making child care and other domestic work public and communal rather than private and individual[41]—and would find other ways for women to be economically independent. All of this would remove the economic basis for male privilege and men's ability to exploit women's labor, reproductive ability, and sexuality. Since Marxism sees economics as the basis for all other forms of power, economic equality would bring about general social equality between women and men.

Marxist feminism is useful because it shows how economic life in general and capitalism in particular shape male privilege. In agrarian patriarchies, for example, rather than control the flow of cash income, men own the land and have authority over wives and children. Under industrial capitalism, land ownership is no longer the major basis for wealth and power, and so the economic underpinnings of male privilege shift from the family to wage labor and controlling the occupational marketplace.

As useful as Marxist feminism is, however, its single-minded focus on economics overlooks the essentially patriarchal nature of systems such as feudalism and capitalism. It tells us little about how the interests and dynamics of patriarchy and capitalism overlap and support each other. Nor does it help explain women's continued subordination in noncapitalist societies such as China and the former Soviet Union that failed to live up to socialist ideology's opposition to all forms of privilege and oppression. These societies have shown that although removing capitalism can improve the status of women—as it certainly did in many ways—patriarchy can continue to exist.

Marxist feminism's limitations are understandable, given its origins. In many ways it developed as an attempt by traditional Marxists to accommodate the challenges raised by the modern women's movement. Using ideas they were most familiar with, Marxists forced male privilege into a relatively narrow framework of capitalist class relations. This inevitably came up against the limitations of trying to reduce everything to economics. Marxists were onto something important, however, when they identified capitalism as a powerful force to be reckoned with in opposing patriarchy. Capitalism is organized around control and domination—whether of workers or technology or markets and competitors—and economic life is one of the most important arenas in which the patriarchal dynamic of fear and control operates. Marxism also should be credited for focusing long ago on the origins of male privilege. Marx's collaborator Friedrich Engels, for example, argued that social inequality originated in the family and that historically women were the first oppressed group.[42]

Criticism of Marxist feminism produced socialist feminism, which broadens and deepens the Marxist approach by focusing on the complex connection between patriarchy and economic systems such as capitalism, especially as they operate through the family. As Heidi Hartmann argues, for example, privilege and oppression involve more than psychology and social roles, for they are always rooted in the material realities of production and reproduction.[43] In other words, historically women have been oppressed primarily through male control over women's labor and women's bodies—their sexuality and reproductive potential—especially in families. The goods women produce have been appropriated by men, women have been bought and sold in marriage arrangements between men, and control over women's sexuality and the children they bear has been a staple ingredient of patriarchal marriage. The institution of monogamous heterosexual marriage has enabled men to control women's bodies through conjugal rights of sexual access, to keep women dependent on men (through control over land or, more recently, control over the "bread winner" role), and to ensure a clear male line of inheritance. Although women are now challenging the male monopoly over the provider role, this arrangement has served men's interests for a long time, especially in the middle and upper classes. It has enabled them to benefit from women's personal services and to enhance their competition with other men over the resources and rewards that determine social class position.

One of the great values of socialist feminism is that it shows how the status of women and men has both shaped and been shaped by economic arrangements. Patriarchy and capitalism are so deeply intertwined with each other that some socialist feminists argue against even thinking of them as separate systems:

> Under capitalism as it exists today, women experience patriarchy as unequal wages for work equal to that of men; sexual harassment on the job; uncompensated domestic work. . . . Earlier generations of women also experienced patriarchy, but they lived it differently depending on the dynamics of the reigning economic system. . . . A feudal system of gender relations accompanied a feudal system of class arrangements, and the social relations of class and gender grew together and evolved over time into the forms we now know (for example, the capitalist nuclear family). To say that gender relations are independent of class relations is to ignore how history works.[44]

The basic insight of socialist feminism is that patriarchy is not simply about gender, but is bound up with the most fundamental aspects of social life. Justice for women involves more than changing how men and women think, feel, and behave in gendered relationships, for any deeply rooted challenge to patriarchy will profoundly affect the prevailing economic system. This also applies to other institutions such as the state, religion, education, the law, and the mass media that support and reflect both economic and patriarchal interests.

## Feminism: Being and Doing

As a way of thinking, feminism is invaluable to anyone who wants to help unravel the patriarchal gender knot. It gives us a way to question every aspect of human life. Liberal feminism provides a place to start, but sooner or later we have to move toward the roots of the problem, beyond relatively superficial change to a more fundamental restructuring and redefinition of what life is to be about. This is precisely where we are early in the twenty-first century: standing at the edge of where liberal feminism has brought us and wondering what to do next. Some people, perhaps sensing that liberalism has taken us as far as it can, have declared a postfeminist era. But we aren't in postfeminism. We are in a backlash coming at the tail-end of a temporarily exhausted women's movement.

Patriarchy is like a fire burning deep underground, spreading and burning into the Earth for thousands of years. We notice what breaks through the surface and may think that's all there is. We may focus on not getting burned in the moment even though we can sense something larger and deeper down below. But if we're serious about change, we have to wake up to the fact that there's more going on than gendered brushfires springing up in episodes of miscommunication, harassment, discrimination, violence, and all the other day-to-day occurrences that add up to life under patriarchy. If we're serious about this, we've got to dig, preferably with plenty of company and with a full appreciation of the fact that although we didn't start the fire, it belongs to us now.

Many people feel threatened by feminism, especially its nonliberal aspects, because it raises questions that invite us to look more closely not only at the world, but at the complex fullness of who we are in relation to it. Feminism is a window on the world and our connection to it, and it is a mirror reflecting what our lives are about. Above all, it is a powerful framework for making sense of what we're participating in, for digging beneath the surface of status quo ideology and what we take to be reality to discover the unarticulated terms on which we actually live our lives.

But at the same time that feminism can frighten us or make us feel uncomfortable, it can also empower us by making sense of what's going on and what this has to do with us. Feminism embodies an enduring truth that male privilege and women's oppression are real and problematic for all of us, and that not only *can* we understand what's happening, we *must* understand if we are ever to be part of the solution and not just part of the problem.

As reluctant as many women are to embrace feminism, it's even harder for men, who often see themselves as excluded members of an enemy class and therefore personally to blame for patriarchy and its consequences. Even men who don't go to this extreme are often careful not to identify too closely or too openly with feminism. This includes many men who actively support the struggle against patriarchy. The National Organization for Men Against Sexism, for example, describes itself as "pro-feminist" rather than feminist. In some ways a "feminist-once-removed" identity helps counter the dominant group tendency to co-opt and take over anything of value produced by subordinate groups—from white people's appropriation of Native American spirituality to the "new men's movement" claim that it parallels the women's movement.[45] The pro-feminist label also honors the fact that whatever their politics, men cannot call themselves feminists as a kind of safe-conduct pass that obscures or denies the reality of male privilege, of their inherently problematic status *as men* under patriarchy, and of the legitimacy of women's anger. Insofar as feminism has to do with *being* rather than with *thinking* or *doing*, insofar as it reflects women's actual experience under patriarchy, then men shouldn't call themselves feminists.

But men's seemingly appropriate distance from feminism also reinforces the idea that deep down, patriarchy, like housework, is really a women's problem. This limits men to a supportive role in which they can "do the right thing" and count themselves among the "good guys." To be pro-feminist is to support women in *their* fight, but it doesn't name the fight against patriarchy as inherently *men's* responsibility and therefore their fight as well. This is especially important if we think of feminism as more than a way to think about gender oppression and how to advance women's interests in relation to men. Because patriarchy isn't simply about gender, because every major social institution is grounded in core patriarchal values, feminism is, in its broadest sense, about the way the whole world is organized.[46]

For all of feminism's potential, the simple truth is that if people want to dismiss it, they'll have an easy time of it, given how effectively feminism has been distorted and marginalized. All one need do is point to the disagreeable views of one feminist or another in order to feel the approving nod of the mainstream that, "Yes, isn't that odd?" or "Isn't she outrageous?" and then move along. But any complex body of thought coupled with social movements against a system as deeply entrenched as patriarchy can't help but produce enough excesses and contradictions to provide opponents with an inexhaustible supply of ammunition. Settling for that, however, accomplishes nothing more than leaving us in the mess we're in, surrounded by familiar stereotypes yet knowing on some level that something is seriously wrong with what patriarchy makes of gender and human life and the world beyond.

Ultimately, either we believe patriarchy exists or we don't. And if we do, we need to know more about feminism, because regardless of what branch of it we might lean toward, feminism is the only ongoing conversation about patriarchy that can lead to a way out. But in the patriarchal mainstream, this is just the problem, because as the following chapters show, there's little there that doesn't make it harder to see patriarchy for what it is.

# Part II
## Sustaining Illusions, Barriers to Change

# 6

# Thinking about Patriarchy:
# War, Sex, and Work

To be part of the solution to patriarchy, we have to think about it in new ways, but to do this we have to work through how we *already* think about it. This is easier said than done, because in many ways what we take to be reality is up for grabs. It's easy to get lost in patriarchy's superficial sideshows, to fixate on male guilt, or "gender roles," or the communication "styles" of "men from Mars" and "women from Venus." Whether we see women and men as different species or as more alike than different is a matter of social definition that's been shaped and reshaped for centuries in an ongoing struggle over the kind of reality we will live in. How we see patriarchy—not to mention whether we see it at all—is no less contentious. Because patriarchy is the status quo, it's easy to see it as normal and unproblematic. Culture provides no end of smoke and mirrors that normalize and shield the status quo from view and criticism. Culture is our main resource for defining what's real, and it cannot help but reflect the experience and interests of groups with the most power and privilege, such as whites, men, and the upper classes.

There's no conspiracy here, for this is how every social system operates. Reality is always being socially constructed. Whatever groups have the most access to and control over resources and institutions through which

reality is shaped—from education to the media to religious dogma to political ideology—will see their views and interests reflected in the results. This
means that those with the biggest stake in changing the world—lower classes,
white women, and people of color—typically have the *fewest* resources and
the most difficult time getting their experience accepted as "real," much less
as a legitimate basis for social criticism and change.

As a social system, patriarchy has an elaborate and thick ideology that
justifies its existence, and this chapter is the first of several that will explore
what it looks like and how it works in everyday life. Perhaps the bedrock of
patriarchal ideology is the belief that it is necessary, socially desirable, and
rooted in a universal sense of tradition and history. Upon this foundation
are built core ideas about social life, especially in relation to the family, war,
economics, reproduction, and sex.

## Patriarchy: Gotta Have It

Central to patriarchy's continued existence is the idea that we can't do without it. As the argument goes, societies have needs that must be met in order to
survive, and these require a division of labor by gender and more power for
men than for women.[1] From this perspective, the stereotypical middle-class
white family ideal, with its homebound housewife and breadwinning husband, makes sense as a way for families and societies to survive because it's
the most efficient way to raise children. It's "efficient" to allocate child care
and other domestic work to wives and mothers and breadwinning to husbands and fathers because under industrial capitalism, family life happens
in one place and work in another, because mothers have a closer physical tie
to children, and so on.[2] David Gilmore uses this approach in his study of
masculinity in tribal societies:

> Manhood ideals make an indispensable contribution both to the con-
> tinuity of social systems and to the psychological integration of men
> into their community. I regard these phenomena not as givens, but
> as part of the existential "problem of order" that all societies must
> solve by encouraging people to act in certain ways, ways that fa-
> cilitate both individual development and group adaptation. Gender
> roles represent one of these problem-solving behaviors.[3]

Gilmore uses an idea that's been around in sociology and anthropology
for quite a while and that has a lot of intuitive appeal—that social life has
a "wholeness" about it. This lends itself to the idea that various aspects
of social life are woven together to form a functioning unit. By itself, this

isn't bad idea. In fact, it's useful for drawing attention to how everything is connected to everything else, how things are usually more complicated than they seem, and how changing one thing touches everything it's connected to. We can see, for example, that while poverty ruins many people's lives, it also benefits others by providing a supply of people who are willing to take jobs that no one else wants. If we get rid of poverty, then we also have to figure out a way to get people to clean motel rooms and do other dirty work that pays poorly and earns workers little respect.

So, looking at societies in terms of form and function certainly has its uses. But the idea that something like patriarchy exists because societies *need* it is something else. In fact, it's nothing but trouble, because while we reassure ourselves that male privilege is a key aspect of society as we know it, we forget to ask what kind of society would need such a thing and whether we ought to be thinking about changing *that*. After all, drug addicts need drugs and alcoholics need alcohol to such a degree that they may die if they suddenly go without. But I haven't heard anyone use this to argue in favor of alcoholism or drug addiction. By definition, every social system is a form of social order that solves the "problem of order" by resisting the universal tendency of things to fall apart.[4] Just because a system exists, however, doesn't mean it's a good thing or has to stay the way it is, or that the particular way that it solves the problem of order is inevitable or necessary. If that were so, then all forms of privilege and oppression would be self-justifying.

When we evaluate some aspect of social life, such as who does what in families or how men and women communicate, it isn't enough to point out that it appears to be an "efficient" way to organize things because it "fits" with society as it is now. We also have to ask how this way of or- ganizing things is connected to other aspects of social life such as women's subordination. We have to ask, for example, how it props up male privilege at women's expense or how it increases women's vulnerability to abuse or economic hardship.

In her books on gender "styles" in communication, Deborah Tannen often asserts that each gender's style makes sense and is legitimate in its own way.[5] Like an anthropologist who is loathe to indulge in ethnocentric criticism of another culture, Tannen is respectful in all directions. But what this misses is that men and women do not come from two different societies, and even if they did, what they do is legitimate only when judged within a particular cultural context. Since that context is patriarchy, what Tannen observes in women and men makes sense only to the extent that we think patriarchy makes sense. If we step back and put things in their larger context and see how style is connected to privilege and its oppressive consequences, how it serves men's power and status interests, it becomes not only possible but incumbent upon us to question their legitimacy and whether this is really how we want life to be. The alternative is the kind of self-justifying spiral that the paralysis around gender inequality has become.

Explaining patriarchy away as useful or necessary has become a popular way to deal with gender inequality. Robert Bly, for example, extols "Zeus energy," which he defines as a "positive male energy that . . . is male authority accepted for the sake of the community . . . in all the great cultures."[6] Leaving aside the question of why Bly would celebrate a god with Zeus's reputation for degrading and raping women,[7] he doesn't explain why *either* gender should be elevated over the other or why it should be men rather than women. Nor does he tell us what the "sake of the community" consists of, or what makes patriarchal cultures—and only patriarchal cultures—"great." Such lack of clarity serves patriarchy well by making male privilege more acceptable, serving a greater good that couldn't possibly contribute to something as awful as oppression. It also lends itself to mythological allusions that abound in such visions of patriarchy. Consider, for example, how Bly describes "genuine patriarchy":

> The patriarchy is a complicated structure. Mythologically, it is matriarchal on the inside; and a matriarchy is equally complicated, being patriarchal on the inside. The political structure has to resemble our interior structure. And we know each man has a woman inside him and each woman has a man inside her.
>
> The genuine patriarchy brings down the sun through the Sacred King, into every man and woman in the culture; and the genuine matriarchy brings down the moon, through the Sacred Queen, to every woman and every man in the culture. The death of the Sacred King and Queen means that we live now in a system of industrial domination, which is not patriarchy.[8]

As is typical of such arguments, Bly explains none of this. Not only does he portray men and women as split in two, but when he tells us that social systems must mirror the individual psyche, he ignores most of what we've learned from sociology, anthropology, and even psychology about societies, individuals, and how they are related. He goes on to imply that "genuine patriarchy" can somehow coexist with its counterpart, "genuine matriarchy," to everyone's benefit, but in this he ignores what the terms actually mean. By definition, patriarchy is fundamentally about power and *is distinguished from* matriarchy in the elevation of fathers and men over mothers and women, just as matriarchy—which, as far as we know, has never existed[9]—would subordinate fathers and men to mothers and women.

This kind of thinking also ignores the highly *un*-mythological day-to-day realities of patriarchal privilege and oppression. Bly, for example, blames "industrial domination" for the death of the Sacred King and Queen and the demise of "genuine patriarchy." Long before the Industrial Revolution, however, this supposedly golden era of "genuine patriarchy" produced an abundance of oppression, including medieval witch burnings, chronic warfare, and the class oppression of feudalism. Exhibiting a limited sense of history, Bly also ignores the connection between the emergence of industrial capitalism and the high value patriarchy places on control, competition, and domination.

In other words, industrial capitalism didn't come out of the blue and "do in" patriarchy. Instead, it was and is an economic expression of core patriarchal values that are more powerful today than ever. The problem with Bly's reasoning is that he uses the term *patriarchy* to name a mythical society that never existed. He then tells us that "genuine patriarchy" was destroyed by very unmythical social forces such as industrialization. This implies either that patriarchy (and with it, male privilege and the oppression of women) no longer exists, or that now we are stuck with a "false patriarchy." In either case, he suggests that some form of benevolent male privilege is not only possible, but something whose passing is cause for mourning and regret.

In another widely read book on men, Sam Keen suggests that patriarchy was an adaptive part of human social evolution that "saved" humankind from the gynocentrism of early goddess-oriented societies. Before patriarchy, Keen writes, societies labored under a "servitude to nature" that was broken by "the transcendent male God" who "sanctioned the development of individualism and the technological impulse to seize control and have dominion over the earth."[10] This rebellion—and, presumably, the ascendancy of masculine gods and men—was supposedly fomented by women and men alike. Given how much women had to lose, this doesn't make a lot of sense unless we want to resurrect the idea of female masochism. Like many new men's movement writers, Keen implies that patriarchy and its male-identified principle of control were an upward leap in social evolution, to be regretted only for their limited success and fleeting glory:

> This God, who stands above the fatedness of nature, commands men to stand above nature and society *and woman* and take charge of his own destiny. . . . Life in the garden of the goddess was harmonious but the spirit of history called for man to stand up and take charge. . . . [I]t is easy to forget the triumph of that moment when men rebelled against their fate, threw off their passivity, and declared: Thank you, Mother, but I can do it myself.[11] [emphasis added]

Keen uses some peculiar reasoning here. He argues both that men and women participated in evolutionary rebellion as equals, and that it was men who rejected women (Mother) and ascended to a dominant position over women, nature, society, domestic animals, coal reserves, and all the rest. He links "harmony" with "passivity" for no apparent reason and perpetuates the patriarchal idea that the only alternative to passivity is domination and aggression. And in the spirit of Bly's mythological haze, Keen invokes vague magical forces such as the "spirit of history" (*whose* history?) to explain a complex social transformation brought about by real people. Although Keen goes on to argue that this new order has now "outlived its usefulness," he leaves undisturbed the idea that patriarchy delivered us all from the menacing throes of gynocentric "harmony" run amok.

Keen is right in step with patriarchal ideology when he aligns women with nature and against men and civilization, and suggests that true human progress occurs only among men and then only through rebellious separation from the "mother," or, as Bly puts it, "a revolt against the earthly, conservative, possessive, clinging part of the maternal feminine."[12] By default, women and mothers stunt individual development and social progress, which means they must be controlled so that men can be free to pursue masculine individualism and control. Keen's description of our "servitude to nature" stands reality on its head, as if servitude, hierarchy, control, exploitation, and oppression are inventions of nature and not of patriarchal society. But in Keen's and Bly's scheme of things, women, not nature, are the real problem, getting in the way of patriarchal manhood's fullest expression.

## Warfare: Defending Hearth and Home

A key defense of patriarchy invokes the mysteries of warfare as crucial to understanding the "natural" gender order. As the argument goes, men must be aggressive and develop a capacity for violence in order to defend society and family.[13] As Keen puts it, sacrifice is at the center of men's lives as they put the welfare of others above their own: "Most men went to war, shed blood, and sacrificed their lives with the conviction that it was the only way to defend those whom they loved.... [S]hort of a utopian world... someone must be prepared to take up arms and do battle with evil."[14] The violent-man-as-protector image is connected to patriarchy through the idea that men's capacity for violence and aggression inevitably leads to male dominance over women, children, and property, since men must be more powerful than those they protect.[15] "Men... must be manly," David Gilmore tells us, "because warfare demands it."[16] But it is no less reasonable to also argue that warfare itself exists because patriarchal manliness and its related structures of control and dominance demand *it*.

There are two major problems with using warfare to justify patriarchy. First, romantic images of war don't fit much of what we know of it. The idea that men are motivated primarily by self-sacrifice, for example, doesn't square with the high value patriarchal cultures place on male autonomy and freedom. According to Keen, autonomy and independence, not self-sacrifice for women and children, were a key to the patriarchal rebellion against goddess religions and men's "servitude to nature."

The warfare argument for patriarchy also fits poorly with the reality of warfare as most people experience it. I don't know which wars Keen has in mind, but most that I can think of were fought for anything but defense of loved ones, and men in privileged racial and economic classes— who presumably love their families as much as the next man—have been all too willing to allow those less fortunate than they to serve in their place.

Was it love that motivated the endless bloodshed of the Roman conquests, the slaughter of countless religious wars and crusades, the Napoleonic wars, the U.S. Civil War, or the two world wars? Was it to protect women and children that the United States "liberated" the Philippines from the Spanish following the Spanish–American war and then brutally suppressed Philippine resistance to becoming a U.S. colony and gateway to Asian markets? Was it for the sake of hearth and home that U.S. soldiers went to Korea, Vietnam, Grenada, Panama, and Iraq, or Soviet troops to Afghanistan? Does love of family explain the ethnic slaughter in Eastern Europe and the brutality of civil wars from Cambodia to Somalia to El Salvador?

It would seem not. Closer to the truth is that war allows men to reaffirm their masculine standing in relation to other men, to act out patriarchal ideals of physical courage and aggression, and to avoid being shamed and ridiculed by other men for refusing to join in the fight. As Keen himself tells us, war is "a heroic way for an individual to make a name for himself" and to "practice heroic virtues."[17] It is an opportunity for men to bond with other men—friend and foe alike—and reaffirm their common masculine warrior codes. If war was simply about self-sacrifice in the face of monstrous enemies who threaten men's loved ones, how do we make sense of the long tradition of respect between wartime enemies, the codes of "honor" that bind them together even as they bomb and devastate civilian populations that consist primarily of women and children? Could soldiers fighting only out of such lofty motives as love for home and hearth accumulate such an extensive and consistent record of gratuitous rape and other forms of torture, abuse, and wanton violence inflicted on civilian populations?[18] Certainly there are men who go to war with the sense of self-sacrificing mission that Keen describes, but to attribute warfare as a system to such altruistic motives is the kind of romantic thinking that warfare thrives on. In spite of the horrible price that many men pay for their participation in war, we shouldn't confuse the fact of their *being* sacrificed with self-sacrificing personal motivations, especially when trying to explain why warfare exists as a social phenomenon.

The second problem with using warfare to explain male aggression and patriarchal dominance is that it's a circular argument. As much as we like to divide the world into good guys and bad guys, every nation going to war sees itself as justified in defending what it defines as the good. Each side believes in and glorifies the use of male-identified armed force to resolve disputes and uphold deeply held principles, from the glory of Allah to ethnic or racial purity to spreading democracy and defending against terrorism or defeating imperialism. Even the most reluctant government may welcome a breakdown of negotiations that will justify using force (unless they think they'll lose), and it has become commonplace for national leaders to use war as a way to galvanize public support for their regimes, especially in election years. The heroic male figure of western gun-slinging cowboys is almost always portrayed as peace-loving and unwilling to use violence "unless he has to." But the whole point of his heroism and the story is the audience *wanting* him to "have to." The spouses, children, territory, honor, and various underdogs who are defended with heroic violence serve as excuses for the violent demonstration of a particular version of patriarchal manhood. They aren't of central importance, which is why their experience is rarely the focus of attention.

The real interest lies in the male hero and his relation to other men—as victor or vanquished, as good guy or bad guy. Indeed, the hero is often the only one who remains intact (or mostly so) at the end of the story. The raped wife, slaughtered family, and ruined community get lost in the shuffle, with only passing attention to their suffering as it echoes across generations with no mention of how they've been used as a foil for patriarchal masculine heroism. Note, however, that when female characters take on such heroic roles, as in *Thelma and Louise*, the social response is ambivalent if not hostile. Many people complained that the villains in *Thelma and Louise* made men look bad, but I've never heard anyone complain that the villains in male-heroic movies make men look bad. It seems that we have yet another double standard: It's acceptable to portray some men as villainous but only if it serves to highlight the heroism of other men.

To support male aggression and therefore male dominance as society's only defense against evil, we have to believe that evil forces exist "out there," in villains, governments, and armies. In this, we have to assume that the bad guys actually see themselves as evil and not as heroes defending loved ones and principles against bad guys like us. The alternative to this kind of thinking is to realize that the same patriarchal ethos that creates our masculine heroes also creates the violent villains they battle and prove themselves against, and that both sides often see themselves as heroic and self-sacrificing for a worthy cause. For all the wartime propaganda, good and bad guys play similar games and salute a core of common values, not to mention one another on occasion. At a deep level, war and many other forms of male aggression are *manifestations* of the same evil they supposedly defend against. That evil is the patriarchal religion of control and domination that encourages men to use coercion and violence to settle disputes, manage human relations, and affirm masculine identity.

None of this criticism means that men can't feel compelled to sacrifice themselves. It also doesn't mean there's no place for ferocity in the face of danger, as the females of many species, including our own, demonstrate in defense of their young. But as we saw in Chapter 2, there is a difference between patriarchy as a system and the personal motivations of the people who participate in it. When a man goes off to war, that man may feel full of love for family and community, but this doesn't explain why warfare exists as a social institution or what compels men to march off to it.

In similar ways, men may put family needs before their own simply out of love, but this happens *in spite of* a patriarchal system that encourages them to value their competitive masculine standing above all else. How else do we explain the men who abandon families rather than work at jobs they consider "beneath them" and leave behind wives who are far less reluctant to do whatever is necessary to support their children? How else do we understand men who insist on "sacrificing" themselves only in ways that tend to impress other men? I suspect that most men would rather work overtime or fight another man, for example, than diaper babies or risk true emotional intimacy, *even if the latter provided loved ones with what they needed most.* The patriarchal path of least resistance for a man whose wife is raped isn't to take care of her, but to wreak heroic revenge on the rapist, an act that, if anything, makes things worse for her. But in a patriarchy, her well-being is secondary to his rights and standing as a man in relation to other men. In this sense, the rapist does more than assault a woman, for he also violates a man's proprietary rights of sexual access and casts doubt on that man's ability to defend his sexual property against other men. The husband's revenge uses violence in true patriarchal fashion to reestablish his masculine rights and standing in relation not only to the rapist, but to men in general.

When we romanticize patriarchy or define it as noble and socially necessary, we blind ourselves to what's going on and paralyze our capacity to work for change. In truth, patriarchy is everywhere, from family, sexuality, and reproduction to global politics and economic production, and not seeing it won't save us from its consequences.

## Things Aren't What They Used to Be, and They Never Were: Gender, Work, and Who Depends on Whom

To account for patriarchy's past, it helps to see how it works now. It's easy to get it wrong—to shroud patriarchy in a haze of "tradition," to ignore its connection to industrial capitalism, religion, or warfare, or simply to deny its existence altogether. Robert Bly, for example, organizes a lot of *Iron John* around a longing for a lost pre-industrial, pre-urban era of maleness in which older men passed along to younger men the precious secret essence of being men in the world: "During the nineteenth century, grandfathers and uncles lived in the house, and older men mingled a great deal. Through hunting parties, in work that men did together in farms and cottages, and through local sports, older men spent much time with younger men and brought knowledge of male spirit and soul to them."[19]

Bly and Keen get almost wistful about the supposed loss of traditional visions of manhood. "Old male bonding rituals—sports, war, business, woman bashing, drinking, hunting—are *no longer sufficient or appropriate*" (emphasis added).[20] Neither, however, seems curious to dig beneath the surface of this supposedly golden era when men knew who they were and liked it. What, for example, did "knowledge of the male spirit and soul" *consist* of? What was its content, and how did men actually live it in relation to women, children, and other men? If there was a time when such things as war, drinking, and woman bashing *were* "sufficient and appropriate," just what kind of times were those? Bly refers often to a pre-industrial, agrarian past in which men owned land and felt as rooted in themselves as they did in the land. What he doesn't ask about is women in such societies, their lack of civil rights, their devalued status, or how they were often numbered among a man's possessions and defended against other men—along with the land, cattle, sheep, and other domestic livestock that men "husbanded"—as part of fulfilling patriarchal manhood.

This kind of selective history generalizes from one period to the whole of human experience, as if things are now the way they've always been. It's become cliché, for example, to refer to breadwinning as men's "traditional" role, and unproductive "domestic chores"—including childbearing and child rearing—as women's. Men's Rights advocate Warren Farrell, for example, divides history into two stages, with the entire human experience prior to World War II lumped into one of them. During this period, he tells us, and presumably across all known cultures, things were pretty simple: "the woman raised the children, and the man raised the money" and saved the woman and children from starvation. Women did little more than produce children who consumed the food men provided.[21] In his cross-cultural study of masculinity, David Gilmore echoes Farrell by portraying women in nonindustrial societies as little more than passive performers of insignificant tasks whose main function is to free men to do the real work of providing for families:

> Work defines manhood, but not just work as energy spent but as labor that supports life, constructive labor. . . .Hunting provides more than food alone; it also furnishes tools and clothing as well as critical ritual and religious materials. . . . [T]he Mbuti too have an image of . . . manhood [that] connects directly with male prowess in securing food, clothing, and magical objects for the group.[22]

This kind of imagery is used as easily with modern industrial societies as with hunting and gathering tribes. Men, Keen and Farrell tell us, are known for their willingness to work even when they're tired or don't like the job, an observation that underlies the rueful joke that men have three choices in life—work, work, and work. As Anthony Astrachan argues, this means that technological change and the most recent influx of women into the workplace radically shifts the lives of men, who historically "grew up expecting to provide for themselves and for their family. . . . A 'man's job' once required skill, strength, and the ability to work long hours—all admirable qualities that used to be thought of as exclusively male."[23]

If hard work, providing, and "breadwinning" define manhood, and if manhood exists, by definition, in contrast to womanhood, then it's hard not to conclude that women don't work and never have. If we extend Gilmore's and Astrachan's observations just a bit further, women's labor hasn't been notably constructive, life-supporting, or difficult, and men somehow found a way to hunt for clothing, pottery, housing, bread, bedding, healing herbs, utensils, religious objects, and all the other goods that women have produced over the millennia through their vision, skill, and hard work. Gilmore tells us that the cultural ideals of manhood are necessary to force men to perform the critical providing function, which, it seems, women cannot handle. Farrell makes a similar assertion about the "protecting" function.[24] Without men, we'd all starve, freeze, or be devoured by wild beasts.

That such ridiculous notions persist and seem to have little trouble finding a receptive audience says a lot about the power of social mythology and ideology to shape beliefs and perceptions.[25] Even today, women perform an estimated two thirds of the economically productive work in the world, provide almost half of the food, and yet receive only 10 percent of all income and own only 1 percent of property.[26] In horticultural societies in which most food is grown in small, hand-worked gardens rather than large plowed fields, the imbalance has been even more lopsided, with women providing most food and other essentials, often including the building of houses.[27] In spite of this, however, women's labor is largely invisible, especially as recorded by modern economics. As Marilyn Waring shows, United Nations accounting systems assign economic value only to what is traded in cash markets, a standard that excludes an enormous amount of the work that women do.[28] Water carried through a pipeline and sold at the other end, for example, is counted as part of a country's gross national product. But the labor of women who walk for several miles each day to carry water to their homes isn't counted:

> A young, middle-class North American housewife spends her days preparing food, setting the table, serving meals, clearing food and dishes from the table, washing dishes, dressing and diapering her children, disciplining children, taking the children to day-care or to school, disposing of garbage, dusting, gathering clothes for washing, doing the laundry, going to the gas station and the supermarket, re-pairing household items, ironing, keeping an eye on or playing with the children, making beds, paying bills, caring for pets and plants, putting away toys, books, and clothes, sewing or mending or knit-ting, talking with door-to-door salespeople, answering the telephone, vacuuming, sweeping, and washing floors, cutting the grass, weed-ing, and shoveling snow, cleaning the bathroom and the kitchen, and putting her children to bed. [She] has to face the fact that she fills her time in a *totally* unproductive manner. She...is economically inactive, and economists record her as unoccupied.[29]

This is how Farrell can make the mistake of seeing women through the ages as economically unproductive dependents "supported for life" by their husbands and other men. When he describes men as "raising money" while women raise children, he ignores the fact that money has been an important factor in economic life for only a tiny portion of human existence in his pre-World War II stage. The cash market is a recent invention, prior to which people largely consumed what they produced and bartered the rest.

In portraying men as the primary providers, patriarchal culture promotes seeing men as independent, autonomous, and self-sufficient and women as dependent on them, as if women were large children. Historically, however, the only way that most men and women could survive was to work together in economically productive families. In hunting and gathering societies, for example, men may have ranged far and wide in search of game, but with-out women, there wouldn't have been much to come home to—no shelter, clothing, pottery, or cooking or other implements, nor, for that matter, enough food to live on, since meat has usually been a supplemental source of protein for essentially vegetarian societies.

The capitalist Industrial Revolution transformed the close economic interdependency between men and women so profoundly that it *seemed* to disappear altogether. This happened through a system in which, for the first time in history, goods were produced primarily for sale in cash-driven markets. Most people became employees who sold their time in exchange for wages, not independent workers who produced goods primarily for consumption by themselves and their families. This meant that people lost control over work and production, but it also meant they could rely on cash earnings to support themselves and live independently of families. Children no longer depended on inheriting a portion of a family farm but instead could leave home and find jobs. This was especially true for middle- and upper-class white men, whose gender, race, and class privilege and freedom from child care and other domestic work enabled them to shape the emerging political economy to accommodate themselves and largely exclude women. As a result, married women became economically dependent on men *for the first time in human history.*

As men took over the cash economy, earning power not surprisingly became the only legitimate measure of productivity, worth, and independence, with the result that most women were defined as economically dependent "nonworkers." But if we think of production and economic value in terms of providing people with what they need, then it's clear that women have always worked, and husbands and wives have never stopped being economically interdependent. A woman who shops for food and prepares and serves meals for her family, for example, is just as engaged in productive work as any restaurant worker, and she plays a key role in making it possible for other workers to sustain themselves and perform paid labor. Even when only the husband works for pay, women sustain families as much as, if not more than, men do.

The reality of marital interdependency, however, is masked by cultural beliefs about men's and women's economic roles. As women's domestic labor has been devalued and redefined as nonwork, it has also been made socially invisible, resulting in images of women as dependent, passive, unproductive, and primarily concerned with child care and "chores" (what women's work is typically called when done by other household members). In its most extreme form, such imagery produces the culturally despised "welfare mother" who, to judge by popular mythology, sits around all day indulging herself at public expense, when reality is closer to a numbing daily grind full of deprivation, worry, struggle, and despair.

The devaluing of women's work is, of course, complemented by images of men as hard-working, self-sufficient, autonomous, and even heroic bread-winners who carry on their shoulders the sole burden of family support. Most men do work hard, of course, and many feel burdened by it. But this doesn't mean that women don't also work hard or that the taking on of this kind of adult responsibility has somehow become the sole province of men.[30]

Cultural mythology is often used in this way to distort what goes on between subordinate and dominant groups. It enables dominant groups to avoid seeing how much they depend on others to perform disagreeable labor in return for the low wages that help make privilege possible. Members of the upper class, for example, typically are portrayed as "wealth producers," the ones who build buildings, bridges, and empires, even though most of the work is performed by others, by "little people" who pay taxes and often live lives of chronic anxiety about making ends meet. Donald Trump, we're told, "built" Trump Tower, just as turn-of-the-century robber barons "built" the railroads and steel mills that made vast personal fortunes possible. Entire nations also indulge in this kind of magical thinking. In the United States, for example, we rarely realize how much Third World poverty subsidizes our standard of living. We like to believe that our affordable abundance is solely our own doing, unaware of how much it has always depended on a steady supply of cheap labor and raw materials provided by countries in which most of the world's population lives in poverty.

Part of what makes such mental magic possible is confusion between independence and autonomy. Dominant groups are generally autonomous in the sense that they aren't accountable to those below them and don't have to ask for permission to do what they want. This doesn't make dominant groups *independent*, however. The upper class may not be accountable to the working class, but their lives would fall apart without working-class labor. In similar ways, when men aspire to autonomy in relation to women, they're not looking for independence. They aren't trying to live without using women to meet their needs. What autonomy means to many men is the privilege to do what they want *and* get their needs and wants met.

It's a relationship that looks a lot like what many teenagers try to have with parents, except that teenagers, being relatively powerless, usually don't get away with it. Dominant groups, however, have the advantage of far greater control over how reality gets defined and can use this to mask what's going on. The truth that most men depend on women—in many ways far more than women depend on men—is routinely covered up or trivialized. When men do acknowledge their dependency, especially in relation to sex, they often do so resentfully, as if women should be so accessible that men wouldn't experience their need for women as dependency at all. In this way, women are expected to act like the accomplished servant who plays the provider role without ever making the masters aware of how dependent on the servant they really are. At its most successful, the perception is just the opposite—that it's the upper classes who "take care of" their servants, the slave masters who bear the burden of caring for their slaves, and the husbands who "provide" for wives and children.

On some level, of course, both women and men know how men depend on the domestic and caring work that women perform. Men eat the food that women buy and prepare for them, slide into bed and feel the clean, freshly changed sheets that have been laid out for them, accept caring when they're sick, grieving, or in despair, take emotional support when they feel doubt or fear; and benefit from countless other things that sustain them. But when men acknowledge need, they make themselves vulnerable, which under patriarchy is threatening for men to do, especially within sight of other men. As a result, men and, to some degree, the women who share lives with them often feel compelled to maintain a pretense of dependent women and independent men.

In this way, patriarchal culture makes it difficult to see the profound *inter*dependence that's always been at the core of gender relationships. Even stickier is patriarchal thinking about heterosexuality, a key to human life that's become a linchpin of male privilege.

## Sex in the Patriarchy

One thing that makes gender issues difficult to deal with is that they often seem so *natural* that they aren't something we can make choices about. This is especially true of sexuality, which we tend to see as entirely rooted in nature, embedded in emotion and body, and so immediate that it's hard to imagine how it could be shaped by something as remote as society. Surely something like orgasm isn't a social invention. But that doesn't mean sexuality is all hard-wired biology unshaped by the conditions of social life.

As the species with the big brain, we can't separate how we perceive and experience sexuality from how we *think* about it. And how we think about it is so tied up with the society we live in that we can't talk about "sexuality" as having some kind of pure existence independent of society.[31] What we take to be "normal" human sexuality is actually a set of cultural ideas about sexuality, and as such we have to ask how these ideas are shaped and how they affect life and our experience of it. Less than two centuries ago, for example, "good" women weren't supposed to enjoy sex, much less have orgasms, and were sometimes subjected to clitoridectomies in order to "cure" them of an "excessive" interest in it. Today, however, healthy women are supposed to have multiple orgasms and might think there's something wrong with themselves or their partners if they don't.

How we think about heterosexuality is key to patriarchy because *ideas about gender are at the core of patriarchy, and heterosexuality and gender are defined in terms of each other.* Whether a man is considered a real man, for example, or whether a woman is considered a real and legitimate woman depends on their sexual feelings, behavior, and relationships. In particular, as defined in most Western cultures, "real" women and men are exclusively heterosexual. The definition of a "man" is so bound up with being hetero-sexual that gay men are routinely accused of not being men at all. This is also why lesbians are often likened to men because they, like "real men," are sexually oriented to women. Since "real men" and "real women" are by definition heterosexual, anyone who is gay, lesbian, or bisexual is stigma-tized as a deviant outsider who threatens the status quo and doesn't deserve a socially legitimate identity. As such, they are suspect and vulnerable to ostracism, discrimination, and abuse.

Heterosexuals, however, can move through the world as socially legit-imate men or women. They have the privilege of being able to assume ac-ceptance as "normal" members of society, express physical affection with their partners in public, refer openly to their private lives, live in a world full of cultural images that confer a sense of legitimacy and social desirability, and live without fear that others will find out who they are. All of this is a form of privilege because it is systematically denied to gays, lesbians, and bisexuals.[32] As with most forms of privilege, heterosexuals take it so much for granted that they don't experience it as privilege at all. It's just the way things are. But, as Charlotte Bunch points out, it wouldn't take much for heterosexuals to realize just how much their privilege amounts to: "[I]f you don't have a sense of what privilege is, I suggest that you go home and an-nounce to everybody that you know—a roommate, your family, the people you work with—that you're a queer. Try being queer for a week."[33]

Under patriarchy, cultural ideals of masculine manhood and feminine womanhood are organized on a heterosexual model. This means that a real man is someone who can act out core patriarchal values by orienting himself to the task of controlling sexual access to women. He makes it clear, especially to other men, that he has a sexual interest in women and does nothing to shake the presumption that he can act on that interest and get what he wants. A real woman is one who accepts and relates to men on these terms, who subordinates her reality and sense of self to male control (such as by having sex whether she wants to or not) and defines sex from a masculine point of view. As Marilyn Frye suggests, from a patriarchal perspective, "having sex" typically means sexual intercourse through which the man has an orgasm, and his orgasms are the measure of how many times "it" has occurred.[34] As such, whether her orgasms are real or faked or whether she even enjoyed herself is largely beside the point of whether they've actually "had sex," although this may reflect on his sexual performance (i.e., control) and, hence, his masculine standing.

The patriarchal form of heterosexuality is male dominated, male identified, male centered and organized around an obsession with control. As such, its social significance goes beyond sexuality per se, because it also serves as a general model for male dominance and for dominance and aggression in general. Whether the authority figure is a father, lover, husband, or employer, the underlying dynamic of control typically involves cultural themes tied to sexuality in one way or another. The common expression, "Fuck you!" for example, heterosexualizes aggression by identifying the aggressor with men who fuck and the object of aggression with women who are fucked. Similarly, being hurt or taken advantage of is often linked to heterosexual imagery, as in "I've been screwed," "had," "taken," or "fucked."[35] The language of warfare is full of heterosexual imagery, from ditties chanted by recruits in basic training ("This is my rifle, this [my penis] is my gun; this is for fighting, this is for fun") to high command metaphors for nuclear destruction such as "going all the way" and "wargasm."[36]

Power is also heterosexualized, as in "screwing the competition," the use of "fucking" as an adjective indicating something of awesome proportions (as in "fucking fantastic"), or the idea that men have the right to sexualize all women, including employees, co-workers, strangers on the street, and daughters.[37] There is a popular romanticized notion that fathers should guard the sexual integrity of their daughters and maintain their own proprietary interest until they turn it over, reluctantly and sometimes with displays of jealousy, to husbands. The film *Father of the Bride*, for example, shows how far a father will go to act out jealousy over his daughter's impending marriage. We're supposed to take this as cute foolishness in spite of its clear basis in cultural images of daughters as romantic sexual property, images rooted in core patriarchal ideas about heterosexuality and its relation to male privilege and women's oppression.

Patriarchy isn't the only kind of society in which sexuality is socially shaped and defined. In every society, the human potential for sexual feeling, experience, and behavior is constructed and regulated in one way or another. Everywhere people are socialized to see themselves, other people, and sexuality in certain ways. They're taught what to expect, how to interpret sensations and feelings, and how to identify what's considered appropriate and with whom. But when power and privilege are added to the mix, the universal practice of shaping sexuality as a social reality takes on much greater significance. The major actors in heterosexuality are female and male, and women and men are also main points of reference for defining patriarchy as a system. This means that how we view heterosexuality will have a profound effect on how we view patriarchy. If we treat the patriarchal version of heterosexuality as "natural," we'll treat *patriarchy* as "natural," and if patriarchy is seen as natural, then criticism of it will be taken as an affront to human nature and our deepest sense of who we are. It's in this way that patriarchal heterosexuality serves as what Catharine MacKinnon calls the "linchpin of gender inequality."[38]

Seeing patriarchal heterosexuality as the linchpin of gender inequality seems to contradict a longstanding feminist argument that women are oppressed primarily through the demands of motherhood. In pre-industrial patriarchies, for example, if breastfeeding requires mothers to stay close to home, they can't participate in activities such as hunting and warfare that are tied to status and power. In industrial patriarchies, the greatest barrier to women's advancement in the workplace is conflict between work and childcare roles. Historically, however, the oppressive consequences of motherhood may be less than they seem. As we saw earlier, raising children in pre-industrial societies has never prevented women from participating fully in production, often producing more than half of necessary goods and services.

Motherhood has been more limiting under industrial capitalism, where the physical separation of work and home forces women to choose between caring for children and working outside the home. Even this, however, hasn't meant much to working- and lower-class women, most of whom routinely work both inside and outside the home. This has been especially true of women of color who perform domestic work for white women during the day and then go home at night to care for their own families. Mothering thus keeps women in their place primarily in a limited economic sense that may be a relatively short-lived and class-bound phenomenon as the percentage of middle-class mothers in the labor force continues to rise.

A stronger explanation of women's subordination isn't their relation to children but to men, beginning with fathers and extending to husbands and other male authority figures. As Miriam Johnson argues, the socialization that goes on between fathers and daughters centers more on preparing daughters to be good wives than to be good mothers. And it's a relationship often charged with romantic heterosexual ideals (as in *Father of the Bride*) that are much less likely to be found between mothers and sons. It's quite acceptable for a daughter to be a "daddy's girl," for example, but a curse for a son to be called a "mama's boy."

This double standard is tied to cultural ambivalence about father–daughter incest. There's little ambivalence, however, about mother–son incest, which, as Johnson argues, may be prohibited not for deep psychosexual reasons but because a sexual relationship between a male and a more powerful woman violates core patriarchal values.[39] To get a vivid sense of what this means, try to imagine the box-office appeal of a movie entitled *Mother of the Groom*. In *Father of the Bride*, the man is the subject, and although it's a comedy, he's not portrayed as dangerous to his daughter's well-being, only carried away by what are regarded as appropriate feelings of jealousy. Movies that portray mothers with obsessive attachments to married sons, however, are still male-centered but now regard the parent as neurotic and destructive in ways unlikely to be viewed as funny.

The subordination of wives is supported by a host of cultural beliefs and expectations such as valuing her husband's work and needs above her own or defining and judging her sexuality in relation to his experience and needs. When men want sex more often than women, the difference is usually interpreted as indicating something wrong with women but not with men. Men may feel deprived, angry, rejected, confused, or hurt, but patriarchal culture doesn't encourage them to feel guilty or sexually flawed because of it. They may feel pressure to change by being more tolerant, sensitive, or understanding of women, but this doesn't alter the perception of women and *their* sexuality—not men and theirs—as problematic and thereby needing tolerance and understanding.

Women, however, are more likely to attribute differences in sexual rhythm, desire, or forms of expression entirely to themselves and feel responsible for doing something about it, such as by agreeing to have sex more often or in ways they don't like. Fittingly, the English language includes well-known terms such as "frigidity" for women who are reluctant to have sex with men when and how men want it, but nothing in most people's vocabulary identifies men with excessive sexual desire.[40] As with so much else in patriarchal systems, standards against which "normal" human experience is defined and evaluated are male identified and male centered.

The kind of patriarchal heterosexuality we live with is one version of a universal phenomenon, for every culture has ideas about sexuality and the forms it can take, from heterosexual to bisexual to lesbian and gay to polymorphous eroticism, from egalitarian pleasuring to sado-masochism, from sacred ritual to profane recreation. At its heart, the problem with patriarchal sexuality is how it joins sexuality with control, dominance, and, therefore, violence as a means for achieving both. For years, many feminists in the antiviolence movement denied this by arguing that sexual violence is solely about power and not about sex. This overlooks, however, the possibility that, under patriarchy, violence is about power *and* sex.

This could mean that sex and power operate as two independent motivations (sexual violence as "sex + power"). On a deeper level, however, it's important to see how patriarchal culture defines mainstream sexuality *in terms of* power and male privilege, and how power and male dominance are routinely conceived in sexual terms. All of this means it's hard to participate in heterosexual relations without issues of power coming up, or to deal in power without invoking sexual imagery. If we deny this linkage to avoid seeing how sexuality has been contaminated with the potential for violence, we can't see the problem for what it truly is or what needs to be changed.

What's true of sexual violence is also true of pornography, which carries its own load of cultural confusion and ambivalence. To many feminists, pornography is the "theory" on which the "practice" of sexual violence is based.[41] As John Stoltenberg argues, pornography reveals the connection between patriarchal oppression, on the one hand, and cultural ideas about sexuality on the other:[42]

> Male-supremacist sexuality is important to pornography, and pornography is important to male supremacy. Pornography *institutionalizes* the sexuality that both embodies and enacts male supremacy. Pornography says about that sexuality, . . . Here's how to act out male supremacy in sex. . . . Here are the acts that impose power over and against another body. And pornography says about that action, . . . Here's who you should do it to and here's who she is: your whore, your piece of ass, yours. Your penis is a weapon; her body is your target. And pornography says about that sexuality, "Here's why": Because men are masters, women are slaves; men are superior, women are subordinate; men are real, women are objects; men are sex machines, women are sluts. . . . Pornography also *eroticizes* male supremacy. It makes dominance and subordination feel like sex; it makes hierarchy feel like sex; it makes force and violence feel like sex; it makes hate and terrorism feel like sex; it makes inequality feel like sex.[43]

It's no wonder there's so much confusion—especially among men—about the difference between abusive and nonabusive sex, about what sexual harassment is and isn't, about how to reconcile the need for intimacy with patriarchal paths of least resistance leading toward domination. The more invested men are in patriarchal masculinity, the more they value being in control and detached from their feelings and vulnerability. Vulnerability and feeling are rooted in the body, which means that in taking men away from their feelings, the pursuit of masculinity also takes them away from a sense of connection with their own bodies.

In this sense, patriarchy encourages men to leave behind their sense of themselves as *embodied* sexual beings. Masculine heterosexuality becomes something outside men's own bodies, to seek, "get," and control as a commodity or prize buried in and controlled by women. Men are encouraged to see sexuality as something women have and men don't, and therefore as a source of women's power over men and an occasion for male resentment, rage, and aggression. This can reduce men's sexual lives to a choice between chronic sexual deprivation and finding ways to buy, earn, win, seduce, or seize it. It can set men up to feel responsible for women's sexual pleasure—always under pressure to perform to women's satisfaction—as a way to demonstrate the artistry of masculine control. It's also a way to earn access to the sexuality women supposedly possess and give in carefully measured portions to deserving men. All of this may be the closest many men can get to a genuine sense of connection to their own sense of being alive as sexual beings.[44]

It's also no wonder that so many men and women can be involved as victims or victimizers in sexual coercion, abuse, harassment, or violence without seeing it for what it is. And no wonder there's so much confusion about the difference between the erotic and the pornographic, so that those who attack the latter are often accused of having hang-ups about the former.[45] In an important sense, it's true that those who condemn pornography *are* anti-sex, not "sex" in a generic sense, but patriarchy's oppressive brand of it.[46]

To find a way out of patriarchy, we have to deal with the powerful social connection that links gender and sexuality with core patriarchal values. Perhaps here, more than any other area of human life, male privilege is *embodied* in ways that make it difficult to see beyond our seemingly natural experience of sexuality to what's really happening and what it has to do with us. For this and all the other forms of myth and misperception that cloud our vision, we need to realize that we aren't simply prisoners of a socially constructed reality. Reality is being constructed and reconstructed all the time, and the part we play in that, however small and unconscious, gives us the chance and the responsibility to choose in ways that might make a difference.

# 7

# What Patriarchy?

**P**erhaps the most efficient way to keep patriarchy going is to promote the idea that it doesn't exist in the first place. Patriarchy, we might say, is just a figment of angry feminist imagination. Or, if it does exist, it's by reputation only, a shadow of its former self that no longer amounts to much in people's lives. To pull this off, you have to be willing to engage in a lot of denial, but you can also use some key supporting arguments—that patriarchy doesn't exist because many women seem better off than many men, that the generally miserable lot of the modern man contradicts the idea of male privilege, that women and men are each affected by parallel versions of a common oppression, and that men and women are equal co-creators of every aspect of social life, including patriarchy. This mind-numbing mixture serves patriarchy well by leading us in every direction but the one that counts— toward a clear understanding of what's really going on.

## Now You See Him, Now You Don't: The Paradox of Male Invisibility

A key to maintaining male privilege is to devalue women by making them and what they do invisible. This happens, for example, when cleaning the house or taking care of children is viewed as "nonwork," or when a woman's ideas are ignored, only to be noticed and adopted when suggested by a man. But social life is full of paradox, for men are also made invisible in important ways. As is usually the case with dominant groups, however, invisibility, rather than working against their interests, works *for* them.

One way this works is through the male-identified aspect of patriarchy itself. Because patriarchal culture designates men and masculinity as the standard for people in general, maleness is the taken-for-granted backdrop, making it the last thing to stand out as remarkable. When we refer to humanity as *man,* for example, maleness blends into humanness, and men can enjoy the comfort and security of not being marked as *other.* In contrast, *female* stands out as a marked category of outsiders in relation not simply to men, but to humanity in general.[1] If "every*man*" is every*one*, then woman is something *else* and therefore problematic, something that needs to be figured out.

The same kind of invisibility occurs around race: We hardly ever call attention to the race of whites in the news, for example, because in a white-identified society, whiteness is the standard—the *assumed* race. Only deviations from the dominant group are marked for special attention. So it is routine to mark white women and people of color as exceptions (police-woman, black physician, Native American artist, Asian American executive, and so on), a practice that underscores the normative and therefore taken-for-granted standing of men and whites. What is ironic in such cases is that male gender and white race so dominate social life that they become, in a sense, socially invisible. Unlike the invisibility of women and people of color, this supports privilege by allowing men and whites to move through the world with relatively little awareness of the causes or consequences of *male* privilege and *white* privilege and the social oppression they produce.

In general, women are made invisible when they do something that might elevate their status, such as raising children into healthy adults or coming up with a brilliant idea in a business meeting. Men, however, are often made invisible when their behavior is socially undesirable and might raise questions about the appropriateness of male privilege. Although the vast majority of violent acts are perpetrated by men, for example, news accounts rarely call attention to the gender of those who rape, kill, beat, torture, and make war on others. Instead, we read about mobs, crowds, people, students, gangs, citizens, youths, fans, workers, militants, party members, teenagers, insurgents, soldiers, and so on—ungendered categories that presumably can include both women and men. If a crowd of women gather to make a news-worthy event, however, one can be sure they will be identified as women, not merely as a crowd. But such attention is rarely paid to maleness per se. And on those rare occasions when someone mentions statistics on male violence and suggests this might be a problem worth looking at, the response is yawning impatience ("Oh, *this* again?") or, more likely, a torrent of objections to the male-bashing straw man defense: "You're accusing *all* men of being murderers and rapists!"

When the media do identify male gender, they rarely make much of it. With numbing regularity, we hear reports of violent crimes perpetrated by men, from wife beating, stalking, rape and murder to the gunning down of workers and bystanders by disgruntled employees to the September 11 disaster to mass murder as an instrument of national policy. Yet rarely do we hear the simple statement that the perpetrators of such acts are almost always men. Nor do we take seriously the idea that men's pervasive involvement in such violence provides a clue to understanding it and why it happens. No one suggests, for example, that an ethic of masculine control might be connected to the use of violence or that there is good reason to limit the male population's opportunities to harm others. Note, however, the radically different response when subordinate groups are the focus. The fact that most early AIDS victims were gay men, for example, brought demands to quarantine and repress the entire gay population, even though most gay men didn't have AIDS. Teenage *pregnancy*—a state that describes women, not men—is a hot topic in the United States, but not male *insemination* of teenage girls. And if people of color did violence to whites at the rate that the male population produces violence against women, there would be national mobilization to do something to contain this "dangerous population."

Selective male invisibility shapes how we perceive and think about gender issues. The oppression of women, for example, is routinely discussed as a *women's* issue rather than as a *men's* issue, making male gender invisible as part of the problem. Whether it's job discrimination or harassment and violence, gender issues typically are seen as problems for women—the category of people who are victimized. Gender issues are rarely seen as problems for men, the category of people who actually do the victimizing and whose privilege is rooted in the same system that promotes women's oppression.

If male gender is invisible, then patriarchy also is invisible, and it's easy to go around acting as though men have nothing to do with something that is, by definition, organized around gender. In the simplest sense this is illogical, because something can't be about gender and yet only be about women. If something happens to women simply because they are women, then we also have to understand why it *doesn't* happen to men simply because they happen to be men. But male invisibility is more than illogical, for it also loads both responsibility and blame onto the victim by implying that oppression is an issue for those who suffer from it but not for those who benefit from or perpetrate it.

Defining oppression as a problem only for the oppressed is as old as oppression itself. It doesn't protect or enhance the status of men, whites, and the upper classes to look critically at systems that privilege them over women, people of color, and the working and lower classes. Instead, the path of least resistance is to be charitable or to focus on how oppressed groups can solve "their" problems, resolve "their" issues, or advance "their" standing as having "special interests." But advantaged, dominant groups are rarely portrayed as problematic or even as groups, much less as special-interest groups.

Dominant groups avoid scrutiny because their position enables them to define their own interests as those of society as a whole. This lays down a path of least resistance for men to protect their privilege by coasting along with the patriarchal status quo—mentoring and promoting people who look like them, avoiding domestic work, and passing laws and setting policies that reflect a male-centered, male-identified, male-dominated world. Nothing much is made of it. No "special interests" at work here. But those who struggle against the consequences of patriarchy are another story. They are the "other," the outsiders trying to get in, the seekers after affirmative action and other "special" considerations that would advance them at the expense of others.

If privilege and oppression are visible only as issues for oppressed groups, then privileged groups don't have to feel responsible or accountable or even involved. Men can feel good—even virtuous—when they show any concern for "women's issues" or just don't behave in overtly sexist ways. They can regard the slightest gesture in support of gender equality—from saying they favor equal pay to doing the dinner dishes—as a sign of what good people they are. And men can take comfort from the illusion that women can achieve justice for themselves by resolving *women's* issues with some help from benevolent men but without radically affecting men's lives or how patriarchal society is organized, including its male-identified core values.

Many men will object to the very idea that male privilege exists, but their objection also insists on a kind of invisibility that patriarchy depends on. Few men realize how much their lives would change if women weren't treated as subordinate. Instead, men take credit for their hard work and achievements without taking into account how much harder it would have been if they had to compete with women on a level playing field or do without the supportive (and unpaid) domestic labor that so many wives and mothers perform. Because patriarchy defines women as subordinate and "other," men can take women's exclusion from serious competition for granted. As a result, many men have been rudely awakened by women's entry into hitherto male-only workplaces. When men complain about the advantage some women gain from affirmative action, they ignore centuries of pro-male affirmative action that, in spite of the women's movement, continues as the largely unexceptional default condition under patriarchy.

The more invisible male gender is, the more gender problems like violence and discrimination are identified with women and the less likely we are to notice that patriarchy even exists as an oppressive system. When we don't see the significance of the gender categories to which rapists and their victims belong, individual men who aren't rapists don't have to consider how their connection to patriarchal privilege also connects them to the sexual violence of men who *are*.

# Denial

Denial can be a powerful and useful psychological defense mechanism. When something is too horrible to deal with, denial can be a lifesaver, especially for children. Usually, however, denial exacts a price by standing between us and our power to see our lives clearly and to do something to make them better. The denial that saves a girl from confronting the reality of her abuse, for example, can eventually cripple her ability to function as an adult and drive her into therapy as a way to free herself from it and what lies behind it.

Denial can be even worse when it is built into the culture of an entire social system. When a family defines abuse as love, for example, or when a nation calls war keeping the peace, or when patriarchy defines male dominance as human nature, we're up against a lot more than a personal reluctance to look at the truth. For a girl to acknowledge her own abuse, she must set aside her own denial as a defense against pain and terror. She has to give up the only safe place she's ever known—the place where she can pretend that none of this is really happening. But she also has to go up against her family's collective denial that defines love, abuse, violence, and "family" in ways that make her and everyone else's denial possible. In this sense, she risks even more by having to challenge an entire system that she depends on for a sense of belonging and identity.

Similar risks occur on a larger scale. Antiwar protestors who object to a popular war, for example, risk everything from the goodwill of their neighbors and how well their children are treated at school to their sense of themselves as true citizens who have a right to be there. "America: Love it or leave it" was a standard challenge thrown at people protesting the Vietnam War, as if only those who bought into the prevailing collective denial could count themselves among those who loved their country. And anyone who doubts that massive denial was at work from the highest levels on down need only read former Secretary of Defense Robert McNamara's regretful memoir[2] or see the film, *Fog of War*.

Similar antipathy was present when the U.S. invaded Iraq in 2003. Members of Congress who spoke out against or even questioned the war were often accused of being unpatriotic and aiding the enemy, as were citizens who engaged in various forms of protest.

Denial takes a variety of forms. There is the denial that a problem even exists ("Rape isn't an issue on this campus."), or, if it does, that it's serious enough to worry about ("It happens once in awhile, but women get over it."). When that fails, the next line of defense is to blame the victim ("Of course women get raped, but they have only themselves to blame. They should be more careful and watch how they dress.") or call it something else ("It's just a case of bad sex. A misunderstanding, really. It's not like it's actual *violence*."). And, then, as Stanley Cohen argues in his book, *States of Denial*, when it becomes impossible to avoid seeing the reality of things, additional levels of denial come into play—not feeling anything about it or feeling something but not seeing it as a moral issue or, if all else fails, denying there's anything we can do.[3]

Given how risky it can be to acknowledge painful realities, it's not surprising that we might deny that patriarchy exists rather than risk ridicule, rejection, or worse by seeing it for what it is. For men in particular, denial can be militant and confrontational, but it usually appears as a stubborn inability to see or understand. It may begin with something as simple as calling gender issues "women's issues," an easy way for men to disassociate themselves from the problems of the "other." From there, denial gets thicker and harder to penetrate. On the subject of sexual harassment, for example, men's renowned ability to solve problems can suddenly take a holiday as they look to women to tell them what to do and what not to do. Many men complain that they don't know the "rules" anymore and can't seem to figure them out. It's as if harassment were some kind of female mystery that only women can understand. For some equally mysterious reason, although men control every major social institution, and although this is supposedly based at least in part on their superior power to make objective sense of things, they can become surprisingly slow when they enter the alien territory of "women's issues." They may retreat into a kind of earnest "not getting it" or "I'm just not good at that sort of thing."

Denial is a reliable defense serving all forms of privilege. To some degree, denial operates in every society because societies are organized to be self-justifying and self-perpetuating. No social system has a culture that values the kind of serious ongoing criticism of itself that could lead to its transformation. Instead, the status quo typically is defined as normal, legitimate, and unremarkable, and slides along paths of least resistance that assume everything is basically alright. If troublemakers come along to suggest otherwise, it's easy enough to blame them instead of listening to what they're saying—to attribute a system's problems to anything but something wrong with the system itself. "Outside agitators" are the problem, or disgruntled groups who won't face up to their individual failings and get on with it.

Because every system of privilege is organized to protect the interests of privileged groups, denial serves privilege by making it tough for anyone to challenge the system. Dominant groups can maintain privilege simply by going about business as usual and riding the rolling inertia of the status quo. The last thing that will occur to them is to go out of their way to understand how privilege works, who gets hurt by it, and what it's got to do with them. This can make the most privileged groups the ones who see the least. The classic BBC television series, *Upstairs, Downstairs,* for example, portrayed life among the privileged (upstairs) and servant (downstairs) classes in Edwardian England at the turn of the twentieth century. In this rigid class system, servants did virtually everything for their employers, from cooking and serving meals to keeping house to drawing baths, polishing boots, and helping family members dress themselves. In one scene, Richard Bellamy, the master of the house, must deal with a personal problem among the servants, which his inept handling has only made worse. As he attempts to deal with the situation, he mutters in exasperation, "Servants! I don't know *why* we put up with them!"

On one level, the statement is simply insensitive and blind, even silly, and it's tempting to write it off as a personality flaw—just as some conclude that men who don't get it are simply jerks. The truth, however, is more complicated. When we participate in a social system, we feel drawn toward paths of least resistance that shape how we perceive and make sense of things. Every system of privilege is organized to encourage subordinate groups to keep quiet and pretend there's no oppression going on lest the wrath of those above them make things a whole lot worse than they already are. And dominant groups are encouraged toward the subtle arrogance of not paying attention to the reality of the oppression that supports their privilege.

Not surprisingly, if anyone breaks the silence, it is usually those nearest the bottom, who also tend to have the fewest resources for making change. As a result, oppressed groups often feel backed into a corner where making trouble seems the only way to draw attention to what's going on. Making trouble, in turn, routinely evokes official disgust, charges of "extremism," and even violent repression.[4] In democracies like the United States, a certain amount of troublemaking is tolerated in order to avoid openly compromising democratic values. But after a while, patience runs out, and dominant groups rise up and say "Enough!"[5]

Denial is so thick that women who manage to penetrate it for themselves often have to drag the men in their lives into awareness and keep them focused long enough to act. At the same time, women must also struggle with the everyday facts of gender oppression and stay healthy, clearheaded, and aware in spite of a mainstream culture permeated with the message that privilege and oppression aren't real to begin with and that what is real about them isn't such a big deal.

A common dynamic begins when a woman tries to explain why a man's behavior is offensive or threatening, why he should feel responsible for cleaning the house, why describing what he thinks isn't the same as describing what he feels, why his focus on being in control all the time is oppressive, or why his behavior is inappropriate for an employer and makes it impossible for her to do her work, and so on. He, innocently, perhaps earnestly, says he doesn't get it, and asks her to explain. She does, but he argues some fine point—a definition of terms, or an exception to the rule. Or his attention wanders and still he doesn't get it, or he gets it but then loses it again an hour or a week later.

It goes on this way until she gives up, which may not take very long, since this is exhausting work. Then he may feel stung by her impatience because he thinks he's trying to be sensitive. She feels frustrated, trapped, furious at his often calm inability to get it (he being calm because somewhere inside himself he feels—even if unconsciously—the male-privileged knowledge that he doesn't *have* to get it). She may go to extremes to get him to move, to see, to do *something*. Depending on the relationship, she may threaten to break up, divorce, quit the job, file a complaint, or sue, any of which can be risky for her—from the breakup of her family to losing her job to coping with violent retaliation for being "a crazy woman" or "such a bitch."

Sometimes her efforts work, and for a while he may take an interest in "women's issues." He may even help others become more aware, including other men. But as he swims against the steady current of his own privilege and the paths of least resistance that patriarchy holds out to him, he's likely to lose interest before long. So it goes with virtually every form of privilege—the great yawn tinged with waning patience capping the conversation, "Do we have to talk about this again?"

Patriarchy is denied in every setting, from bedrooms to boardrooms. The owner of an "exotic dance" club near Hartford, Connecticut, for example, advertised his business on a highway billboard that pictured two

162 SUSTAINING ILLUSIONS, BARRIERS TO CHANGE

women wearing low-cut tops and gazing vampily toward the stream of passing traffic. A few people complained, but there wasn't much interest until two members of the National Organization for Women scaled the heights and spray-painted "Stop Graphic Rape" in large letters across the ad. *Now* the public stood up and paid attention from living rooms to radio talk shows, but not to the issue of "graphic rape," not to the multibillion dollar business of objectifying, appropriating, and exploiting women's bodies and how it might encourage sexual and other violence, not to men and why they run to spend their money in such businesses. People wanted to talk about whether the spray-painters had violated the advertiser's free speech rights, whether breaking the law was an appropriate or effective strategy for change, and whether it was fair to criticize the strippers for choosing this kind of work. A chorus of clicking tongues arose, admonishing women to be reasonable and engage men in constructive dialogue. Within a few weeks the tempest died down, interest shifted to other things, and the billboard remained, while the business of men buying a chance to watch and fantasize about women's bodies went on as usual.

One theme running throughout the billboard controversy was the idea that the women from NOW were being stereotypical uptight feminist prudes, all worked up over what amounted to nothing more than normal heterosexuality. This kind of argument is a staple ingredient in the denial of patriarchy: The portrayal of what goes on around gender as obvious and natural, if sometimes a bit annoying or offensive to delicate sensibilities (but always in an ultimately charming and inconsequential way, as in "naughty").[6] If women want to take their clothes off in front of men in order to support themselves and their children—well, women have been doing that sort of thing for ages, and after all, it's their choice, isn't it? And if men don't "get it," there's no point to making an issue of it, because men just aren't good at getting it. Judging from the best-seller lists, women and men not only speak different languages but come from different planets (Venus and Mars, respectively), which means we should be grateful for those rare moments when they actually understand each other. It seems to go without saying that when it comes to the attention and skills required for human intimacy, men simply aren't very good at that sort of thing (in spite of dominating the mental health profession and nearly monopolizing advice to parents). So, they're readily forgiven when they don't get it and applauded when they do, however quickly they might lose it again.

But not getting the reality of patriarchy and male privilege is more than a charming or regrettable incapacity. Whether conscious or not, it's also an effective way to deny patriarchy, men's involvement in it, and their potential to be part of the solution.[7]

## "She Did It, Too!": Consensus and Collusion

Openly oppressive systems of privilege like apartheid in South Africa or slavery in the United States provide a comforting clarity because it is easy to see who oppresses whom and how it is done. You can always tell one group from the other, differences in privilege are obvious, abuse and exploitation are public, and the entire system is organized around rigid segregation. The world seems neatly divided into the innocent who are victimized on the one side and the bad who victimize on the other.

It would be easier to see how patriarchy works if it fit this kind of model, but it doesn't. Social life has always revolved around women and men living and working together in families and communities, an arrangement that doesn't lend itself to the stark contrasts separating oppressor and oppressed evident in other systems. As far as we know, women's and men's lives have always been bound together in one way or another. Men have always been born to and, with relatively few exceptions, raised by women, and women's lives have always been bound up with those of men, whether fathers, brothers, husbands, lovers, sons, uncles, nephews, cousins, or grandfathers. Intimacy across gender has always been a hallmark of human experience, and this can make it difficult to see how it works, or to see it at all.

One way this difficulty shows itself is through the idea that since both genders share in a common social reality of everyday life, they must be equally responsible for creating and maintaining it. This implies that neither gender dominates the overall scheme of things. On one level this is of course true since unless people live as hermits, they have to participate in one society or another. And unless they're going to live in open rebellion all the time— with all the risks that go with it—they will "go along to get along." So it's inevitable that both women and men will to some degree go along with and support patriarchy, because it's the only way of life they know.

But going along with patriarchy also makes us part of the consequences it produces, even if we simply stay silent about it. When all the details of our lives are shaped to reflect patriarchal reality, oppression can blend into the rest of social life in a seamless field of mundane normality. Pain, loss, and conflict appear not as something remarkable or out of place, but simply as what life *is*, or as personal problems caused by faulty personalities, bad childhoods, or some bit of bad luck that could happen to anyone. What is harder to see is how systems like patriarchy promote individual troubles and connect them to one another.

The tendency to fuse privilege and oppression with visions of ordinary life is most common where the lives of dominant and subordinate groups are integrated in close and interdependent ways. This was true to some degree of the upper and servant classes in Victorian England and of slavery in the United States, but neither of these systems compares with the intermeshing of men's and women's lives over thousands of years of human experience. As a result, the path of least resistance is to experience patriarchy as normal, consensual, and serving everyone's needs and values—except for the occasional misfit. It shouldn't surprise us, then, to find no shortage of women who seem to accept their lot, and not a few who do their part to keep it going in the "natural" order of things. But this doesn't mean women and men are *equal* co-creators of patriarchy, or that patriarchy is a system that serves men's and women's interests equally. It's one thing to participate in a system and accommodate to it even to the point of identifying with and perpetuating it. It's quite another to knowingly choose to create it.[8] Just because we lie down in a bed doesn't mean we made it or even that we'd sleep in it if we had a better alternative.

Consider, for example, African blacks who were brought to the United States as slaves. Black parents who wanted their children to survive undoubtedly taught them how to avoid white violence by deferring to whites, doing as they were told, and doing nothing to question the status quo. Whites could—and often did—point to a seeming consensus underlying this way of life and claim that blacks were content or even happy as participants in a system that supposedly benefited everyone, at least in keeping with their different stations in life (which, of course, were "natural" and God given).

But this is false consensus based on choosing the lesser of the evils offered by an oppressive society. Equally false is attributing the kind of responsibility that goes with free and considered choice to those who agree to accommodate themselves to a system that oppresses them. A coal miner's son, for example, may be said to freely choose to be a coal miner instead of a Wall Street lawyer in that no one overtly coerces him to make that choice. We could also say that a Wall Street lawyer's son might freely choose to follow in his father's footsteps rather than be a coal miner. But to argue that both are equally responsible for the consequences of their choices on the grounds that each exercised "free choice" ignores how societies limit the alternatives that people perceive as available to chose from, which is a direct result of living in a particular kind of society that privileges certain classes, genders, and races over others.

Of course, no society can exist without some degree of consensus, and both women and men do participate in life under patriarchy. But we have to ask what this consensus is based on, what different groups of people get out of it, what their alternatives are, and what the terms on which they participate are. When women go along with the inferior social standing that goes with being female, they do *not* do so because it's an attractive and enviable thing to do in patriarchal culture. It is true that "feminine" virtues and "women's work" are valued, but primarily through their usefulness to men and in sentimental, romantic ways (Mothers Day, Secretaries Day) that have little standing in comparison with what's widely regarded as serious life and work.

Many men are quick to protest that the family is the most important of all social institutions—next to which "men's work" is second best. Women, they say, should feel privileged to call the family their turf. Although the family *should* be among the most important of all institutions, if we judge from how resources and rewards are distributed and what men in particular choose as their own priorities, the family clearly ranks well down the list. Consider, for example, the tolerance of widespread violence and abuse in families, the fact that children are more likely to live in poverty than any other age group, the nationwide child-care crisis, men's routine lack of concern for taking responsibility for contraception and, therefore, the consequences of unprotected sex, and the steadfast mainstream refusal of most husbands and fathers to see themselves as equally *responsible* for the domestic labor that makes up family life. All these examples highlight the gulf between public rhetoric and sentimentality, on the one hand, and the reality of family life and its place in the larger society, on the other.

Most women accept their status because it's all they know or the best they can get. The alternative is to risk challenging a system defended by powerful interests, which makes going along with male privilege women's path of least resistance. To choose different paths is of course possible, as the frequent heroism of women makes clear, but not without considerable effort and risk.

But don't men also feel compelled to bend themselves to fit patriarchal standards? Do they freely choose to go along with patriarchy any more than women do? And don't they pay a price for challenging the status quo? The answer is yes on all counts, but here the similarity between men and women ends, for men's and women's lack of freedom comes with very different consequences.

Under patriarchy, when a woman embraces her subordinate, devalued gender status, she gains precious little in return. But when a man assumes his gender status, he can identify with some of society's highest cultural values—values associated with manhood, such as control, reason, strength, industry, courage, decisiveness, dominance, emotional control and inexpressiveness, toughness, wisdom, abstract principles, intellectual and artistic genius, even God. A man can take advantage of male privilege and the rewards for suc-cessfully embodying patriarchal values. By identifying himself as a man, he gains privilege by associating himself with what's socially defined as the best that *humanity* can be. No matter what his social standing might otherwise be, he can know that something in his masculine being connects him with ideals that elevate him above even the most highly placed woman or, for that matter, other men who, although superior in relation to other forms of privilege, seem insufficiently masculine. So, the working-class carpenter can feel superior to a president's wife because he's a man and she isn't, or he can feel more of a man than a male professional who for all his class privilege seems to lack toughness and grit.

Like men, women participate in the patriarchy into which they were born and raised because they don't see any alternative. They inevitably identify with that society and even defend it to some degree. This is a far cry, however, from the notion that women share control over the shape of patriarchal society on some kind of equal footing with men. As a system, patriarchy is a lot more than a bad case of co-dependency or sexual game-playing. It is not a grand "battle of the sexes" in which men and women pursue equal but conflicting interests as "sexual superpowers." Patriarchy is an oppressive system in which women, like all subordinate groups, make the best of what they've got and build whatever basis of power and influence they can. If women are turned into sexual property, then they will find ways to control that property for their own advantage. If they become the emotional caretakers, then they will develop ways to use emotion as leverage. The fact that women can hurt or deprive men doesn't mean that patriarchy doesn't exist or that women and men are equal partners in it. After all, white slaveholders depended on and often lived in fear of their slaves, but this didn't make blacks partners in a slave society.

What we're seeing here is an inherent paradox in the social dynamics of oppressive power: The more invested people are in dominance and control, the more frightened they are of having those same forces and values turned against them—and the more powerful those beneath them may seem as a result.[9]

For both men and women, participating in patriarchy puts us in the middle of a huge contradiction. On the one hand, we may feel we have little choice but to live within the limits imposed by a patriarchal system that privileges men at women's expense. On the other hand, we bring to one another some of our most compelling personal needs—whether as parents, siblings, children, lovers, or spouses—needs that are invariably distorted and perverted by a system organized around privilege and oppression. The contradiction is so deep and the stakes so high that we don't want to know what's going on. Many men are so afraid of being blamed (just as women are of blaming them), that we find it easier to pretend that women and men are equals. We are tempted to respond to every statement about oppression with "But women do it, too," or "What about men?" It's easier to cast women as a bizarre variety of people who for some reason choose to help produce their own oppression. It drives otherwise intelligent people into corners where they turn and fight their way out with absurd arguments that women like being dominated and knocked around or naturally find pleasure in pain and humiliation—the convenient myth of female masochism. It is a crazy dynamic, but no less crazy than patriarchy itself, a system that pits one half of humanity against the other.

## False Parallels

Drawing false gender parallels creates a particularly effective smoke screen around the reality of patriarchy. To see women and men as co-equal conspirators who together created and maintain patriarchy, we have to ignore the fact that patriarchy gives men and women different interests, resources, and experience. We can't lump the two genders together and treat them as an undifferentiated whole, no more than we can act as if all races, classes, and ethnic groups participate and benefit equally in societies and their development. The terms of social life aren't equally under the control of women and men, whites and people of color, people with and without disabilities, bosses and workers, or rich and poor. Everyone does participate in social life, and as such we all play some role in creating it, including its consequences. This doesn't mean, however, that all groups participate in the same way, for the same reasons, or with the same results.

Nonetheless, it's become routine to respond to criticism of patriarchy or men's participation in it with false parallels that portray women and men as interchangeable in various social situations, their experience and behavior parallel if not equivalent. One way to do this is to match each statement about women's oppression with something comparable about men, not seeing how patriarchy shapes men's and women's lives in different ways.

Cultural mythology, for example, often associates femaleness with evil, with images of the castrating bitch, the whore, the temptress who brings about a good man's downfall, the morally weak vessel ripe for the devil's seductions, the wicked witch who eats small children, and so on. "But what about the Christian devil?" comes a ready retort. Isn't *he* an evil figure who parallels and in some sense balances negative images of women? Isn't this therefore a *human* thing rather than a *gender* thing?

Although male and female images of evil may seem equivalent and parallel, in fact they're quite different. The devil may be male, but his evil isn't based on the simple fact of his *being* male. He isn't regarded as evil *because* he's male, because maleness itself is associated with evil. Instead, the devil is evil because of his particular and special relation to God.[10] If anything, this elevates him as a fallen angel who began as God's moral sparring partner, formidable enough to be a worthy adversary of none less than God *Him*self.

In contrast, the evil attributed to female figures such as Eve, Pandora, and witches is associated with femaleness itself. In patriarchal culture, females are seen as *naturally* weak, carnal, corruptible, and corrupting.[11] What power they do have is portrayed as disgusting, contemptible, lacking in character, and destructive. This is very different from the power attributed to the devil, who, like Hitler and other larger–than–life, monstrous figures, earns at least some degree of awe and fascination, if not respect, for his power. It's hard to imagine how patriarchal Christianity would ever develop an evil female figure powerful and substantial enough to challenge God, for this would require that women be taken seriously. In other words, under patriarchy, women aren't *good* enough to be the devil.

False gender parallels are a powerful kind of thinking that easily lends itself to the idea that patriarchy doesn't exist. If everything one could say about women is matched by something comparable about men, what basis is there for talking about male privilege or female oppression? The word "sexism," for example, is often used to describe any prejudice based on gender, including negative stereotypes about men. Many men complain that affirmative action programs are sexist ("reverse sexism"), that judges who routinely award child custody to mothers are sexist, and that women who suggest that men are jerks are sexist. Others point out that it's becoming more common for women to focus on men's physical attractiveness in ways that seem to parallel the sexual objectification of women. Women talk more openly about men's bodies, male nightclub strippers play to audiences of cheering women, and the media are quick to focus on the occasional female executive who sexually harasses a male subordinate, whether the harassment is actual or, as in the novel and movie *Disclosure*, imagined. The cosmetics industry for men is booming in a seeming move toward the kind of preoccupation with personal appearance that's long been a burden borne almost entirely by women.

Like kids arguing over who's to blame for a fight ("He hit me!" "Yeah, well, she . . ."), parallel complaints about antimale sexism are a routine response to any kind of serious attention to male privilege. Women complain that life's rough for them and then men complain it's rough for them, too. Heads nod amid a collective sigh of relief at once more avoiding honest talk about privilege. Sometimes it's women who save the day by hastening to point out that for every female who is disadvantaged, men suffer some ill effect of their own. But no matter who does it, the typical result is a dead end or a conversation that focuses more on men's woes than women's, taking attention from patriarchy and male privilege and reinforcing male centeredness. In this way, even when the subject is privilege and oppression, somehow the path of least resistance is to turn the conversation toward focusing on and taking care of men.

The problem with false gender parallels is that the significance of what happens to people differs profoundly from one gender to the other. On the surface, the experience and behavior of women and men may appear to be similar, but this impression falls apart if we look at the larger reality of people's lives. Negative stereotypes about men, for example, can make them uncomfortable and hurt their feelings. This seems to be the most common cause for men's complaint and a major reason for women's reluctance even to talk about sexism when men are around. But antimale stereotypes come primarily from women, a subordinate, culturally devalued group that lacks authority in a male-identified, male-dominated, male-centered society. In other words, if the source is a woman, the damage stereotypes can do is pretty much confined to personal hurt (as in making men feel foolish in bed), with little if any effect in the larger world. This is because antimale stereotypes aren't rooted in a culture that regards maleness itself as inherently dangerous, inferior, ridiculous, disgusting, or undesirable. Such stereotypes can therefore be written off as the bitter ravings of a group beneath being taken seriously.

Antimale stereotypes also can't be used to keep men down as a group, to lock them into an inferior and disadvantaged status, to justify abuse and violence against them, or to deprive them of fair treatment.[12] When women refer to men as jerks, for example, they aren't expressing a general cultural view of men as jerks. If our culture really regarded men as jerks, the population would be clamoring for female presidents, senators, and CEOs. Instead, we routinely look to men for leadership and expertise in every area of social life, whether philosophy, government, business, law, religion, art, science, cooking, or child care. To the extent that men are culturally portrayed as jerks, it's only in areas of life defined as relatively unimportant, which is to say, in their intimate relations with women. Ultimately this damages women more than men, for the capacity to make superiors look foolish is one of the many ways that subordinate groups of all kinds are portrayed as dangerous and in need of control.

Prejudice against women, however, has deep and far-reaching consequences that do a lot more than make them feel bad, for it supports an entire system that privileges men at women's expense. Sexist prejudice doesn't just target individual women, for it is fundamentally *about* women and strikes at femaleness itself in every instance. Each expression of antifemale prejudice *always* amounts to more than what is said, for it reaffirms a cultural legacy of patriarchal privilege and oppression. When a particular woman is treated as less intelligent, less serious, and less important than the men she works with, for example, this specific view of her is easily linked to the patriarchal idea that women in general are inferior to men. When men ignore her ideas and suggestions or pay more attention to her looks than to her work, they do so with a cultural authority that damages her far more than similar treatment directed at a man. Since patriarchal culture values maleness, the weight behind antimale prejudice is limited primarily to the individual woman who expresses it and is therefore easier to discount ("She must not like men"). And however hurt men might feel, they can always turn to the compensations of male privilege and a mainstream culture that sends continuing messages of inherent male value. In this sense, the issue isn't whether prejudice hurts—it hurts everyone it touches. But prejudice against women wounds in deeper and more complex ways than does prejudice against men because the hurt is magnified by a patriarchal system that spreads it by association to *all* women and that systematically links it to male privilege.

Because prejudice affects women and men so differently, calling antimale prejudice "sexism" distorts the reality of how systems of privilege work. Prejudice against women not only harms individual women, but perpetuates an oppressive system based on gender that harms women more deeply than any isolated instance of hurtful speech or discrimination. Antimale prejudice may hurt individual men, but it isn't connected to a system that devalues maleness and oppresses men as a result. The difference between the two is so great that we need to distinguish the one from the other, and that's what words like "sexism" and "racism" are for. *Sexism* distinguishes simple gender *prejudice*—which can affect men and women both—from the much deeper and broader consequence of expressing and perpetuating privilege and oppression. Without this distinction, we treat all harm as equivalent without taking into account important differences on both the personal and the social levels in what causes it and what it does to people.

For example, when a man strips off his clothes in a nightclub act, he doesn't also take off his dignity, autonomy, and power as a human being, because there's nothing in patriarchal culture that would interpret his behavior as giving up anything of real value to the women who watch him perform. If anything, he can get the male-centered satisfaction of having his body admired by women who lack the social power to treat his body like admired *property*. His relation to women in the audience doesn't reflect a larger social reality in which men's bodies are routinely regarded as objects to be sought after and controlled by women. But a woman who strips *does so in a very different social context* that changes entirely the meaning of her behavior and that of the men who watch her. In a patriarchal culture, her body has significance primarily in relation to men who value rights of access and use through various forms of contract, force, or purchase, from the bonds of love or marriage to prostitution to rape. Men who pay women to strip in front of them do far more than pay to watch someone they find beautiful or arousing take off her clothes. They also participate in a much wider social pattern that defines women's existence in relation to pleasing men, to meeting male standards of attractiveness, and to being available for men's appropriation and use. To some degree, the price of admission buys men the right to feel, if only in short-lived fantasy, a sense of indirect control over women's bodies. Women who watch men strip, on the other hand, will find little in mainstream patriarchal culture that supports viewing or treating men in this way.

There are, of course, similarities between male and female strippers, but they don't have much to do with gender. Both men's and women's bodies, for example, are often used as commodities under market capitalism. Many male athletes are treated as so much meat to be used and then thrown away when no longer needed, and men working in dangerous occupations are routinely treated as expendable. This kind of exploitation also exists in the commercialization of men's growing attention to personal appearance, from body building to cosmetics.[13]

But the commercial exploitation of women's bodies isn't simply about social class and capitalism, for it also involves a patriarchal system that normalizes and promotes sexual exploitation. When a female executive sexually harasses a male subordinate, for example, she abuses both her organizational authority and her class privilege. But she doesn't take advantage of female *gender* privilege or a general social subordination of men, because these don't exist for her to use in the first place. Her behavior is inappropriate and harmful, and she should be held accountable for it. But this doesn't make it the same as male harassment of women, because it doesn't have the formidable *social* power of patriarchy and male privilege behind it.

## Men as Victims

One of the trickiest patriarchal paradoxes is that although patriarchy privileges men, many, if not most men don't *feel* privileged, powerful, or in control of much of anything, especially at work.[14] To judge from what many men say about their lives, they often feel victimized, deprived, put down, disposable, and trapped. Such feelings are often associated with costs that are at least statistically tied to being male. Men die at younger ages than women and are more vulnerable to almost every cause of death (with a few exceptions such as ovarian and breast cancer). Men are more likely to work at dangerous occupations, to kill themselves—dramatically so at older ages—and to be killed by others. They are more likely to suffer from alcohol, drug, and psychotic disorders,[15] to commit violent crimes, to be arrested and imprisoned, and to be homeless. Compared with women, men's same-sex friendships tend to be fewer, shallower, and shorter, and men don't do as well at surviving the loss of a spouse, especially at older ages. The high priority on work in men's lives takes them away from family and intimacy. Some men feel demeaned by popular culture, such as TV sitcoms that portray men as bumbling and foolish at home and around women. And in the controversy over affirmative action, many men complain that women are getting jobs and promotions men should have had, although there is still no evidence that this is anything more than anecdotal.

How can we say that patriarchy exists if men feel so little sense of privilege in their lives and seem to pay a substantial cost for being male? Can men be both privileged and miserable? The answer is yes, because most of men's loss and misery is linked to what is required of men in order to participate in the very system that privileges them. As Marilyn French argues:

> A person who values control over anything else is incapable of any relation that might weaken or penetrate that surface of control; thus such a person becomes almost incapable of intimacy, equality, or trust, each of which requires the abdication of control. Needing to hold oneself apart and above so that the appearance of control may not be shattered . . . one is terrified at the nakedness and vulnerability that seem to hover beyond the carefully maintained wall of control. . . . [16]
>
> If the traditional patriarchal image of women has constricted them greatly, depriving them of most of life's activities and pleasures, the traditional patriarchal image of men has deprived them greatly, of the core of life, its central "purposes" and values: pleasure, love, intimacy, sharing, and community. Women have been imprisoned in the core, and men on the fringe; and the two areas have been renamed.[17]

The paradox between male privilege and male misery is often used to argue that women's oppression is balanced by a similar or even worse lot for men. Warren Farrell, for example, writes that societies such as that in the United States are *both* patriarchal and matriarchal, with each gender having its own areas of oppressive domination.[18] As with other false parallels, Farrell draws attention away from patriarchy to men as victims who deserve sympathy as much as women do. At the extreme, men's woes are used to blame women for the price men pay for privilege, even though the price usually is exacted by other men. Men's reluctance to open themselves fully to their inner emotional lives, for example, is based far more on fear of being vulnerable to other men or of being seen as insufficiently manly— not in control and controlled by others—than on worries about women. In similar ways, the competitive grind, insecurity, or fear of violence that many men experience is overwhelmingly in relation to other men, not women.

Men's misery *does* deserve sympathy, but not if it means we ignore how men contribute to that misery, where it comes from, and what men get in exchange for it. It's all too easy to go from sympathy for men to forgetting that patriarchy and male privilege even exist. Part of what makes it so easy is misunderstanding what privilege is, where it comes from, and how it is distributed. Many men argue, for example, that men *are* privileged only to the degree that they *feel* privileged. A key aspect of privilege, however, is to be unaware of it *as* privilege. In addition, even though men as a group are privileged in society, factors such as race, class, sexual orientation, and disability status affect how much privilege each man gets to enjoy and how he experiences it.

Privilege can take many forms, and its distribution among people in a society is a complicated process. Privilege can be something as simple as being heard and taken seriously when we say something, of being served promptly and courteously in a store or restaurant, or of being free to move around or express an opinion. It can take the form of wealth or power or having other people clean up after us and take care of our needs. In every case, what makes something privilege is the unequal way in which it is distributed and the effect it has of elevating some people over others.[19] When men are listened to in a meeting and women are ignored, for example, what would otherwise be a common courtesy of human conversation—taking people seriously enough to listen to them—is turned into a form of privilege.

How much privilege people have depends on the combination of the social positions they occupy and how those positions are located and valued in society. The privilege that goes with wealth, for example, depends on other factors such as race, ethnicity, education, occupation, class background, and gender. Winning the lottery isn't enough to send a working-class family into the upper class, just as no amount of professional training, occupational achievement, or income can erase the stigma of race attached to people of color in the United States. It doesn't matter if a family of color has enough money to live in white neighborhoods if real estate agents won't show them houses in those neighborhoods. It doesn't matter if women earn medical degrees, if patients assume they are nurses and male colleagues treat them as second rate. And all the class or race privilege in the world won't protect women from being targeted for sexual and domestic violence.

In short, although we experience privilege as individuals, it is conferred upon us by systems through a process that depends far more on social characteristics such as gender and race than on the personal characteristics that make us unique individuals. The distinction between the personal and the social is crucial, because it means that the only way to affect privilege is to change our social positions—go back to school, for example, pass for white, or marry someone from a higher class—or change social systems. We can change many of our social characteristics if we're willing to make the effort, but it's much harder when it comes to gender and race. When such characteristics are a basis for privilege and oppression, then the usual routes to privilege such as education and occupation often aren't enough. The only way out is to change the systems and social machinery through which privilege is created and distributed.

We can draw two points from this discussion that relate to the paradox of males *being* privileged under patriarchy but not necessarily *feeling* privileged. First, the fact that all men aren't better off than all women doesn't mean male privilege doesn't exist. Racism undermines men of color's access to male privilege, for example, by making it more difficult for them to earn a good living and claim the patriarchal position of "male provider." In similar ways, the dynamics of class undermine access to male privilege for lower- and working-class men. This doesn't mean, however, that there's no such thing as male privilege or a patriarchal system that promotes and legitimates it on behalf of *all* men. Even the poorest men of color have access, for example, in the widespread social presumption that they *should* be able to assume the position of heads of families and realize the patriarchal ideal—just like white men.

In short, because male privilege is socially generated and distributed, it exists regardless of whether men *know* it or *want* it. When I go out at night for a walk alone, for example, I rarely think of how the mere fact of my being male grants me the freedom to move about with relatively little fear in a world that is far more threatening to women. I don't feel imprisoned in my own home after dark, but instead enjoy a taken-for-granted sense of safety that is a form of male privilege. The fact that I don't consciously *feel* privileged isn't because I'm *not* privileged. In part it's because my privilege consists of otherwise unremarkable aspects of everyday life. Being able to take a late night walk by myself simply because I feel like it or need a quart of milk isn't the kind of thing that makes me feel privileged. But it is a privilege when a society is organized in ways that systematically deny it to some while allowing it for others. This is what Peggy McIntosh calls an "unearned advantage," an entitlement that "none of us should have to earn."[20] Since privileged groups don't *have* to earn it, they don't see it as a form of privilege.

Men's blindness to male privilege is also based on the dynamics of how we compare ourselves to other people as a way to judge our relative standing. When we gauge how well off we are, we tend to look sideways and upward, not downward. In other words, if our neighbors, friends, and co-workers seem to be better off than we are, we take little comfort in noting that others are worse off, especially if the "others" don't resemble us in ways we consider important. So, it doesn't make people living in poverty in the U.S. feel better if you tell them that poverty is worse in India or Somalia, or if you tell white women bumping up against the corporate glass ceiling that working-class women are a lot worse off than they are.

Because of this, people usually don't have to be reminded of their relative deprivation, but they may refuse to acknowledge even the possibility of their relative privilege. This is why a man in a corporation may feel unfairly disadvantaged when he's passed over in favor of a woman, in spite of the fact that he's surrounded by a patriarchal system in which the overwhelming majority of women are undervalued, underpaid, and locked into a small number of dead-end occupations. It's also why people often object to Take Your Daughters to Work Day with cries of "What about the boys?" For a man passed over in favor of women, the path of least resistance is never to consider that if there had always been a level playing field for men and women, he might never have been in the running for that promotion he just missed. And male privilege is so normalized that it's easy to miss the fact that without special attention to occupational possibilities and role models, girls are unlikely to get what boys can get simply by turning on the television, opening a textbook, or going to the movies: visible confirmation that people of their gender can and do perform all manner of occupations, especially those valued most highly in society. The real transgression of Take Your Daughters to Work Day isn't that it actually deprives boys of something they can't get elsewhere. It's that it shifts attention away from boys—if only for a day—and onto girls, and thereby challenges the patriarchal principle of male centeredness.

A second point about the paradox of male privilege is that many men believe that an oppressive system like patriarchy can't exist unless the dominant group is happy, prosperous, and well-adjusted. Oppression, it seems, is about pleasure and the good life for the dominant group that keeps "all the joys and privileges of the earth for themselves."[21] This would make an unhappy member of an oppressor group a contradiction in terms. Sam Keen argues that since "oppressors have greater access to comfort and health care, and thus live longer lives," men's shorter average life span proves that an oppressive relationship between men and women doesn't exist, except, perhaps, for the possibility that *women* oppress *men*.[22]

But if we think for a moment about the kind of grinding daily suffering and injustice that oppression involves, the last thing we should expect is that participating in the oppression of more than half the human race—including some of the most important people in men's lives—could ever be the basis for a thriving, pleasurable life. As Marilyn French writes:

> Domination is an ill, not because of some abstract moral principle but because of a concrete moral fact: it makes people unhappy. Domination makes impossible the most essential and felicitous element in life: trusting mutual affection . . . .
>
> It is always true that those whom we control control us. Insofar as a sense of freedom, autonomy, is a basic human good, dominators, pressured and threatened on all sides, have less personal freedom than an itinerant laborer . . . . To keep a slave in a ditch, one must stay there oneself, or appoint an overseer to guarantee the slave's obedience. But then it is necessary to appoint a supervisor who will make sure that the slave and the overseer do not collude . . . and so on. There is no place of safety for a dominator, ever; there is no security, peace, or ease. The urge to control others backfires; it cannot be satisfied and it entraps the controller . . . . The dominators of the world never have a day off.[23]

It's apparent from this that systems don't merely create and distribute privilege. They also create and distribute risk and cost of various kinds, depending on how privilege is organized. Under European feudalism, for example, privilege was organized as a social system linking nobility, peasants, and landed estates, enforced ultimately through the elite's monopoly over military hardware and expertise. For much of this period, the nobility maintained their monopoly by not allowing peasants to fight in wars (just as, though for somewhat different reasons, men have kept women out of combat). Noblemen paid a price for this, of course, because it meant their privilege required them to risk life and limb on behalf of their sovereigns, who granted them rights to land in exchange for military support. We don't know how the average life span of these warriors compared with that of men in peasant households, but it's entirely possible that the privilege of noble birth was as life threatening for these men as it was life enhancing.[24]

For all the perils of warfare and chivalrous codes of "women and children first," in pre-industrial patriarchies male survivability is generally enhanced at the expense of females—from "excess" female mortality in nineteenth-century Ireland[25] to census reports of millions of "missing" female children in Asia, largely as a result of infanticide and selective neglect.[26] Females may enjoy some sentimental attention, but this doesn't protect them from being neglected, starved, left to die as infants, or sold into various forms of servitude—including forced prostitution—when money gets tight at home.[27]

In industrial societies, things are less extreme and male dominance doesn't include socially sanctioned life-and-death control over girls and women. Men do, however, control major social institutions such as the state, church, and the economy. That women in industrial societies typically live longer than men doesn't mean male dominance is a thing of the past, but instead reflects the shifting *costs* of male dominance brought on by a changing world that uses different social mechanisms to generate and distribute privilege.

Systems of privilege are rarely neat and unambiguous, with dominant groups having everything good and oppressed groups having everything bad. More often, privilege is a mixed bag. This doesn't deny the reality of privilege, it merely complicates it. White privilege for example, was an undeniable fact of life in the U.S. South before the Civil War, but the same economic system that produced white enslavement of blacks also produced a large class of poor whites, many of whom had little interest in fighting a bloody civil war to defend the slave property of wealthier whites.[28] Although lower- and working-class whites probably would have laughed at the idea that they were privileged, there's no doubt that they were regarded as superior to blacks and used the racist cultural presumption of white superiority as a way to compensate themselves for their economic and social deprivation, especially after slavery was abolished.[29]

For many reasons, the reality of life in systems of privilege is difficult for privileged groups to grasp, much less appreciate. The path of least resistance is to deny and turn reality on its head with false parallels and misperceptions of what privilege is and how it works. There are so many ways to distort and obscure the existence of patriarchy that it's a wonder we're able to see it at all. But as the next chapter shows, the prize for patriarchy's boldest defense probably should go to the idea that the real problem isn't patriarchy at all, but women.

# 8

# It Must Be Women

When all else fails in defense of patriarchy, what could be more magical than turning the critical eye to women as the real problem? As the argument goes, *women* are the really powerful ones in social life, not men, because women are mothers, and, as every little boy knows, nothing compares with mom.

The idea that motherhood makes women the more powerful and valued gender is often tossed off as a self-evident aside—"Well, of course, women are mothers and that means they do what *really* counts, you know." Or it comes out in earnest, with resentment, anger, or outrage that men are seen as dominant when women are the powerful ones. Women, after all, bear and raise children who depend on them for their most profound needs and whose personalities are shaped through a lifelong dependency. Since everyone has a mother and every mother is a woman, it's easy to go along with cultural images of maternal power that controls men by giving or withholding what they need.

In its mildest form, mother power supposedly produces envy in men who feel insignificant and left out of the life-giving process. Although men live in a male-identified and male-centered world, they may feel peripheral to life around them. They may feel stuck on the sidelines of their children's birth, left out as fathers, or unable to grasp the mysteries of human intimacy. Feeling left out touches feelings of powerlessness, in response to which men may project power onto women as the true insiders—selfish keepers of the keys to life. At its most extreme, the idea of mother power is used to explain patriarchy itself as a way for men to defend themselves against otherwise overwhelming odds: Male dominance and all that goes with it are seen as just a troubled response to women's power, a way for men to establish themselves, hang on to their identities, and find some compensation for not having the *real* power.[1]

Warren Farrell organized his entire book, *The Myth of Male Power*, around the idea that men are powerless and women have the potential to be corrupted by "absolute power."[2] To make the argument work, however, he defines power only as "having control over one's life," a very narrow definition that excludes the "power over" that makes oppressive systems of privilege work. People of color, for example, aren't oppressed simply in that they lack control over their own lives. The power that oppresses them is collective white control of economic, political, and other resources and both passive and active use of that control to privilege whites. Controlling our own personal lives certainly can be viewed as a form that power can take, as well as a consequence of having other kinds of power. But it isn't the kind of power through which one group rules (the *archy* in patriarchy), exploits, or oppresses another. After all, the most powerful people in the world often complain that they don't have lives of their own because they're under such scrutiny and have so many obligations to meet. But few would suggest that the power of presidents and prime ministers is therefore mythical and of no consequence.

## Babies, Blood, and Power

It's easy for men to see themselves as outsiders to the mystery of life and reproduction—scientists trying to tease nature's secrets from *her*, male gynecologists and obstetricians trying to control the life process, tribal males excluded from women's sacred mysteries, or modern Lamaze birth coaches trying to help without getting in the way. Biology supposedly renders men inadequate and estranged from reproduction, and stuck with second-best compensations such as building cities, composing symphonies, conquering nature, tuning the family car, or running the world. Women, however, are seen as biologically endowed with a core connection to life that men simply cannot have.[3] From this perspective, women can appear as powerful creators of life—envied by men, feared, hopelessly loved, and held in awe by their children, and, until the advent of patriarchy some seven thousand years ago, firmly seated at the symbolic center of goddess-based religions.

In fact, men often do report feeling left out of family life and other things close to the life process. As Sam Keen recounts his experience as a father, for example, the birth of his children left him feeling not only awestruck, but profoundly inadequate:

> In that hour, all my accomplishments—books I had written, works of will and imagination, small monuments to my immortality—shrank into insignificance. Like men since the beginning of time I wondered: What can I ever create that will equal the magnificence of this new life?
>
> ...She gives birth to meaning out of her body. Biology alone assures her of a destiny, of making a contribution to the ongoing drama of life. A man responds to her challenge by simulating creation, by making, fabricating, and inventing artifacts. But while she creates naturally and literally, he creates only artificially and metaphorically.[4]

Keen seems to see having babies as something that women *do*—like building a house or writing a book or sculpting a statue—rather than something that women experience, participate in, and become part of.[5] Keen feels challenged to do something equally "magnificent," and feels inadequate and left out because he can't. He seems to believe that biology is the root of the problem, but in fact it has more to do with how patriarchy encourages men to organize their lives around control. When control is at the center, it's hard to settle for merely being part of something or witnessing someone else's powerful experience. Everything comes down to gaining or losing status awarded according to the ability to control and do.

Since she can do this thing and he can't, patriarchy offers three paths of least resistance: He can devalue what she does, he can find a way to control it, or he can feel lousy about himself. It is easiest to devalue her and what she does—by being indifferent to birth and babies—because devaluing women is a staple of patriarchal culture. Asserting control takes more effort: A man can become an obstetrician or a child-care expert, or, more simply, come into the delivery room as a "coach." But the life process is far more than the mechanical process patriarchal medicine has turned it into. It is soul and body work, and it may be the lack of this that leaves many men feeling left out, diminished, and not up to the "challenge."

When men feel left out, it isn't because they aren't women. They feel left out because participating in patriarchy leaves them disconnected from their own sense of aliveness. We can't practice a religion of control without alienating ourselves from everything we might seek to control.

Inevitably, control becomes a standard for measuring our worth. As Keen puts it,

> When men define themselves by power... they are able to feel their manhood only when they have the ability to make things happen, only when they can exert control over events, over themselves, over women. Therefore they are condemned to be forever measuring themselves by something exterior to themselves, by the effects of their actions, by how much change they can implement, how much novelty they can introduce into the slowly evolving history of nature. I did it; I made it happen; I exist.[6]

If men's sense that they even exist depends on having control, then it takes very little to threaten their sense of identity and worth. Almost anything can trigger this—having to say "I don't know," losing a job, not having an erection, or having to stand by and watch someone else "have" a baby. To avoid feeling threatened, men may devalue or ignore whatever doesn't support the feeling of being in control and focus instead on what does. It's no surprise that men typically seem less interested in the uncontrollable emotional and spiritual aspects of life and are drawn to whatever enhances feelings of control, from sports to computers to business to carpentry to orgasms to arguing about politics to getting into the *Guinness Book of Records* for doing something longer or faster or more times than anyone else. It's also no surprise that men so often place a premium on presenting themselves as independent and self-sufficient in relation to women: "In Andalusia, as in Cyprus or Algeria, a man is expected to spend his free time outdoors, backslapping and glad-handing. This world is the street, the bar, the fields—public places where a man is seen. He must not give the impression of being under the spell of the home, a clinger to wife or mother."[7]

This disconnected sense of standing alone and independent takes many forms. Men, for example, routinely diminish their connection to nature. They often ignore their own pain and mortality by pretending they're fine when they're not and acting as though they don't need help when they do. They may put on a tough, stoic front and make a point of being able to "take it" or do it on their own. Many live as though the body and its needs are repugnant (no smelly diapers for us), as though mind, spirit, and body can be separated into neat little compartments, as though the body were merely a machine, as though a life that denies or even punishes the body is superior to a fully embodied life. Nature, the body, and women become the "other," objects of repressed desire and longing as well as fear—"a great swamp into which men slide when they forget to maintain control."[8]

For men to feel inadequate because they can't feel in control around life's great mysteries is silly, but it also makes perfect sense in a patriarchy that encourages men to think they're supposed to control everything worth anything and to feel connected to things through controlling them. The problem is that feeling a deep sense of connection and aliveness—that we belong and matter within the mystery of life—isn't about control. On the contrary, control poisons and contradicts the inherently unpredictable and messy nature of aliveness. When life is about status, control, and competition, then everything becomes an occasion to feel vindicated or challenged (even by a woman giving birth to a child the two of you have created), to feel superior or inferior, included or excluded, chosen or rejected, elevated or diminished, "magnificent" or "insignificant." Any limitation can make men feel vulnerable by exposing them to someone else's pursuit of competitive advantage or simply to the private worry that they don't measure up.

As the father of two children, I know what it's like to wonder a little enviously at women's birth experience. But the fact that I can't give birth doesn't make me inadequate, marginal, or insignificant. It doesn't mean I can't connect my life to the blood mysteries of existence, a primal tie to my children that's rooted in flesh, cells, and nerves. It doesn't exclude me from the everyday mingling of lives, from changing diapers to the mysteries of language and talk to the struggle for a sense of who we are and what we're doing here. If the powerful feelings I have for these beings whom I never carried in my body don't involve me in something mysterious, awesome, powerful, and magnificent, I don't know what does. This doesn't make *me* powerful or magnificent, for the mystery is simply *there* as mystery and all I can do is choose how to participate in it without trying to *do* it or control it or use it. Men who find this mystery unappealing, who turn away from it in favor of competition, achievement, and "success," do so not because their biology sticks them on the periphery of life. It's because they're trapped on patriarchal paths that lead everywhere but into the mystery, the awe, and the vulnerable, messy realities of life, the body, and ourselves.

## The Hand That Rocks the Cradle

Arguments about mother power go beyond the ability to give birth, because in the broadest sense, it takes many years to "reproduce" human beings with adult capabilities. In Dorothy Dinnerstein's analysis of the intense relationship between mothers and children, for example, she argues that infants experience mother power as both overwhelming and ambivalent. It's overpowering because mothers have so much control over what happens, and it's ambivalent because mothers can use their power to cause everything from the greatest misery to the most ecstatic fulfillment of deepest needs.[9] This supposedly produces a sense of love–hate in both boys and girls, who want and long for their mothers, on the one hand, and are terrified of them on the other. The key part of Dinnerstein's argument is that the love–hate relationship translates into male dominance and misogyny in men and into self-hatred and subservience in women. Boys, she argues, will long for the mother's power to meet their needs, but also fear an engulfing dependency on them. This produces the paradox of patriarchal male possessiveness of women coupled with misogyny—wanting women and hating them at the same time.

From this perspective, patriarchy can appear be to just a countervailing force that provides shelter for both men and women from the despotism inherent in women's monopoly over child care. For boys, it requires them to both separate from and reject their mothers and the femaleness and femininity mothers represent. And if boys grow up to be emotionally inexpressive, dominant, misogynist, hostile toward women, aggressive, and obsessed with control, it's seen as just a way to fend off this dangerously seductive mother power. Patriarchy, then, is interpreted as an adaptive response to a system that has made the mistake of leaving mothering exclusively to women, which also implies that if mothering were left exclusively to men, the result would be an oppressive matriarchy. Dinnerstein's solution to all of this is a system of shared parenting.

There are many problems with such arguments, primarily because they make patriarchy and male privilege invisible.[10] In the broadest sense, they try to reduce complex social systems to simple and supposedly universal psychological mechanisms of child development, a kind of determinism that ignores most of what we know about history, cross-cultural variation, and how societies actually work.

Arguments like Dinnerstein's also greatly exaggerate how powerful mothers actually are. Connected to this are shaky assumptions about how infants experience mother power and about how this, in turn, carries over into adulthood. Just because mothers can withhold what infants need to survive, for example, doesn't mean infants actually *experience* mothers as omnipotent, threatening, or frightening. Adults might imagine what it would be like for *them* to be as helpless as infants, but, not actually *being* infants, they can't substitute this kind of imagining for what infants actually feel. The idea that baby boys lie in their cribs worrying about what mom might do with her power is more an adult fantasy than a credible account of infant experience. Even if infants felt these things on an unconscious level, Dinnerstein gives little credit to the human ability to reach some point where we stop relating to the world like infants.[11]

As anyone who spends much time with children knows, mother power erodes rapidly as children move beyond infancy and start to realize their own sense of agency and power. There's a lot of truth in the old saying that children raise parents as much as they're raised by them, and anyone who's ever watched parents and children in supermarkets knows that it's often unclear who's controlling whom. This shift in power can turn into a full-blown crisis when children hit adolescence and, regardless of gender, discover how easily they can drive parents to distraction by pushing the limits of adult control. If mothers have so much power to overwhelm children, they and their children certainly don't *act* like it most of the time. Instead, mothers are more likely to complain of doubt, worry, frustration, helplessness, bewilderment, and guilt because although they invariably feel responsible for how their children turn out, they know they're not really in control of this process or its outcome.

An additional factor that seriously limits mothers' potential for power is the cultural principle that "good mothers" are self-sacrificing and love unconditionally. "Bad mothers" put their own interests first or openly embrace power, like that favorite terror of psychiatric mother lore, the "domineering mother." Saddled with such heavy cultural baggage, women's potential to overwhelm children turns out to be largely hollow, since *women dare not use it if they value their social standing as good mothers.*

This is why the misogynist stereotype of the "wicked stepmother" has so much cultural clout and why the public reacts with special horror when a mother abuses or kills her children—it serves to warn any mother of what might happen to her if she uses the potential power of mothers without the social restraints of mother*hood*. In typical patriarchal fashion, cultural images of mother power do less to empower women than to ensnare them in a disempowering web of guilt and impossible expectations. The mother-power myth keeps women distracted and unclear about themselves and their abilities and makes it easier for husbands, fathers, physicians, therapists, child development experts, and other agents of patriarchal authority to control them.

The argument that patriarchy is a form of self-defense against mother power also doesn't fit very well with what we know about how families actually operate, especially historically. Patriarchy developed long before child care was defined as the core of women's existence, for example, and long before children and mothers were confined in small and isolated nuclear families. Even these patterns still don't describe most of today's nonindustrial patriarchies. For most of human history—including all but the last few centuries of the patriarchal period—children grew up in extended families, cared for by men and women alike and integrated at an early age into productive life. Mothers had their hands full with work that included far more than child care. This isn't the kind of world that would support formidable mother power, a world in which little boys would worry about how to get free of mom. If anything, fathers are the ones who would inspire fearful childhood images of omnipotence, for under patriarchy, a father's moral and legal authority *has* been formidable—often including the right to abuse, kill, trade, lend, sell, or otherwise dispose of children or wives. Even Freud argued that the most fearsome figure in little boys' nightmares isn't omnipotent mama but castrating papa. And when boys become men, the real power to "unman" them lies not with women, but with other men.[12]

The myth of overwhelming maternal power seems to be told most often by white, middle-class men like Sam Keen. As such, the myth is more about men's anxiety and insecurity than about the nature of child development; and in patriarchal systems, it isn't women's power that makes men feel anxious and insecure. If a chronic worry dogs men's heels, it's the worry that they'll lose status by not being able to measure up to patriarchal standards of manhood defined and enforced by other men.

If mothers contribute to men's insecurity and anxiety, it's more likely because mothers are in a position to know how preposterous the patriarchal charade of masculine power and control really is. Mothers know firsthand how vulnerable and human people really are. After all, mothers are the ones who changed men's diapers when they were little and wiped their noses and quieted their night fears and watched them stumble their way through childhood, all of which gives them the unique potential to unmask the pretense on which patriarchal privilege rests.

But, again, even this "power" really isn't about women—for men's fear of being exposed as weak and not in control ultimately is related to other men, who control and enforce images of manhood and the privilege that goes with them. It's easier and safer, however, to focus on mothers as the problem than to face the fear–control dynamic with other men that drives patriarchy. If men can see mom as the core of their problems, then they won't have to look at themselves or other men or what they're participating in. In the process, male privilege and solidarity stay hidden and unchallenged.

## Boys into Men, Girls into Women

Ideas about how male identity develops are key to the argument that patriarchy is just a response to mother power. Supposedly, male identity is formed in quite different ways from female identity and with very different results for men, women, and societies. The relationship between sons and mothers supposedly compels boys to reject their mothers and "women's ways" in order to take on a socially acceptable male identity. As this version of child development goes, both boys and girls experience a sense of closeness with their mothers that is organized around safety, pleasure, and meeting emotional and physical needs. Each boy or girl needs to develop a stable gender identity—"the simple emotional, cognitive, and bodily grounded conviction of being male or female and to being able to take this conviction for granted as a comfortable and desirable reality."[13] Body, mind, and feeling come together to form some stable sense of who the individual is and how that identity fits in an acceptable way into the larger world.

As the argument goes, a girl can achieve this simply by staying with her mother and modeling herself after her, but a boy must distinguish himself from his mother by separating and building a masculine identity that clearly marks him as "not mother." Boys have to shape their broad human potential to fit a narrow masculine mold—to devalue emotional attachment, tenderness, vulnerability, and nurturing. They must objectify themselves and others, organize their lives around issues of control, dominance, and competition, and develop their potential for aggression.

This is hard and sometimes risky work, and, not being fools, boys would have good reason to hang on to what they have with their mothers, touching deep feelings, body memories, and enduring needs. But "manly virtues" such as control, reason, and aggression are so important to society that powerful rewards and punishments would be required to motivate boys to walk the path to patriarchal manhood. According to this view, the core inducement is male bonding around male privilege, reinforced by various kinds of coercion, from schoolyard teasing to the kidnapping and ritual mutilation practiced in some tribal societies.[14] In other words, boys will get the pleasure and privilege of being one of the guys and avoid the ostracism and punishment of *not* being one of the guys.

The first piece of this argument suggests that patriarchal manhood is a necessary cultural creation that men must achieve and preserve throughout their lives. A man can't become a man simply by going through puberty and coming out looking like one. He has to *do* something, go out of his way to *become* something, in order to be counted as a man among men. On the face of it, this makes good sociological sense, since just about everything that human beings are and do is shaped by culture in one way or another. Behind this view of manhood, however, lies a false assumption about women and womanhood that undoes the whole argument.

By definition, patriarchal manhood is a negation of womanhood. Thus, if manhood is special because it has to be achieved and held through effort and courage, then womanhood must *not* be these things. Otherwise there would be no reason to elevate and privilege manhood above womanhood. Such an assumption, however, forces us to view womanhood as something other than a socially constructed status that women must achieve through effort, training, and sacrifice. It reduces womanhood to a natural result of a girl's physical maturation into an adult female. All she has to do is wait passively for puberty and do as mom does and womanhood will just happen.

By comparison, becoming a man is portrayed as the stuff of great and noble drama, struggle, and heroism, like the stirring lines of Rudyard Kipling's poem "If—," whose long list of virtues—from "keep[ing] your head when all about you are losing theirs" to dreaming great dreams, living in moderation, enduring defeat and starting all over again, taking risks, working hard, and not giving up—leads inevitably to the patriarchal payoff:

Yours is the Earth and everything that's in it,
And—which is more—you'll be a Man, my son![15]

"If—" made quite an impression on me when I was a boy, judging from how familiar its verses are to me in middle age. How could it not, holding out manhood as a prize more valued than "the Earth and everything that's in it"? And to *win* it, all I had to do was be what might be described as a healthy, fully functioning adult who knew how to live with integrity and take responsibility—not easy by any means, but a reasonable aspiration.

But there was one more little requirement, and that was that I be a boy to begin with. I don't think it ever occurred to me that "If—" was about me, my brother, or my father, but not about my sister or my mother or the girl across town I had a crush on. As I read "If—" now, however, I realize that it couldn't possibly be about girls turning into women ("Yours is the Earth and everything that's in it . . . "!), even though there's nothing particularly male or female in its list of qualities and virtues. In patriarchy, "If—" can't end with a woman, because womanhood can't command such reverence or rewards without encroaching on male privilege, which it's not allowed to do. "If—" couldn't end that way because womanhood isn't even regarded as an accomplishment. It just happens if a girl waits long enough.

But in reality the lives of girls and women aren't this simple. If we consider what a woman has to be and do in order to be socially acceptable, there's clearly a lot more going on than growing into biological womanhood. In spite of the fact that she's a full human being, a woman is expected to content herself with being something less than half of that. She's expected to allow men to see themselves as superior to her, to subordinate her needs and interests to his; to accept lesser occupations, slower promotions, lower pay, higher standards, to shape and mute her intelligence to avoid threatening men's egos, to endure being ignored, unheard, and invisible because she's a woman in a man's world, to do the work he won't do because it's beneath his status as a man. She's expected to accommodate herself to often impossible patriarchal standards of female beauty, an accommodation that often involves relating to her own body as an enemy or a failure, and molding, squeezing, and even starving herself in order to satisfy the male gaze. And she has to do all of this on top of being an adult in her family and community, holding up at least half the world with her labor, keeping herself and her family together whether her husband is there or not, raising children, and maintaining ties with extended kin.

None of this comes naturally to any girl simply by physically maturing into a woman. The extent of her "obligations" requires her to deny, mask, and distort the fullness of who she really is or could be. The only work that clearly hinges on biological femaleness is reproduction, but this has *never* been the central defining element of women's daily lives except perhaps in the recent sentimental patriarchal mythology of Western industrialized societies, and even then primarily in the white middle class.[16] In short, there is nothing "natural" about the social transformation from girlhood to womanhood. It requires effort, training, commitment, and a certain amount of coercion, as a girl who doesn't measure up discovers all too quickly when boys don't want to have anything to do with her. It's certainly true that *being* a woman is culturally devalued in patriarchal societies, but that doesn't mean that *becoming* a woman isn't a social process organized around cultural ideas about womanhood. Learning to fit into a subordinate, devalued status is no more "natural" and no less a matter of training and sacrifice than is learning how to claim and maintain privilege. The only reason patriarchal culture considers adult standing an achievement among males is precisely because it is associated with privilege, while women's transition is not. The other side of manhood as achievement is male privilege as entitlement.

The second piece of the argument connecting male development to patriarchy is the idea that boys must reject their mothers. At least in Western societies, there's a consensus that healthy development does require children to separate and differentiate from parents to some degree.[17] As applied to gender, however, this principle picks up the added assumption that boys must develop differently from girls by rejecting their mothers and femininity. In the romantic, mythological view of some male writers, older men must take boys—forcibly, if necessary—and introduce them to manly ways that are incompatible with "women's ways." Male initiation often includes painful and frightening rites of passage and an overt rejection of the once cherished female figure and her place in boys' lives.

The presumed goal of all this is to ensure "appropriate" male development and the survival of society as a whole. But the *process*, according to David Gilmore's cross-cultural study of masculinity in tribal societies, is to prevent boys from giving in to "the temptation to drown in the arms of an omnipotent woman, to withdraw into a puerile cocoon of pleasure and safety."[18] Boys, he tells us, must be forced to renounce their mothers and join the company of men in order to discharge their responsibility to protect and provide for their families. Otherwise they would be drawn irresistibly to the passive, pleasure-oriented world of women, hanging around and having a good time while society went to hell around them, with women leading the way.

Even if we accept the idea that psychological separation from parents is necessary for healthy development, it's quite a leap from that to the assumption that boys must reject their mothers and women in general as "other." It's an assumption that rests on a grossly distorted view of women and their role in social life. It also ignores the fact that whether something is regarded as necessary depends almost entirely on its social context. When patriarchy is the context, the rejection of mothers may be "necessary" only to the extent that it helps perpetuate a patriarchal system by enabling boys and men to assume their privileged position in it.

The assumption that boys will be passive and inactive if they don't reject their mothers depends on the myth that the world of women is organized around passivity and inactivity. It's hard to imagine more inappropriate terms to describe the historical and cross-cultural reality of women's lives and their enormous and irreplaceable contributions to the survival and thriving of families, communities, and societies. The *only* area where inactive passivity is ever encouraged in women is in submitting themselves to husbands and fathers, and this is an important clue to what the rejection of mothers and women is really about.

The worry behind breaking boys' connections with their mothers isn't that men won't work, contribute to their families, or ensure their children's safety and survival. After all, if men joined the world of most women, they'd be in for a lifetime of hard work and sacrifice, including risking their lives to protect home and children. The real worry is that men won't feel solidarity with other men and won't assume their superior position in relation to women, and will thereby undermine male privilege and patriarchal masculine identity. The real worry is that a boy who values and retains a deep connection with his mother evokes disturbing questions about a gender system that elevates and privileges male over female, including sons over mothers. The real worry is that a boy who doesn't reject his mother will continue to value aspects of his humanity that don't fit with core patriarchy values and rela-tions. *Only in a patriarchal context does it "make sense" to require boys to reject their mothers and, by extension, all women as a way to form a stable masculine identity and promote male solidarity.*

Ironically, boys are encouraged to separate from their mothers in a way almost guaranteed to keep them *connected* to their mothers and women in general in neurotic, conflicted relationships. To be real men, they are expected to reject their mothers and women and repress anything that seems remotely feminine. But this doesn't mean "feminine" aspects of themselves no longer exist or that they can live full lives by pretending they don't. Instead, the more men reject and devalue their mothers and the qualities that patriarchal culture associates with women, the more limited their inner and outer lives become. It precludes them from knowing true intimacy with other people, estranges them from their own feelings and the bodies through which feelings are felt, and denies them powerful inner resources for coping with stress, fear, and loss.

On some level, many men know what they're missing, and feel envy and anger and longing for what they don't have. They may fear women's anger because they need women to compensate them for what they've lost, to refrain from unmasking men's illusions of control, and to leave male privilege unchallenged. In this social climate, it's no surprise to find theories of male development that cast mothers as awesome figures in relation to adult men *imagining* themselves to be helpless, vulnerable infants again in a world organized around oppressive uses of power.

In a nonpatriarchal world, boys would become men without having to reject their mothers or women. They would embrace the fact that where they came from and who they are have as much to do with their mothers as with their fathers. But patriarchy makes this all but impossible by wrapping masculine identity in male privilege and measuring men's lives by control and success at not being like women. Men cannot both take their place as the dominant gender and honor and develop those aspects of themselves most associated with women and with their childhood connection to women. That so many men feel confused, incomplete, and resentful is inevitable under such conditions, as is the hope and belief that women somehow can make everything better.

The problem and its solution, however, lie primarily in men's relation-ships with other men and in the patriarchal order through which they define themselves and live. Many men see themselves as selling out their souls in response to women's power to give or withhold, to approve or disapprove. The truth, however, is that the successful achievement of patriarchal man-hood requires boys to give up a portion of their humanity—primarily at the urging of fathers, teachers, coaches, male peers, and a culture drenched in masculine mythology. If they want it back, they won't find it in women, but in themselves.

## Kings, Queens, and Wild Men

One of the most popular versions of the mother-power myth is Robert Bly's tale of Iron John, a mythic Wild Man who represents the "true masculine"— the creative, vibrant, passionate potential inherent in every man. Bly is a poet who founded the mythopoetic men's movement in the 1980s. He uses the tale of Iron John as a way to present his analysis of gender and how it operates in the world, especially in relation to men. According to Bly, the Wild Man was destroyed by the grinding forces of industrialization and, most important, by alienation between older and younger men, especially fathers and sons.[19] But the relationship between sons and mothers is never far from the center of the story.

The hairy Wild Man is discovered in a lake and locked in a cage by the townspeople. The King gives the key to the Queen, who places it beneath her pillow, an act of great significance when we consider that the Wild Man represents the true masculine nature of both the King and the young prince. The son wants to free the Wild Man, but is certain the Queen won't give him the key and is reluctant to steal it.

Why does the Queen have the key? Bly offers two different explanations, both of which ignore the fact that it was the King who *gave* the key to the Queen for reasons that Bly doesn't relate.

He begins by observing that it's a mother's job to civilize her son "and so it is natural for her to keep the key."[20] Over the last century or so this may have been somewhat true of European and U.S. cultures, but historically this kind of role for mothers has been the exception, not the rule that Bly's use of the word "natural" implies. Women generally have not been granted moral authority in patriarchal societies, even as mothers. On the contrary, fathers have been the ones with the moral authority to socialize children, since women were widely assumed to have an inherently weak and inferior moral character and therefore to be unsuited to such vital work.[21]

Bly mentions the interesting question of how the Wild Man threatens larger social interests, but he doesn't ask what social interests these are. Given that every *king*dom ever known has been, by definition, patriarchal, the interests of "society" can't help but reflect masculine control and male privilege. Rather than ask how patriarchy affects the father's behavior and the repression of the Wild Man, Bly moves to his second explanation for the Queen having the key to the Wild Man's—and hence her son's—freedom. It is simply part of a condescending, contemptuous effort to possess her son:

> Attacking the mother, confronting her, shouting at her, . . . probably does not accomplish much—she may just smile and talk to you with her elbow on the pillow. . . .
> "I want to let the Wild Man out!"
> "Come over and give Mommy a kiss."
> Mothers are intuitively aware of what would happen if he got the key: they would lose their boys. *The possessiveness that mothers typically exercise on sons . . . can never be underestimated.*[22] (emphasis added)

In just a few paragraphs, Bly shifts the power away from the King who authorized the Wild Man's imprisonment and who gave the Queen responsibility for keeping the key to his cage. Now the problem is the mother and her unexplained—but "never to be underestimated"—need to possess her son's life, to imprison and deny him his own essence. The father—his motives, interests, and power—are all invisible. Bly tells us that few mothers dream of their sons growing up to be Wild Men, but doesn't speculate about what fathers dream. And as fathers become invisible, so too does patriarchy as a powerful force shaping both the story and what Bly makes of it.

Bly, for example, says nothing about how a patriarchal world organized around the oppression of women might encourage mothers to hang on to sons in various ways, including unhealthy ones. Instead, he presents possessive maternal tendencies as universal and inherent in the relationship between mothers and sons. "That's just the way mothers *are,*" he remarked in one of his workshops for men.

With fathers, however, Bly takes a very different approach, asserting that fathers' routinely neglect and abandon their sons, not because that's just the way fathers *are,* but because fathers are victimized by social forces that separate them from their families. The implication is clear that men can be good fathers under the right social conditions, to which Bly longs to return. Mothers, however, are by nature selfish, possessive, and bent on denying their sons the passion and fullness of their own lives—provided, of course, that dad hands over the key.

Given what patriarchy does to men, it shouldn't surprise us that mothers often have powerful and ambivalent feelings about giving their sons up to it. It's a staple of mother love to want children to "fit in," and to anguish over sons coming home from school after having been taunted, ostracized, or beaten up for not being accepted as "one of the guys." As much as mothers want their sons to be socially acceptable men, however, their work as mothers makes it difficult to live with the consequences.

As Sara Ruddick argues in her book, *Maternal Thinking*, the kind of work we do affects how we think, and taking care of children is work.[23] Maternal work is so rooted in nurturing and so close to the raw basics of human need and vulnerability that you can't do it without appreciating what it takes to make a human life and what pain and suffering really amount to in human experience. This gives mothers powerful incentives to notice the destructive potential of patriarchal masculinity and to resist it. It was Argentinean mothers—not fathers—who organized protests demanding accountability for the thousands of sons and daughters who'd been "disappeared" at the hands of the military. There is a *Mother's* March for Peace and a *Mothers* Against Drunk Driving and Women in Black, but nothing comparable for fathers. Mothers support their sons' entry into patriarchal manhood because they want them to fit in and succeed, even though sons will suffer at the hands of patriarchy no matter what mothers do. And that suffering—and the root of the problem of turning boys into men—isn't inflicted primarily by women. It comes from men and boys acting on core patriarchal values and building and defending personal identities and an entire world based on them.

It also shouldn't surprise us that mothers don't welcome their sons' rejection of women and the breaking of a powerful emotional bond that patriarchal culture dismisses as unworthy and inferior. A mother's ambivalence about letting go of her son reflects a classic double bind. If she lets him go, she gives him up to patriarchal manhood, aids and abets her own oppression, and risks being blamed for it. If she hangs on, she's accused of being a bad, selfish, devouring mother who makes her son weak and neurotic.[24]

The root of the problem doesn't lie with mothers. But blaming fathers isn't the answer, either. At its core, patriarchy isn't about villains and victims, although there's no shortage of either. It's about paths of least resistance that encourage mothers and fathers to participate on different and highly unequal terms in a powerful process that shapes their own lives and the lives of their daughters and sons. And it's about how we choose to live in relation to those paths and how we might learn to choose differently.

## Who's Afraid of the Wild Man?

If Bly's story is telling us that the Wild Man is caged in order to safeguard the interests of civilization, then we have to ask whose interests are most closely associated with what we call "civilization." Since civilization as we know it is patriarchal, safeguarding the interests of civilization has less to do with Queens and mothers than with Kings and fathers and the patriarchal system that promotes male privilege.

Why, however, should an archetypal figure of manhood like the Wild Man threaten a system dominated by, identified with, and centered on men? A clue can be found in a closer look at the Wild Man himself, for although Bly makes much of the Wild Man's connection to manhood, ironically, the Wild *Man* has a deeper connection to what is culturally associated with women. He is a symbolic link to life energy, the earth, pleasure, and the body, all of which are tied to cultural images of womanhood, especially in industrial patriarchies. Early in the story of Iron John, for example, Bly notes that as the boy leaves for the forest, riding on the Wild Man's shoulders, "he has to overcome, at least for the moment, his fear of wildness, irrationality, hairiness, intuition, emotion, the body, and nature."[25]

In other words, the Wild Man represents what is most difficult for humans to control, which from a patriarchal perspective looks more female than male. The most uncontrollable force in human life is nature, which patriarchal culture routinely characterizes as female. Women are regarded as irrational beings ruled by emotion, intuition, and the rhythms, needs, and desires of the body. In patriarchal culture, truly dangerous wildness is female, for it is female wildness that threatens male privilege.

This is why so much energy is expended trying to control girls and women. It is why sexually active girls are more likely to be institutionalized as incorrigible than are sexually active boys. It's why openly sexual women are often regarded by men as "asking for" men to assert control by raping them. It's why the Wild Woman is so often portrayed as a nymphomaniac whose "wildness" isn't true wildness at all, but a compulsion that winds up primarily serving men's sexual fantasies. It's why "a good fuck" is the standard patriarchal "cure" for women whose "condition" is the wildness of female autonomy and power and a hairy, carnal juiciness that defies male control.

Ultimately, the Wild Man symbolizes defiance of the patriarchal obsession with control. Since patriarchy makes control primarily a man's game, men and not women are the ones most threatened by the Wild Man. As Bly tells us, the persecution of the Wild Man has been going on for centuries. He doesn't mention, however, that the power behind this always has been male-dominated institutions such as church and state. The Wild Man is imprisoned and murdered by a patriarchal system whose core values contradict everything he represents.[26] The Grand Inquisitor is never a woman, because women cannot be allowed such power. This is especially so when power is combined with wildness, which is why Bly's story is about the Wild *Man* and not the Wild Woman.

To control the passionate Wild Woman and what she represents, patriarchy makes her invisible or defines her as pathological or evil, to be co-opted, "cured," exorcised, tortured, burned, murdered, raped, tamed, or otherwise transformed. In the Middle Ages she was burned as a witch. In ancient China her feet were bound and crippled in the name of beauty. Today her Western counterpart is poured into a tight dress and jacked up onto high heels so she can barely move, much less run. In nineteenth-century Europe and the United States she was treated with "rest cures" and clitoridectomies to curb "excessive" female pleasure and desire. In many parts of Africa and the Middle East her genitals are mutilated and sewn up. Around the world she is sold and treated as marital and other sexual property. And advertising routinely exploits her sexuality to sell everything from spark plugs to alcohol. Her life is medicalized to justify intervention from patriarchal medical institutions—from weight loss to mood control to PMS, menopause, and childbirth. Murdering the Wild Woman draws on a rich cultural legacy that defines women as sexually passive and subservient in relation to men, that dismisses clitoral orgasms as immature and female physiology as pathological, that still labels women who avoid sex with men as "frigid," and that defines women's sexuality primarily in terms of its appeal and accessibility to men.[27] The particulars change, but the overall result stays the same.

Neither the King nor the Queen in Bly's story has the power to free the Wild Woman/Man, but patriarchy places the King a lot closer than the Queen to the heart of what keeps him locked up. As Miriam Johnson argues in *Strong Mothers, Weak Wives*, the real power in turning boys into men comes from fathers, male peers, and a culture that provides few alternatives to male dominance, patriarchal masculinity, and the rejection of mothers and women.[28] Research shows, for example, that U.S. fathers are far more concerned than mothers about children behaving in culturally defined gender-appropriate ways. It also shows that if sexual orientation is linked to social factors, it has more to do with how children relate to fathers than to mothers. Outside the family, boys soon learn to fear the potential violence and ostracism other boys use to establish masculine identities and compete for status in the male hierarchy. Boys who don't go along with rejecting things female are easy targets for male aggression.

Boys don't devalue their mothers and women in response to some overwhelming mother power that imprisons the Wild Man in every male. There's nothing inherent in child development that requires boys to reject their mothers in order to find themselves as men. It doesn't take much for a boy to see

how he resembles his father or to want to be like him. It does take some doing, however, to get a boy to deny and devalue how he resembles his mother,
to reject his tie with her, to deny his own human needs, and to embrace
dominance and control as guiding values in his life.

The struggle for boys is to respond to a patriarchal ultimatum: Either you
identify with and join men as a dominant group defined by rejecting women
and privileged by promoting solidarity and competitive abuse among men;
or you struggle to live at the margins of male society, excluded or excluding
yourself, sexually suspect, distrusted if not persecuted by other men, and yet
not fully acceptable to the company of women. Of course, it's not all one
or the other, and many men wind up somewhere between the two extremes.
But the tension between these two polarities is powerful, and every boy and
every man must come to terms with it in his own way. And every woman
must come to terms with the consequences of how men do that.

When boys reject their mothers as a requirement to join the patriarchal
order, they break a connection to a profoundly important human being in
their lives. But they also damage their own internal erotic and life-giving
sense of humanity, which, under patriarchy, they experience first and most
powerfully through the mother–son relationship. The damage often takes
the form of a hole in men's being, which they will try to fill. But so long as
they're stuck in the denial that brought them to patriarchal manhood in the
first place, the hole will remain.

Patriarchy discourages other men from making up the difference, for
they are all in the same boat. Men have reason to fear other men even
*knowing* they feel something lacking in themselves, and rarely do they dare to
identify, much less question, the patriarchal basis of what's going on. And so,
ironically, men often turn to women and feel daunted by what can seem to be
women's power to save them or not. But this often amounts to handing over
responsibility for men's dilemma to women and holding them accountable
for what men lack and for what men do with their feelings about that lack.

## What's Wrong with Dad?

The great power falsely attributed to women is often associated with men
feeling empty, devalued, dependent, excluded, or simply not good enough.
Sam Keen, for example, portrays women as holding tremendous power to
make men feel good or bad about themselves, intimidating men with their
anger, and evoking sometimes frantic efforts to satisfy women in exchange
for approval, affection, and sex. When men talk about gender, they often
report feeling vulnerable to women—feminist women in particular—who

can withhold what men need, make men feel bad, and undermine masculinity by refusing to play their complementary role as "real" women.

New men's movement writers such as Keen and Bly make an issue of men not feeling very good about themselves or their lives. They attribute most of this to relationships with women and their mysterious powers. As Keen puts it:

> The average man spends a lifetime denying, defending against, try-ing to control, and reacting to the power of WOMAN. . . . We have invested so much of our identity, committed so much of our energy, and squandered so much of our power in trying to control, avoid, conquer, or demean women because we are so vulnerable to their mysterious power over us. Like sandy atolls in a monsoon-swept ocean, the male psyche is in continual danger of being inundated by the feminine sea. And this fragility is not psychological, not neurotic, not a symptom of abnormality, but is an ontological fact rooted in our being.[29]

Many men probably do feel bad about their lives, but we can't make sense of this by ignoring the patriarchal context that shapes those lives. If men feel bad about themselves in relation to women, it isn't because of who women are, what they have, or how they behave. This pervasive pattern of feeling is rooted in men's participation in patriarchy that shapes who they are, what they lack, and the resources patriarchy provides for dealing with it. As with other aspects of patriarchal societies, the price men pay for male privilege has more to do with their relationships with other men and the social institutions that men control than it does with women. It's easier and safer to project power and responsibility onto women, but, like so many paths of least resistance, it takes us away from the truth.

Consider, for example, one of Bly's favorite themes, the lack of close, supportive relationships between young males and older men. On the surface, he seems to attribute this to industrialization, but it doesn't take long to realize that he thinks women are the real problem. The desire to control sons, he tells us, is only the tip of the maternal-possessiveness iceberg. To hang on to her son, a mother will do almost anything. She'll tear the father down to compete for the son's affection, draw her son into a conspiracy to oust the father from the family's emotional circle, and abandon the father to face alone the ravages of alienated industrial society. In Bly's version of history, "Those sensitive mothers who prefer[red] white curtains and an elevated life" undermined the father's position in the family by playing a key role in the cultural devaluing of physical labor so that fathers would abandon manual occupations and take their place in alienated offices.[30] And with fathers absent much of the time, sons can only experience their fathers through their mothers' eyes, which, Bly claims, always see the father's masculinity in negative, disparaging terms. Instead of clear male models from which to derive a stable sense of himself as a man, the son is left with a negative, trashed image promoted by his mother.

The image of absent fathers and their sons struggling to sort out manhood is a powerful one, but Bly's understanding of where all this comes from is rooted more in myth and misogyny than in the facts of history and family life. His explanation of what carried fathers away from both manual labor and their families completely ignores industrial capitalism and the emerging class system that turned manual labor into a commodity and subordinated and demeaned the men and women who performed it. He also ignores the fact that most women's domestic work is overwhelmingly *manual* and anything but genteel. It is women, after all, who clean most people's houses, who learn to take feces, urine, garbage, dirt, roaches, rats, and vomit in their stride. This isn't true of upper-class and upper-middle-class women, who can hire other women to do such work for them, but to attribute to the vast majority of women some general cultural devaluing of physical labor and those who do it doesn't fit the facts of women's lives. If anything, the working-class women Bly refers to were looking for a way out of the crushing class oppression of workers and their families and, perhaps, the common practice of husbands violently venting their misery on wives and children.

Even more difficult to fathom is Bly's argument that wives and mothers— the people most closely associated with nurturing, empathy, softness, self-sacrifice, and emotional support—are systematically trashing, undermining, and shutting out their husbands, their life partners in creating families. These are the same women who are so reluctant to give up on marriages with alcoholic or abusive husbands and who, more often than not, are roundly criticized for *staying* and enduring it all long after they should have walked out and saved themselves.

Undoubtedly, many men *feel* devalued and diminished as fathers, but the reason isn't that wives and mothers, for mysterious "feminine" reasons, tear them down. And the problem isn't simply industrial capitalism, which cannot be invoked out of thin air as if it has nothing to do with patriarchy and its core values. The competition that patriarchy encourages among men positions men in relation to industrial capitalism as workers or managers, and this profoundly affects how men feel about themselves. Industrial capitalism, for example, doesn't explain men's absence from family life. Millions of women, after all, work at full-time jobs and then go home to cook supper, help their children with homework, clean house, pay the bills, and tuck the children into bed. A substantial percentage of working-class and lower-class women of color in the United States have always done this kind of double duty, often by taking care of white people's houses and children by day and their own by night.[31]

If men are absent from family life, it's because patriarchy makes that choice a path of least resistance that men who identify with patriarchal values find hard to resist. Their choice isn't an easy one, just as such choices are difficult for women, but they are choices nonetheless. This doesn't mean that men are to blame for what's become of fatherhood in industrial capitalist patriarchies, for they didn't create the paths of least resistance that shape their lives. But if they want better paths to follow, they'll have to do something to acknowledge and resist existing paths and create and support new ones.

Men who feel devalued and powerless as fathers are often caught up in patriarchal notions of what fatherhood is about.[32] In patriarchal terms, fatherhood was once a linchpin of male privilege because fathers were the heads of families and families were the primary owners of land and producers of wealth. When industrial capitalism transformed economic life, both land and families lost much of their economic and political significance, which took away much of fatherhood's appeal as a way to enhance status and control. As the family shrank in social importance to an intimate group organized around meeting personal needs, men's ambivalence grew. What remains of fatherhood is often a romanticized way to feel special, emotionally fulfilled, looked up to and admired by one's children, or to share in tender yet fleeting moments of play and special family occasions.

Regardless of which era of fatherhood we look at, patriarchy shapes it to overlook the daily job of taking care of children, of cleaning up, watching, soothing, worrying, disciplining, transporting here and there, being constantly on call, and generally keeping track of who's where and doing what. Patriarchal fatherhood overlooks such domestic work because domestic work is culturally devalued labor that men typically regard as beneath them because it does nothing to enhance or preserve status.[33] Cleaning and ongoing child care are kinds of work that most men simply won't do except under exceptional circumstances, and even those who do such work on a more regular basis typically see themselves as doing wives a favor. When it comes to shunning the dirty domestic work of the world, no one holds a candle to men in patriarchal societies, regardless of their social class.[34] When mothers complain about fathers, it isn't to tear them down in some competition for sons' loyalty and affection. More likely it's because they resent the division of labor that works against women whether or not they work outside the home, that leaves to them most of the domestic work and denigrates that work at the same time.

If men feel bad about their lives, it isn't because women tear them down or don't build them up. The answer lies primarily among and within men and their participation in patriarchy. This doesn't mean that individual women don't behave in ways that undermine men or make them feel bad. But this can't explain the widespread *patterns* of disaffection and unhappiness that Bly, Keen, and others see among men. At most, what goes on between women and men is only symptomatic of the deeper contradictions and tensions created by life in patriarchy. If men project great power onto women, feel rejected, denied, and shut out by them, it's because men's participation in patriarchy sets them up to feel powerless, vulnerable, and inadequate and yet to deny they feel that way. The path of least resistance is to cut themselves off from the core of human life, making it difficult to get what they need from anyone, and to project all of that onto women rather than deal with the reality of patriarchy and the role men play in it.

## Paradoxes of Power

Men's frequent complaints about their lives often reflect the patriarchal paradox that organizing yourself around control, power, and privilege usually makes you feel worse rather than better. The paradox can produce surprising consequences, such as men feeling relatively powerless or envying women's position in society even though they aren't about to assume it for themselves. There really is no safe place in oppressive systems of privilege, and the lack of safety can, paradoxically, make dominant groups feel powerless, frightened, vulnerable, dependent, and even worse off than those they dominate.

Many men, for example, complain of feeling less in charge of their lives than women feel. Typically, men project such feelings outward and downward: Men feel this way because women have more power than men do, because they make men feel bad about themselves, because they cut men down. In reality, men are set up to feel vulnerable, powerless, and bad about their lives in two ways: by cutting themselves off from other people and their own sense of humanity, and by depending on women to go along with male privilege, to prop up men's egos, and to compensate men for what male privilege costs them as human beings.

Many men feel powerless, for example, not because *women* are so powerful but because men follow the patriarchal path of organizing their lives around control. This not only sets men up to expect absurd levels of control in their own lives, it also deeply affects how they experience others and themselves. The more that men pursue control and judge themselves by their success at it, the more they experience everyone and everything outside themselves as objects. This happens in part because one way to justify control over others is to see them as "less than"—as adults often see children or the elderly as inferior, incomplete, or damaged, as employers often see workers, or as teachers may see students. Unlike full-blown people, objects don't have wills or complex inner lives and needs that must be taken into account. They can simply be handled, used, or dealt with as their betters see fit. This provides a rationale for controlling others: that male superiority gives men the *right*, if not the obligation, to control women, or controlling women is for their own good or reflects the natural order of things. "To husband" is an active verb that takes an object which the subject manages "with prudent economy," whether it be livestock, money, or wives.

To objectify people is to strip them of their essential character, their "subjectness," experience, wants, needs, and desires. This is why we feel diminished by "paternalistic" treatment, even when it's supposedly for our own good.[35] This is a core element of dominant–subordinate relationships, the arrogant freedom to substitute our own experience for that of the "other," to assume their experience isn't important enough to consider, that they need or want only what we let them have, that we are all that really matters. In this way, we see them as estranged *from us* (rather than us from them or all of us from one another), as "other," as objects in relation to us as subjects. This is why it's commonly assumed that animals can't feel pain or terror, or that wartime enemies don't value human life as "we" do.

Stripping people of their "subjectness," however, also does something to the objectifiers by making it difficult to relate to the "others" in anything like a full way. When we objectify, we close ourselves not only to who the "others" really are, but to how *they* experience *us*. In this way, objectification disconnects us both from others and from ourselves. The human self is highly relational in the sense that who we think we are and how we experience ourselves can't be separated from how other people mirror and treat us. The more invested we are in controlling "them," however, the less reason there is to care about how they see us and the more limited our own sense of self becomes. This is one reason why those most obsessed with control are so often flat and dull figures, the Eichmanns, the lifeless bureaucrats, the schoolyard bullies.

The patriarchal obsession with control also diminishes men's lives when they turn it upon themselves as objects of control, with "self-control" as one of the hallmarks of a "real man." Instead of experiencing emotion (except for anger and rage) as a simple aspect of who they are, for example, men are encouraged to see it as something to control, a "feminine side" split off from the rest of themselves, threatening to become a loose cannon that threatens their status. When my mother died, for example, I went through a period of grieving that made me feel like crying much of the time, whether I was driving down the road or turning the corner in a supermarket aisle. When people asked me how I was, I often told them—sad, in grief, missing my mother, struggling to grasp the reality that death really meant she was gone utterly and forever, that I was now someone in the world without a mother.

In mainstream patriarchal culture, this kind of emotional openness often makes men feel uncomfortable because the line separating it from seeming out of control or woman-like is too thin. Living authentically in the emotional moment is too close to messy, chaotic, unpredictable, and uncontrollable Wildness. If you buy into control as a core value, you need to shield yourself from such possibilities, and many men compartmentalize their emotional lives and carefully control who—including themselves—is aware of what. They cultivate transcendence—the ability to "rise above" it all—as a value, holding themselves above the inherently uncontrollable flesh-and-blood realities of human existence. They cling to abstract principle and theory, or immerse themselves in the concrete, predictable world of machines and other selfless objects. The result is self reduced to a collection of objectified parts, aspects, and potentials to be managed for best effect and advantage and for minimal vulnerability.[36]

The more that men organize their lives around control, the more they disconnect from everyone, including themselves. They become trapped in avoidance of attachment, denial of need, and an endless quest to substitute abstract "meaning" for what Joseph Campbell called "the authentic feeling of being alive."[37] Living this way often brings with it feelings of emptiness, a simultaneous longing for and denial of what's lacking, creating monuments to control and achievement as a substitute for a self. Since most men have little actual power, they may struggle between acting as if they were in control, on the one hand, and feeling frustrated, angry, and helpless on the other, between powerful needs for connection at one moment and the safety of disconnection in the next, between seeming to have control of things and acting like children in relation to women, whether whining, complaining, or bullying. They may live with little real pleasure rooted in feeling and the body. They may feel anxious and uncertain, which often comes out as feeling powerless.

Another paradox is how patriarchy sets men up to depend on women in ways that make men feel vulnerable and, therefore, powerless in relation to them. In one sense, this is a common feature of systems of privilege that depend on subordinate groups to go along, to ratify privilege as legitimate, and to refrain from challenging the status quo. The potential to *not* go along, however, is always present as a form of power, and dominant groups know it. Unlike most systems of privilege, patriarchy generates an interdependency that goes deeper than merely going along with the status quo. Because ideas about manhood and masculinity play such a prominent role in patriarchal dynamics, men need women to present themselves in ways that make men's claim to a unique and privileged gender identity credible. Because patriarchal masculinity is defined as *not* female or feminine, men need women to provide a clear counterpoint that highlights masculine identity.

A major reason why women aren't supposed to be aggressive, for example, is so that men *can* be aggressive as a way to demonstrate true manhood. When women don't play this complementary role, they undermine men's ability to distinguish themselves as what women are *not*. If women can be just like men, then masculinity as the negation of femininity loses its meaning as a basis for privilege. Women's potential to be like men allows women to use the simple choice of how to be as women to influence how men feel about themselves as men. Women's power to pull the rug out from underneath men in this way is often attributed to women as some kind of negative personality trait—the castrating bitch, for example, or Bly's image of mothers who undermine fathers in competition for a son's loyalty and affection. But it's actually the system of patriarchy that sets up this dynamic and the feelings that go with it.

In patriarchy, men also need women to support patriarchal images of men as powerful and larger than life, what an Avon Cosmetics ad describes as, "What every man wants, what every woman wants him to have: That sense of triumph."[38] Patriarchy encourages men to use women as what Virginia Woolf described as mirrors that reflect them at twice their natural size. Without this power,

> ...the earth would still be swamp and jungle. The glories of all our wars would be unknown.... [M]irrors are essential to all violent and heroic action. That is why Napoleon and Mussolini both insist so emphatically upon the inferiority of women, for if they were not inferior, they would cease to enlarge. That serves to explain the necessity that women so often are to men. And it serves to explain how restless they are under her criticism; how impossible it is for her to say to them that this book is bad, this picture is feeble, or whatever it may be.... For if she begins to tell the truth, the figure in the looking-glass shrinks; his fitness for life is diminished. How is he to go on giving judgement, civilizing natives, making laws, writing books...unless he can see himself at breakfast and at dinner at least twice the size he really is?[39]

There's nothing about being born male that means you have to see yourself as larger than life, but there is something about patriarchal manhood that makes it tough to feel secure about being merely life size when control and competition are the order of the day. Most men know they're neither extraordinary nor powerful. In patriarchy, however, every man is diminished if he can't sustain a self-image in which somewhere, in someone's eyes, he's seen as triumphant, a winner, dominant, heroic, or at least in control. Since competition makes it hard to get this from other men, heterosexual men typically turn to women to pump them up, and may complain openly to women who don't actively make them feel like more than they are. Women—often out of a sense of compassion and caring—may respond in a supportive way to bolster male pride that, ironically, is a cornerstone of women's oppression.

This use of women to anchor male identity doesn't run equally in the other direction, for men feel little if any obligation to avoid appearing feminine in order to protect women's sense of themselves as women. When men are insufficiently masculine, women may disapprove or feel uncomfortable, but women rarely respond as though their own identity were seriously threatened. In part, this is because gender is a basis of real privilege for men and therefore entails higher stakes than it does for women. Women can play with the cultural lines separating the genders with relatively little risk, but a man who does so takes the much bigger risk.

While much about patriarchy works in such paradoxical ways, there are also many ways that men can work for change if they can see how they participate in ways that maintain and perpetuate it. The path of least resistance, however, is to project power and therefore responsibility onto women in general and mothers and wives in particular. When men feel inconsequential, it's easier to blame women than it is to confront patriarchy—the true source of the diminishment and lack of meaning in so many men's lives. When men feel unloved and disconnected, it's easier to accuse women of not loving them well enough than it is to consider men's own alienation from life. It's easier to think of women as keeping men from the essence of their own lives than it is to see how men's participation in patriarchy can suffocate and kill the life within themselves. It's easier to theorize about powerful, devouring mothers than to confront the reality of patriarchy.

Beneath the massive denial of men's power and responsibility and its projection onto women is an enormous pool of rage, resentment, and fear. Rather than look at patriarchy and their place within it, many men will beat, rape, torture, murder, and oppress women, children, and one another. They will wage mindless war and offer themselves up for the slaughter, chain themselves to jobs and work themselves to numbed exhaustion as if their lives had no value or meaning beyond controlling or being controlled or defending against control, and content themselves with half-lives of confused, lost deprivation. What men lack, women didn't take from them, and it isn't up to women to give it back.

# Part III
## Unraveling the Patriarchal Legacy

# 9

# Shame, Guilt, and Responsibility

I f this book has done what I intended it to do, it should be clear by now that no amount of denial or cultural magic can alter the simple fact that patriarchy exists and no one is personally to blame for it. Patriarchy is, however, a legacy in which we all share ownership. It involves everyone—men and women alike—although in different ways, especially when we take into account other factors such as social class, race, and sexual orientation.

Patriarchy is driven by a powerful and self-perpetuating dynamic between control and fear. This dynamic is coupled to a system of male privilege that is paradoxically grounded in competitive solidarity among men. As in every social system, patriarchal paths of least resistance can make it seem natural, even invisible. These paths encourage men to perpetuate an oppressive system that privileges them at women's expense, and encourage women to accept the terms of their own oppression even to the extent of resisting change. Instead of seeing patriarchy for what it is, we are more likely to dwell on gender differences, masculinity and femininity, and "gender roles." We normalize discrimination, prejudice, coercion, and violence against women. We confuse systems with individuals, personalize patriarchy, and get stuck in cycles of guilt and blame. We devalue, discount, and dismiss feminism and feminists. We get lost in denial, blaming the victim, and false gender parallels.

So where do we go from here? How can we build on this kind of understanding and awareness? What can we *do*? The first step is to realize that doing something about patriarchy is taking responsibility for it. Taking responsibility entails responding rather than merely reacting. It is acting from a clear sense of why things are as they are, and what about them needs changing. It is seeing how different aspects of patriarchy are connected to one another, to other aspects of social life, and to each of us. Taking responsibility is proactive, not passive. It means taking the initiative to become more aware, going out of our way to pay attention to what's going on. It means not waiting to be told something's wrong, but paying attention in such a way that we can see for ourselves. Taking responsibility means doing whatever it takes to come up with our share of analysis and insight—reading, watching, listening, and learning to question our assumptions. It requires an ongoing commitment to see and understand what we're participating in, how we participate in it, and the consequences this produces.

Without this commitment, we stay stuck in merely being part of the problem rather than *also* being part of the solution. Men, for example, who commit themselves to understanding patriarchy and its paths of least resistance, are unlikely to complain about the "changing rules" of sexual behavior and to ask women to "explain" sexual harassment to them. They will come to know intuitively what is appropriate and what is not in each situation, and when they aren't sure, they'll at least sense that something is wrong and needs their attention.

Dominant groups, however, typically don't show this kind of attention and commitment to the dynamics of their own dominance. They might see themselves as burdened with the responsibility that comes with power—bosses for workers, or "protecting" and "providing" husbands for wives and children. There are few incentives, however, for them to assume responsibility for the systems that give them power and for the consequences that result.

Instead, dominant groups typically take responsibility for whatever affirms their superior status and reinforces their privileged position. Warren Farrell, for example, and other "men's rights" activists complain that many men feel stuck with the breadwinning role in families.[1] Undoubtedly, many men *do* feel stuck, but this isn't the whole story. It ignores, for example, the well-documented relationship between earnings and decision-making power in families, the common tendency to see the breadwinner as the "head of household," men's resistance to letting wives share the breadwinning role (especially when women earn more than men), and the cultural devaluing of people who don't "work" (i.e., earn money) for a living and the respect and elevated status for those who do.

Taking responsibility for patriarchy means not only trying to be aware of what's going on and to understand it, but also daring to *act* from this understanding in ways that do more than make us comfortable with things as they are. To do this, we have to lay claim to patriarchy and own it as something we have an obligation to act upon. If we keep thinking that it's someone else's problem or some cosmic force that has nothing to do with us, we won't take responsibility for doing something about it. We have to act from some sense of obligation—that it's up to us to act—because without that, when things get tough, it's too easy to let go and leave it for someone else to deal with.

Responsibility begins with simply acknowledging that patriarchy exists to be understood, that we're connected to it and its consequences, and that we have both the power and obligation to do *something* about it and how we participate. Its present and its future have some small thing to do with the choices each of us makes, and taking responsibility means living with an open awareness of that simple fact. To paraphrase William James, we must act as though what we do makes a difference. We may not be able to do much, but it doesn't take much from each of us to produce change.

## Who Takes Responsibility?

What we're prepared to do about patriarchy depends on how we see ourselves in relation to it. Most men do nothing about the problem of sexual violence, for example, because they see it as an individual problem: "Unless *I* do it or it's done to someone I care about, it's someone else's problem, not mine." Women who succeed in male-dominated professions may take a similar attitude toward women who haven't, especially by denying the existence of male privilege, discrimination against women, and other aspects of patriarchy they think they've avoided in their own lives.

Not surprisingly, the ones most likely to take responsibility for systems like patriarchy are the people oppressed by it, usually as a matter of survival. Just as people of color have done most of the work in the struggle against racism, women have contributed most to figuring out patriarchy. With few exceptions, women have been the personal and public risk-takers. They've formed consciousness-raising groups to probe how patriarchy shapes their lives. They've written a huge literature analyzing the history, sociology, psychology, philosophy, anthropology, economics, politics, and everyday details of life under patriarchy. And they've paid attention, watched, listened, questioned, confronted, challenged, and taken to the streets. Many women, of course, haven't done such work, but where it's been done, it's almost always women who have done it.

With just enough exceptions to prove the rule,[2] men have taken almost no responsibility for patriarchy. Some men confuse taking responsibility with being sensitive to women, offering emotional support, or tolerating women's anger and frustration. Men can be sensitive, however, without doing anything to challenge or undermine male privilege or to define gender issues as *men's* issues, especially to other men. Even sensitive men can be drawn to the path of least resistance that defines problems such as housework, workplace discrimination, sexual harassment, and violence as women's issues. This makes it easy for men to see themselves as "good guys"—loving helpers, loyal supporters, or valiant defenders who help women in a patient and caring way.

What such men often don't do is the work of taking the initiative to decide what needs to be said, asked, listened to, discussed, fought over, attended to, and cared for in order to overcome the status quo's foot-dragging inertia. When women get tired or confused or distracted by the everyday details of their lives, the responsibility these men take often lies dormant until the next time a woman feels compelled to risk making trouble by raising a "women's issue." And when women express anger at always having to carry the burden of figuring out patriarchy and doing something about it, these sensitive and supportive men may react as if they're being unfairly criticized or even attacked, their exceptional and seemingly generous efforts unappreciated, their supposed immunity from reproach unfairly snatched away.

Sensitive men are particularly likely to feel vulnerable to angry accusations of sexist behavior. Robert Bly, for example, argues that when men respond to feminist criticism and demands by being "soft," "sensitive," and "passive," they set themselves up to be punished and manipulated by vengeful women. This is the sensitive man who turns up his soft underbelly to a woman, only to have her stab him and turn the knife slowly with relentless demands and criticism.[3]

What's going on here, however, isn't men taking responsibility and being punished for their trouble. In my experience, men who take responsibility for patriarchy are the last men most feminist women want to attack. More often than not, the men Bly refers to present the appearance of taking responsibility without the substance, *because they don't have a clear sense of what taking responsibility actually means or what there is to take responsibility for or are unwilling to do the emotional and intellectual work that taking responsibility entails.* They may claim to be on women's side because doing the right thing makes them feel good about themselves or because they value relationships with women and fear women's displeasure and anger, but this merely avoids taking responsibility. It's a stance that dominant groups often take, and women and other minorities rightly distrust it and feel insulted by its implicit condescension.

Why, then, do men avoid taking responsibility for patriarchy? In the simplest sense, men may not realize that patriarchy exists and therefore not be aware there's any responsibility for them to take in the first place. Also, the path of least resistance is to see themselves as not *having* to do anything. The status quo is organized in their image and in their interests, reflecting maleness in its highest ideals and images. Why, then, change it? Why question, much less give up, what they've got and risk *men's* disapproval, anger, and rejection, not to mention feeling disempowered, diminished, and "softened" to a position of equality with women? And why should they do this when they may not feel terribly good about their own lives in the first place?

Many men feel threatened by the idea of taking responsibility not only because they would have to give up a great deal of what they've been taught to value, but also because they would have to confront what they have given up *already* in order to participate in patriarchy. There is among men in modern industrial patriarchies an enormous pool of loss, pain, and grief, some of which, as Bly rightly argues, is tied to the lost relationship between younger and older men. But this reflects a much deeper loss traceable to the portion of men's humanity that they give up as part of their *solidarity* with older men and the patriarchal society whose interests both groups identify with. For men to feel their deep and deadening disconnection from their own and other people's lives is potentially so painful and frightening that most men simply don't want to know about it.

Perhaps the most important barrier to men taking responsibility, however, is their reluctance to expose themselves to the ocean of guilt and shame they believe awaits them if they acknowledge that patriarchy and male privilege exist.[4] The negative power of guilt and shame is especially significant for men who are otherwise most sympathetic to women and most likely to oppose patriarchy. These are the men who are most aware of male privilege and the price women pay in order for men to have it, which also makes them most prone to feeling blameworthy. They're in this trap because (as we saw in Chapter 2) both women and men often confuse individuals with systems and often place blame where it doesn't belong. Add to this how easy it is to confuse guilt and blame with taking responsibility, and it's understandable why even men sympathetic to justice avoid going very far down the road of taking responsibility.

## The Power of Guilt and Blame

Women are bound to have moments when they feel angry at men and blame them for the oppressive consequences of male privilege. For all the ways there are to joke about, rationalize, and sentimentalize male dominance, on some level most people know that it's real and that women pay for it much more than men do. To the degree that women and men find ways to love one another, it's *in spite of* patriarchy and the misogynist paths of least resistance patriarchy holds out for men to follow. Whether women are feminist or not, many know they have reason to resent men *as a group*, for you don't have to go very far beneath the surface of gender relations to see that there's more going on than a lively "battle of the sexes" or a fascinating case of "opposites" who attract. There's an oppressive system of privilege at work here, and men are its beneficiaries. Not only that, but, as Marilyn French points out, men have also been primarily responsible for perpetuating it:

> We must face the fact that the greatest impediment to the acceptance of women as full members of the human race comes from men. . . . If we put aside subjectivity, if we stop insisting that we, or our spouses or relatives, are not like that, and look quietly at the account of women's past, the facts are clear.
>
> On every level, men block women's use of their abilities outside the private sphere. . . . There can be no question that men as a class have made a continuous, unremitting effort to keep women under male control.[5]

Regardless of individual men's behavior, the facts of patriarchy give women ample reason to resent men collectively simply because "male" is a privileged social category in relation to which women experience oppression. This is quite different, however, from holding individual men accountable for the existence of patriarchy and blaming them simply for being men. In other words, when a woman says, "I hate men," this doesn't necessarily mean she hates *me*, Allan. But, living in a society dominated by individualistic thinking makes it easy to lose sight of the crucial distinction between men as individuals and men as a category of people. A woman may get angry at a specific man when it's patriarchy and male privilege she's really mad at, or overreact to his behavior by piling anger at the system on top of appropriate anger at him. There probably isn't much we can do about it, except be aware that it's going to happen from time to time and deal with it as best we can.

Men in particular can learn not to take it personally, to develop thicker skins, to let it slide rather than get sidetracked into arguments about whether they deserve this particular bit of anger. Women's anger is an important engine for change, and if women have to tiptoe around worrying about whether it might hurt a man's feelings, they're going to be silenced. I've seen this over and over again in workshops where women take care of men by silencing themselves rather than voice feelings about male privilege. Certainly there's room to talk about how women express anger at men, to sort out the individual man from the group as we go along. But occasional misplaced anger is no reason for men to get huffy and defensive if their real concern is doing something about patriarchy. Making room for the anger is a price men have to pay for privilege, and as prices go, it isn't very high.

The problem, though—and a major reason men may feel blamed even when they aren't being blamed—is that most men's identification with patriarchy runs so deep (consciously or not) that they experience criticism of the system as a personal attack. The evidence of women's oppression is everywhere, and it's hard not to know that cultural misogyny is real and that maleness is culturally defined as superior. When men and women list women's disadvantages in the workplace, their lists match to a degree that surprises everyone. In other words, many men know what's going on and yet find it hard to resist going along with the status quo and basing their identities at least in part on the rejection and negation of femaleness. So, when most men hear criticism of patriarchy, they have a hard time not taking it personally and feeling defensive because on some level, the criticism *does* involve them. Since each man's participation benefits him at women's expense—regardless of his personal attitudes or behavior—it's hard not to feel bad about it, which easily brings up feelings of blame and guilt.

## Why Guilt and Blame Don't Work

Guilt can be a powerful motivator to change behavior, but often only in the short run. In the long run, personal guilt doesn't give enough leverage for social change, and almost always provokes a backlash. People have a limited tolerance for feeling bad about themselves or for making other people feel bad about themselves. This is especially true around gender, because women's and men's lives are so bound up with one another. We've become so wary of invoking bad feelings that we've stripped ourselves of the ability even to talk about what's really going on. Words like "feminist," "oppression," "patriarchy," "sexism," and "radical" have become such buzzwords that the only people who dare use them are the very people who are most likely to be stereotyped as man-hating extremists. Because patriarchy is real, however, and since feminism and its radical, root-seeking varieties are fundamental to figuring it out, if we don't dare talk for fear of retaliation, we retreat into powerless silence.

Dominant groups typically show the least tolerance for allowing themselves to feel guilt and shame. Privilege, after all, should exempt one from having to feel such things. This means that, sooner or later, dominant groups experience reminders of their potential for feeling guilt as an affront that infringes on their sense of entitlement to a life unplagued by concern for how their privilege affects other people. The right to deny that privilege exists is an integral part of privilege itself, so men can be quick to complain about being made to feel guilty without actually *feeling* guilty. I've met few men who seem genuinely guilt-stricken over male privilege, just as I rarely meet white people who seem guilt-stricken over racism. Such people exist, but they aren't the ones who complain so loudly about being made to feel guilty.

Guilt also fails as a strategy for social change because it relies on a false model of how social life works. A system like patriarchy can't be blamed or made to feel guilty, because systems don't actually *do* or feel anything and therefore can't be held accountable as people can. This means that blame and guilt psychologize and individualize something that's also rooted in *systems*.

The guilt strategy also doesn't work because it disempowers people to act for change. Fear can get people to look at what's going on as a way to survive. Guilt, on the other hand, typically has just the opposite effect. For every man whose guilt has spurred him to dig deeper into the reality of patriarchy, there are thousands more who'd rather dig a deep hole of denial to hide in. To make men feel guilty simply because they are men puts them in a box, which all but ensures they'll never make a move toward changing themselves or anything else. They're far more likely to detach from whatever the guilt is about ("I wasn't there, I never knew, it never even happened") or angrily defend themselves against the unfairness of being blamed simply for being male or get off the hook by saying they're sorry or seem to change their ways, promising to be more careful in the future.

A different response to guilt is the overt celebration of maleness, as in the mythopoetic men's movement. While guilt can make men feel culpable for patriarchy, singing the praises of being male goes the other way by ignoring patriarchy in the rush to make men feel better.[6] This is part of an increasingly widespread denial that male privilege even exists, which in the hands of the men's rights movement often takes the form of self-pity and angry defensiveness.

A good example of denial is Warren Farrell's *The Myth of Male Power,* which reflects men's fear of being blamed and how far some will go to avoid it. Farrell seems obsessed with blame, from his early days as an ally of the women's movement, when he enjoyed women's approval for his public criticism of *other* men as Neanderthals, to his recent work, in which he repudiates feminism and promotes "men's rights." The purpose of *The Myth of Male Power* is to persuade readers that men aren't inherently bad or solely responsible for the evil in the world.[7] A feminist understanding of how patriarchy works leads to the same conclusion, but Farrell gets there by an entirely different route and from different motives.

Farrell seems so worried and angry about guilt and blame that he goes off the deep end to argue that men aren't powerful at all and are, instead, worse than slaves. He does this in part by adopting a narrow definition of power that has little to do with how systems of privilege actually work.[8] But the weight of his argument is a breathless series of thumbnail observations and assertions that are often illogical and groundless.

He tells us, for example, that since men may die trying to protect property (even though it's largely theirs), this makes them somehow of less value than property and therefore of less value than women, who he acknowledges *are* treated like men's property. He asks us to believe that men and boys taunt and challenge one another for not being masculine enough for no other reason than to develop men's capacity and willingness *to protect* women. He goes on to argue that culturally sanctioned torture such as Chinese foot binding is about female beauty and nothing else, that engagement rings symbolize the amount of physical protection a man offers a woman ("The bigger the diamond . . . the greater the protection"), that gay men are persecuted solely because of "their unwillingness to protect women," that no one ever jokes about women being raped, that people routinely ridicule unemployed men, that the only reason men don't share their feelings with women is to keep from worrying *them*, and that men routinely support women for life. He tells us that men's high suicide rate reflects the powerlessness of men as a group, ignoring the fact that blacks have dramatically lower suicide rates than whites, and black women the lowest rates of all, which would seem to imply that black women are the *really* powerful ones and that white males are at the bottom of the heap. And since slaves open doors for masters and help them put on their coats, Farrell reasons, and men are often expected to do the same for women, men are therefore deferential and subservient to women just as slaves are to their masters.[9] He tries to make it all right again by saying that men and women are *both* dominant *and* subservient to one another, but in different areas of life. Like Farrell's definition of power, this all but mocks what social domination and subordination are really about.

The real problem here isn't how Farrell turns reality on its head. It's the individualistic guilt and blame model that drives him and other men to such extremes to avoid feeling bad about themselves as men[10] and, whether they intend it or not, to perpetuate male privilege through massive denial. And the problem is the chord Farrell still touches in many men who feel bad about their lives, who measure themselves by control and power, and who welcome permission to deny there's anything going on around male privilege that might explain their predicament and call for taking some responsibility. The mere fact of being a man, of belonging to the social category that dominates the patriarchal system, is *not* a basis for feeling guilty or being blamed by anyone. It is, however, a reason to feel responsible for making informed choices about how we participate. The struggle to end patriarchy needs men with the courage to face a powerful system and other men, and there's no way this can happen if men are fixated on guilt and blame.

How, then, can we think about taking responsibility in a way that gets us beyond the individualistic model?

## Claiming the Legacy

To take responsibility for patriarchy we have to *feel* responsible for it, which means we have to look at how we're connected to it without being swallowed up by a sea of men's guilt or women's rage. Patriarchy is a *legacy* that's been handed down to us without our ever being asked about it. Growing up in patriarchy, the path of least resistance is to see it as normal, unexceptional, and how things ought to be. Like people in most social systems, we're largely oblivious to what we're participating in and fall easily into denial and rationalization when the status quo is challenged. But beneath our lack of awareness, the legacy and our connection to it remain. Simply by living under its terms and going along its paths of least resistance, we keep it going and pass it on.

Since everyone participates in patriarchy, everyone shares in the legacy. But like dominant and subordinate groups in general, men and women are connected to patriarchy in different ways. This means they share in the legacy and responsibility for it in different ways and to different degrees. Like all subordinate groups, women play a role in their own oppression, and a lot of feminist work focuses on reminding women of this and identifying alternative paths. Like all dominant groups, however, men are far more problematic because patriarchy gives them so many reasons to actively or passively perpetuate male privilege. Since patriarchy exists in men's name and primarily for their benefit, men have a special responsibility to face the patriarchal legacy and themselves in it, to know what's been passed on to them and why it matters.

To take responsibility for patriarchy, men will have to claim it without guilt or shame. Men can't hide behind arguments that patriarchy is about someone else, that others benefit from it more or suffer from it less, or that we're the exceptional nice guys who never hurt anyone. We can't pass off the enormous complexity of patriarchy to bad parenting or flawed personalities. We can't hide behind the damage we do to ourselves as we participate in patriarchy ("Leave me alone. It hurts me, too"), for how we damage our own lives doesn't remove responsibility for how patriarchy destroys the lives of others. Suicide doesn't balance homicide, just as men's abuse of themselves and one another doesn't balance men's abuse of women. Men can't hold out until women agree to take care of men's wounds along with their own or even to stop blaming men individually or collectively, fairly or not. And we can't take refuge in issues of race or class by reducing patriarchy to the power of upper-class white males. Men privileged by race and class are in a better position to benefit from core patriarchal values, but they don't have a monopoly on identifying with and defending them. Patriarchy is about all of us.

## Involving Men

Sooner or later, finding a way out of patriarchy has to involve men, in part because they collectively control most social systems and resources, but also because men's and women's lives are so bound up with one another.[11] On a deeper level though, men can have a unique perspective on the reality of male privilege, just as only women can fully understand the reality of female subordination.

Coming to grips with patriarchy poses special challenges to men. This is apparent across the spectrum of men, from diehard defenders of "men's rights" to the "pro-feminist" men's movement. There have always been a small number of men who openly ally with women in search of equality and justice, from John Stuart Mill to Frederick Douglass to Alan Alda.[12] There are now a small but growing number of men's studies courses in colleges and universities, a handful of journals devoted to understanding and exploring alternatives to patriarchal masculinity, and an expanding literature of men trying to figure out how patriarchy works and what they can do about it. It's hard work, not only because no one likes to focus on human suffering or give up privilege or risk feeling guilty, but also because the path of least resistance in a male-centered system is for men to focus on themselves and their own needs and concerns, not on male privilege and the oppression of women.

Contemporary men's movements are a varied lot, but they all call for some scrutiny simply because as "men's" movements they're organized around membership in a category of people that is socially dominant and privileged. Inevitably, such groups must resist being drawn to their own interests and maintaining their privilege. We wouldn't expect a "white people's movement," for example, to do much for people of color, or a "rich people's movement" to advance the interests of the working class, or a "men's movement" to end male privilege and female oppression.

Some men's movements are openly hostile to the women's movement, especially those organized around fathers' rights and divorced men's associations, known loosely as the "men's rights movement." At the other extreme are academics who write and teach about patriarchy and male privilege, and men's groups that work to mitigate some of the worst aspects of patriarchy, especially violence against women. On a larger level, the National Organization for Men Against Sexism (NOMAS) sponsors annual conferences on gender and organizes task forces on gender issues that include pornography, homophobia, fathering, male–female relationships, spirituality, and men's violence. In its statement of purpose, NOMAS

> strongly supports the feminist movement and the continuing struggle of women for full equality. We work to end crimes and injustices toward women such as domestic and sexual violence, attacks on choice and reproductive rights, sexual harassment, lack of parity, and the global feminization of poverty. We understand pro-feminism to mean challenging ourselves and other men on the ways in which we benefit from sexist behaviors. At the same time, we are celebrating the many ways in which men are becoming caring, strong, and non-abusive.[13]

Although NOMAS supports the women's movement, it calls itself a men's movement in part to stress that male privilege gives men a special responsibility for doing something about patriarchy. This also avoids the appearance of trying to co-opt the women's movement. Even among pro-feminist men, however, there are problems with identifying a social movement with male gender. By casting a men's movement as parallel to the women's movement, it's easy to see men as parallel to women in other ways as well, such as being oppressed or victimized as men. This makes it relatively easy for men's movements to drift toward blaming women for men's troubles or ignoring patriarchy and male privilege in a self-centered rush to make men feel better.

While NOMAS, for example, hasn't fallen into the trap of blaming women, it has been seen by some as focusing too much on heterosexism and gay rights and too little on the dynamics of male privilege that go beyond issues of sexual orientation. Part of the NOMAS emphasis on gay issues is based on the realization that heterosexual privilege and the oppression of gay men are links in the chain of patriarchal oppression of women. It may also reflect, however, a patriarchal path of least resistance that encourages men to focus on their own interests.

In some ways, this phenomenon is similar to white women who advance their concerns—such as breaking corporate and professional glass ceilings—and ignore white racism, in the mistaken belief that an analysis of male privilege from a white, middle-class point of view will also work for women of color. They may think that because they know what it's like to be oppressed as women, they also understand what racial oppression is like, even though they belong to the privileged race.[14] In similar ways, gay men may believe their own experience with oppression obviates the need to look at sexism.

A related danger is that men's sympathy with women's oppression may sensitize but not radicalize their view of patriarchy. It may make men more caring in the face of women's pain, for example, and turn them into more sympathetic listeners or supportive partners or co-workers. But if it doesn't also take them toward the roots—the "radicals"—of that pain to confront its connection with male privilege, they're in danger of becoming "sensitive New Age guys" who mean well but don't share in the hard and risky work of confronting privilege.

Many men are, of course, no strangers to radical thought and action, having been radicalized through experiencing their own oppression around issues other than gender. Some men have become radicalized around issues that require them to denounce one or more of their own privileged statuses, as when whites work openly against white privilege. Typically, however, people who have various forms of are privilege will cling to at least one of them while fighting against others. It's a rare person who renounces them all, and, for men, the hold-out is often gender. Radical feminism was born out of white women's experience of blatant sexism from men in the New Left antiwar movement of the 1960s. These men were on the leading edge of struggles against class and white privilege, but they were oblivious to their own male privilege and contemptuously defensive when women called attention to it. For men to be radicalized around gender is far more difficult than with other forms of oppression, because men have no experience of being oppressed *as men*, and because all men, regardless of race or class, have access to some degree of male privilege.

## Mythopoetics and the Men's Movement

The tendency of men to focus on themselves as victims rather than on patriarchy is nowhere more evident than in the mythopoetic men's movement,[15] most closely associated with the work of Robert Bly, Sam Keen, and various Jung-inspired writers and activists. Through books, journals, and workshops, the movement brings men together to focus on men and manhood and to heal the suffering and loss many men experience—spiritual damage, emotional impoverishment, poor relationships with women and children, and estrangement from other men, especially fathers.

Such problems are prominent in many men's lives, but this is no organized male response to the patriarchal system whose dynamics produce much of men's loss, suffering, and grief. Contrary to Bly's claim, it is not a parallel to the women's movement that is merely on a "different timetable."[16] It may be a response to genuine emotional and spiritual needs that are met by bringing men together to drum, chant, and share stories and feelings from their lives. It may help to heal some of the damage patriarchy does to men's lives.[17] But it is not a movement aimed at the system and the gender dynamics that actually *cause* that damage.

As such, the mythopoetic men's movement does more harm than good by encouraging men to pursue private solutions to what are social problems. Drumming, chanting, and storytelling may help men feel more connected to one another and to a mythic essence of manhood, but it does nothing to illuminate or transform the patriarchal system that creates the wounds they want to heal.

In some ways it's hard to see the mythopoetic men's movement as a movement at all, since it focuses on personal rather than social transformation— in contrast, for example, to the civil rights, environmental, and women's movements.[18] A social movement is more than a group of people trying to change their individual lives. It's also an organized effort to change the *collective* terms on which those lives are lived. In this sense, this men's movement is no more parallel to the women's movement or the civil rights movement than is the tendency of many in the United States to use psychotherapy or 12-step programs as a way of coping with life. More than anything, the mythopoetic men's movement is about self-discovery, personal redefinition, and catharsis among members of a relatively privileged group trying to ameliorate the emotional, spiritual, and social consequences that go along with that privilege. The only time the movement shows any interest in social forces is to portray fathers and other men as mere victims of those forces, and to defend men against feeling guilty about women's oppression by pretending that men and women are equally oppressed or that men are worse off than women. But this men's movement shows no interest in the idea of men taking any responsibility for something larger than themselves, such as patriarchy, or their participation in it.

The pursuit of private solutions to social problems reduces the dynamics of whole societies to individual psychic experience and interpersonal relations. This is related to a general social tendency to psychologize social problems. To judge from Bly and Keen, societies amount to little more than

what goes on between parents, children, and spouses; and social problems—
from war to oppression—can be reduced to bad parenting, interpersonal
misunderstanding, or bad habits.[19] If masculinity is a problem, they argue,
it isn't because it's connected to privilege and oppression, but because it's
"worn out," "undependable," "unsatisfying," and "no longer works" in
men's lives. The solution isn't social change but the individual, transforming, heroic inner journey.[20]

Intense individualism, combined with denial that patriarchy even exists, backs the mythopoetic men's movement into a corner from which it
invariably looks for someone to blame for men's pain and loss. Usually it
isn't industrialization. More often than not, anger and resentment go toward
women. Sometimes the blame is out in the open, sometimes hidden. Mothers
and wives come up a lot in discussions of men feeling diminished, incomplete, and unfulfilled. At one of Bly's day-long workshops, it wasn't talk
about the evils of industrialization that aroused grumbling recognition from
a huge roomful of men. Rather, it was the "Great Mother" who keeps men
from developing discipline; "the earthly, conservative, possessive, clinging
part of the maternal feminine" that suffocates men's souls and denies them
their manhood; the mother whose power over infants is so awesome that
boys and men have to organize their lives in response to it; the Queen who
keeps the key to the Wild Man's freedom beneath her pillow, whose tendency to cling to her son can never be overestimated, who competes for her
son's affection by diminishing, undermining, and trashing her husband and
refusing to redeem him from his own "dark side." It's women—especially
feminist women—who want men to be docile, soft, and weak, rather than
bold, independent, and courageous. It's women whose anger and demands
inspire fear and guilt in men.

Strangely enough, husbands and fathers are nowhere to be seen in the
definition of the problem. Bly mentions that fathers are rule makers and that
the King is the one who gives the Queen the key to the Wild Man's cage.
But otherwise, men come out as hapless victims at the mercy of women
and social forces such as industrialization. Apparently, male dominance isn't
privilege but only a burden men must bear—this business of having to be on
top all the time. Fathers slouch about in the shadows, drowning in their own
darkness, pushed from their families by women and the demands of work,
their fierceness and pride gone. Every once in a while someone mentions
that, yes, of course, some pretty awful things are happening to women in all
this, but that's quickly forgotten in the rush to portray women as, almost
magically, the truly powerful and privileged ones.

Although the mythopoetic men's movement claims to have no political
agenda, in effect it is profoundly political in its denial of the very existence

of patriarchy and any need to take responsibility for it. It routinely renders women as other, outsider, and the ultimate source of men's problems. It portrays patriarchal masculinity as problematic only insofar as it makes men unhappy, not as an ideology for an oppressive system that privileges men. The movement doesn't protest male dominance per se, only the price it exacts from men (it doesn't work anymore), and seeks more satisfying ways for men to be in society as it is:

> [The men's movement] is not, fundamentally, about uprooting sex-ism or transforming patriarchy, or even understanding masculinity in its various forms. When it comes to the crunch, what it is about is *modernizing* hegemonic masculinity. It is concerned with finding ways in which the dominant group—the white, educated, hetero-sexual, affluent males ...—can adapt to new circumstances without breaking down the social-structural arrangements that actually give them power.[21]

Coming to terms with patriarchy is hard work, and men have good reason to support one another in it. But there are serious problems with male solidarity around the common experience of men as men, because male solidarity too easily ignores how patriarchy privileges men *as males*. The mythopoetic men's movement perpetuates patriarchy and its consequences for *both* men and women, including the pain, loss, and grief that draw many men together in the first place.

In spite of all this, the various men's movements have at least helped many men acknowledge that there's something deeply wrong in their lives and that this has to do with their status as men. This awareness has opened up avenues of communication, experience, and expression among men that encourage them to explore their inner lives. But whatever books, workshops, and weekend retreats in the woods may accomplish in terms of men's feelings, these won't move us toward a society in which those feelings are lived openly. They will, instead, live on as personal solutions extending not much further than the relatively privileged subculture that shapes and nurtures them.

A key step for men who want to participate in change is to connect their inner lives to the outer reality of patriarchy, to go beyond vague attribu-tions to "society" to a clearer understanding of how social systems work and how our participation makes them happen. If the new men's movement is to be part of the solution rather than merely a self-absorbed, increasingly entrenched part of the problem, men are going to have to learn how to take responsibility for this social system that bears their name. Becoming part of the solution involves a fundamental moral choice about whether to use

gender privilege to further that privilege or to join women in taking responsibility for the patriarchal legacy. Men should either empower themselves to
move toward taking their share of responsibility or they should make way
for those who will. Until men begin to share seriously in the emotional, intellectual, and practical aspects of struggling with our legacy, not only will
change be seriously limited, but men and women will continue to feel at odds
with one another, because in fact they *will be* at odds.

Men's alternatives aren't appealing, but neither are the alternatives for
women or racial and ethnic minorities trying to deal with oppression. Like
all dominant groups, men are often stuck in a state of arrested development
that can wrap them in an almost childlike obliviousness, grandiosity, and
sense of entitlement in relation to women.[22] This insulates them from the
adult responsibility to know what's going on and to move toward doing
something about it, a responsibility that includes coming to terms with the
reality of privilege and the oppression that supports it. The reality of life
under patriarchy has forced many women to change in order to survive and
work for something better for us all. It demands nothing less from men.

# 10

# Unraveling the Gender Knot

What is the knot we want to unravel? In one sense, it is the complexity of patriarchy as a system—the tree, from its roots to the smallest outlying twig. It is misogyny and sexist ideology that keep women in their place and men in theirs. It is the organization of social life around core patriarchal principles and the powerful dynamics of fear and control that keep it going.

But the knot is also about our individual and collective paralysis around gender issues. It is everything that prevents us from seeing patriarchy and our participation in it, from the denial that patriarchy even exists to false parallels, individualistic thinking, and cycles of blame and guilt. Stuck in this paralysis, we can't think or act to help undo the legacy of privilege and oppression.

To undo the patriarchal knot we have to undo the knot of our paralysis in the face of it. A good place to begin is with two powerful myths about how change happens and how we contribute to it.

## Myth #1: "It's Always Been This Way, and It Always Will Be"

Given thousands of years of patriarchal history, it's easy to slide into the belief that things have always been this way. Even thousands of years, however, are a far cry from what "always" implies unless we leave out the more than 90 percent of humanity's time on Earth that preceded it. Given all the archaeological evidence pointing to the existence of goddess-based civilizations and the lack of evidence for perpetual patriarchy, there are plenty of reasons to doubt that life has always been organized around some form of privilege (see Chapter 3). So, when it comes to human social life, the smart money should be on the idea that *nothing* has always been or will be this way or any other.

In short, the only thing we can count on is change. Reality is always in motion. Things may appear to stand still, but that's only because we have limited attention spans. If we take the long view—the *really* long view—we can see that everything is in process all the time.

Some argue that everything *is* process, the space between one point and another, the movement from one thing toward another. What we may see as permanent end points—world capitalism, Western civilization, advanced technology, and so on—are actually temporary states on the way to other temporary states. Even ecologists, who used to talk about ecological balance, now speak of ecosystems as inherently unstable. Instead of always returning to some steady state after a period of disruption, ecosystems are, by nature, a continuing process of change from one arrangement to another and never go back to just where they were.

Social systems are also fluid. A society isn't some *thing* that sits there forever as it is. Because a system only happens as people participate in it, it can't help but be a dynamic process of creation and recreation from one moment to the next. In something as simple as a man following the path of least resistance toward controlling conversations (and a woman letting him), the reality of patriarchy in that moment comes into being. This is how we *do* patriarchy, bit by bit, moment by moment. It is also how individuals can contribute to change—by choosing paths of greater resistance.

Since we can always choose paths of greater resistance or create new ones entirely, systems can only be as stable as the flow of human choice and creativity, which certainly isn't a recipe for permanence. In the short run, patriarchy may look stable and unchangeable. But the relentless process of social life never produces the same result twice in a row, because it's impossible for everyone to participate in any complex system in an unvarying and uniform way. Added to this are the dynamic interactions that go on among systems—between capitalism and the state, for example, or between families and the economy or religion—that also produce powerful and unavoidable tensions, contradictions, and other currents of change. Ultimately, systems can't help but change, whether we notice it or not.

Social systems often *seem* stable because they limit our lives and imaginations so much that we can't see beyond them. This is especially true when a social system has existed for so long that its past extends beyond collective memory of anything different. As a result, it lays down terms of social life—including various forms of privilege—that can easily be mistaken for some kind of normal and inevitable human condition.

But this masks a fundamental long-term instability caused by the dynamics of privilege and oppression. Any system organized around an obsession with control is ultimately a losing proposition because it contradicts the uncontrollable nature of reality and does such violence to basic human needs and values. As the last two centuries of feminist thought and action have begun to challenge the violence and break down the denial, patriarchy has become increasingly vulnerable. This is one reason why men's resistance, backlash, and defensiveness are now so intense. Many men complain about their lot, especially their inability to realize ideals of control in relation to their own lives,[1] women, and other men. Fear and resentment of women are pervasive, from railing against affirmative action to worrying about being accused of sexual harassment. Even the mildest criticism of men or mention of patriarchy is enough to elicit angry—and worried—charges of male bashing.

Patriarchy is also destabilized as the illusion of masculine control breaks down. Corporate leaders alternate between arrogant optimism and panic, while governments lurch from one crisis to another, barely managing to stay in office, much less solving major social problems such as poverty, violence, terrorism and war, health care, middle-class angst, and the excesses of global capitalism. Computer technology supposedly makes life and work more efficient, but it does so by chaining people to an escalating pace of work and giving them less rather than more control over their lives. The loss of control in pursuit of control is happening on a larger level, as well. As the patriarchal obsession with control deepens its grip on everything from governments and corporations to schools and religion, the overall degree of control actually becomes less, not more. The scale on which systems are out of control simply increases. The stakes are higher and the capacity for harm is greater, and together they fuel an upward spiral of worry, anxiety, and fear.

As the illusion of control becomes more apparent, men start doubting their ability to measure up to patriarchal standards of manhood. We have been here before. At the turn of the twentieth century, there was widespread white male panic in the United States about the "feminization" of society and the need to preserve masculine toughness. From the creation of the Boy Scouts to Teddy Roosevelt's Rough Riders, a public campaign tried to revitalize masculinity as a cultural basis for revitalizing a male-identified society and, with it, male privilege.[2] A century later, the masculine backlash is again in full bloom. The warrior image has re-emerged as a dominant masculine ideal, from *Diehard* and *XXX* to right-wing militia groups to corporate takeovers to New Age Jungian archetypes in the new men's movement to terrorist groups and the president of the United States taunting enemy Iraqi combatants to "bring it on."[3]

Neither patriarchy nor any other system will last forever. Patriarchy is riddled with internal contradiction and strain. It is based on the false and self-defeating assumption that control is the answer to everything and that the pursuit of more control is always better than contenting ourselves with less. The transformation of patriarchy has been unfolding ever since it emerged seven thousand years ago, and it is going on still. We can't know what will replace it, but we can be confident that patriarchy will go, that it *is* going at every moment. It's only a matter of how quickly, by what means, at what cost, and toward what alternatives, and whether each of us will do our part to make it happen sooner rather than later and with less rather than more destruction and suffering in the process.

## Myth #2: The Myth of No Effect, and Gandhi's Paradox

Whether we help change patriarchy depends on how we handle the belief that nothing we do can make a difference, that the system is too big and powerful for us to affect. In one sense, the complaint is valid: If we look at patriarchy as a whole, it's true that we aren't going to make it go away in our lifetime. But if changing the entire system through our own efforts is the standard against which we measure the ability to do something, then we've set ourselves up to fail. It's not unreasonable to want to make a difference, but if we have to *see* the final result of what we do, then we can't be part of change that's too gradual and long term to allow that.

We also can't be part of change that's so complex that we can't sort out our contribution from countless others that combine in ways we can never grasp. Problems like patriarchy are of just that sort, requiring complex and long-term change coupled with short-term work to soften some of its worst consequences. This means that if we're going to be part of the solution to such problems, we have to let go of the idea that change doesn't happen unless we're around to see it and that what we do matters only if we *make* it happen. In other words, if we free ourselves of the expectation of being *in control* of things, we free ourselves to act and participate in the kind of fundamental change that transforms social life.

To get free of the paralyzing myth that we cannot, individually, be effective, we have to change how we see ourselves in relation to a long-term, complex process of change. This begins by changing how we relate to time. Many changes can come about quickly enough for us to see them happen. When I was in college, for example, there was little talk about gender

inequality as a social problem, whereas now there are women's studies programs all over the country. But a goal like ending male privilege takes far
more time than our short lives can encompass. If we're going to see ourselves as part of that kind of change, we can't use the human life span as a
significant standard against which to measure progress.

To see our choices in relation to long-term change, we have to develop
what might be called "time constancy," analogous to what psychologists call
"object constancy." Infants lack object constancy in the sense that if you hold
a cookie in front of very young children and then put it behind your back
while they watch, they can't find the cookie because they apparently can't
hold on to the image of it and where it went. In other words, if they can't see it,
it might as well not exist. After a while, children develop the cognitive ability
to know that objects or people exist even when they're out of sight. In thinking about change and our relation to it, we need to develop something similar in relation to time that enables us to carry within us the knowledge—the
faith—that significant change happens even though we aren't around to see it.

Along with time constancy, we need to get clear about how our choices
matter and how they don't. Gandhi once said that nothing we do as individuals matters, but that it's vital that we do it anyway. This touches on a powerful
paradox in the relationship between society and individuals. In terms of the
patriarchy-as-tree metaphor, no individual leaf on the tree matters. Whether
it lives or dies has no effect on much of anything. But collectively, the leaves
are essential to the whole tree because they photosynthesize the sugar that
feeds it. Without leaves, the tree dies.

So, leaves matter and they don't, just as we matter and we don't. What
each of us does may not seem like much, because in important ways, it *isn't*
much. But when many people do this work together, they can form a critical
mass that is anything but insignificant, especially in the long run. If we're
going to be part of a larger change process, we have to learn to live with
this sometimes uncomfortable paradox rather than going back and forth
between momentary illusions of potency and control and feelings of helpless
despair and insignificance.

A related paradox is that we have to be willing to travel without knowing
where we're going. We need faith to do what seems right without necessarily
knowing the effect our actions will have. We have to think like pioneers
who may know the *direction* they want to move in or what they would like
to find, without knowing where they will wind up. Because they are going
where they've never been before, they can't know whether they will ever
arrive at anything they might consider a destination, much less what they
had in mind when they first set out. If pioneers had to know their destination
from the beginning, they would never go anywhere or discover anything.

In similar ways, to seek out alternatives to patriarchy, it has to be enough to move *away* from social life organized around dominance and control and to move *toward* the certainty that alternatives are possible, even though we may not have a clear idea of what those are or may never experience them ourselves. It has to be enough to question how we think about and experience different forms of power, for example—how we see ourselves as gendered people, how privilege and oppression work and how we participate—and then open ourselves to experience what happens next. When we dare ask core questions about who we are and how the world works, things happen that we can't foresee, but they don't happen unless we *move*, even if only in our minds. As pioneers, we discover what's possible only by first putting ourselves in motion, because we have to move in order to change our position—and hence our perspective—on where we are, where we've been, and where we might go. Alternatives begin to appear as we imagine how things might be, but first we have to get past the idea that things will always be the way they are.

In relation to Gandhi's paradox, the myth of no effect obscures the role we can play in the long-term transformation of patriarchy. But the myth also blinds us to our own power in relation to other people. We may cling to the belief that there is nothing we can do precisely because we know how much power we do have and are afraid to use it because people may not like it. If we deny our power to affect people, then we don't have to worry about taking responsibility for how we use it or, more significant, how we don't.

The reluctance to acknowledge and use power comes up in the simplest everyday situations, as when a group of friends starts laughing at a sexist joke and we have to decide whether to go along. It's a moment in a sea of countless such moments that constitutes the fabric of all kinds of oppressive systems. It is a crucial moment because the group's seamless response to the joke reaffirms the normalcy and unproblematic nature of it and the system of privilege behind it. It takes only one person to tear the fabric of collusion and apparent consensus.

On some level, we each know we have this potential, and this knowledge can empower us or scare us into silence. We can change the course of the moment with something as simple as visibly not joining in the laughter, or saying "I don't think that's funny." We know how uncomfortable this can make people and how they may ward off their discomfort by dismissing, excluding, or even attacking us as bearers of bad news. Our silence, then, isn't because nothing we do will matter. Our silence is our not *daring* to matter.

Our power to affect other people isn't simply about making them feel uncomfortable. Systems shape the choices people make primarily by providing paths of least resistance. We typically follow those paths because alternatives offer greater resistance or because we aren't even aware that alternatives exist. Whenever we openly choose a different path, however, we make it possible for people to see both the path of least resistance they're following and the possibility of choosing something else.

The choice is both radical and simple. When most people get on an elevator, for example, they turn and face front without ever thinking why. We might think it's for purely practical reasons—the floor indicators and the door we'll exit through are at the front. But there's more going on than that, as we'd discover if we simply walked to the rear wall and stood facing it while everyone else faced front. The oddness of what we were doing would immediately be apparent to everyone, and would draw their attention and perhaps make them uncomfortable as they tried to figure out why we were doing that. Part of the discomfort is simply calling attention to the fact that we make choices when we enter social situations and that there are alternatives, something that paths of least resistance discourage us from considering. If the possibility of alternatives in situations as simple as where to stand in elevator cars can make people feel uncomfortable, imagine the potential for discomfort when the stakes are higher, as they certainly are when it comes to how people participate in oppressive systems like patriarchy.

If we choose different paths, we usually won't know if we affect other people, but it's safe to assume we do. When people know that alternatives exist and witness other people choosing them, things become possible that weren't before. When we openly pass up a path of least resistance, we *increase* resistance for other people around that path because now they must reconcile their choice with what they've seen us do, something they didn't have to deal with before. There's no way to predict how this will play out in the long run, and there's certainly no good reason to think it won't make a difference.

The simple fact is that we affect one another all the time without knowing it. When my family moved to our house in the woods of northwestern Connecticut, one of my first pleasures was blazing walking trails through the woods. Sometime later I noticed deer scat and hoof prints along the trails, and it pleased me to think they had adopted the trail I'd laid down. But then I wondered if perhaps I had followed a trail laid down by others when I cleared "my" trail. I realized that there is no way to know that anything begins or ends with me and the choices I make. It's more likely that the paths others have chosen influence the paths I choose. This suggests that the simplest way to help others make different choices is to make them myself, and to do it openly so they can see what I'm doing. As I shift the patterns of my own participation in patriarchy, I make it easier for others to do so as well—*and harder for them not to*. Simply by setting an example—rather than trying to change people—I create the possibility of their participating in change in their own time and in their own way. I can thus widen the circle of change without provoking the kind of defensiveness that perpetuates paths of least resistance and the systems they perpetuate.

It's important to see that in doing this kind of work we don't have to go after people to change their minds. In fact, changing people's minds may play a relatively small part in changing systems. Rather than turning diehard misogynists into practicing feminists, we can shift the odds in favor of new paths that contradict core patriarchal values. We can introduce so many exceptions to patriarchal rules that the children or grandchildren of diehard misogynists will start to change their perception of which paths offer the least resistance. Research on men's changing attitudes toward the male provider role, for example, shows that most of the shift occurs *between* generations, not within them.[4] This suggests that rather than trying to change people, the most important thing we can do is contribute to shifting entire cultures so that patriarchal forms and values begin to lose their "obvious" legitimacy and normalcy and new forms emerge to challenge their privileged place in social life. And when this happens, the structures of privilege—the unequal and oppressive distribution of wealth, power, resources, and opportunities—become harder to maintain.

In science, this is how one paradigm replaces another.[5] For hundreds of years, for example, Europeans believed that the stars, planets, and the sun revolved around Earth. But Copernicus and Galileo found that too many of their astronomical observations were anomalies that didn't fit the prevailing paradigm: If the sun and planets revolved around Earth, then they wouldn't move as they did. The accumulation of such observations made it increasingly difficult to hang on to an Earth-centered paradigm. Eventually the anomalies became so numerous that Copernicus offered a new paradigm, for which he, and later Galileo, were persecuted as heretics. Eventually, however, the evidence was so overwhelming that a new paradigm replaced the old one.

In similar ways, we can think of patriarchy as a system based on a paradigm that shapes how we think about gender and organize social life in relation to it. The patriarchal paradigm has been under attack for several centuries and the defense has been vigorous, with feminists widely regarded as heretics who practice the blasphemy of "male bashing." The patriarchal paradigm weakens in the face of mounting evidence that it produces un-acceptable consequences. We help weaken it by openly choosing alternative paths in our everyday lives and thereby providing living anomalies that don't fit the prevailing paradigm. By our example, we contradict patriarchal assumptions and their legitimacy over and over again. We add our choices and our lives to tip the scales toward new paradigms that don't revolve around control, privilege, and oppression. We can't tip the scales overnight or by ourselves, and in that sense we don't amount to much. But on the other side of Gandhi's paradox, it is crucial where we "choose to place the stubborn ounces of [our] weight."[6] It is in such small and humble choices that patriarchy and the movement toward something better actually happen.

## Stubborn Ounces: What Can We Do?

There are no easy answers to the question of what can we do about patriarchy. There is no 12-step program, no set of instructions that will turn it into something else. Most important, there is no way around or over it—the only way out is through.

We won't end oppression by pretending it isn't there or that we don't have to deal with it. Some may complain that working for change is "divisive" by drawing attention to oppressive systems of privilege. But when members of dominant groups "mark" differences by excluding or discriminating against subordinate groups and treating them as "other," they aren't accused of being divisive. Usually it's only when someone calls attention to how differences are used as a basis for privilege that the charge of divisiveness comes up.

In a sense, it *is* divisive to say that oppression and privilege exist, but only insofar as it points to divisions that already exist and to the perception that the status quo is normal and unremarkable. Privilege and oppression promote the worst kind of divisiveness because they cut us off from one another and, by silencing us, cut us off from ourselves as well. Not only must we participate in privilege and oppression by living in society, we also must act as though they don't exist, denying the reality of our own experience and its consequences for people's lives, including our own.

What does it mean to go out by going through? What can we do about patriarchy that will make a difference?

### Acknowledge That Patriarchy Exists

A key to the continued existence of every oppressive system of privilege is people being unaware of what's going on, because privilege contradicts so many basic human values that it invariably arouses opposition when people know about it. The Soviet Union and its East European satellites, for example, were riddled with contradictions that were so widely known among their people that the regimes fell apart with barely a whimper when given half a chance. An awareness of privilege compels people to speak out, breaking the silence on which continued privilege depends. This is why most cultures mask the reality of privilege by denying its existence, trivializing it, calling it something else, blaming it on those most damaged by it, or drawing attention away from it to other things.

It's one thing to become aware and quite another to stay that way. The greatest challenge when we first become aware of a critical perspective on the world is simply to hang on to it. Every system's paths of least resistance invariably lead *away* from critical awareness of how the system works. Therefore, the easiest thing to do after reading a book like this is to forget about it. Maintaining a critical consciousness takes commitment and work. Awareness is something we either maintain in the moment or we don't. And the only way to hang on to an awareness of patriarchy is to make paying attention to it an ongoing part of our lives.

## Pay Attention

Understanding how patriarchy works and how we participate is essential for change. It's easy to have opinions, but it takes work to know what you're talking about. The easiest place to begin is by reading, and making reading about patriarchy part of your life. Unless you have the luxury of a personal teacher, you can't understand patriarchy without reading, just as you need to read about a foreign country before you travel there for the first time. Many people assume they already know what they need to know about gender since everyone has a gender, but they're usually wrong. Just as the last thing a fish would discover is water, the last thing we'll discover is society itself and something as pervasive as gender dynamics.

This means you have to be open to the idea that what you think you know is, if not wrong, so deeply shaped by patriarchy that it misses most of the truth. This is why feminists talk with one another and spend time reading one another's work—seeing things clearly is tricky and difficult work. This is also why people who are critical of the status quo are so often self-critical as well, for they know how complex and elusive the truth really is and what a challenge it is to work toward it. People working for change are often accused of being orthodox and rigid, but they are also among the most self-critical people around.

There is a huge feminist literature available through any decent library, although you'd never know it to judge from its invisibility in the mass media and mainstream bookstores. In fact, it's a good idea not to rely on the mass media for meaningful analysis of any form of privilege. The media ignore most of what is known about privilege, and routinely focus on issues that have the least to do with it ("Do men and women use different parts of their brains?"), that reflect the most flawed models of social reality

("Men are from Mars, . . ."), and that set women against one another, especially when women attack other women. Most feminist work is virtually invisible to book reviewers, journalists, editorial writers, columnists, and publishers. So, to know what's going on, it may take an interlibrary loan request or a special order at the bookstore. But we can do more than that—we can also tell librarians and bookstore managers how surprised we are that they don't stock such essential reading for understanding the world.

As you educate yourself, it's important to avoid reinventing the wheel. Many people have already done a lot of work that you can learn from. There's no way to get through it all, but you don't have to in order to develop a clear enough sense of how to act in meaningful and informed ways. A good place to start is a basic text on women's studies. Men who feel there is no place for them in women's studies might start with books about patriarchy and gender that are written by men. Sooner or later, however, men will have to turn to what women have written, because women have done most of the work of figuring out how patriarchy works.[7] Those who expect women's feminist writings to be full of animosity toward men should prepare themselves for a surprise. And while it's important never to swallow anything whole and uncritically, it's also important that men believe what women say about their experience of oppression under patriarchy. These are, after all, our mothers, sisters, daughters, lovers, wives, and friends telling us in a resounding collective voice of centuries of oppression from perspectives that we as men cannot duplicate. When the stories originate from women of so many racial, class, and ethnic backgrounds, and when they echo across cultures and the span of history, they call on men to have enough respect and humility to be silent for a while and just listen.

Reading, though, is only a beginning. At some point you have to look at yourself and the world to see if you can identify what you're reading about. Once the phrase "paths of least resistance" entered my active vocabulary, for example, I started seeing them all over the place. The more aware I am of how powerful a path is, the more I can decide whether to go down it each time it presents itself. When this kind of awareness is shared openly among people, the possibilities for alternative paths multiply rapidly, especially when you realize that you don't have to feel guilty for what you're leaving behind. If you focus on paths and your choices in relation to them rather than on the content of your character, you can leave guilt behind and work to identify new paths and support yourself and other people in choosing them. It doesn't have to be about continually pointing to "what's wrong with me," because the truth is that we aren't the problem. The primary problem is the system we're participating in and the consequences that result from the choices we make in relation to it. Seeing this and seeing how we can participate differently isn't easy or fun. But it is a way for women and men to reclaim important parts of their lives that are now compromised, distorted, and damaged under patriarchy.

There are endless opportunities to participate in change, because paths of least resistance connect us to all kinds of systems. At work, the path of least resistance for managers is to mentor and promote people who most resemble themselves, which in most companies turns out to be white men. Whether at work or on the street, sexual harassment results from men following paths that define both male and female sexuality in male-dominated, male-identified, and male-centered terms. In everyday conversation, the path of least resistance is for men to dominate and be heard, and for women to defer and be unheard. In school, patriarchal paths draw teachers to pay more and better attention to boys than to girls, draw boys to take advantage of it, and draw girls to expect less than they need or deserve. And on it goes, from one social situation to another, as patriarchy shapes how we perceive alternatives and how we choose among them without even knowing it. The challenge *is* to know it by becoming more aware of both the paths inherent in those situations and the choices we make in relation to them.

It helps to be like anthropologists, participant observers who watch and listen to others and ourselves, who notice patterns that come up over and over in social life. We can pretend we're strangers in a strange land who know nothing about where we are and *know* we know nothing. This keeps us open to mistaken assumptions and the surprise of realizing that things aren't what they seem.

This is especially challenging for men, whose privilege tells them they shouldn't have to work to figure out someone else, that it's up to others to figure them out. It's easy for men to fall into the trap of being like impatient, arrogant tourists who don't take the initiative to educate themselves about where they are and their place in it. But taking responsibility means men not waiting for women to tell them what to do, to point out what's going on, or to identify alternatives. If men are going to take their share of responsibility, it's up to men to listen, watch, ask, and listen again, to make it their business to find out for themselves. If they don't, they'll slide down the comfortable oblivious path of male privilege. And then they will be *just* part of the problem and they *will* be blamed and they'll have it coming.

### Learn to Listen

This is especially difficult for members of dominant groups. If someone confronts you with your own behavior that supports privilege, step off the path of least resistance that encourages you to defend and deny. Don't tell them they're too sensitive or need a better sense of humor, and don't try to explain away what you did as something else than what they're telling you it was. Don't say you didn't mean it or that you were only kidding. Don't tell them what a champion of justice you are or how hurt you feel because of what they're telling you. Don't make jokes or try to be cute or charming, since only privilege can lead someone to believe these are acceptable responses to something as serious as privilege and oppression. Listen to what's being said. Take it seriously. Assume for the time being that it's true, because given the power of paths of least resistance, it probably is. And then take responsibility to do something about it.[8]

A student of color in one of my classes, for example, once told me that she noticed me cutting her off during class, something she didn't think I did with white students. I could have weighed in with my professorial authority and said it wasn't true, that she was imagining it, that I treat all my students the same, that she was being too sensitive, that I travel all over the country speaking about issues of inequality and injustice, so certainly I was above such things. But what I said to her was that I was truly sorry she'd had that experience. I wasn't aware of doing that, I told her, but the fact that I didn't consciously mean to was beside the point.

To respond in this way, I had to de-center myself from my position of privilege and make her experience and not mine the point of the conversation. I ended by telling her I would do everything I could to pay attention to this in the future to make sure it didn't happen in my classes.

It's important to note that my goodness or badness as a person was not the issue. The issue was the existence of pervasive racist patterns through which privilege is enacted every day and whether I was unconsciously reproducing those patterns and, most important, whether I was willing to take responsibility for paying attention to my own behavior as a participant. I believe that most of the time, members of subordinate groups are not looking for dominant groups to feel ashamed or guilty, because this will do nothing in itself to improve their own lives. In my experience, the true goal is to end privilege and oppression and to get dominant groups to commit themselves to doing whatever they can to make that happen.

## Little Risks: Do Something

The more you pay attention to what's going on, the more you'll see opportunities to do something about it. You don't have to mount an expedition to find them, because they're all over the place, beginning in ourselves.

As I became aware of how I gravitated toward controlling conversations, for example, I also realized how easily men dominate group meetings by controlling the agenda and interrupting, without women objecting to it. This pattern is especially striking in groups that are mostly female but in which most of the talking nonetheless comes from a few men. I would find myself sitting in meetings and suddenly the preponderance of male voices would jump out at me, an unmistakable hallmark of male privilege in full bloom.

As I've seen what's going on, I've had to decide what to do about this little path of least resistance and my relation to it that leads me to follow it so readily. With some effort, I've tried out new ways of listening more and talking less. At times it has felt contrived and artificial, like telling myself to shut up for a while or even counting slowly to ten (or more) to give others a chance to step into the silence. With time and practice, new paths have become easier to follow and I spend less time monitoring myself. But awareness is never automatic or permanent, for patriarchal paths of least resistance will be there to choose or not as long as patriarchy exists.

You might be thinking at this point that everything comes down to changing individuals after all since doing something is a matter of people's behavior. In a sense, of course, it's true that, for us, it all comes down to what we do or don't do as individuals since that's what we are. But the key is to always connect our choices to the systems we participate in. When you *openly* change how you participate in a system, you do more than change your own behavior, for you also change how the system itself happens. When you change how a system operates, you change the social environment that shapes other people's behavior which, in turn, further changes how the system operates. And when you do that, you also change the consequences that come out of the dynamic relationship between systems and individuals, including patterns of privilege and oppression.

Sometimes stepping off the path of least resistance is a matter of directly calling attention to the system and how it's organized. As you'll see below, for example, it might involve calling attention to the distribution of power and resources in an organization—why are all the secretaries women and all the executives men? Why is the custodial staff mostly people of color and the management staff entirely white? Choosing to call attention to such patterns means changing your own behavior, but it does more than that because the focus of your actions is the system itself.

In short, since the world happens as it does through the dynamic relationship between individuals and social systems, changing the world has to involve both.

As you see more of what's going on, questions come up about what goes on at work, in the media, in families, in communities, in religion, in government, on the street, and at school—just about everywhere. The questions

don't come all at once (for which we can be grateful), although they sometimes come in a rush that can feel overwhelming. If you remind yourself that
it isn't up to you to do it all, however, you can see plenty of situations in
which you can make a difference, sometimes in surprisingly simple ways.
Consider the following possibilities:

- *Organize, organize, organize.* Work with other people. This is one
  of the most important principles of participating in social change.
  From expanding consciousness to taking risks, it makes all the difference in the world to be in the company of people who support
  what you're trying to do. You can read and talk about books and
  issues and just plain hang out with other people who want to understand and do something about patriarchy. Remember that the
  modern women's movement's roots were in consciousness-raising
  groups in which women did little more than sit around and talk
  about themselves and their lives and try to figure out what that had
  to do with living in patriarchy. It may not have looked like much
  at the time, but it laid the foundation for huge social movements.
  One way down this path is to share a book like this one with someone and then talk about it. Or ask around about local groups and
  organizations that focus on gender issues, and go find out what
  they're about and meet other people. After reading a book or article that you like, write to the author in the care of the publisher
  or by email. It's easy to think authors don't want to be bothered
  by interested readers, but the truth is, they usually welcome it and
  respond. Make contact and connect to other people engaged in the
  same work. Do whatever reminds you that you aren't alone in this.
- *Make noise, be seen.* Stand up, volunteer, speak out, write letters,
  sign petitions, show up. Like every oppressive system of privilege,
  patriarchy feeds on silence. Breaking the silence is especially important for men, because it undermines the assumption of male
  solidarity that patriarchy depends on. If this feels too risky, men
  can practice being aware of how silence reflects their investment in
  solidarity with other men. This can be a place to begin working on
  awareness: "Today I said nothing, colluded in silence, and this is
  how I benefited from it. Tomorrow I can try something different."
- *Find little ways to withdraw support from paths of least resistance
  and people's choices to follow them, starting with yourself.* It can be
  as simple as not laughing at a sexist joke or saying you don't think
  it's funny. Or writing a letter to the editor objecting to sexism in
  the media. When my local newspaper ran an article whose headline

referred to sexual harassment as "earthy behavior," for example, I wrote a letter pointing out that harassment isn't "earthy."

The key is to interrupt the flow of "business as usual." You can disrupt the assumption that everyone is going along with the status quo by *simply not going along.* When you do this, you stop the flow, if only for a moment, but in that moment other people can notice and start to think and question. It's a perfect time to suggest the possibility of alternatives such as humor that isn't at someone else's expense or of ways to think about harassment and violence that do justice to the reality of what's going on and how it affects people.

We often like to think of ourselves as individuals—especially in the United States. But it's amazing how much of the time we compare ourselves to other people as a way to see how well we fit in. Anything that disrupts this process in even the smallest way can affect taken-for-granted assumptions that underlie social reality. It might help to think of this process as inserting grains of sand in an oyster to irritate it into creating a pearl of insight, or as a way to make patriarchy itch, stir, and scratch and thereby reveal itself for others to see, or as planting seeds of doubt about the desirability and inevitability of the way things are, and, by example, planting seeds of what might be.

• *Dare to make people feel uncomfortable, beginning with yourself.* At the next local school board meeting, for example, ask why principals and other administrators are almost always men, while the teachers they control are mostly women. Consider asking the same thing about church, workplaces, or local government. If the video store carries pornography, ask the owners if they've thought about how pornography harms women. Ask how they'd feel if their daughters "chose" that kind of work or if their daughters married men who treated them the way men treat women in pornographic films. Tell them you don't like having pornography in your community and would feel much better about bringing your business to them if you didn't have to know you were subsidizing it. You don't have to win or even make an argument, for just asking questions in an open way can make a difference (if not *the* difference).

It may seem that such actions don't amount to much until you stop for a moment and feel your resistance to doing them—your worry, for example, about how easily you could make people feel uncomfortable, including yourself. If you take that resistance to action as a measure of power, then your potential to make a difference is plain to see. The potential for people to feel uncomfortable is a measure of the power for change inherent in such simple acts of not going along with the status quo.

Some will say that it isn't "nice" to make people uncomfortable, but patriarchy does a lot more than make people feel uncomfortable, and it certainly isn't "nice" to allow it to continue. Besides, discomfort is an unavoidable part of any meaningful process of education. You can't grow without being willing to challenge your assumptions and take yourself to the edge of your competencies, where you're bound to feel uncomfortable. If you can't tolerate ambiguity, uncertainty, and discomfort, then you'll never go beneath the superficial appearance of things or learn or change anything of much value, including yourself.

- *Openly choose and model alternative paths.* As you identify paths of least resistance—such as women being held responsible for child care and other domestic work—you can identify alternatives and then follow them openly so that other people can see what you're doing. Patriarchal paths become more visible when people choose alternatives, just as rules become more visible when someone breaks them. Modeling new paths creates tension in a system, which moves toward resolution (like the irritated oyster). You don't have to convince anyone of anything. As Gandhi put it, the work begins with us as we simply try to be the change we want to see happen in the world. Anyone who thinks this has no effect need only watch how people react to the slightest departures from paths of least resistance, at how much effort people expend trying to ignore or explain away or challenge those who choose alternative paths.
- *Actively promote change in how systems are organized around patriarchal values and male privilege.* There are almost endless possibilities here because social life is complicated and patriarchy is everywhere. You can, for example,
  - Speak out for equality in the workplace.
  - Promote awareness and training around issues of privilege.
  - Support equal pay and promotion for women.
  - Oppose the devaluing of women and the work they do, from the dead-end jobs most women are stuck in to the glass ceilings that keep women out of top positions.
  - Support the well-being of mothers and children and defend women's rights to control their bodies and their lives.
  - Object to the punitive dismantling of welfare and attempts to limit women's access to reproductive health services.

- Speak out against violence and harassment against women wherever they occur, whether at home, at work, or on the street.
- Support government and private support services for women who are victimized by men's violence.
- Volunteer at the local rape crisis center or battered women's shelter.
- Call for and support clear and effective anti-harassment policies in workplaces, unions, schools, professional associations, churches, and political parties, as well as public spaces such as parks, sidewalks, and malls.
- Join and support groups that intervene with and counsel men who perpetrate violence against women.
- Object to pornography in theaters, video stores, and on the internet. This doesn't require a debate about censorship—just the exercise of freedom of speech to articulate pornography's role in patriarchy and to express how its opponents feel about it.
- Ask questions about how work, education, religion, family, and other areas of family life are shaped by core patriarchal values and principles. Some accept women's entry into combat branches of the military or the upper reaches of corporate power as "progress," for example. But others question what happens to people and societies when political and economic institutions are organized around control, domination, "power over," and, by extension, competition and the use of violence. Is it progress to allow selected women to share control with men over oppressive systems?

• *Openly support people who step off the path of least resistance.* When you witness someone else taking a risk—speaking out, calling attention to privilege and oppression—don't wait until later to tell them in private you're glad they did. Waiting until you're alone makes it safer for you, but does the other little good. Support is most needed when the risk is being taken, not later on, so don't wait. Make your support as visible and public as the courageous behavior that you're supporting.[8]

• *Because the persecution of gays and lesbians is a linchpin of patriarchy, support the right of women and men to love whomever they choose.* Raise awareness of homophobia and heterosexism. For example, ask school officials and teachers about what's happening to gay and lesbian students in local schools. If they don't know, ask them to find out, since it's a safe bet that gays and lesbians are being harassed by other students and in other ways oppressed at one of the most vulnerable stages of life. If you find alternatives to heterosexuality to be unacceptable for moral or religious reasons, then consider how the treatment of gays and lesbians is used to perpetuate patriarchy and the oppression of women. Whether in the media or among friends, when sexual orientation is discussed, raise questions about its relation to patriarchy. Remember that it isn't necessary to have *answers* to questions in order to ask them.

- *Because patriarchy is rooted in principles of domination and control, pay attention to racism and other forms of oppression that draw from those same roots.* There has been a great deal of struggle within women's movements about the relationship between patriarchy and other forms of privilege, especially those based on race, social class, and sexual orientation. There has also been debate over whether some forms of privilege are more important to attack first or produce more oppressive consequences than others.

  One way out of this conflict is to realize that patriarchy isn't problematic just because it emphasizes *male* dominance, but because it promotes dominance and control as ends in themselves. In that sense, all forms of privilege draw support from common roots, and whatever we do that draws attention to those roots undermines them *all*. If working against patriarchy is seen simply as enabling some women to get a bigger piece of the pie, then some women probably will "succeed" at the expense of others who are disadvantaged by race, class, or sexual orientation. But if we identify the core problem as *any* society organized around privilege, then changing *that* requires us to pay attention to all forms of privilege and oppression. Whether we begin with race or gender or disability status or class, if we name the problem correctly, we'll wind up going in the same general direction.

- *Don't keep it to yourself.* A corollary of looking for company is not to restrict your focus to the tight little circle of your own life. It isn't enough to work out private solutions to social problems like patriarchy and other forms of privilege and keep them to yourself. It isn't enough to clean up your own act and then walk away, to find ways to avoid the worst consequences of patriarchy at home and inside yourself and think that's taking responsibility. Patriarchy isn't a personal problem and it can't be solved through personal solutions. At some point, taking responsibility means acting in a larger context, even if that means just letting one other person know what you're doing. It makes sense to start with yourself, but it's equally important not to *end* with yourself.

If all of this sounds overwhelming, remember again that you don't have to deal with everything. You don't have to set yourself the impossible task of letting go of everything or transforming patriarchy or even yourself. All you can do is what you can *manage* to do, secure in the knowledge that you're making it easier for other people—now and in the future—to see and do what *they* can do. So, rather than defeat yourself before you start:

- *Think small, humble, and doable rather than large, heroic, and impossible.* Don't paralyze yourself with impossible expectations. It takes very little to make a difference. Small acts can have radical implications. If the main requirement for the perpetuation of evil is that good people do nothing, then the choice isn't between all or nothing, but between nothing or *something.*

- *Don't let other people set the standard for you.* Start where you are and work from there. Make a list of all the things you could actually imagine *doing*—from reading another book about gender inequality to suggesting policy changes at work to raising questions about who cleans the bathroom at home—and rank them from the most risky to the least. Start with the least risky and set reasonable goals ("What small risk for change will I take *today?*"). As you get more experienced at taking risks, you can move up your list. You can commit yourself to whatever the next steps are for you, the tolerable risks, the contributions that offer some way—however small it might seem—to help balance your inability to avoid being part of the problem. As long as you do something, it counts.

In the end, taking responsibility doesn't have to be about guilt and blame, about letting someone off the hook or being on the hook yourself. It is simply to acknowledge your obligation to make a contribution to finding a way out of patriarchy, and to find constructive ways to act on that obligation. You don't have to do anything dramatic or Earth-shaking to help change happen. As powerful as patriarchy is, like all oppressive systems, it cannot stand the strain of lots of people doing something about it, beginning with the simplest act of speaking its name out loud.

# Appendix: Resources for Unraveling the Knot

Here are some resources for acting on the suggestions in Chapter 10. They fall into four general categories—periodicals and books, feminist bookstores, Web sites, and examples of how women and men can organize to work together on these issues.

## Readings

In putting together a collection of recommended periodicals and books, I've thought primarily of what might be useful after reading *The Gender Knot*. The titles listed below are only a tiny portion of the huge literature that's available. I tried to choose books that have interesting things to say, whether I agree with them or not, that are readable and available in paperback, that don't assume a lot of prior knowledge of gender issues or any particular academic discipline, and that touch on one or more of the major issues involved in patriarchy and gender inequality. To make the list easier to use, I've grouped the suggested readings by type of publication and subject matter.

### Periodicals and Journals

*Affilia: Journal of Women and Social Work*
*Asian Journal of Women's Studies*
*Australian Feminist Studies*
*Berkeley Women's Law Journal*
*Canadian Women's Studies*
*Columbia Journal of Gender and Law*
*European Journal of Women's Studies*

*Feminism and Psychology*
*Feminist Economics*
*Feminist Media Studies*
*Feminist Review*
*Feminist Studies*
*Feminist Teacher*
*Gender and Development*

Gender and Education
Gender and History
Gender and Society
Gender, Place, and Culture
Harvard Women's Law Journal
Hypatia
Indian Journal of Gender Studies
Irish Journal of Feminist Studies
Journal of Feminist Studies in Religion
Journal of Gender Studies
Journal of Lesbian Studies
Journal of Women and Aging
Journal of Women's Health
Journal of Women's History
Lesbian Review of Books
Ms.
National Women's Studies
    Association Journal
Nordic Journal of Women's Studies
Off Our Backs
Psychology of Women Quarterly
Sex Roles

Signs
Social Politics: International Studies
    in Gender, State, and Society
Sojourner: The Women's Forum
U.S.-Japan Women's Journal
Violence Against Women
Womanist Theory and Research
Women and Criminal Justice
Women and Politics
Women and Therapy
Women's Health
Women's Health Issues
Women's History Review
Women's International Network News
Women's Review of Books
Women's Rights Law Reporter
Women's Studies
Women's Studies in Communication
Women's Studies International Forum
Women's Studies Quarterly
Yale Journal of Law and Feminism

## Texts, References, and General Anthologies

Andersen, Margaret L. *Thinking about Women: Sociological Perspectives on Sex and Gender.* 6th ed. New York: Macmillan, 2002.

Anzaldua, Gloria, ed. *Making Face, Making Soul/Haciendo Caras: Creative and Critical Perspectives by Feminists of Color.* San Francisco: Aunt Lute Books, 1990.

Arliss, Laurie P. *Women and Men Communicating: Challenges and Changes.* 2nd ed. Prospect Heights, IL: Waveland, 2000.

Collins, Patricia Hill. *Black Feminist Thought.* 2nd ed. New York: Routledge, 2000.

Day, Sharon, Lisa Albrecht, Jacqui Alexander, and Mab Segrest. *Sing Whisper Shout Pray: Feminist Visions for a Just World.* EdgeWork Books, 2003.

Disch, Estelle. *Reconstructing Gender: A Multicultural Anthology.* 3rd ed. New York: McGraw-Hill, 2002.

Ehrenreich, Barbara, and Arlie Russell Hochschild. *Global Woman.* New York: Owl Books, 2004.

Fenstermaker, S., and C. West, eds. *Doing Gender, Doing Difference: Inequality, Power, and Institutional Change.* New York: Routledge, 2002.

Findlen, Barbara, ed. *Listen Up: Voices from the Next Feminist Generation.* 2nd ed. New York: Seal Press, 2001.

Gornick, Vivian, and Barbara K. Moran, eds. *Woman in Sexist Society.* New York: Basic Books, 1971.

Grewal, Inderpal, and Caren Kaplan, eds. *Introduction to Women's Studies: Gender in a Transnational World.* New York: McGraw-Hill, 2001.

Hernández, Daisy, and Bushra Rehman, eds. *Colonize This! Young Women of Color on Today's Feminism.* New York: Seal Press, 2002.

Hyde, Janet Shibley. *Half the Human Experience: The Psychology of Women.* 6th ed. Boston: Houghton Mifflin, 2003.

Jackson, Donna. *How to Make the World a Better Place for Women in Just Five Minutes a Day*. New York: Hyperion, 1992.

Jaggar, Alison M., and Paula S. Rothenberg, eds. *Feminist Frameworks*. 3rd ed. New York: McGraw-Hill, 1993.

Kimmel, Michael, and Amy Aronson, eds. *The Gendered Society Reader*. 2nd ed. New York: Oxford, 2003.

Lorber, Judith. *Paradoxes of Gender*. New Haven: Yale University Press, 1995.

Minas, Anne, ed. *Gender Basics: Feminist Perspectives on Women and Men*. 2nd ed. Belmont, CA: Wadsworth, 2000.

Morgan, Robin, ed. *Sisterhood Is Global*. New York: Feminist Press, 1996.

Peterson, V. Spike, and Anne Sisson Runyan. *Global Gender Issues*. Boulder, CO: Westview Press, 1999.

Richardson, Laurel, Verta Taylor, and Nancy Whittier, eds. *Feminist Frontiers*. 6th ed. New York: McGraw-Hill, 2003.

Sapiro, Virginia. *Women in American Society: An Introduction to Women's Studies*. 5th ed. New York: McGraw-Hill, 2002.

Walker, Barbara G. *The Woman's Encyclopedia of Myths and Secrets*. San Francisco: Harper and Row, 1983.

———. *The Woman's Dictionary of Symbols and Sacred Objects*. San Francisco: Harper and Row, 1988.

Walker, Rebecca, ed. *To Be Real: Telling the Truth and Changing the Face of Feminism*. New York: Doubleday/Anchor, 1995.

### Economy and Work

Blau, Francine S., Marianne A. Ferber, and Anne E. Winkler. *The Economics of Women, Men, and Work*. 4th ed. Englewood Cliffs, NJ: Prentice-Hall, 2001.

Cockburn, Cynthia. *In the Way of Women: Men's Resistance to Sex Equality in Organizations*. Ithaca, NY: ILR Press, 1991.

Michelson, William M. *From Sun to Sun: Daily Obligations and Community Structure in the Lives of Employed Women and Their Families*. Totowa, NJ: Rowman and Allanheld, 1985.

Molyneux, Maxine, and Shahra Razavi, eds. *Gender Justice, Development, and Rights*. New York: Oxford University Press, 2002.

Waring, Marilyn. *If Women Counted: A New Feminist Economics*. San Francisco: HarperCollins, 1988.

Williams, Christine L. *Still a Man's World: Men Who Do Women's Work*. Berkeley: University of California Press, 1995.

### Family

Crittenden, Ann. *The Price of Motherhood: Why the Most Important Job in the World Is Still the Least Valued*. New York: Owl Books, 2001.

Davey, Moira. *Mother Reader: Essential Writings on Motherhood*. New York: Seven Stories Press, 2001.

Gerson, Kathleen. *No Man's Land: Men's Changing Commitments to Family and Work*. New York: Basic Books, 1994.

Griswold, Robert L. *Fatherhood in America: A History*. New York: Basic Books, 1993.

Hochschild, Arlie. *The Second Shift: Working Parents and the Revolution at Home*. New York: Viking/Penguin, 2003.

Johnson, Miriam M. *Strong Mothers, Weak Wives: The Search for Gender Equality.* Berkeley: University of California Press, 1990.
Oakley, Ann. *Woman's Work: The Housewife, Past and Present.* New York: Vintage, 1976.
Rich, Adrienne. *Of Woman Born.* New York: W. W. Norton, 1995.

### Feminism

Baumgardner, Jennifer, and Amy Richards. *Manifesta: Young Women, Feminism, and the Future.* New York: Farrar, Straus and Giroux, 2000.
Frye, Marilyn. *The Politics of Reality: Essays in Feminist Theory.* Freedom, CA: Crossing Press, 1983.
———. *Willful Virgin: Essays in Feminism, 1976–1992.* Freedom, CA: Crossing Press, 1992.
Lorber, Judith. *Gender Inequality: Feminist Theories and Politics.* 2nd ed. Los Angeles: Roxbury, 2001.
McCann, Carole, and Seung-Kyung Kim. *Feminist Theory Reader: Local and Global Perspectives.* New York: Routledge, 2002.
Schneir, Miriam, ed. *Feminism: The Essential Historical Writings.* New York: Vintage, 1972.
———. *Feminism in Our Time: The Essential Writings, World War II to the Present.* New York: Vintage, 1994.
Tong, Rosemarie. *Feminist Thought: A More Comprehensive Introduction.* Boulder, CO.: Westview Press, 1998.

### Global Perspectives

Afshar, Haleh, and Stephanie Barrientos, eds. *Women, Globalization and Fragmentation in the Developing World.* New York: St. Martin's Press, 1999.
Basu, Amrita, and C. Elizabeth McGrory, eds. *The Challenge of Local Feminisms: Women's Movements in Global Perspective.* Boulder, CO: Westview Press, 1995.
Burn, Shawn Meghan. *Women across Cultures: A Global Perspective.* New York: McGraw-Hill, 1999.
Kramarae, Cheris, and Dale Spender, eds. *Routledge International Encyclopedia of Women: Global Women's Issues and Knowledge.* New York: Routledge, 2000.
Narayan, Uma. *Dislocating Cultures: Third World Feminism and the Politics of Knowledge.* New York: Routledge, 1997.

### Health and the Body

Bordo, Susan. *The Male Body: A New Look at Men in Public and Private.* New York: Farrar Straus & Giroux, 2000.
———. *Unbearable Weight: Feminism, Western Culture, and the Body.* Berkeley: University of California Press, 1995.
Chernin, Kim. *The Obsession: Reflections on the Tyranny of Slenderness.* New York: Harper and Row, 1981.
———. *Reinventing Eve: Modern Woman in Search of Herself.* New York: Times Books, 1987.
Dyck, Isabel, Nancy Davis Lewis, and Sara McLafferty, eds. *Geographies of Women's Health: Place, Diversity and Difference.* New York: Routledge, 2001.
Ehrenreich, Barbara, and Deidre English. *For Her Own Good: 150 Years of Experts' Advice to Women.* New York: Doubleday/Anchor, 1989.

Hall, Kim Q., ed. "Feminist Disability Studies." Special issue, *National Women's Studies Association Journal* 14, no. 3 (2002).

Leavitt, Judith Walzer. *Women and Health in America*. 2nd ed. Madison: University of Wisconsin Press, 1999.

Smith, Bonnie, and Beth Hutchinson, eds. *Gendering Disability*. New Brunswick, NJ: Rutgers University Press, 2004.

Wendell, Susan. *The Rejected Body: Feminist Philosophical Reflections on Disability*. New York: Routledge, 1996.

Wolf, Naomi. *The Beauty Myth: How Images of Beauty Are Used against Women*. New York: William Morrow, 1991.

## Heterosexism, Homophobia, and Sexual Orientation

Abelove, Henry, Michele Aina Barale, and David M. Halperin, eds. *The Lesbian and Gay Studies Reader*. New York: Routledge, 1993.

Fausto-Sterling, Anne. *Sexing the Body: Gender Politics and the Construction of Sexuality*. New York: Basic Books, 2000.

Halberstam, Judith. *Female Masculinity*. Durham, NC: Duke University Press, 1998.

McNaught, Brian. *Gay Issues in the Workplace*. New York: St. Martin's Press, 1993.

Miller, Neil. *Out of the Past: Gay and Lesbian History from 1869 to the Present*. New York: Vintage, 1995.

Myron, Nancy, and Charlotte Bunch, eds. *Lesbianism and the Women's Movement*. Baltimore: Diana Press, 1975.

Pharr, Suzanne. *Homophobia: A Weapon of Sexism*. Exp. ed. Inverness, CA: Women's Project. 1997.

## History

Anderson, Bonnie S., and Judith P. Zinsser. *A History of Their Own: Women in Europe*. 2 vols. New York: HarperCollins, 1999.

Baxandall, Rosalyn, Linda Gordon, and Susan Reverby, eds. *America's Working Women: A Documentary History—1600 to the Present*. Rev. ed. New York: W. W. Norton, 1995.

Degler, Carl N. *At Odds: Women and the Family in America from the Revolution to the Present*. New York: Oxford University Press, 1990.

Echols, Alice. *Daring to Be Bad: Radical Feminism in America 1967–1975*. Minneapolis: University of Minnesota Press, 1989.

Eisler, Riane. *The Chalice and the Blade*. New York: HarperSanFrancisco, 1988.

Evans, Sara M. *Born for Liberty: A History of Women in America*. New York: Free Press, 1997.

Fisher, Elizabeth. *Woman's Creation: Sexual Evolution and the Shaping of Society*. New York: McGraw-Hill, 1979.

Kerber, Linda K., and Jane Sherron De Hart, eds. *Women's America: Refocusing the Past*. 6th ed. New York: Oxford University Press, 2003.

Lerner, Gerda. *The Creation of Feminist Consciousness: From the Middle Ages to 1870*. New York: Oxford University Press, 1994.

———. *The Creation of Patriarchy*. New York: Oxford University Press, 1987.

Sanday, Peggy Reeves. *Female Power and Male Dominance: On the Origins of Sexual Inequality*. Cambridge: Cambridge University Press, 1981.

*Men (by or about)*

Abbot, Franklin, ed. *Men and Intimacy.* Freedom, CA: Crossing Press, 1990.
Brittan, Arthur. *Masculinity and Power.* Oxford: Basil Blackwell, 1989.
Connell, Robert W. *Gender and Power: Society, the Person, and Sexual Politics.* Stanford: Stanford University Press, 1988.
———. *Masculinities.* Berkeley: University of California Press, 1995.
Gibson, James William. *Warrior Dreams: Violence and Manhood in Post-Vietnam America.* New York: Hill and Wang, 1994.
Gonzalez, Ray, ed. *Muy Macho: Latino Men Confront their Manhood.* New York: Anchor, 1996.
Hagan, Kay Leigh, ed. *Women Respond to the Men's Movement.* San Francisco: Harper-Collins, 1992.
Kaufman, Michael, ed. *Beyond Power: Essays by Men on Pleasure, Power, and Change.* Toronto: Oxford University Press, 1987.
———. *Cracking the Armor: Power and Pain in Men's Lives.* New York: Penguin, 1993.
Kimmel, Michael. *Manhood in America.* New York: Free Press, 1996.
Kimmel, Michael S., ed. *The Politics of Manhood: Profeminist Men Respond to the Mythopoetic Men's Movement (And the Mythopoetic Leaders Answer).* Philadelphia: Temple University Press, 1995.
Kimmel, Michael, R. W. Connell, and Jeff Hearn, eds. *Handbook on Studies of Men and Masculinities.* Thousand Oaks, CA: Sage, 2004.
Kimmel, Michael S., and Michael A. Messner, eds. *Men's Lives.* 6th ed. Boston: Allyn and Bacon, 2003.
Kimmel, Michael S., and Tom Mosmiller. *Against the Tide: Pro-Feminist Men in the United States, 1776–1990.* Boston: Beacon Press, 1992.
Messner, Michael A. *Power at Play: Sports and the Problem of Masculinity.* Boston: Beacon Press, 1992.
Rotundo, E. Anthony. *American Manhood: Transformations in Masculinity from the Revolution to the Modern Era.* New York: Basic Books, 1993.
Schwalbe, Michael. *Unlocking the Iron Cage: The Men's Movement, Gender Politics, and American Culture.* New York: Oxford University Press, 1996.
Stoltenberg, John. *The End of Manhood: A Book for Men of Conscience.* New York: Dutton, 1993.
———. *Refusing to Be a Man.* New York: Meridian, 1989.

*Patriarchy and Gender Inequality*

Anzaldua, Gloria, ed. *Making Face, Making Soul/Haciendo Caras: Creative and Critical Perspectives by Feminists of Color.* San Francisco: Aunt Lute Books, 1990.
Caputi, Jane. *Gossips, Gorgons, and Crones.* Santa Fe, NM: Bear and Co., 1993.
Diamond, Irene, and Gloria Feman Orenstein, eds. *Reweaving the World: The Emergence of Ecofeminism.* San Francisco: Sierra Club Books, 1990.
Epstein, Cynthia Fuchs. *Deceptive Distinctions: Sex, Gender, and the Social Order.* New Haven: Yale University Press, 1990.
Faludi, Susan. *Backlash: The Undeclared War against American Women.* New York: Crown, 1991.
Firestone, Shulamith. *The Dialectic of Sex: The Case for Feminist Revolution.* New York: William Morrow, 1970.
French, Marilyn. *Beyond Power: On Men, Women, and Morals.* New York: Summit Books, 1985.
———. *The War against Women.* New York: Ballantine Books, 1993.

Gorilla Girls, The. *Confessions of the Gorilla Girls*. New York: HarperCollins, 1995.

Janeway, Elizabeth. *Man's World, Woman's Place: A Study in Social Mythology*. New York: Dell, 1971.

Kaschak, Ellyn. *Engendered Lives: A New Psychology of Women's Experience*. New York: Basic Books, 1993.

Lakoff, Robin. *Language and Woman's Place*. New York: Harper Collins 1989.

———. *Talking Power: The Politics of Language in Our Lives*. New York: Basic Books, 1990.

Lorde, Audre. *Sister Outsider: Essays and Speeches*. Freedom, CA: Crossing Press, 1984.

MacKinnon, Catharine A. *Feminism Unmodified: Discourses on Life and Law*. Cambridge: Harvard University Press, 1987.

Miller, Casey, and Kate Swift. *Words and Women*. Updated ed. New York: HarperCollins, 1991.

Miller, Jean Baker. *Toward a New Psychology of Women*. 2nd ed. Boston: Beacon Press, 1986.

Pollitt, Katha. *Reasonable Creatures: Essays on Women and Feminism*. New York: Vintage, 1994.

Ruddick, Sara. *Maternal Thinking: Towards a Politics of Peace*. Boston: Beacon Press, 1995.

Spender, Dale. *Man Made Language*. London: Pandora, 1980.

Walker, Barbara G. *The Skeptical Feminist: Discovering the Virgin, Mother, and Crone*. New York: Harper and Row, 1987.

Woolf, Virginia. *A Room of One's Own*. New York: Harcourt Brace and World, 1929.

## Race, Class, and Gender

Andersen, Margaret L., and Patricia Hill Collins, eds. *Race, Class, and Gender*. 5th ed. Belmont, CA: Wadsworth, 2003.

Davis, Angela Y. *Women, Race, and Class*. New York: Random House, 1981.

Frankenberg, Ruth. *White Women, Race Matters*. Minneapolis: University of Minnesota Press, 1993.

hooks, bell. *Ain't I a Woman: Black Women and Feminism*. Boston: South End Press, 1981.

———. *Feminist Theory: From Margin to Center*. Boston: South End Press, 1984.

———. *Sisters of the Yam: Black Women and Self-Recovery*. Boston: South End Press, 1993.

———. *Talking Back: Thinking Feminism, Thinking Black*. Boston: South End Press, 1989.

Hurtado, Aida. *The Color of Privilege*. Ann Arbor: University of Michigan Press, 1999.

Moraga, Cherríe, and Gloria Anzaldúa, eds. *This Bridge Called My Back: Writings by Radical Women of Color*, 3rd ed. New York: Third Woman Press, 2002.

Rothenberg, Paula S. *Invisible Privilege: A Memoir about Race, Class, and Gender*. Lawrence: University Press of Kansas, 2000.

St. Jean, Yanick, and Joe R. Feagin. *Double Burden: Black Women and Everyday Racism*. Armonk, NY: M. E. Sharpe, 1999.

## Religion and Spirituality

Christ, Carol. *Womanspirit Rising: A Feminist Reader in Religion*. San Francisco: HarperSanFrancisco, 1992.

Daly, Mary. *Beyond God the Father*. Boston: Beacon Press, 1973.
Gimbutas, Marija. *The Civilization of the Goddess: The World of Old Europe*. San Francisco: Harper and Row, 1991.
———. *The Language of the Goddess*. New York: HarperCollins, 1989.
Stone, Merlin. *When God Was a Woman*. New York: Harcourt Brace Jovanovich, 1976.


## Schools and Learning

American Association of University Women. *Gender Gaps: Where Schools Still Fail Our Children*. Washington, DC: AAUW Educational Foundation, 1998.
———. *Growing Smart: What's Working for Girls in Schools*. Washington, DC: American Association of University Women, 1995.
———. *How Schools Shortchange Girls*. Washington, DC: American Association of University Women, 1992.
———. *A License for Bias: Sex Discrimination, Schools, and Title IX*. Washington, DC: AAUW Educational Foundation, 2001.
Belenky, Mary Field, Blythe McVicker Clinchy, Nancy Rule Goldberger, and Jill Mattuck Tarule. *Women's Ways of Knowing: The Development of Self Voice, and Mind*. New York: Basic Books, 1997.
Hall, Roberta M., with Bernice R. Sandler. *The Classroom Climate: A Chilly One for Women?* Washington, DC: Association of American Colleges, 1986.
Sadker, Myra, and David M. Sadker. *Failing at Fairness: How America's Schools Cheat Girls*. New York: Charles Scribner's Sons, 1995.
Thorne, Barrie. *Gender Play: Girls and Boys in School*. New Brunswick, NJ: Rutgers University Press, 1993.


## Science

Benderly, Beryl L. *The Myth of Two Minds: What Gender Means and Doesn't Mean*. Garden City, NY: Doubleday, 1987.
Bleier, Ruth. *Science and Gender: A Critique of Biology and Its Theories on Women*. New York: Pergamon Press, 1984.
Fausto-Sterling, Anne. *Myths of Gender: Biological Theories about Women and Men*. 2nd rev. ed. New York: Basic Books, 1992.
Lederman, Muriel, and Ingrid Bartsch, eds. *The Gender and Science Reader*. New York: Routledge, 2001.
Sonnert, Gerhard, and Gerald Holton. *Who Succeeds in Science? The Gender Dimension*. New Brunswick, NJ: Rutgers University Press, 1995.
Zuckerman, Harriet, J. R. Cole, and J. T. Bruer, eds. *The Outer Circle: Women in the Scientific Community*. New York: W. W. Norton, 1991.


## Violence, Harassment, and Pornography

Brownmiller, Susan. *Against Our Will: Men, Women, and Rape*. New York: Simon and Schuster, 1975.
Buchwald, Emilie, Pamela R. Fletcher, and Martha Roth, eds. *Transforming a Rape Culture*. Minneapolis: Milkweed Editions, 1993.
Comstock, David Gary. *Violence against Lesbians and Gay Men*. New York: Columbia University Press, 1991.
Cornell, Drucilla, ed. *Feminism and Pornography*. New York: Oxford, 2000

Dworkin, Andrea. *Woman Hating*. New York: E. P. Dutton, 1974.

Fisher, Bonnie S., Francis T. Cullen, and Michael G. Turner. "The Sexual Victimization of College Women." Bureau of Justice Statistics, National Institute of Justice, U.S. Department of Justice, Washington DC, 2000.

Gardner, Carol Brooks. *Passing By: Gender and Public Harassment*. Berkeley: University of California Press, 1995.

Gilbert, Paula Ruth, and Kimberly K. Eby, eds. *Violence and Gender: An Interdisciplinary Reader*. Englewood Cliffs, NJ: Prentice Hall, 2004.

Griffin, Susan. *Pornography and Silence: Culture's Revenge against Nature*. New York: Harper and Row, 1981.

Herman, Judith Lewis. *Trauma and Recovery*. New York: Basic Books, 1997.

Hosken, Fran P. *The Hosken Report: Genital and Sexual Mutilation of Females*. 4th rev. ed. Lexington, MA: Women's International Network News, 1994.

Jones, Ann. *Next Time She'll Be Dead: Battering and How to Stop It*. Boston: Beacon Press, 2000.

Kimmel, Michael S., ed. *Men Confront Pornography*. New York: Meridian, 1990.

Kivel, Paul. *Men's Work: How to Stop the Violence that Tears Our Lives Apart*. New York: Ballantine, 1992.

Lederer, Laura, ed. *Take Back the Night: Women on Pornography*. New York: William Morrow, 1980.

Levinson, David. *Family Violence in Cross-Cultural Perspective*. Thousand Oaks, CA: Sage, 1989.

MacKinnon, Catharine A. *Only Words*. Cambridge: Harvard University Press, 1993.

———. *Sex Equality: Rape Law*. New York: Foundation Press, 2001.

Manderson, Lenore, and Linda Rae Bennett, eds. *Violence against Women in Asian Societies*. Curzon Press, 2003.

Messner, Michael A., and Donald F. Sabo. *Sex, Violence, and Power in Sports: Rethinking Masculinity*. Freedom, CA: Crossing Press, 1994.

Paludi, Michele A. *Sexual Harassment on College Campuses*. Albany: State University of New York Press, 1996.

Russell, Diana. *The Secret Trauma: Incest in the Lives of Girls and Women*. New York: Basic Books, 1986.

———. *Sexual Exploitation: Rape, Child Sexual Abuse, and Workplace Harassment*. Beverly Hills, CA: Sage, 1984.

Russell, Diana, ed. *Making Violence Sexy: Feminist Views on Pornography*. New York: Teachers College Press, 1993.

Russell, Diana E. H., and Roberta A. Harmes. *Femicide in Global Perspective*. New York: Teachers College Press, 2001.

Sanday, Peggy Reeves. *Fraternity Gang Rape: Sex, Brotherhood, and Privilege on Campus*. New York: New York University Press, 1990.

———. *A Woman Scorned: Acquaintance Rape on Trial*. New York: Doubleday, 1996.

## Feminist Bookstores

Feminist bookstores are a great source not only of books you'd have to special order anywhere else, but of like-minded people and news of events and groups and other opportunities to stretch ourselves and do something about patriarchy. They vary in their emphasis—especially around gay and lesbian issues—but have something to offer everyone who cares about gender issues.

## Resources on the Web

There are numerous excellent starting places on the Web for finding all kinds of resources related to gender inequality and patriarchy.

*American Association of University Women*
www.aauw.org
*American Medical Women's Association Information*
www.amwa-doc.org
*Boston Women's Health Book Collective*
www.ourbodiesourselves.org
*Bureau of Justice Statistics, Sexual Victimization of College Women*
www.ojp.usdoj.gov/bjs/abstract/svcw.htm
*Center for American Women and Politics*
www.rci.rutgers.edu/~cawp
*Center for Reproductive Law and Policy*
www.crlp.org
*Domestic Violence Statistics (National Criminal Justice Reference Service)*
www.ncjrs.org
*Ecofeminism*
www.ecofem.org
*Factbook on Global Sexual Exploitation*
www.catwinternational.org/fb/index.html
*Family Violence Prevention Fund*
www.fvpf.org
*Femina Gateway*
www.femina.com
*Feminist.com*
www.feminist.com
*Gay/Lesbian Politics and Law*
www.indiana.edu/~glbtpol
*Gender Watch*
www.softlineweb.com/softlineweb/genderw.htm
*Institute for Law and Justice (domestic violence and sexual assault links)*
www.ilj.org/projects.html

*Institute for Women's Policy Research*
www.iwpr.org
*Men's Bibliography*
www.mensbiblio.xyonline.net
*MensNet (Canada)*
www.conscoop.ottawa.on.ca/mensnet
*National Coalition for Women and Girls in Education*
www.ncwge.org
*National Women's Health Information Center*
www.4woman.gov
*Rape, Abuse, Incest National Network Statistics*
www.rainn.org/statisticsarc.html
*Rape on Campus*
www.u.arizona.edu/~sexasslt/arpep/researchabstracts2.html#College
*Rape by Fraternities and Gangs*
www.mensbiblio.xyonline.net/violence.html#Gangs
*Religion and Women*
www.womenshistory.about.com/od/religion
*Society for Women's Health Research*
www.womens-health.org
*United Nations Global Campaign to End Violence against Women*
www.undp.org/unifem/campaign/violence
*United Nations Development Fund for Women*
www.unifem.undp.org
*U.S. Department of Justice, Office on Violence Against Women*
www.ojp.usdoj.gov/vawo
*Women Artists Archive*
http://library.sonoma.edu/regional/waa.html
*Women in Music*
www.iawm.org

*Women in the Arts*
www.nmwa.org
*WomensNet (news and gateway)*
www.igc.org/igc/gateway/
  wnindex.html
*Women's Studies Core Lists*
www.library.wisc.edu/libraries/
  WomensStudies/core/coremain.htm

*Women's Studies Listserv*
http://research.umbc.edu/~korenman/
  wmst/wmst-l_index.html
*Women Watch (United Nations
  Gateway)*
www.un.org/womenwatch

You'll find a wide range of approaches as you explore this territory. This is especially true of the Men's Bibliography, which includes everything from the address for the National Organization of Men Against Sexism to men's rights organizations that deny patriarchy even exists and believe women have all the privilege and power. I found many of these in Virginia Sapiro, *Women in American Society: An Introduction to Women's Studies*, 5th ed. (New York: McGraw-Hill, 2003). My thanks to the author.

## Doing It Together

How you work with other people on these issues depends in part on what you want to accomplish. You can do a lot to deepen your understanding of patriarchy and how it works, for example, by reading and getting together with other people to talk about it and how it relates to your own lives. This can be done in consciousness-raising groups, study groups, adult education classes, and, if you have access to a local college or university, women's or men's studies courses. This kind of work doesn't require formal organizations—all it takes is people who want to do it and a place to meet.

If you want to work with other people to change patriarchy, there are lots of organizations already in existence. And there is always the possibility of starting your own, especially around local concerns. To get some idea of what people are doing, consider the following.[1] There are hundreds of women's organizations that focus on everything from how to succeed in business to securing health care for women to combating violence. There are women's associations in law, medicine, business, public administration, engineering, science, sport, and the media. There are organizations focusing especially on the perspectives of black women and of Hispanic women. Some, such as the National Organization for Women and the American Association of University Women, have state and local chapters as well as a national organization. Here's a sampling:

*American Association of University
  Women*
*1111 16th Street, NW*
*Washington, DC 20036*
*www.aauw.org*

*American Jewish Conference
  Commission on Women's Equality*
*2027 Massachusetts Avenue*
*Washington, DC 20036*

*Canadian Women's Health Network*
*419 Graham Street, 3rd Floor*
*Winnipeg, Manitoba R3C OM3*
*Canada*
*www.cwhn.ca*

*National Committee on Pay Equity*
*1126 16th Street, NW, Suite 411*
*Washington, DC 20036*
*www.pay-equity.org*

*National Council for Research on
  Women*
*11 Hanover Sq. 24th Floor*
*New York, NY 10005*
*www.ncrw.org*

*National Organization for Women*
*1000 16th Street, NW, Suite 700*
*Washington, DC 20036*
*www.now.org*

NOW Legal Defense and Education
Fund
395 Hudson Street
New York, NY 10014
www.nowldef.org

Older Women's League 1750
New York Ave NW, Suite 350
Washington, DC 20006.
www.owl-national.org

Religious Network for Equality for
Women
475 Riverside Drive
New York, NY 10115

The Feminist Majority Foundation
1600 Wilson Boulevard, Suite 801
Arlington, VA 22209
www.feminist.org

9 to 5: National Association of
Working Women
152 W. Wisconsin Ave., Suite 408
Milwaukee, WI 53203
www.9to5.org

## Working against Violence against Women

From rape crisis services to shelters for women who have been battered, there are thousands of local services that need volunteers in all kinds of capacities. For information on how you can connect to this effort, there are several possibilities. The National Domestic Violence hotline is 800–799–7233. It is a 24-hour crisis intervention line. For information on what you can do, contact one or more of the following:

Battered Women's Justice Project: 800–903–0111
Center for the Prevention of Sexual and Domestic Violence: 206–634–1903
Health Resource Center on Domestic Violence (focusing on health-care issues):
800–313–1310
National Resource Center on Domestic Violence: 800–537–2238
Resource Center on Child Protection and Custody: 800–527–3223

## Men Working with Men

Men have formed a number of organizations that use varying mixes of small group meetings, education, and political action to raise consciousness, deepen understanding, and do something about sexism and violence against women.

DC Men Against Rape
c/o Washington Peace Center
2111 Florida Ave, NW
Washington, DC 20008
Tel. 202–882–5898

Men Against Domestic Violence
32 West Anapamu Street, #348
Santa Barbara, CA 93101
Tel. 805–563–2651

Men Against Racism and Sexism
517 Sacramento Drive
Austin, TX 78704
www.conscoop.ottawa.on.ca/
    mensnet/MARS_org.html.

Men as Peacemakers
320 West 2nd Street, Room 503
Duluth, MN 55802
Tel. 218–726–2067
www.menaspeacemakers.org

Men Can Stop Rape
P.O. Box 57144
Washington, DC
www.mencanstoprape.org

National Men's Resource Center
P.O. Box 800
San Anselmo, CA 94979

National Organization for Men
Against Sexism
798 Pennsylvania Avenue, Box 5
Pittsburgh, PA 15221
www.nomas.org

Oakland Men's Project
1222 Preservation Park Way
Oakland, CA 94612
Tel. 510–835–2433

Rape and Violence End Now
7314 Manchester, 2nd Floor
St. Louis, MO 63143
www.members.tripod.com/
~raventeaches

Real Men
PO Box 1769
Brookline, MA 02146
Tel. 617–422–1650
e-mail treefrog@usal.com or
conejomiel@aol.com

The Violence Intervention Project
159 Margaret Street, #201
Plattsburg NY 12901
Tel. 518–563–8206

Twin Cities Men's Centers
3255 Hennepin Avenue, South,
Suite 55
Minneapolis, MN 55401
[and]
986 Forest Street
St. Paul, MN 55106
www.tcmc.org

Unitarian Universalist Men's
Network
1240 Washington Road
Mount Lebanon, PA 15228
www.uua.org

In Canada, the Men for Change network has branches in major cities throughout the country. For more information, write to:

Men For Change P.O. Box 33005
Quinpool Postal Outlet
Halifax, Nova Scotia, Canada B3L 4T6
www.chebucto.ns.ca/CommunitySupport/Men4Change/

All of these groups began when women and men were willing to start talking about the reality of gender inequality, how it affects people's lives, and what we can do about it. If you don't live in communities that have such groups, you can do what they did: Talk with people about what's going on and what it has to do with all of us.

# Notes

## Chapter 1

1. See Marilyn French, *Beyond Power: On Men, Women, and Morals* (New York: Summit Books, 1985), 303.
2. For more on gender and dominant/subordinate relationships, see Jean Baker Miller, *Toward a New Psychology of Women*, 2nd ed. (Boston: Beacon Press, 1986).
3. There is a lot of research that shows how such uses of language affect people's perception. See, for example, Mykol C. Hamilton, "Using Masculine Generics: Does Generic 'He' Increase Male Bias in the User's Imagery?" *Sex Roles* 19, nos. 11/12 (1988): 785–799; Wendy Martyna, "Beyond the 'He/Man' Approach: The Case for Nonsexist Language," *Signs* 5 (1980): 482–493; Casey Miller and Kate Swift, *Words and Women*, updated ed. (New York: HarperCollins, 1991); and Joseph W. Schneider and Sally L. Hacker, "Sex Role Imagery in the Use of the Generic 'Man' in Introductory Texts: A Case in the Sociology of Sociology," *American Sociologist* 8 (1973): 12–18.
4. See, for example, Carole Levin's *The Heart and Stomach of a King: Elizabeth I and the Politics of Sex and Power* (Philadelphia: University of Pennsylvania Press, 1994).
5. See Carol Brooks Gardner, *Passing By: Gender and Public Harassment* (Berkeley: University of California Press, 1995).
6. See Paula England and D. Dunn, "Evaluating Work and Comparable Worth," *Annual Review of Sociology* 14 (1988): 227–248.
7. Mary Daly, *Beyond God the Father: Toward a Philosophy of Women's Liberation* (Boston: Beacon Press, 1973).
8. For some research on gender differences in friendship, see R. Aukett, J. Ritchie, and K. Mill, "Gender Differences in Friendship Patterns," *Sex Roles* 19, nos. 1/2 (1988): 57–66; R. J. Barth and B. N. Kinder, "A Theoretical Analysis of Sex Differences

in Same-sex Friendship," *Sex Roles* 19, nos. 5/6 (1988): 349–363; Z. Kiraly, "The Relationship between Emotional Self-disclosure of Male and Female Adolescents' Friendship," *Dissertation Abstracts International* (2000), 60(7-B), p. 3619: and D. G. Williams, "Gender, Masculinity-Feminity, and Emotional Intimacy in Same-Sex Friendships," *Sex Roles* 12, nos. 5/6 (1985): 587–600.

9. For more on gender and interaction, see Laurie P. Arliss, *Women and Men Communicating: Challenges and Changes*, 2nd ed. (Prospect Heights, IL: Waveland, 2000); Robin Lakoff, *Language and Woman's Place* (New York: Harper and Row, 1975) and *Talking Power: The Politics of Language in Our Lives* (New York: Basic Books, 1990). See also Deborah Tannen, *Conversational Style: Analyzing Talk among Friends* (Norwood, NJ: Ablex, 1984) and *You Just Don't Understand: Women and Men in Conversation* (New York: William Morrow, 1990).

10. See American Association of University Women, *How Schools Shortchange Girls* (Washington, DC: American Association of University Women, 1992); idem, *Gender Gaps: Where Schools Still Fail Our Children* (Washington, DC: AAUQ Educational Foundation, 1998); idem, *A License for Bias: Sex Discrimination, Schools, and Title IX* (Washington, DC: AAUW Educational Foundation, 2001); and Myra Sadker and David M. Sadker, *Failing at Fairness: How America's Schools Cheat Girls* (New York: Charles Scribner's Sons, 1994).

11. Virginia Woolf, *A Room of One's Own* (New York: Harcourt Brace and World, 1929), 35.

12. My thanks to Nora L. Jamieson, who helped me navigate through this psychological territory.

13. French, *Beyond Power*, 132.

14. See American Association of University Women, *How Schools Shortchange Girls; Gender Gaps: Where Schools Still Fail Our Children; A License for Bias: Sex Discrimination, Schools, and Title IX;* and Sadker and Sadker, *Failing at Fairness.*

15. See Susan Brownmiller, *Against Our Will: Men, Women, and Rape* (New York: Simon and Schuster, 1975); Andrea Dworkin, *Woman Hating* (New York: E. P. Dutton, 1974); Susan Faludi, *Backlash: The Undeclared War Against American Women* (New York: Crown Publishers, 1991); Marilyn French, *The War Against Women* (New York: Summit Books, 1992); Gardner, *Passing By;* Laura Lederer, ed., *Take Back the Night: Women on Pornography* (New York: William Morrow, 1980); Catharine MacKinnon, *Only Words* (Cambridge: Harvard University Press, 1993); Catherine MacKinnon, *Sex Equality: Rape Law* (New York: Foundation Press, 2001); "Medical News and Perspectives," *Journal of the American Medical Association* 264, no. 8 (1990): 939; Diana E. H. Russell, *Rape in Marriage* (New York: Macmillan, 1982); idem, *Sexual Exploitation: Rape, Child Sexual Abuse, and Workplace Harassment* (Beverly Hills, CA: Sage Publications, 1984); Diana E. H. Russell, ed., *Making Violence Sexy: Feminist Views on Pornography* (New York: Teachers College Press, 1993); Diana E. H. Russell and Roberta A. Harmes, *Femicide in Global Perspective.* (New York: Teachers College Press, 2001).

16. This is true even in socialist societies such as Sweden. For research on men and domestic work, see R. L. Blumberg, ed., *Gender, Family, and Economy: The Triple Overlap* (Newbury Park, CA: Sage Publications, 1991); C. Goldin, *Understanding the Gender Gap: An Economic History of American Women* (New York: Oxford University Press, 1990); L. Haas, *Equal Parenthood and Social Policy: A Study of Parental Leave in Sweden* (Albany: State University of New York Press, 1992); Arlie Hochschild, *The Second Shift* (New York: Viking, 1989); M. J. Intons-Peterson, *Gender Concepts of Swedish and American Youth* (Hillsdale, NJ: Lawrence Erlbaum Associates, 1988);

and J. R. Wilkie, "Changes in U.S. Men's Attitudes Towards the Family Provider Role," *Gender and Society* 7, no. 2 (1993): 261–279.

17. For thorough accounts, see Faludi, *Backlash*, and French, *War Against Women*. For more recent information, see Women's Action Coalition, *WAC Stats: The Facts about Women* (New York: New Press, published annually).

18. I first saw the use of the tree metaphor to describe aspects of system in Roosevelt Thomas's *Beyond Race and Gender* (New York: American Management Association, 1991).

19. For a provocative and insightful argument about what becomes of the values supporting free speech and those opposed to oppression and inequality, see MacKinnon, *Only Words*.

20. Michel Foucault, *History of Sexuality* (New York: Vintage Press, 1980).

21. Neil Miller, *Out of the Past: Gay and Lesbian History from 1869 to the Present* (New York: Vintage, 1995); and David S. Reynolds, *Walt Whitman's America: A Cultural Biography* (New York: Alfred A. Knopf, 1995).

22. See, for example, Gary Kinsman, "Men Loving Men: The Challenge of Gay Liberation," in *Beyond Patriarchy*, edited by Michael Kaufman (New York: Oxford University Press, 1987), 108–110; Suzanne Pharr, *Homophobia: A Weapon of Sexism*, exp. ed. (Inverness, CA: Women's Project, 1997); Reynolds, *Walt Whitman's America*; and Jeffrey Weeks, *Coming Out: Homosexual Politics in Britain from the Nineteenth Century to the Present* (London: Quartet, 1977).

23. For more on sex and gender as socially constructed categories, see Anne Fausto-Sterling, "The Five Sexes: Why Male and Female Are Not Enough," *The Sciences* (March/April 1993): 20–24; Judith Lorber, *Paradoxes of Gender* (New Haven: Yale University Press, 1995); M. Kay Martin and Barbara Voorhies, *Female of the Species*, chap. 4 (New York: Columbia University Press, 1975); John Money and Anke A. Ehrhardt, *Man and Woman, Boy and Girl* (Baltimore: Johns Hopkins University Press, 1972).

24. Foucault, *History of Sexuality*.

25. Martin and Voorhies, *Female of the Species*.

26. For more on this, see Marilyn Frye, *The Politics of Reality: Essays in Feminist Theory* (Freedom, CA: Crossing Press, 1983).

27. Sam Keen, *Fire in the Belly: On Being a Man* (New York: Bantam, 1991), 203.

28. See, for example, Susan A. Ostrander, *Women of the Upper Class* (Philadelphia: Temple University Press, 1984).

29. See Frye, *Politics of Reality*, 1–16.

30. Christian G. Appy, *Working-Class War: American Combat Soldiers in Vietnam* (Chapel Hill: University of North Carolina Press, 1993).

31. Warren Farrell, *The Myth of Male Power* (New York: Berkley Books, 1993).

32. It is useful to note that in thirteenth-century Europe peasants were not allowed to participate in battle, since the nobility's monopoly over the tools and skills of warfare was its main basis for power and domination over land and peasants. Although knights undoubtedly suffered considerably from their endless wars with one another, one could hardly argue that their obligation to fight rendered them an oppressed group. Whatever price they paid for their dominance, the concept of oppression is not the word to describe it. For a lively history of this era, see Barbara Tuchman, *A Distant Mirror* (New York: Alfred A. Knopf, 1978).

33. Save the Children. Study results reported in *The Boston Globe*, 17 November 1994, 23.

34. Keen, *Fire in the Belly*, 133.

## Chapter 2

1. Sam Keen, *Fire in the Belly: On Being a Man* (New York: Bantam, 1991), 207.
2. Robert Bly, *Iron John: A Book about Men* (Reading, MA: Addison-Wesley, 1990); Keen, *Fire in the Belly.*
3. Although the game analogy is useful, social systems are quite unlike a game in important ways. The rules and other understandings on which social life is based are far more complex, ambiguous, and contradictory than those of a typical game and much more open to negotiation and "making it up" as we go along.
4. For some insightful analyses of why men fight, see Dave Grossman, *On Killing* (Boston: Back Bay Books, 1996); J. Glenn Gray, *The Warriors: Reflections on Men in Battle* (Lincoln: University of Nebraska Press, 1970); Charles Moskos, "Why Men Fight: American Combat Soldiers in Vietnam," *Transaction 7*, no. 1 (1969); and E. A. Shils and Morris Janowitz, "Cohesion and Disintegration in the Wehrmacht in World War II," *Public Opinion Quarterly* 12 (summer 1948). For a powerful personal account of experiences in Vietnam, see Philip Caputo, *A Rumor of War* (New York: Holt, Rinehart and Winston, 1977).
5. For historical discussion of the social forces underlying war, see Barbara W. Tuchman, *The Guns of August* (New York: Macmillan, 1962); idem, *The March of Folly: From Troy to Vietnam* (New York: Alfred A. Knopf, 1984). In relation to the Vietnam War, see David Halberstam, *The Best and the Brightest* (New York: Random House, 1972); Stanley Karnow, *Vietnam: A History* (New York: Viking Press, 1983); and John Keegan, *The History of Warfare* (New York: Alfred A. Knopf, 1993).
6. I'll have more to say about the "new men's movement" in later chapters. For a more thorough treatment than I can offer here, see Michael Kimmel, ed., *The Politics of Manhood: Profeminist Men Respond to the Mythopoetic Men's Movement (And the Mythopoetic Leaders Answer)* (Philadelphia: Temple University Press, 1995) and Michael L. Schwalbe, *Unlocking the Iron Cage: The Men's Movement, Gender Politics, and American Culture* (New York: Oxford University Press, 1996).
7. For a history of American fatherhood, see Robert L. Griswold, *Fatherhood in America: A History* (New York: Basic Books, 1993).
8. For a thorough discussion of this distinction, see Marilyn French, *Beyond Power: On Men, Women, and Morals* (New York: Summit Books, 1985).
9. See Carol Cohn, "Sex and Death in the Rational World of Defense Intellectuals," *Signs* vol. 12, no. 4 (1987): 687–728; Brian Easlea, "Patriarchy, Scientists, and Nuclear Warriors," in *Beyond Patriarchy: Essays by Men on Pleasure, Power, and Change,* edited by Michael Kaufman (New York: Oxford University Press, 1987); and Myriam Miedzian, "'Real Men,' 'Wimps,' and Our National Security," in *Boys Will Be Boys: Breaking the Link Between Masculinity and Violence* (New York: Doubleday, 1991).
10. For discussion of language and gender, see Jane Caputi, *Gossips, Gorgons, and Crones* (Santa Fe: Bear and Company, 1993); Mary Daly, *Gyn/Ecology: The Metaethics of Radical Feminism* (Boston: Beacon Press, 1978); Margaret Gibbon, *Feminist Perspectives on Language* (New York: Longman, 1999); Dale Spender, *Man Made Language* (London: Pandora, 1980); Barbara G. Walker, *The Women's Encyclopedia of Myths and Secrets* (San Francisco: Harper and Row, 1983); idem, *The Woman's Dictionary of Symbols and Sacred Objects* (San Francisco: Harper and Row, 1988). For a very different slant on gender and language, see Mary Daly (in cahoots with Jane Caputi), *Webster's First New Intergalactic Wickedary of the English Language* (Boston: Beacon Press, 1987).

11. See Arlie Hochschild (with Anne Machung), *The Second Shift* (New York: Penguin, 2003).

12. See, for example, Rosalyn Baxandall, Linda Gordon, and Susan Reverby, eds., *America's Working Women: A Documentary History—1600 to the Present* (New York: Vintage Press, 1976); Ashley Montagu, *The Natural Superiority of Women* (New York: Collier, 1974); Robin Morgan, ed., *Sisterhood Is Global* (New York: Feminist Press, 1996); and Marilyn Waring, *If Women Counted: A New Feminist Economics* (San Francisco: HarperCollins, 1990).

13. Elizabeth Janeway, *Man's World, Woman's Place: A Study in Social Mythology* (New York: Dell, 1971), 37.

14. Some would no doubt argue, with good reason, that our social selves mask more essential selves, but that's another argument for another place.

15. There is a substantial research literature documenting such genderized patterns of conversation. See, for example, Laurie P. Arliss, *Women and Men Communicating: Challenges and Changes*, 2nd ed. (Prospect Heights, IL: Waveland, 2000); N. Henley, M. Hamilton, and B. Thorne, "Womanspeak and Manspeak: Sex Differences and Sexism in Communication," in *Beyond Sex Roles*, edited by A. G. Sargent (New York: West, 1985), 168–185; P. Kollock, P. Blumstein, and P. Schwartz, "Sex and Power in Interaction," *American Sociological Review* 50, no. 1 (1985): 34–46; L. Smith-Lovin and C. Brody, "Interruptions in Group Discussions: The Effect of Gender and Group Composition," *American Sociological Review* 51, no. 3 (1989): 424–435; and Mary M. Talbot, *Language and Gender: An Introduction* (Malden, MA: Blackwell, 1999).

16. Harry Brod, "Work Clothes and Leisure Suits: The Class Basis and Bias of the Men's Movement," in *Men's Lives*, edited by Michael S. Kimmel and Michael A. Messner (New York: Macmillan, 1989), 280.

17. U.S. Census Bureau, *Statistical Abstract of the United States: 2003* (Washington, DC: U.S. Government Printing Office, 2003); Joint Economic Committee, *The Concentration of Wealth in the United States* (Washington, DC: Joint Economic Committee of the U.S. Congress, 1986); John Schmitt, Lawrence Mishel, and Jared Bernstein. "Trends in Economic Well-Being in North America," presented at Canadian Economic Association Meetings, Ottawa, May 31, 1998. Found online at http://www.csls.ca/events/cea1998/rtw.asp#T7. Similar patterns are found throughout the industrialized world, although the United States has the highest level of inequality among them and the lowest level of social support, such as universal health care, for the poor.

18. United Nations. Reported in the Boston *Globe*, July 23, 1997, p. A06. See also Brenda C. Coleman, "Harassment Is Cited by Many Female Physicians." Boston *Globe*, February 23, 1998, p. A03; "Medical News and Perspectives," *Journal of the American Medical Association* 264, no. 8 (1990): 939; M. A. Paludi, *Sexual Harassment on College Campuses* (Albany: State University of New York Press, 1996); and Diana Russell, *Sexual Exploitation: Rape, Child Sexual Abuse, and Workplace Harassment* (Beverly Hills, CA.: Sage, 1984).

19. See, for example, Susan Brownmiller, *Against Our Will: Men, Women, and Rape* (New York: Simon and Schuster, 1975); Paludi, *Sexual Harassment*; and Russell, *Sexual Exploitation*.

20. For example, the more dominant males are in a society, the more frequent sexual violence becomes. See Peggy Reeves Sanday, *Female Power and Male Dominance: On the Origins of Sexual Inequality* (Cambridge: Cambridge University Press, 1981).

21. As Masters and Johnson documented in their classic studies of human sexuality, intercourse isn't a reliable way for most women to have orgasms; but as Nora L. Jamieson

points out, this doesn't prevent filmmakers from routinely portraying women having orgasms during intercourse (personal conversation).

22. See Marilyn Frye, "Some Reflections on Separatism and Power," in *The Politics of Reality* (Trumansburg, NY: Crossing Press, 1983).

23. My thanks to Donna Garske of Marin Abused Women's Services for emphasizing to me the importance of this aspect of men's violence against women.

24. See Michel Foucault, *The History of Sexuality: An Introduction* (Harmondsworth: Penguin, 1981). See also Arthur Brittan, *Masculinity and Power* (Oxford: Basil Blackwell, 1989).

25. Brownmiller, *Against Our Will*, 15.

26. For a classic discussion of the forms that privilege takes, see Peggy McIntosh, "White Privilege and Male Privilege: A Personal Account of Coming to See Correspondences Through Work in Women's Studies," in *Gender Basics: Feminist Perspectives on Women and Men*, 2nd edited by Anne Minas (Belmont, CA: Wadsworth, 2000).

## Chapter 3

1. See, for example, John Gray, *Men Are from Mars, Women Are from Venus* (New York: HarperCollins, 1993); Steven Goldberg, *The Inevitability of Patriarchy*, new ed. (New York: William Morrow, 1993); and Lionel Tiger, *Men in Groups* (London: Nelson, 1969). For a view of feminist essentialism, see Rosemarie Tong, *Feminist Thought: A More Comprehensive Introduction* (Boulder, CO: Westview Press, 1998).

2. Which, of course, some feminists—lesbian separatists in particular—have suggested.

3. E. O. Wilson, "Biology and the Social Sciences," *Daedalus* 106 (Fall 1977): 127–140. See also Ruth Bleier, *Science and Gender: A Critique of Biology and Its Theories on Women* (New York: Pergamon Press, 1984); Anne Fausto-Sterling, *Myths of Gender: Biological Theories about Men and Women*, 2nd rev. ed. (New York: Basic Books, 1992); Katharine B. Hoyenga and Kermit T. Hoyenga, *Gender-Related Differences: Origins and Outcomes* (Needham Heights, MA: Allyn and Bacon, 1993); and Eleanor E. Maccoby and Carol N. Jacklin, *The Psychology of Sex Differences* (Standford: Standford University Press, 1974).

4. See Riane Eisler, *The Chalice and the Blade* (New York: Harper and Row, 1987); Elizabeth Fisher, *Woman's Creation: Sexual Evolution and the Shaping of Society* (New York: McGraw-Hill, 1979); Marilyn French, *Beyond Power: On Men, Women, and Morals* (New York: Summit Books, 1985); Marija Gimbutas, *The Civilization of the Goddess: The World of Old Europe* (San Francisco: Harper and Row, 1991); idem, *The Language of the Goddess* (New York: HarperCollins, 1989); Richard Lee and Richard Daly, "Man's Domination and Woman's Oppression: The Question of Origins," in *Beyond Patriarchy: Essays by Men on Pleasure, Power, and Change*, edited by Michael Kaufman (New York: Oxford University Press, 1987), 30–44; Gerda Lerner, *The Creation of Patriarchy* (New York: Oxford University Press, 1986); and Marlin Stone, *When God Was a Woman* (New York: Harcourt Brace Jovanovich, 1976).

5. See, for example, Maria Lepowsky, "Women, Men, and Aggression in an Egalitarian Society," *Sex Roles* 30, nos. 3/4 (1994); 199–211; Margaret Mead, *Sex and Temperament in Three Primitive Societies* (New York: William Morrow, 1963); Henrietta L. Moore, *Feminism and Anthropology* (Minneapolis: University of Minnnesota Press, 1988); Peggy Sanday, *Female Power and Male Dominance: On the Origins of Sexual Inequality* (Cambridge: Cambridge University Press, 1981); and idem, "The Socio-Cultural Context of Rape: A Cross-Cultural Study," *Journal of Social Issues* 34, no. 7 (1981): 5–27.

6. See Fausto-Sterling, *Myths of Gender.*
7. See, for example, W. T. Bielby and D. D. Bielby, "Family Ties: Balancing Commitments to Work and Family in Dual Earner Households," *American Sociological Review* 54, no. 5 (1989): 776–789; Maccoby and Jacklin, *The Psychology of Sex Differences*; B. J. Risman, "Intimate Relationships from a Microstructuralist Perspective: Men Who Mother," *Gender and Society* 1, no. 1 (1987): 6–32; and Naomi Weisstein, "Psychology Constructs the Female," in *Woman in Sexist Society: Studies in Power and Powerlessness*, edited by Vivian Gornick and Barbara K. Moran (New York: Basic Books, 1971) 207–224.
8. See, for example, Deborah S. David and Robert Brannon, eds., *The Forty-Nine Percent Majority: The Male Sex Role* (Reading, MA: Addison-Wesley, 1976); Clyde W. Franklin, *Men and Society* (Chicago: Nelson-Hall, 1988); Michael Kaufman, ed., *Beyond Patriarchy: Essays by Men on Pleasure, Power, and Change* (New York: Oxford University Press, 1987); Sam Keen, *Fire in the Belly: On Being a Man* (New York: Bantam, 1991); Michael Kimmel, *Manhood in America* (New York: Free Press, 1996); Michael S. Kimmel and Michael A. Messner, eds., *Men's Lives*, 6th ed. (Boston: Allyn and Bacon, 2004); Joseph H. Pleck and Jack Sawyer, *Men and Masculinity* (Englewood Cliffs, NJ: Prentice-Hall, 1974); and Andrew Tolson, *The Limits of Masculinity* (New York: Harper and Row, 1977).
9. For a history of European women's early awareness of and resistance to patriarchal oppression, see Gerda Lerner, *The Creation of Feminist Consciousness: From the Middle Ages to Eighteen-Seventy* (New York: Oxford University Press, 1993).
10. The following discussion draws on many sources, especially Robert Connell, *Gender and Power: Society, the Person, and Sexual Politics* (Stanford: Stanford University Press, 1987); Eisler, *The Chalice and the Blade*; Fisher, *Woman's Creation*; French, *Beyond Power*; David D. Gilmore, *Manhood in the Making: Cultural Concepts of Masculinity* (New Haven: Yale University Press, 1990); Miriam M. Johnson, *Strong Mothers, Weak Wives: The Search for Gender Equality* (Berkeley: University of California Press, 1988); Lee and Daly, "Man's Domination"; and Lerner, *The Creation of Patriarchy.*
11. For more on this, see, for example, Michael Kaufman, "The Construction of Masculinity and the Triad of Men's Violence," in *Beyond Patriarchy*, edited by Michael Kaufman, 1–29.
12. A form of ritual aggression most often associated with African American males in which the contest is to trade progressively harsher insults until one or the other contestant either gives up or cannot better the previous insult.
13. French, *Beyond Power*, 337.
14. See Doris Kearns Goodwin, *Lyndon Johnson and the American Dream* (New York: St. Martin's Press, 1991).
15. French, *Beyond Power,* 508.
16. Simone Weil, "Analysis of Oppression," in *Oppression and Liberty*, translated by Arthur Wills and John Petrie (Amherst: University of Massachusetts Press, 1973), quoted in French, *Beyond Power*, 508.
17. This was the subject of a now-classic experiment in social psychology. See Manford Kuhn and Thomas McPartland, "An Empirical Investigation of Self Attitudes," *American Sociological Review* 19 (1954): 68–76.
18. Anyone who doubts this needs look no further than the nearest school playground and the persecution endured by boys who show any interest in playing with girls. Among adults, woe betide the man who openly prefers the company of women. See Barrie Thorne, *Gender Play: Girls and Boys in School* (New Brunswick, NJ: Rutgers University Press, 1993).

19. I haven't done the research, but I'd guess that men comprise the overwhelming majority of entries in the *Guinness Book of World Records*.
20. David Halberstam, *The Best and the Brightest* (New York: Random House, 1972), 76.
21. See William G. Domhoff, *The Bohemian Grove and Other Retreats* (New York: Harper and Row, 1974).
22. Women in this position, of course, would only lose.
23. See Joseph H. Pleck, "Men's Power with Women, Other Men, and Society: A Men's Movement Analysis," in *Men's Lives*, 2nd ed. edited by Michael S. Kimmel and Michael A. Messner (New York: Macmillan, 1992), 25.
24. See Johnson, *Strong Mothers, Weak Wives*, 117–118; and Pleck, "Men's Power with Women," 22–25.
25. See, for example, Frank Browning, *The Culture of Desire: Paradox and Perversity in Gay Lives Today* (New York: Crown Publishers, 1993); Tim Carrigan, Robert Connell, and John Lee, "Hard and Heavy: Toward a New Sociology of Masculinity," in *Beyond Patriarchy*, edited by Michael Kaufman, 139–192; and Suzanne Pharr, *Homophobia: A Weapon of Sexism*, exp. ed. (Inverness, CA: Women's Project, 1997).
26. John Stoltenberg, "Pornography and Freedom," in *Men's Lives*, edited by Michael S. Kimmel and Michael A. Messner (New York: Macmillan, 1989), 482–488.
27. This is a confused area of thinking about gender that I try to clear up in Chapter 4.
28. See J. M. Golding, "Division of Household Labor, Strain, and Depressive Symptoms among Mexican American and Non-Hispanic Whites," *Psychology of Women Quarterly* 14, no. 1 (1990): 103–117; E. Litwak and P. Messeri, "Organizational Theory, Social Supports, and Mortality Rates," *American Sociological Review* 54, no. 1 (1989): 49–66; and J. Mirowsky and C. E. Ross, *Social Causes of Psychological Distress* (New York: Aldine de Gruyter, 1989).
29. See, for example, Jessie Bernard, "The Good Provider Role," *American Psychologist* 36, no. 1 (1981): 00–00; R. C. Kessler and J. A. McRae, Jr., "The Effects of Wives' Employment on the Mental Health of Married Men and Women," *American Sociological Review* 47 (April 1982): 216–227; W. Michelson, *From Sun to Sun: Daily Obligations and Community Structure in the Lives of Employed Women and Their Families* (Totowa, NJ: Rowman and Allanheld, 1985); and J. R. Wilkie, "Changes in U.S. Men's Attitudes Towards the Family Provider Role, 1972–1989," *Gender and Society* 7, no. 2 (1993): 261–279.
30. See Heidi I. Hartmann, "The Unhappy Marriage of Marxism and Feminism: Towards a More Progressive Union," in *Women and Revolution*, edited by Lydia Sargent (Boston: South End Press, 1981), 1–41.
31. For some revealing case studies of how this works, see Arlie Hochschild, *The Second Shift: Working Parents and the Revolution at Home* (New York: Viking/Penguin, 1989).
32. This phenomenon is part of most oppressive systems, including racist ones. See Gerda Lerner, "Reconceptualizing Differences Among Women," in *Feminist Frameworks*, edited by Alison M. Jaggar and Paul S. Rothenberg, 3rd ed. (New York: McGraw-Hill, 1993), 237–248.
33. See David R. Roediger, *The Wages of Whiteness: Race and the Making of the American Working Class* (New York: Verso, 1991).
34. See Ann Jones, *Next Time She'll Be Dead: Battering and How to Stop It* (Boston: Beacon Press, 2000).
35. See Andrea Dworkin, *Woman Hating* (New York: E. P. Dutton, 1974); Susan Faludi, *Backlash: The Underclared War Against Women* (New York: Crown Publishers, 1991); Marilyn French, *The War Against Women* (New York: Summit Books, 1992);

and Catharine A. MacKinnon, *Only Words* (Cambridge: Harvard University Press, 1993).

36. It is notable that although a word for the hatred of maleness exists—*misandry*—it wasn't included in most dictionaries until very recently. The closest the English language comes to the hatred of males is *misanthropy*, which actually refers to the hatred of people in general. Once again, patriarchal culture identifies males as the standard of humanity while women are marginalized as a hate-worthy "other."

37. See B. Dijkstra, *Idols of Perversity: Fantasies of Feminine Evil* (New York: Oxford University Press, 1987); and S. Pomeroy, *Goddesses, Whores, Wives, and Slaves* (New York: Schocken, 1975).

38. See N. Ben-Yehuda, "The European Witch Craze of the 14th and 17th Centuries: A Sociologist's Perspective," *American Journal of Sociology* 86, no. 1 (1980): 1–31; Kim Chernin, *The Obsession: Reflections on the Tyranny of Slenderness* (New York: Harper and Row, 1981); C. P. Christ, "Heretics and Outsiders: The Struggle over Female Power in Western Religion," in *Feminist Frontiers*, edited by L. Richardson and V. Taylor (Reading, MA: Addison-Wesley, 1983), 87–94; Dworkin, *Woman Hating*; Barbara Ehrenreich and Deidre English, *For Her Own Good: 150 Years of Experts' Advice to Women* (New York: Anchor Books/Doubleday, 1989); Faludi, *Backlash*; French, *War Against Women*; and MacKinnon, *Only Words*.

39. It's true that "prick" is a form of insult, but it doesn't have nearly the weight of likening men to women.

40. Barbara G. Walker, *The Woman's Encyclopedia of Myths and Secrets* (San Francisco: Harper and Row, 1983).

41. A metaphor I first heard from Nora L. Jamieson.

42. For some accounts of how this works, see Studs Terkel, *Race* (New York: New Press, 1992).

43. It should come as no surprise that abusive men tend to be very emotionally dependent on the women they abuse. See Ann Jones, *Next Time She'll Be Dead*; and Thomas J. Scheff and Suzanne M. Retzinger, *Emotions and Violence: Shame and Rage in Destructive Conflicts* (Lexington, MA: Lexington, 1991). See also Claire M. Renzetti, *Violent Betrayal: Partner Abuse in Lesbian Relationships* (Newbury Park, CA: Sage, 1992).

44. I suspect a similar phenomenon occurs in other forms of oppression. Whites, for example, often look upon stereotypical characteristics of people of color with a mixture of contempt and envy. I've heard some whites say they would like to have the feeling of strength and wisdom that many African Americans have developed in order to survive in a racist society.

45. See Ehrenreich and English, *For Her Own Good*; and Viviana A. Zelizer, *Pricing the Priceless Child: The Changing Social Value of Children* (New York: Basic Books, 1985).

46. Today custody has become a hotly contested terrain as children's emotional value has increased and its potential as a weapon in marital disputes has been recognized. For some history and analysis, see Susan Crean, *In the Name of the Fathers* (Toronto: Amanita Enterprises, 1988).

47. See Bonnie S. Anderson and Judith P. Zinsser, *A History of Their Own: Women in Europe from Prehistory to the Present*, vols. 1 and 2 (New York: Harper Collins, 1999); Rosalyn Baxandall, Linda Gordon, and Susan Reverby, eds., *America's Working Women: A Documentary History—1600 to the Present* (New York: Vintage, 1976); Elise Boulding, *The Underside of History: A View of Women Through Time* (Boulder, CO: Westview Press, 1976); and Marilyn Waring, *If Women Counted: A New Feminist Economics* (San Francisco: HarperCollins, 1988).

48. See Waring, *If Women Counted.*
49. Except, perhaps, in the upper classes, in which such dependency was more common. In the United States, it also wasn't true of most working- and lower-class women and women of color, who have always had to work both inside and outside the home.
50. Willard Libby, "Man's Place in the Physical Universe," in *New Views of the Nature of Man,* edited by John R. Platt (Chicago: University of Chicago Press, 1965), 14–15. See also Brian Easlea, "Patriarchy, Scientists, and Nuclear Warriors," in *Beyond Patriarchy,* edited by Michael Kaufman, 200.
51. Arthur Brittan, *Masculinity and Power* (Oxford: Basil Blackwell, 1989), 97.
52. Robert Bly, *Iron John: A Book about Men* (Reading, MA: Addison-Wesley, 1990), 19–21, 98 and Keen, *Fire in the Belly,* 33, 56, 60, 105.
53. Henderson, who describes herself as a futurist and alternative economist, made this remark at a conference at Western Connecticut State University, March 31, 1989. See also *Creating Alternative Futures: The End of Economics* (Bloomfield, CT: Kumarian Press, 1996); *The Politics of the Solar Age* (Garden City, NY: Doubleday, 1988); and *Paradigms in Progress: Life Beyond Economics* (Indianapolis: Knowledge Systems, 1991). Socialist feminists might object that there's nothing inherently patriarchal about socialism in theory, contrary to socialism as it has thus far been practiced in modern times. Capitalism, however, with its emphasis on control, competition, and the inherently exploitative relationship between capitalists and labor, embodies core patriarchal values both in theory and in practice.
54. I base what follows on my understanding of a sizable literature that, for reasons of space, I won't try to summarize in a comprehensive way. Readers who want more should consult the fascinating and well-written sources cited throughout this section and decide for themselves.
55. See, for example, Jack Goody, *Production and Reproduction* (New York: Cambridge University Press, 1976); Ruby Leavitt, "Women in Other Cultures," in *Woman in Sexist Socitey,* edited by Vivian Gornick and Barbara K. Moran (New York: Mentor, 1971), 393–427); M. Kay Martin and Barbara Voorhies, *Female of the Species* (New York: Columbia University Press, 1975); Margaret Mead, *Sex and Temperament in Three Primitive Societies* (New York: William Morrow, 1963 and Henrietta L. Moore, *Feminism and Anthropology* (Minneapolis: University of Minnesota Press, 1988).
56. In *matrilineal* societies, lineage is traced through the mother's blood relatives, not the father's. In *matrilocal* societies, a married couple must live near and be integrated with the wife's family.
57. See David Levinson, *Family Violence in Cross Cultural Perspective* (Thousand Oaks, CA: Sage, 1989); Peggy Reeves Sanday, "The Socio-Cultural Context of Rape: A Cross-Cultural Study," *Journal of Social Issues* 37 (1981): 5–27; and idem, "Rape and the Silencing of the Feminine," in *Rape: An Historical and Social Enquiry,* edited by Sylvana Tomaselli and Roy Porter (Oxford: Basil Blackwell, 1986), 84–101.
58. See, for example, Eisler, *The Chalice and the Blade;* Fisher, *Woman's Creation;* French, *Beyond Power;* Gimbus, *The Language of the Goddess* and *The Civilization of the Goddess;* Lee and Daly, "Man's Domination"; Lerner, *The Creation of Patriarchy;* and Stone, *When God Was a Woman.*
59. There are historical records of societies in which the male reproductive role was unknown. It also would seem beyond dispute that knowledge of reproductive biology was something humans had to discover, perhaps through the domestication of animals. See Fisher, *Woman's Creation.*
60. Miriam M. Johnson, *Strong Mothers, Weak Wives,* 266. See also French, *Beyond Power,* 46–47, 65.

61. The "locality" of family systems refers to marriage rules governing where married couples live—matrilocal (with the wife's mother) and patrilocal (with the husband's father). Together with the way lineage is figured, locality has profound effects on the degree to which social relationships are woman identified or man identified.

62. Much of the discussion that follows depends on my interpretation of several sources, the most important of which are Eisler, *The Chalice and the Blade*; Fisher, *Woman's Creation*; French, *Beyond Power;* Lee and Daly, "Man's Domination"; and Lerner, *The Creation of Patriarchy*. For an important sociological discussion of the origins of social inequality in general, see Gerhard Lenski, *Power and Privilege: A Theory of Social Stratification* (Chapel Hill: University of North Carolina Press, 1984).

63. This is based on Lenski, *Power and Privilege*. For a recent test of Lenski's theory, see A. Haas, "Social Inequality in Aboriginal North America: A Test of Lenski's Theory," *Social Forces* 72, no. 2 (1993): 295–313.

64. See French, *Beyond Power*, 47.

65. See Fisher, *Woman's Creation*, p. 190–197.

66. Ibid., p. 197.

67. This is also true of racism in some respects. Slavery, for example, is most common in agricultural societies. See Patrick Nolan and Gerhard Lenski, *Human Societies*, 9th ed. (New York: Paradigm, 2004).

68. Eisler, *The Chalice and the Blade*.

69. See, for example, Keen, *Fire in the Belly*, and Lee and Daly, "Man's Domination."

70. See Brittan, *Masculinity and Power*, 88–92.

71. French, *Beyond Power*.

72. For views on the connection between patriarchy and how we treat the environment, see Irene Diamond and Gloria Feman Orenstein, eds., *Reweaving the World: The Emergence of Ecofeminism* (San Francisco: Sierra Club Books, 1990).

73. See, for example, Richard J. Barnet and John Cavanagh, *Global Dreams: Imperial Corporations and the New World Order* (New York: Simon and Schuster, 1994).

74. Lest anyone conclude that capitalism is the problem, it's important to add that socialism hasn't been any better, at least not in anything we've seen so far. Socialist societies have been as much organized around control and domination as any other patriarchy, if not more so.

75. The men who controlled the Chinese and Russian revolutions said some noble things about gender equality and made a few changes that improved women's standing. In practice, however, they did little to challenge the underlying nature of patriarchy or men's position in it.

## Chapter 4

1. Known in philosophy as epistemic privilege.

2. See Barbara Ehrenreich and Deidre English, *For Her Own Good: 150 Years of Experts' Advice to Women*, chaps. 1–3 (New York: Anchor Books, 1989).

3. A form of female genital mutilation that is still common in many regions of Africa and the Middle East. See Fran P. Hosken, *The Hosken Report: Genital and Sexual Mutilation of Females*, 4th rev. ed. (Lexington, MA: Women's International Network News, 1994); and Anika Rahman and Nahid Toubia, eds., *Female Genital Mutilation: A Guide to Laws and Policies Worldwide* (London: Zed Books, 2000).

4. See Michel Foucault, *The History of Sexuality: An Introduction* (Harmondsworth, England: Penguin, 1981).

5. See S. Bordo, *Unbearable Weight: Feminism, Western Culture, and the Body* (Berkeley: University of California Press, 1995); Kim Chernin, *The Obsession: Reflections on the*

*Tyranny of Slenderness* (New York: Harper and Row, 1981); and Naomi Wolf, *The Beauty Myth: How Images of Beauty Are Used Against Women* (New York: William Morrow, 1991).

6. Sam Keen, *Fire in the Belly: On Being a Man* (New York: Bantam, 1991), 218. Biblical scholar Phyllis Trible has shown Keen to be quite wrong on this. Her translation of the book of Genesis reveals that God created a person named ha'adam, the Hebrew word for person with no specification as to sex. Only when God saw the need for human affiliation did he create women and men. See Trible, *God and the Rhetoric of Sexuality* (Philadelphia: Fortress Press, 1978).

7. Robert Bly, *Iron John: A Book about Men* (Reading, MA: Addison-Wesley, 1990), 93–94.

8. See, for example, Eugene Monick, *Phallos: Sacred Image of the Masculine* (Toronto: Inner City Books, 1987); and Robert Moore and Douglas Gillette, *King, Warrior, Magician, Lover: Rediscovering the Archetypes of the Mature Masculine* (San Francisco: HarperCollins, 1990). I'll have much to say about the new men's movement in later chapters.

9. John Gray, *Men are from Mars, Women are from Venus* (New York: HarperCollins, 1993).

10. Sara Ruddick describes this as "maternal work" in her powerful and insightful book, *Maternal Thinking: Towards a Politics of Peace* (Boston: Beacon Press, 1995). She emphasizes that it can be performed by both women and men, although it is, of course, almost always women's responsibility.

11. Keen, *Fire in the Belly*, 166.

12. Keen, *Fire in the Belly*, 180.

13. Bly, *Iron John*, 14.

14. See, for example, Naomi Weisstein, "'Kinder, Kuche, and Kirche' as Scientific Law: Psychology Constructs the Female," in *Sisterhood Is Powerful: An Anthology of Writings from the Women's Liberation Movement*, edited by Robin Morgan (New York: Vintage, 1970), 228–245. For an interesting discussion of how the social reality of gender is constructed through conversation, see Arthur Brittan, *Masculinity and Power* (Oxford: Basil Blackwell, 1989).

15. From *Dialogues on Love*, quoted in David Gilmore, *Manhood in the Making: Cultural Concepts of Masculinity* (New Haven: Yale University Press, 1990), 155.

16. Anthony Rotundo provides a clear analysis of the historical process through which aggression became defined not as a problem but as a masculine virtue. See Rotundo, *American Manhood: Transformations in Masculinity from the Revolution to the Modern Era* (New York: Basic Books, 1993).

17. See, for example, Bly's reference to women as historically passive and only now becoming "active" (*Iron John*, 60).

18. See Hazel Henderson, *The Politics of the Solar Age* (Garden City, NY: Doubleday, 1981), 169; and Marilyn Waring, *If Women Counted: A New Feminist Economics* (San Francisco: HarperCollins, 1988).

19. Even Andrea Dworkin, who uses much of her provocative book, *Intercourse* (New York: Free Press, 1987) to argue that heterosexual intercourse is inherently aggressive and oppressive, finally acknowledges that it is the patriarchal *version* of heterosexuality that is this way, not heterosexuality per se.

20. See, for example, Emily Martin, "The Egg and the Sperm: How Science Has Constructed a Romance Based on Stereotypical Male-Female Roles," *Signs* 16 (1991): 485–501. See also Ann Cvetkovich, "Recasting Receptivity: Femme Sexualities," in *Lesbian Erotics*, edited by Karla Jay (New York: New York University Press, 1995).

21. Harriet Malinowitz, "Looking for Consensus," *Women's Review of Books* (June 1995): 14. See also the essay that inspired the metaphor, Cvetkovich's "Recasting Receptivity: Femme Sexualities."

22. In *Iron John*, Robert Bly provides vivid examples of this kind of thinking. See, for example, pages 61–63 and 221.

23. Joan Cocks, "Wordless Emotions: Some Critical Reflections on Radical Feminism," *Politics and Society* 13, no. 1 (1984): 48.

24. Nora L. Jamieson first made me aware of this connection.

25. See Robert W. Connell, *Gender and Power: Society, the Person, and Sexual Politics* (Stanford: Stanford University Press, 1987). See also Tim Carrigan, Robert Connell, and John Lee, "Hard and Heavy: Toward a New Sociology of Masculinity," in *Beyond Patriarchy: Essays by Men on Pleasure, Power, and Change*, edited by Michael Kaufman (New York: Oxford University Press, 1987), 139–192.

26. For the best such statement that I have seen, see Carrigan et al., "Hard and Heavy."

27. Although the association of gender with "wife" and "husband" may see obvious, it is less so in light of the fact that in some societies women may marry other women and even in the United States there is a growing recognition of marriage among gays and lesbians. One can be a woman's spouse without being a man, which means that the relationship between husbands and wives bears a particular relationship to gender, a relationship that varies from one society to another. We should also note that just as "to husband" had meaning beyond the confines of marriage, being a good wife has similar cultural connotations about caring, support, and self-sacrifice in relation to one's spouse that need not necessarily be confined to women. As Judy Syfers put it, "My God, who *wouldn't* want a wife?" (*Ms.*, December 1979).

28. Beyond informal everyday usage, "sane" and "insane" are primarily legal terms.

29. R. N. Proctor, *Racial Hygiene: Medicine under the Nazis* (Cambridge: Harvard University Press, 1988).

30. See, for example, E. Stover and E. O. Nightingale, *The Breaking of Bodies and Minds: Torture, Psychiatric Abuse, and the Health Professions* (New York: St. Martin's Press, 1985).

31. This has been particularly true of the authority the male-dominated health profession has used to determine what constitutes a healthy adult woman. See Phyllis Chesler, *Women and Madness* (New York: Doubleday, 1972); and Ehrenreich and English, *For Her Own Good*.

32. See Frank Browning, *The Culture of Desire: Paradox and Perversity in Gay Lives Today* (New York: Crown, 1993); Carrigan et al., "Hard and Heavy"; and David Gary Comstock, *Violence Against Lesbians and Gay Men* (New York: Columbia University Press, 1991).

33. Which is not to say that gay men can't be misogynist.

34. See Gilmore, *Manhood in the Making*.

35. For an insightful discussion of such issues in the history of American manhood, see Rotundo, *American Manhood*.

36. See Frantz Fanon, *The Wretched of the Earth* (New York: Grove Press, 1963), 38–40.

37. Albert Memmi, *Dominated Man* (New York: Orion Press, 1964), 190.

38. For insightful criticism of dichotomous thinking about gender, see Anne Fausto-Sterling, *Myths of Gender*; and Carole Pateman, *The Sexual Contract* (Stanford: Stanford University Press, 1988).

39. The cultural association of women with nature is not universal in patriarchal societies, but whatever is associated with women tends to be devalued in favor of what is associated with men.

40. For criticism of the concept of androgyny, see Miriam M. Johnson, *Strong Mothers, Weak Wives: The Search for Gender Equality* (Berkeley: University of California Press, 1988) 57–60; and Bernice Lott, "A Feminist Critique of Androgyny," in *Gender and Nonverbal Behavior*, edited by C. Mayo and Nancy M. Henley (New York: Springer-Verlag, 1981), 171–180.

## Chapter 5

1. See Marilyn French, *Beyond Power: On Women, Men, and Morals* (New York: Summit Books, 1985), 484–488.
2. Katherine Roiphe, *The Morning After: Fear, Sex, and Feminism on College Campuses* (Boston: Little, Brown, 1993).
3. See, for example, Arthur Brittan, *Masculinity and Power* (Oxford: Basil Blackwell, 1989); Robert W. Connell, *Gender and Power: Society, the Person, and Sexual Politics* (Stanford: Stanford University Press, 1987); Michael Kaufman, ed., *Beyond Power: Essays by Men on Pleasure, Power, and Change* (Toronto: Oxford University Press, 1987): Michael Kimmel, *Manhood in America* (New York: Free Press, 1996); Michael S. Kimmel and Michael A. Messner, eds., *Men's Lives*, 6th ed. (Boston: Allyn and Bacon, 2004); Michael S. Kimmel and Tom Mosmiller, eds., *Against the Tide: Pro-Feminist Men in the United States, 1776–1990* (Boston: Beacon Press, 1992); E. Anthony Rotundo, *American Manhood: Transformations in Masculinity from the Revolution to the Modern Era* (New York: Basic Books, 1993); John Stoltenberg, *Refusing to Be a Man* (New York: Meridian, 1989); idem, *The End of Manhood* (New York: Plume, 1993).
4. For more on this point, see bell hooks, *Feminist Theory: From Margin to Center*, chap. 5 (Boston: South End Press, 1984).
5. Far more than I can cover here. For a more complete look at feminist thinking, an excellent place to start is Margaret L. Andersen, *Thinking about Women: Sociological Perspectives on Sex and Gender,* 6th ed. (New York: Macmillan, 2002); and Rosemarie Tong, *Feminist Thought: A More Comprehensive Introduction* (Boulder, CO: Westview Press, 1998).
6. See, for example, Wendy Kaminer, "Feminism's Identity Crisis," *Atlantic* (October 1993): 51–68.
7. Sharon Lerner, "V-Day's Charismatic Cuntism Rocks the Garden Clit Club." *Village Voice*, February 14–20, 2001.
8. Sam Keen, *Fire in the Belly: On Being a Man* (New York: Bantam Books, 1991), 196*ff.*
9. Keen, *Fire in the Belly*, 196.
10. Limbaugh routinely refers to feminists in this way on his radio and television talk shows. Paglia made this statement on the television show *Sixty Minutes*, 1 November 1992.
11. Naomi Wolf, *The Beauty Myth: How Images of Beauty Are Used Against Women* (New York: William Morrow, 1991).
12. For a powerful analysis of the difference between motherhood as experience and motherhood as a patriarchal institution, see Adrienne Rich, *Of Woman Born* (New York: W.W. Norton, 1976). For some insight into how patriarchy shapes fatherhood, see Robert L. Griswold, *Fatherhood in America: A History* (New York: Basic Books, 1993).
13. Women may make jokes among themselves that play off their subordinate position (as also do blacks, Jews, and other groups targeted by prejudice) that would never be tolerated coming from members of dominant groups. The difference is that when it comes from other women, it heightens awareness of their common standing as women and can help reinforce their sense of solidarity with one another; but when

it comes from men it is more of an assertion of men's dominant position under patriarchy.

14. Quoted by John S. Wilson in *The Boston Globe* Magazine, 8 November 1992, p. 43.

15. Marilyn French, *Beyond Power*, 280.

16. See, for example, Judith Levine, *My Enemy, My Love: Man-Hating and Ambivalence in Women's Lives* (New York: Doubleday, 1993).

17. At a lecture on 11 April 1991, at Trinity College, in Hartford, Connecticut, Davis made this comment in response to a young black man who supported black women's struggle for equality but felt stung by their negative comments about men in general.

18. See bell hooks, *Feminist Theory*, chap. 15.

19. Valerie Solanas, *The SCUM (Society for Cutting Up Men) Manifesto* (New York: Olympia Press, 1968).

20. See Alice Echols, *Daring to Be Bad: Radical Feminism in America 1967–1975* (Minneapolis: University of Minnesota Press, 1990), 210–241; Marilyn Frye, "Willful Virgin, or, Do You Have to Be a Lesbian to Be a Feminist?" in *Willful Virgin: Essays in Feminism, 1976–1992* (Freedom, CA: Crossing Press, 1992); and Nancy Myron and Charlotte Bunch, eds., *Lesbianism and the Women's Movement* (Baltimore: Diana Press, 1975).

21. See Suzanne Pharr, *Homophobia: A Weapon of Sexism,* exp. ed. (Inverness, CA: Women's Project, 1997).

22. Adrienne Rich, "Compulsory Heterosexuality and Lesbian Existence," *Signs: A Journal of Women in Culture and Society 5*, no. 4 (summer 1980).

23. Ellyn Kaschak, *Engendered Lives: A New Psychology of Women's Experience* (New York: Basic Books, 1992), 5. Kaschak provides a provocative discussion of the concept of the "indeterminate" male viewer whose gaze is everywhere in women's lives.

24. See also Marilyn Frye, "In and Out of Harm's Way: Arrogance and Love," in *The Politics of Reality: Essays in Feminist Theory* (Trumansburg, NY: Crossing Press, 1983), 52–83.

25. See Wolf, *Beauty Myth*.

26. See, for example, Roiphe, *Morning After*; Christine Hoff Sommers, *Who Stole Feminism?* (New York: Simon and Schuster, 1994); and Wolf, *Fire with Fire*. NY: Fawcett, 1994.

27. Naomi Wolf, for example, argues that "the right question to ask is simply how to get more power into women's hands—whoever they may be, whatever they may do with it" (*Fire With Fire*, 127).

28. For a more extensive description and analysis of liberal feminism, see Tong, *Feminist Thought*, chap. 1.

29. For some vivid portraits of what these negotiations look like and why they so often fail, see Arlie Hochschild, *The Second Shift: Working Parents and the Revolution at Home* (New York: Viking/Penguin, 1989). See also R. L. Blumberg, ed., *Gender, Family, and Economy: The Triple Overlap* (Newbury Park, CA: Sage, 1991); K. Gerson, *No Man's Land: Men's Changing Commitments to Family and Work* (New York: Basic Books, 1993); F. K. Goldscheider and L. J. Waite, *New Families, No Families? The Transformation of the American Home* (Berkeley: University of California Press, 1991); J. R. Willkie, "Changes in U.S. Men's Attitudes Towards the Family Provider Role, 1972–1989," *Gender and Society 7*, no. 2 (1993): 261–279; and E. O. Wright, K. Shire, S. Hwang, M. Dolan, and J. Baxter, "The Non-Effects of Class on the Gender Division of Labor in the Home: A Comparison of Sweden and the U.S.," *Gender and Society 6*, no. 2 (1992): 25–82.

30. Audre Lorde, *Sister Outsider* (Freedom, CA: Crossing Press, 1984).

31. Wolf, *Fire with Fire*, 139.

32. French, *Beyond Power*, 443.
33. For more on this, see Blumberg, ed., *Gender, Family, and Economy*; C. N. Degler, *At Odds: Women and the Family in America from the Revolution to the Present* (New York: Oxford University Press, 1980); Gerson, *No Man's Land*; Hochschild, *Second Shift*; Miriam M. Johnson, *Strong Mothers, Weak Wives: The Search for Gender Equality* (Berkeley: University of California Press, 1988); Ann Oakley, *Woman's Work: The Housewife, Past and Present* (New York: Vintage, 1976); and Eli Zaretsky, *Capitalism, the Family, and Personal Life*, rev. ed. (New York: Harper and Row, 1986).
34. Deborah Tannen, *You Just Don't Understand: Women and Men in Conversation* (New York: William Morrow, 1990), 15.
35. See Alison M. Jaggar and Paula S. Rothenberg, eds., *Feminist Frameworks* (New York: McGraw-Hill, 1984); and Tong, *Feminist Thought*.
36. See Kate Millet, *Sexual Politics* (Garden City, NY: Doubleday, 1970).
37. See Echols, *Daring to Be Bad*.
38. As we saw in Chapter 3.
39. I have much more to say about the problem of change in Chapters 9 and 10.
40. See Zaretsky, *Captialism, the Family, and Personal Life*.
41. Cooking and child care, for example, might be done collectively in communal living arrangements that break down women's isolation from one another and the larger community.
42. Friedrich Engels, *The Origin of the Family, Private Property, and the State* (New York: Pathfinder Press, 1972).
43. Heidi Hartmann, "The Unhappy Marriage of Marxism and Feminism: Towards a More Progressive Union," in *Women and Revolution: A Discussion of the Unhappy Marriage of Marxism and Feminism*, edited by Lydia Sargent (Boston: South End Press, 1981), 1–41. See also Tong, *Feminist Thought*, chap. 6.
44. Tong in *Feminist Thought* (185) summarizes Iris Young, "Beyond the Unhappy Marriage: A Critique of the Dual Systems Theory," in *Women and Revolution: A Discussion of the Unhappy Marriage of Marxism and Feminism*, edited by Lydia Sargent (Boston: South End Press, 1981).
45. About which I have much to say in Chapter 8.
46. See, for example, Charlotte Bunch, "Bringing the Global Home," in *Passionate Politics: Feminist Theory in Action* (New York: St. Martin's Press, 1987), 328–345. See also Irene Diamond and Gloria Feman Orenstein, eds., *Reweaving the World: The Emergence of Ecofeminism* (San Francisco: Sierra Club Books, 1990).

## Chapter 6

1. In sociology, this view is most often associated with Talcott Parson's functionalist theories of society. In trying to understand how societies hold together with some sense of order, Parsons argued that various aspects of social systems are all related to one another to form a whole society based on a general consensus about core values defining what is most important or desirable. Through these relationships and this consensus, societies function and survive. We can understand each aspect of life in a system—such as male dominance—in terms of its connection to what a particular society needs in order to function, which, of course, varies from one society to another. From this perspective, a key to what makes societies work is a division of labor that allocates tasks to those who can perform them most efficiently and reliably. See *The Social System* (Glencoe, IL: Free Press, 1951); *The Structure of Social Action* (New York: McGraw-Hill, 1937); and Talcott Parsons and Robert F. Bales, *Family, Socialization, and Interaction Process* (Glencoe, IL: Free Press, 1953).

2. Parsons and Bales, *Family, Socialization, and Interaction Process.*

3. David Gilmore, *Manhood in the Making: Cultural Concepts of Masculinity* (New Haven: Yale University Press, 1990), 3.

4. What physicists call *entropy.*

5. Deborah Tannen, *You Just Don't Understand: Women and Men in Conversation* (New York: William Morrow, 1990).

6. Robert Bly, *Iron John: A Book about Men* (Reading, MA: Addison-Wesley, 1990), 22, 23.

7. See Jane Caputi and Gordene O. MacKenzie, "Pumping Iron John," in *Women Respond to the Men's Movement,* edited by Kay Leigh Hagan (San Francisco: Harper-Collins, 1992), 72.

8. Bly, *Iron John,* 98.

9. By matriarchy, I mean a female-dominated, female-identified, and female-centered society in which men are systematically devalued and subordinated to women. There's no evidence that a true matriarchy has ever existed. See Joan Bamberger, "The Myth of Matriarchy: Why Men Rule in Primitive Society," in *Women, Culture, and Society,* edited by Michelle Zimbalist Rosaldo and Louise Lamphere (Stanford: Stanford University Press, 1974), 263–280; and Gerda Lerner, *The Creation of Patriarchy* (New York: Oxford University Press, 1986).

10. Sam Keen, *Fire in the Belly: On Being a Man* (New York: Bantam, 1991), 202.

11. Keen, *Fire in the Belly,* 96.

12. Bly, *Iron John,* 100.

13. See Bly, *Iron John,* 156; Warren Farrell, *The Myth of Male Power* (New York: Berkley Books, 1993), 68, 70, 71, 142; Gilmore, *Manhood in the Making,* 150; and Keen, *Fire in the Belly,* 37, 47–48, 95–96, 113, 138.

14. Keen, *Fire in the Belly,* 47.

15. Farrell, *Myth of Male Power,* 71.

16. Gilmore, *Manhood in the Making,* 150.

17. Keen, *Fire in the Belly,* 95, 113.

18. See Susan Brownmiller, *Against Our Will: Men, Women, and Rape,* chap. 3 (New York: Simon and Schuster, 1975).

19. Bly, *Iron John,* 16.

20. Keen, *Fire in the Belly,* 177.

21. Farrell, *Myth of Male Power,* 42, 70, 93.

22. Gilmore, *Manhood in the Making,* 110, 114, 115.

23. Anthony Astrachan, "Men and the New Economy," in *Men's Lives,* 2nd ed., edited by Michael S. Kimmel and Michael Messner (New York: Macmillan, 1992), 221, 222.

24. Farrell, *Myth of Male Power,* 361.

25. For an insightful look at the role of myth in human culture, especially in relation to gender, see Elizabeth Janeway, *Man's World, Woman's Place: A Study in Social Mythology* (New York: Delta, 1971). For more on women's economic role, see Hazel Henderson, *The Politics of the Solar Age* (Garden City, NY: Doubleday, 1981), 169. See also Teresa L. Amott and Julie A. Matthaei, *Race, Gender, and Work: A Multicultural History of Women in the United States* (Boston: South End Press, 1991); Bonnie S. Anderson and Judith Zinsser, *A History of Their Own: Women in Europe from Prehistory to the Present,* vols. 1 and 2 (New York: Harper Collins, 1999); Rosalyn Baxandall, Linda Gordon, and Susan Reverby, eds., *America's Working Women: A Documentary History—1600 to the Present* (New York: Vintage, 1976); Ester Boserup, *Women's Role in Economic Development* (New York: St. Martin's Press, 1970); Susan Joekes, *Women in the World Economy* (New York: Oxford University Press, 1987); Ann Oakley, *Woman's Work: The Housewife, Past and Present* (New York: Vintage Press,

1976); Irene Tinker, *Persistent Inequalities: Women and World Development* (New York: Oxford University Press, 1990); and Marilyn Waring, *If Women Counted: A New Feminist Economics* (New York: HarperCollins, 1988).

26. Henderson, *Politics of the Solar Age*, 169.

27. Marilyn French, *Beyond Power* (New York: Summit Books, 1985), 39–43.

28. Waring, *If Women Counted*.

29. Waring, *If Women Counted*, 15–16.

30. See Arlie Hochschild, *The Second Shift: Working Parents and the Revolution at Home* (New York: Viking/Penguin, 1989).

31. See Michel Foucault, *The History of Sexuality: An Introduction* (Harmondsworth: Penguin, 1981). See also Arthur Brittan, *Masculinity and Power* (Oxford: Basil Blackwell, 1989).

32. See Charlotte Bunch, "Not for Lesbians Only," *Quest* 11, no. 2 (fall 1975); Purple September Staff, "The Normative Status of Heterosexuality," in *Lesbianism and the Women's Movement*, edited by Nancy Myron and Charlotte Bunch (Baltimore: Diana Press, 1975); 79–83; Gary Kinsman, "Men Loving Men: The Challenge of Gay Liberation," in *Men's Lives*, 2nd ed., edited by Michael S. Kimmel and Michael A. Messner (New York: Macmillan, 1992), 483–496; Brian McNaught, *Gay Issues in the Workplace* (New York: St. Martin's Press, 1993); and Adrienne Rich, "Compulsory Heterosexuality and Lesbian Existence," *Signs: Journal of Women in Culture and Society* 5, no. 4 (summer 1980).

33. Bunch, "Not for Lesbians Only."

34. Marilyn Fryre, "Lesbian Sex," in *Lesbian Philosophies*, edited by Jeffner Allen (Albany: State University of New York Press, 1990).

35. See Robert Baker, "'Pricks and Chicks': A Plea for 'Persons,'" in *Philosophy and Sex*, edited by Robert Baker and Frederick Elliston (Buffalo: Prometheus Books, 1975), 57–64.

36. Brian Easlea, "Patriarchy, Scientists, and Nuclear Warriors," in *Beyond Patiarchy*, edited by Michael Kaufman (New York: Oxford University Press, 1987), 195–215; Marilyn French, *The War Against Women* (New York: Summit Books, 1992), 157–162.

37. See Ellyn Kaschak, *Engendered Lives: A New Psychology of Women's Experience* (New York: Basic Books, 1992), 68.

38. MacKinnon, *Toward a Feminist Theory of the State* (Cambridge: Harvard University Press, 1989), 133.

39. Miriam Johnson, *Strong Mothers, Weak Wives: The Search for Gender Equality* (Berkeley: University of California Press, 1988). See also Catharine A. MacKinnon, "Feminism, Marxism, Method, and the State: An Agenda for Theory," in *Feminist Theory: A Critique of Ideology*, edited by Nannerl O. Keohane, Michelle Z. Rosaldo, and Barbara C. Gelpi (Chicago: University of Chicago Press, 1982).

40. The technical term is *satyriasis*.

41. A characterization first attributed to Robin Morgan. See "Theory and Practice: Pornography and Rape," in *Going Too Far: The Personal Chronicle of a Feminist* (New York: Random House, 1977).

42. John Stoltenberg, "Pornography and Freedom," in *Men's Lives*, edited by Michael S. Kimmel and Michael A. Messner (New York: Macmillan, 1989), 482–488. See also Angela Carter, *The Sadeian Woman and the Ideology of Pornography* (New York: Harper and Row, 1978); Susan Griffin, *Pornography and Silence: Culture's Revenge against Nature* (New York: Harper and Row, 1981); and Laura Lederer, ed., *Take Back the Night: Women on Pornography* (New York: William Morrow, 1980).

43. Stoltenberg, "Pornography and Freedom," 485.
44. See Jack Litewka, "The Socialized Penis," in *A Book of Readings for Men Against Sexism*, edited by John Snodgrass (New York: Times Change Press, 1977), 16–35; and Andy Moye and Martin Humphries, *The Sexuality of Men* (London: Pluto Press, 1985).
45. See Gloria Steinem, "Erotica and Pornography: A Clear and Present Difference," in *Take Back the Night: Women on Pornography*, edited by Laura Lederer, 35–39, and in the same volume Helen E. Longino, "Pornography, Oppression, and Freedom: A Closer Look," 40–54.
46. See Catharine MacKinnon, *Only Words* (Cambridge: Harvard University Press, 1993); and Diana E. H. Russell, ed., *Making Violence Sexy: Feminist Views on Pornography* (New York: Teachers College Press, 1993). See also Carter, *The Sadeian Woman and the Ideology of Pornography*; Griffin, *Pornography and Silence*; and Steinem, "Erotica and Pornography."

## Chapter 7

1. See, for example, M. C. Hamilton, "Using Masculine Generics: Does Generic 'He' Increase Male Bias in the User's Imagery?" *Sex Roles* 19, nos. 11/12 (1988): 785–799; and W. Martyna, "Beyond the 'He/Man' Approach: The Case for Nonsexist Language," *Signs: Journal of Women in Culture and Society* 5 (1980): 482–493. Deborah Tannen also discusses the linguistic concept of "marking" in her books. See, for example, *Conversational Style: Analyzing Talk among Friends* (Norwood, NJ: Ablex, 1984) and *You Just Don't Understand: Women and Men in Conversation* (New York: William Morrow, 1990).
2. Robert S. McNammara, with Brian VanDeMark, *In Retrospect: The Tragedy and Lessons of Vietnam* (New York: Times Books, 1995). See also the 2004 film, *The Fog of War*.
3. Stanley Cohen, *States of Denial: Knowing About Atrocity and Suffering* (Cambridge, UK: Polity Press, 2001).
4. The willingness to make trouble is often a key to bringing about social change. See William A. Gamson, "Violence and Political Power: The Meek Don't Make It," *Psychology Today* 8, no. 2 (July 1974): 35–41; and *The Strategy of Social Protest* (Homewood, IL: Dorsey Press, 1975). See also H. H. Haines, *Black Radicals and the Civil Rights Mainstream* (Knoxville: University of Tennessee Press, 1988); and Doug McAdam, *Political Process and the Development of Black Insurgency 1930–1970* (Chicago: University of Chicago Press, 1982).
5. For more on this point, see Richard Delgado and Jean Stefancic, "Imposition," in *Critical White Studies* (Philadelphia: Temple University Press, 1997), 98–105.
6. A word derived from "naught," meaning "amounting to nothing,"
7. For two contrasting views of this, see Jack O. Balswick and Charles W. Peek, "The Inexpressive Male: A Tragedy of American Society," *Family Coordinator* (October 1971): 363–368; and Jack W. Sattel, "The Inexpressive Male: Tragedy or Sexual Politics?" *Social Problems* 23, no. 4 (April 1976): 469–477.
8. As Sam Keen suggests women and men have done with patriarchy. See *Fire in the Belly* (New York: Bantam, 1991), 176, 205.
9. See Marilyn French, *Beyond Power: On Men, Women, and Morals* (New York: Summit Books, 1985), 337.
10. See Elaine Pagels, *The Origin of Satan* (New York: Random House, 1995).
11. For some interesting views of Eve, see Kim Chernin, *Reinventing Eve: Modern Woman in Search of Herself* (New York: Times Books, 1987); and Barbara G. Walker, *The*

*Skeptical Feminist: Discovering the Virgin, Mother, and Crone* (New York: Harper and Row, 1987).

12. With the possible exception of child custody cases, about which there's a lot of controversy. Women typically get custody of children, for example, but when men actively seek custody, they are successful much of the time. Custody has a long and difficult history, with men automatically getting custody in the nineteenth century, when children had economic value, and custody then routinely going to women when children lost that value and became an economic burden. Now, as the emotional value of children has grown over the past century and custody can be used as a bargaining chip, equal treatment of mothers and fathers in custody decisions has become an issue.

13. See Harry Brod, "Work Clothes and Leisure Suits: The Class Basis and Bias of the Men's Movement," in *Men's Lives*, edited by Michael S. Kimmel and Michael A. Messner (New York: Macmillan, 1989), 276–287.

14. See, for example, Warren Farrell, *The Myth of Male Power* (New York, Berkley Books, 1993); and Andrew Kimbrell, "A Time for Men to Pull Together: A Manifesto for the New Politics of Masculinity," *Utne Reader* (May/June 1991): 66–74.

15. Women are more likely to suffer from depression, a finding that occurs across an enormous range of cultural and racial groupings. They are especially likely to be depressed if they are employed with sole responsibility for child care. See Ellyn Kaschak, *Engendered Lives: A New Psychology of Women's Experience* (New York: Basic Books, 1992), 173–174, 182, 183.

16. French, *Beyond Power*, 323.

17. Ibid., 297.

18. Farrell, *Myth of Male Power*, 18. This is logically impossible—since each refers to a society *ruled by* one gender or the other—unless we distort the meaning of the concepts out of recognition, as Farrell often does. This is similar to Robert Bly's assertion that "genuine matriarchy" and "genuine patriarchy" can coexist in peace and harmony (as discussed in the previous chapter).

19. See Peggy McIntosh, "White Privilege and Male Privilege: A Personal Account of Coming to See Correspondences through Work in Women's Studies," in *Gender Basics: Feminist Perspectives on Women and Men*, 2nd ed., edited by Anne Minas (Belmont, CA: Wadsworth, 2000).

20. Ibid., p. 36.

21. Scott Russell Sanders, "The Men We Carry in Our Minds," *Utne Reader* (May/June, 1991): 77.

22. Keen, *Fire in the Belly*, 203.

23. French, *Beyond Power*, 85, 509.

24. For an engaging history of this period, see Barbara Tuchman, *A Distant Mirror* (New York: Alfred A. Knopf, 1978).

25. Robert E. Kennedy, Jr., "The Social Status of the Sexes and Their Relative Mortality in Ireland," in *Readings in Population*, edited by William Petersen (New York: Macmillan, 1972), 121–135.

26. A considerable number of whom are apparent victims of infanticide and neglect. See Nicholas D. Kristof, "A Mystery from China's Census: Where Have Young Girls Gone?" *New York Times*, 17 June 1991, p. A1.

27. Peter Landesman, "The Girls Next Door." New York Times Magazine, 25 January, 2004.

28. See, for example, James M. McPherson, *Battle Cry of Freedom: The Civil War Era* (New York: Oxford University Press, 1988).

29. See David R. Roediger, *The Wages of Whiteness: Race and the Making of the American Working Class* (New York: Verso Press, 1991).

## Chapter 8

1. See Stephen Goldberg, *Why Men Rule: A Theory of Male Dominancy* (Chicago: Open Court Publishing Company, 1993).

2. Warren Farrell, *The Myth of Male Power* (New York: Berkley Books, 1993), 358.

3. See, for example, Mary O'Brien, "The Dialectics of Reproduction," *Women's Studies International Quarterly* 1 (1978): 233–239; and *The Politics of Reproduction* (Boston: Routledge and Kegan Paul, 1981).

4. Sam Keen, *Fire in the Belly: On Being a Man* (New York: Bantam, 1991), 17, 18.

5. For a powerful discussion of these and other issues related to motherhood, see Adrienne Rich, *Of Woman Born: Motherhood as Experience and Institution* (New York: W. W. Norton, 1976).

6. Keen, *Fire in the Belly*, 103.

7. David D. Gilmore, *Manhood in the Making: Cultural Concepts of Masculinity* (New Haven: Yale University Press, 1990), 52.

8. Marilyn French, *Beyond Power: On Men, Women, and Morals* (New York: Summit Books, 1985), 113.

9. Dorothy Dinnerstein, *The Mermaid and the Minotaur: Sexual Arrangements and the Human Malaise* (New York: Harper and Row, 1976). For some additional views on this subject, see Nancy Chodorow, *The Reproduction of Mothering: Psychoanalysis and the Sociology of Gender* (Berkeley: University of California Press, 1978); Miriam M. Johnson, *Strong Mothers, Weak Wives: The Search for Gender Equality* (Berkeley: University of California Press, 1988); Keen, *Fire in the Belly*; and Marion L. Kranichfeld, "Rethinking Family Power," *Journal of Family Issues* 8, no. 1 (1987): 42–56.

10. For two useful critiques, see Johnson, *Strong Mothers, Weak Wives*; and Rosemarie Tong, *Feminist Thought: A More Comprehensive Introduction* (Boulder, CO: Westview Press, 1998).

11. As Johnson points out in *Strong Mothers, Weak Wives*. See especially pp. 74–77.

12. See Ellyn Kaschak, *Engendered Lives: A New Psychology of Women's Experience* (New York: Basic Books, 1992), 65–66.

13. Johnson, *Strong Mothers, Weak Wives*, 81.

14. See Gilmore, *Manhood in the Making*.

15. Rudyard Kipling, "If—." In *Kipling: A Selection of His Stories and Poems*, vol. 2, edited by John Beecroft (Garden City, NY: Doubleday, 1956).

16. In *Strong Mothers, Weak Wives*, Johnson makes a compelling argument that motherhood is not the key factor determining women's subordinate position under patriarchy.

17. The Japanese, by contrast, find the Western emphasis on separation and individuality somewhat alarming and work to counteract this in their young.

18. Gilmore, *Manhood in the Making*, 39.

19. Robert Bly, *Iron John: A Book about Men* (Reading, MA: Addison-Wesley, 1990). See also Michael S. Kimmel, ed., *The Politics of Manhood: Profeminist Men Respond to the Mythopoetic Men's Movement* (Philadelphia: Temple University Press, 1995); and Michael Schwalbe, *Unlocking the Iron Cage: The Men's Movement, Gender Politics, and American Culture* (New York: Oxford, 1996).

20. Bly, *Iron John*, 11.

21. See Barbara Ehrenreich and Deidre English, *For Her Own Good: 150 Years of Experts' Advice to Women* (New York: Anchor Books/Doubleday, 1989). For a compilation of a long historical tradition of denigrating women's character, see Fidelis Morgan, *A Misogynist's Source Book* (London: Jonathan Cape, 1989).

22. Bly, *Iron John*, 11, 12.

23. Sara Ruddick, *Maternal Thinking* (New York: Ballantine, 1989).
24. Double binds are common for women and other minorities. See the essay by Marilyn Frye, "Oppression," in *The Politics of Reality: Essays in Feminist Theory* (Freedom, CA: Crossing Press, 1983).
25. Bly, *Iron John*, 14.
26. Bly acknowledged in one of his workshops (at "Interface," Watertown, MA, spring 1990) that patriarchy has done terrible things to the Wild Man. But his idea of patriarchy is so confused and he offers virtually no analysis of patriarchy that it's difficult to know just what such statements mean to him. He made this comment in reply to a question I asked him about why patriarchy was never even mentioned during an entire day devoted to men, masculinity, and the tale of Iron John.
27. For histories and analyses of many of these practices and transformations, see C. P. Christ, "Heretics and Outsiders: The Struggle Over Female Power in Western Religion," in *Feminist Frontiers*, edited by L. Richardson and V. Taylor (Reading, MA: Addison-Wesley, 1983), 87–94; Andrea Dworkin, *Woman Hating* (New York: E. P. Dutton, 1974); and Ehrenreich and English, *For Her Own Good*.
28. Johnson, *Strong Mothers, Weak Wives*, chaps. 5, 6.
29. Keen, *Fire in the Belly*, 15.
30. Bly, *Iron John*, 20.
31. See Angela Y. Davis, *Women, Race, and Class* (New York: Random House, 1981); and Judith Rollins, *Between Women: Domestics and Their Employers* (Philadelphia: Temple University Press, 1985).
32. Two excellent discussions of historical shifts in fatherhood and masculinity are Robert L. Griswold, *Fatherhood in America: A History* (New York: Basic Books, 1993), and E. Anthony Rotundo, *American Manhood: Transformations in Masculinity from the Revolution to the Modern Era* (New York: Basic Books, 1993).
33. For a provocative and revealing analysis of why men shun domestic work, see Margaret Polatnick, "Why Men Don't Rear Children: A Power Analysis," in *Sex:Male/Gender:Masculinity*, edited by John W. Petras (New York: Alfred Publishing, 1975), 199–235.
34. Even in upper-class families, it's wives who typically are responsible for overseeing the servants who perform the dirty work and for ensuring that it's done.
35. In my unabridged Random House dictionary, *paternal* has the meaning of intrusive control, but maternal does not.
36. This probably sounds familiar to women as well, since this has become a pervasive model for "normal" human development—yet another example of the male-identified character of patriarchal societies.
37. Joseph Campbell, *The Power of Myth* (New York: Anchor/Doubleday, 1989).
38. Avon 1992 "Summer Preview" catalogue, 41.
39. Virginia Woolf, *A Room of One's Own* (New York: Harcourt Brace and World, 1929), 35–36.

## Chapter 9
1. Warren Farrell, *The Myth of Male Power* (New York: Berkley Books, 1993).
2. See, for example, entries in the appendix for Arthur Brittan, Harry Brod, Robert Connell, Michael Kaufman, Michael Kimmel, Joseph Pleck, Jon Snodgrass, and John Stoltenberg.
3. This attitude is expressed both in Bly's writings—particularly in *Iron John*—and in his workshops.

4. See, for example, Robert Bly, *Iron John: A Book about Men* (Reading, MA: Addison-Wesley, 1990); Farrell, *Myth of Male Power*; and Sam Keen, *Fire in the Belly: On Being a Man* (New York: Bantam, 1991).

5. Marilyn French, *Beyond Power: On Men, Women, and Morals* (New York: Summit Books, 1985), 261.

6. See, for example, Michael S. Kimmel, ed., *The Politics of Manhood: Profeminist Men Respond to the Mythopoetic Men's Movement (And the Mythopoetic Leaders Respond)* (Philadelphia: Temple University Press, 1995).

7. Farrell, *Myth of Male Power*, 12, 22, 27, 98, 356.

8. As I mentioned in the previous chapter, Farrell defines power as merely the ability to control our own lives, with no reference to the power people and groups have to control resources and other people.

9. See Farrell, *Myth of Male Power*, 31, 39, 72–73, 87, 173, 185, 186, 207.

10. Examples abound. See, for example, the cover story for *Time*, 14 February 1994, "Men: Are They Really That Bad?" by Lance Morrow.

11. For a discussion of the necessity of involving men in the struggle against patriarchy, see bell hooks, "Men: Comrades in Struggle," in *Men's Lives*, 2nd ed., edited by Michael S. Kimmel and Michael A. Messner (New York: Macmillan, 1992), 561–571.

12. For a recent history of men working actively against patriarchy, see Michael S. Kimmel and Tom Mosmiller, *Against the Tide: Pro-Feminist Men in the United States, 1776–1990* (Boston: Beacon Press, 1992).

13. NOMAS is headquartered at 798 Pennsylvania Ave., Box 5, Pittsburgh, PA 15221. It is associated with the journal *Changing Men: Issues in Gender, Sex, and Politics*, which is published by Feminist Men's Publications, 306 North Brooks Street, Madison, WI 53715.

14. See bell hooks, *Feminist Theory: From Margin to Center* (Boston: South End Press, 1984), especially chaps. 1–3; Gerda Lerner, "Reconceptualizing Differences Among Women," in *Feminist Frameworks*, 3rd ed., edited by Alison M. Jaggar and Paul S. Rothenberg (New York: McGraw-Hill, 1993), 237–248; and Audre Lorde, "The Uses of Anger: Women Responding to Racism," in *Gender Basics: Feminist Perspectives on Women and Men*, 2nd ed., edited by Anne Minas (Belmont, CA: Wadsworth, 2000).

15. See Kay Leigh Hagan, ed., *Women Respond to the Men's Movement* (San Francisco: Harper Collins, 1992); and Kimmel, *Politics of Manhood*.

16. Bly, *Iron John*, x.

17. See, for example, Michael Schwalbe, *Unlocking the Iron Cage: The Men's Movement, Gender Politics, and American Culture* (New York: Oxford, 1996).

18. Although sociologists recognize "expressive" movements as a form of social movement, such movements differ greatly in method and goals from other types of movement and should not be confused with them. Movements designed to heal individuals or make them feel better through personal transformation are very different from those dedicated to changing social systems.

19. See Keen, *Fire in the Belly*, 95, 171, 213.

20. See especially Keen's list of key questions on p. 131 of *Fire in the Belly*.

21. Tim Carrigan, Robert Connell, and John Lee, "Hard and Heavy: Toward a New Sociology of Masculinity," in *Beyond Patriarchy: Essays by Men on Pleasure, Power, and Change*, edited by Michael Kaufman (New York: Oxford University Press, 1987), 139–192.

22. See Ellyn Kaschak, *Engendered Lives: A New Psychology of Women's Experience* (New York: Basic Books, 1992), 74.

## Chapter 10

1. This is what Warren Farrell means when he describes male power as mythical. In this case, he's right. See *The Myth of Male Power* (New York: Berkley Books, 1993).
2. See Michael Kimmel, *Manhood in America* (New York: Free Press, 1996).
3. See James William Gibson, *Warrior Dreams: Violence and Manhood in Post-Vietnam America* (New York: Hill and Wang, 1994).
4. J. R. Wilkie, "Changes in U.S. Men's Attitudes towards the Family Provider Role, 1972–1989," *Gender and Society* 7, no. 2 (1993): 261–279.
5. The classic statement of how this happens is by Thomas S. Kuhn, *The Structure of Scientific Revolutions* (Chicago: University of Chicago Press, 1970).
6. Bonaro Overstreet, *Hands Laid Upon the Wind* (New York: Norton, 1955), p. 15. and Paula S. Rothenberg, *Invisible Privilege: A Memoir About Race, Class, and Gender* (Lawrence: University of Kansas Press, 2000).
7. I've put together a short reading list in the appendix.
8. The examples in this paragraph are based on suggestions from Joanne Collahan. My thanks to Joanne for making me aware of this issue.

## Appendix

1. I found much of this material on two Web sites—The Feminist Majority Foundation (www.feminist.org) and a section in the Men's Bibliography (www.mensbiblio.xyonline.net) compiled by David Throop. I appreciate the availability of this information and should stress that there are no guarantees that the information provided here is still correct.

# Index

---

[1] Because references to men and women occur on virtually every page, the index lists only selected major topics under those headings.

[2] Because references to men and women occur
on virtually every page, the index lists only
selected major topics under those headings.